THE REMEMBRANCES OF
ELIZABETH FREKE

THE REMEMBRANCES OF ELIZABETH FREKE
1671–1714

edited by

RAYMOND A. ANSELMENT

CAMDEN FIFTH SERIES
Volume 18

CAMBRIDGE
UNIVERSITY PRESS

FOR THE ROYAL HISTORICAL SOCIETY
University College London, Queen Street, London WC1 6BT
2001

Published by the Press Syndicate of the University of Cambridge
The Edinburgh Building, Cambridge CB2 2RU, United Kingdom
40 West 20th Street, New York, NY 10011–4211, USA
10 Stamford Road, Oakleigh, Melbourne 3166, Australia

First published 2001

A catalogue record for this book is available from the British Library

Library of Congress Cataloging-in-Publication Data

Freke, Elizabeth, 1642–1714
    The remembrances of Elizabeth Freke, 1671–1714 / edited by Raymond A.
    Anselment.
        p. cm.— (Camden fifth series; v. 18)
    Includes bibliographical references and index.
    ISBN 0–521–80808–1 (hardback)
        1. Norfolk (England)—Social life and customs—Sources. 2. Terminal
    care—England—Norfolk—History—18th century—Sources. 3.
    Gentry—England—Norfolk—History—Sources. 4.
    Women—England—Norfolk—History—Sources. 5. Married
    women—England—Norfolk—Biography. 6. Widows—England—Norfolk—Biography.
    7. Norfolk (England)—Biography. 8. Freke, Elizabeth, 1642–1714 I. Anselment,
    Raymond A. II. Title. III. Series.

DA20.C15 vol. 18
[DA670.N6]
942.6'106—dc21   2001025756

ISBN 0 521 80808 1 hardback

SUBSCRIPTIONS. The serial publications of the Royal Historical Society, *Royal Historical Society Transactions* (ISSN 0080–4401) and Camden Fifth Series (ISSN 0960–1163), volumes may be purchased together on annual subscription. The 2001 subscription price (which includes postage but not VAT is £60 (US$99 in the USA, Canada and Mexico) and includes Camden Fifth Series, volumes 17 and 18 (published in July and December) and Transactions Sixth Series, volume 11 (published in December). Japanese prices are available from Kinokuniya Company Ltd, P.O. Box 55, Chitose, Tokyo 156, Japan. EU subscribers (outside the UK) who are not registered for VAT should add VAT at their country's rate. VAT registered subscribers should provide their VAT registration number. Prices include delivery by air.

    Subscription orders, which must be accompanied by payment, may be sent to a bookseller, subscription agent or direct to the publisher: Cambridge University Press, The Edinburgh Building, Shaftesbury Road, Cambridge CB2 2RU, UK; or in the USA, Canada and Mexico: Cambridge University Press, Journals Fulfillment Department, 110, Midland Avenue, Port Chester, NY 10573–4930, USA.

SINGLE VOLUMES AND BACK VOLUMES. A list of Royal Historical Society volumes available from Cambridge University Press may be obtained from the Humanities Marketing Department at the address above.

Cover illustration: Detail from a print of the Freke monument in Westminster Abbey. Copyright: Dean and Chapter of Westminster.

Printed and bound in the United Kingdom by Butler & Tanner Ltd, Frome and London

CONTENTS

PREFACE

The British Library Department of Manuscripts granted permission to publish the remembrances of Elizabeth Freke and related documents in its Additional Manuscripts collection. A Chancellor's Research Fellowship and a sabbatical leave from the University of Connecticut as well as grants from its Research Foundation contributed significantly to the completion of the edition.

Throughout the research and writing of this work Lord Peter Carbery and Mary Hussey-Freke were especially supportive. Lord Carbery shared manuscript materials his grandmother Lady Mary Carbery had gathered about the generations of Frekes, and he always found time to answer questions about the seventeenth- and eighteenth-century family. Mrs Hussey-Freke of Hannington Hall was also very kind, responding to queries about the existence of documents and confirming the inscription on the monument of Elizabeth Freke's father in her parish.

Besides those whose specific contributions are acknowledged in the notes, others were generous with their time and information. They include, in particular, John M. Barney, Diarmuid Ó Murchadha, Tim Cadogan, Diana Spelman, Margaret McGregor, Steven Tomlinson, Maija Jansson, Christopher Hilton, Margaret Pelling, Antonia Moon, Helen Orme, Kate D. Harris, Steven D. Hobbs, Susan Maddock, Clive Wilkins-Jones, David A. H. Cleggett, Jeremy Sandford, Reverend David Brooks, Reverend Gordon Taylor, The Venerable Clifford Offer, Andrew Bols, Michael Kelly, and Maureen Moriarity.

Many libraries, record offices, and archives were central to the project. The research was conducted at the Homer Babbidge Library of the University of Connecticut, Yale's Sterling Memorial and Beinecke Libraries, the Widener and Houghton Libraries at Harvard, the British Library, the Bodleian Library, the Public Record Office, the Norfolk Record Office, the Wiltshire and Swindon Record Office, The Welcome Institute for the History of Medicine, the Society of Genealogists in London, The Family Record Center, the Norfolk Family History Society, and the Corporation of London Records Office. The staffs of the Bristol, Bury St Edmunds, Dorset, Essex, Hampshire, Hertfordshire, Ipswich, Somerset, Suffolk, and Surrey Record Offices responded promptly to questions and issues. Others who offered helpful information or guidance include the librarians, archivists, or staff at the Bank of England Archive, Bath Central Library, Bethersden Parish Records Society, Camden Local Studies and Archive Centre, Canterbury Cathedral Archives, Centre for Kentish Studies, College of Arms, Cork City Library, Genealogical Office in Dublin, Huguenot

Society of Great Britain and Ireland, National Archives of Ireland, Norfolk Museum Services, Norfolk Studies, Public Record Office of Northern Ireland, Representative Church Body Library, Royal College of Surgeons, Society of Merchant Venturers, and Wadsworth Atheneum.

Several ideas developed in the introduction were first explored in an essay published in *Tulsa Studies in Women's Literature*; their refinement and the introduction itself reflect my wife Carol's tactful comments. At various stages in this project John J. Manning, John J. Teunissen, and Kenneth G. Wilson offered advice and support. The general editor of the Camden series, Andrew Pettegree, and members of the Cambridge University Press helped make possible the final form and publication of Elizabeth Freke's remembrances.

ABBREVIATIONS

Bennett	George Bennett, *The History of Bandon, and the Principal Towns in the West Riding of County Cork*, 2nd edn. (Cork, 1869)
Black	Henry Campbell Black, *Black's Law Dictionary*, 5th edn. (St Paul, Minn., 1979)
Blomefield	Francis Blomefield and Charles Parkin, *An Essay Towards a Topographical History of the County of Norfolk*, 2nd edn., 11 vols. (London, 1805–10)
Burnet	Gilbert Burnet, *Bishop Burnet's History of His Own Time*, 2nd edn., 6 vols. (Oxford, 1833)
Carthew	George A. Carthew, *The Hundred of Launditch and Deanery of Brisley, in the County of Norfolk*, 3 vols. (Norwich, 1877–9)
Cave-Browne	John Cave-Browne, *The Story of Hollingborne, Its Church and Its Clergy* (Maidstone, 1890)
CB	G. E. Cokayne, ed., *The Complete Baronetage*, 6 vols. (Exeter, 1900–9)
CHAS	*Journal of the Cork Historical and Archaeological Society* (Cork, 1892–)
CJ	*Journals of the House of Commons*
CJI	*Journals of the House of Commons, Ireland*, 2nd edn. (Dublin, 1763)
Commissioned Sea Officers	*The Commissioned Sea Officers of the Royal Navy, 1660–1815*, ed. David Syrett and R. L. DiNardo (Aldershot, 1994)
Cork Remembrancer	Francis H. Tuckey, ed., *The County and City of Cork Remembrancer* (Cork, 1837)
CP	G. E. Cokayne, *The Complete Peerage*, ed. Vicary Gibbs et al., 2nd edn., 13 vols. (London, 1910–59)
CSPD	*Calendar of State Papers, Domestic Series*
CSPI	*Calendar of State Papers, Ireland*
EDD	*The English Dialect Dictionary*, ed. Joseph Wright, 6 vols. (London, 1898–1905)
English Army Lists	Charles Dalton, ed., *English Army Lists and Commission Registers, 1661–1714*, 6 vols. (London, 1892–1904)
Evelyn	John Evelyn, *The Diary of John Evelyn*, ed. E. S. de Beer, 6 vols. (Oxford, 1955)
Fasti Ecclesiae Anglicanae	John Le Neve, *Fasti Ecclesiae Anglicanae, 1541–*

	1857, Ely, Norwich, Westminster and Worcester Dioceses, comp. Joyce M. Horn (London, 1991)
Ffolliott	Rosemary Ffolliott, *The Pooles of Mayfield and Other Irish Families* (Dublin, 1958)
Fifteenth Annual Report	*Reports from the Commissioners Appointed by His Majesty … Respecting the Public Records of Ireland*, 3 vols. (London, 1813–25)
Freemen of Lynn	*A Calendar of the Freemen of Lynn, 1292–1836* (Norwich, 1913)
Harleian Society	*The Publications of the Harleian Society*
Hasted	Edward Hasted, *The History and Topographical Survey of the County of Kent*, 2nd edn., 12 vols. (Canterbury, 1797–1801)
Hatton	Edward Hatton, *New View of London*, 2 vols. (London, 1708)
HC	*The House of Commons, 1660–1690*, ed. Basil Duke Henning, 3 vols. (London, 1983)
Jowitt	Earl Jowitt and Clifford Walsh, *The Dictionary of English Law*, ed. John Burke, 2nd edn., 2 vols. (London, 1977)
Lodge	John Lodge, *The Peerage of Ireland*, rev. Mervyn Archdall, 7 vols. (London, 1789)
Luttrell	Narcissus Luttrell, *A Brief Historical Relation of State Affairs from September 1678 to April 1714*, 6 vols. (Oxford, 1857)
Marriage Licence Bonds	Herbert Webb Gillman, ed., *Index to the Marriage Licence Bonds of the Diocese of Cork and Ross, Ireland, for the Years from 1623 to 1750* (Cork, 1896–7)
Mason	Robert Hindry Mason, *The History of Norfolk*, 2 vols. (London, 1884–5)
Middle Temple Records	*Middle Temple Records*, ed. Charles Henry Hopwood, 4 vols. (London, 1905)
Middle Temple Register	H. A. C. Sturgess, *Register of Admissions to the Honourable Society of the Middle Temple*, 3 vols. (London, 1949)
Norfolk Lieutenancy	*Norfolk Lieutenancy Journal, 1676–1701*, ed. Basil Cozens-Hardy, *Norfolk Record Society*, 30 (1961)
NRO	Norfolk Public Record Office
ODCC	F. L. Cross and E. A. Livingstone, eds., *The Oxford Dictionary of the Christian Church*, 3rd edn. (Oxford, 1997)
Oxford Law	David M. Walker, *The Oxford Companion to Law* (Oxford, 1980)
PRO	Public Record Office

Register of Gray's Inn	*The Register of Admissions to Gray's Inn, 1521–1889*, ed. Joseph Foster (London, 1889)
Rye	Walter Rye, *Norfolk Families*, 2 vols. (Norwich, 1913)
Scots Peerage	*The Scots Peerage*, ed. James Balfour Paul, 9 vols. (Edinburgh, 1904–14)
SG	Society of Genealogists, London
Simms	J. G. Simms, *Jacobite Ireland, 1685–91* (London, 1969)
Smith	Charles Smith, *The Ancient and Present State of the County and City of Cork*, 2nd edn. (Dublin, 1774)
Strype	John Strype, *A Survey Of the Cities of London and Westminster*, 2 vols. (London, 1720)
Venn	*Alumni Cantabrigienses. Part I: From the Earliest Times to 1751*, ed. John Venn and J. A. Venn, 4 vols. (Cambridge, 1922–7)
Wallis	P. J. and R. V. Wallis, *Eighteenth Century Medics*, 2nd edn. (New Castle upon Tyne, 1988)

INTRODUCTION

Among the late seventeenth- and early eighteenth-century manuscripts of Elizabeth Freke in the British Library are two commonplace books. The larger of them, a white vellum-bound volume of 245 folios (BL, Add. MS. 45718), contains among a number of miscellaneous pieces hundreds of preventatives and cures gathered from relatives and acquaintances as well as from contemporary medical authorities. Besides these 'Receipts for my owne use', the manuscript preserves an extensive compendium of remedies abstracted from John Gerard's herbal and long lists of natural medicinal properties derived from the writing of her kinsman Nicholas Culpeper. The other commonplace book of fifty-three folios wrapped in brown wallpaper (BL, Add. MS. 45719) also contains detailed lists, but their enumeration of rents, deeds, and financial transactions emphasizes material rather than medical well-being. Both concerns, however, are bound inextricably together in two of the entries common to both manuscripts: an account of the expenses incurred in the futile attempt to relieve her husband's fatal illness and 'Some few remembrances of my misfortuns [that] have attended me in my unhappy life since I were marryed'. Medicine, money, and misery are inseparably woven into the life Elizabeth Freke constructs and reconstructs in the telling and retelling that characterize her remembrances. Together, the two manuscript versions reveal a sense of self unique among early modern women's autobiographies.

Where previous seventeenth-century women writers of diaries and memoirs saw purpose and meaning in social status, family accomplishments, and religious faith, this Norfolk gentry woman forthrightly emphasizes years of personal struggle and resistance. Her secular and materialistic individualism strikingly redefines the relationships among self, family, and patriarchy characteristic of early women's autobiography. None of her diary-like remembrances ever purports to leave to posterity a record of the family; in fact the only acknowledgment of this conventional desire occurs as she concludes the second version of the expenses related to her husband's sickness, death, and burial: 'This is the usuage I have had in Norfolk; therfore, son, take heed and beware of my fate' (B, below, p. 303). Nor is hers the cultural ideal of maternal strength evoked by the duchess of Newcastle or the traditional role of the supporting, loving wife portrayed by Lady Ann Fanshawe and Lucy Hutchinson. She expresses none of the traditional piety that consoles Alice Thornton, the Yorkshire woman she most closely resembles. In the difficult search for kindness and security from her

husband, son, and male cousin, the patience and fortitude con-
ventionally affirmed in other contemporary memoirs are conspicuously
absent; suffering and sacrifice dominate an extensive ledger of disappointment and bitterness that reveals over time the complex emotions
of a woman seeking both solace and reaffirmation.

Unfortunately Freke's attempts to re-create meaning in her troubled
life are lost in the only published edition of her writing, Mary Carbery's
early twentieth-century publication *Mrs. Elizabeth Freke Her Diary, 1671
to 1714*[1]. Guided apparently by Victorian principles of editing and intent
upon ordering events chronologically, Carbery cut, conflated, and
rearranged the two versions of the life Freke presents in the commonplace books. Though the composition of neither remembrance can
be dated precisely, Carbery assumes that the vellum-bound text
(hereafter W) was 'evidently copied with additions from the "Brown
Book"'[2] (hereafter B). The B text of the memoirs does indeed omit
many of the letters, all of the poetic 'emblems for my own reading', a
narrative of events related primarily to the first years of William III's
reign, and an extensive survey of the West Bilney house found in the
W text; internal evidence suggests, nonetheless, that Freke began the
shorter version some ten years later. Quite explicitly the opening page
of the B text recalls her dreary marriage day 'full forty years past, being
now 1712'. A 1676 entry in W, on the other hand, stresses that her infant
son, crippled soon after birth, now 'goes straight and well, ... the father
of two lovely boys in Ireland, November 14, 1702' (W, below, p. 42).
Other references similarly dated increase the probability that in 1702,
at the age of sixty, Elizabeth Freke began writing her remembrances,
perhaps relying upon earlier notes for the specific details of her first
thirty years of marriage.[3] Differences in the handwriting further suggest
that the increasingly substantial entries in the vellum-bound folio were
written fairly soon after the entry dates. Freke rewrote this account of
her life when at the age of seventy she began the remembrances again
in the brown wallpaper manuscript. Towards the end, parts of both
versions would have been written at about the same time, though the
W text continues the life until 15 February 1714, some ten months
beyond the final entry in the other remembrance of 5 May 1713.

This new edition of both remembrances together with the ledger of
her husband's fatal illness from the wallpaper-bound manuscript and
several miscellaneous pieces from the two commonplace books recovers

---

[1] Published by Guy and Co. Ltd in Cork, 1913; also in *CHAS*, 2nd ser., 16–19 (1910–13).

[2] Carbery, 'Introduction', 12.

[3] The day of the week usually matches the date, indicating she relied on an earlier form of diary notations. Among the miscellaneous sections in the two manuscripts are several versions or drafts of material that appears in the remembrances.

an unusually detailed account of a gentry woman's late seventeenth-
and early eighteenth-century domestic world. Freke's preoccupation
with the sickness, pain, and loss that increase as she ages conveys with
unsentimental immediacy the personal and practical realities of healing
and death. Her own ambivalent attitudes toward the physicians, surgeons, and apothecaries she both scorned and sought provide a rare
view of the patient's plight in a changing yet limited medical marketplace.[4] Her protracted struggle with the bishop of Norwich over the
right to control the parish church and her suits with tenants in the
hundred court, quarter sessions, and assizes show an awareness of
property rights seldom found in earlier women's diaries and memoirs.
Unusual too is the attention to holdings in East India stock and the
Bank of England, mortgages disputed in chancery hearings, and conflicts
about power of attorney. Besides the painstakingly precise inventory
she compiles of all her household possessions or the careful tallies of
expenditures, her penchant for gathering and compiling leads her to
glean from contemporary histories, gazettes, and gossip newsworthy
national and international affairs that reveal how attuned she was to
the world beyond Norfolk. Together, Elizabeth Freke's manuscripts are
unique in their sense of the medical, economic, and political realities
that shaped her daily life.

The edition also recovers a voice new to early autobiography,
an often modern sensibility whose long-suffering but defiant nature
challenges the assumption that domestic memoirs of this period are
limited to *res gestae* narrative and religious meditation. Like Margery
Kempe, the much earlier and more famous spiritual autobiographer
from the nearby town of King's Lynn, Elizabeth Freke depicts her
struggles to overcome domestic constraint. In writing and then rewriting
versions of three decades of marriage and ensuing years of widowhood,
Freke challenges cultural boundaries as she searches for significance and
even vindication in her hardships, frustrations, and disappointments.
Complex feelings of neglect and vulnerability central to her self-
perception suggest an embittered woman, but they are not limited to
disappointment and misery. The infirm woman who eventually found
herself utterly alone remained to the end a contentious, melodramatic,
yet formidable figure – a strong-willed, even sympathetic person intent
upon asserting herself against what she perceived as familial neglect
and legal abuse. By making available both versions of the remembrances
in their entirety, this new, multiple-text edition clarifies the refashioning
inherent in each stage of writing and rewriting. It assumes that in the
case of Elizabeth Freke revisions embody more fully the disposition

---

[4] Raymond A. Anselment, '"The Want of health": An Early Eighteenth-Century Self-
Portrait of Sickness', *Literature and Medicine*, 15 (1996), 225–43.

and circumstances that help determine autobiographical meaning. Her distinctive re-creation becomes apparent when seen in relation to what is known biographically about her life.

I

According to an early eighteenth-century genealogy of the Freke family begun by her father, Elizabeth Freke was 'born at Westminster, Jan. 1, 1641';[5] neither the baptismal register nor her burial monument confirms, however, that year of birth. An entry in the register of St Margaret's Church Westminster records, 'January 3, 1641/2 Elizabeth ffreake d: to Ralph by Dorothy his wife';[6] her Westminster Abbey memorial states, 'She died April 7th 1714, Aged 69 years'. Although Elizabeth's mother was Cicely, not Dorothy, there is little probability of another Freke family; the date, moreover, is correct if the genealogy follows the old style dating, which begins the new year on 25 March. The burial in Hollingbourne of 'A Chrisome of Ralph Freke Esqr and Cicily his wife' on 14 October 1640 further precludes the possibility that the parents could have had another child so shortly after the death of an infant or chrisom no more than a month old. While the remembrances at times imply different years of birth, the explicit statement at the outset of 1714, 'New Years Day and my unhappy birth day thatt I entred my seventy third yeare' (W, below, p. 208), supports the conclusion that she was born in 1642, a date that in this context is not at odds with the Westminster Funeral Book.[7]

Elizabeth was the eldest of the surviving children born to Ralph Freke and Cicely Culpeper, who were married on 18 August 1636 at All Saints Church in the Kent village of Hollingbourne four miles east

---

[5] The Bodleian Library possesses A Pedigree or Genealogy of ye Family of the Frekes, which is 'augmented' by John Freke and 'reduced to this forme by William Freke ... July ye 14th 1706' (MS. Eng. misc. c. 203). The pedigree was also published in 1825 by Middle Hill Press; a condensed version appears in 'The Freke Pedigree', ed. H. B., *The Ancestor*, 10 (July 1904), 179–211; 11 (October 1904), 36–53. Carbery's copy of the 1825 publication (BL, Add. MS. 45721 B) contains corrections by an unidentified author that are incorporated in the published version, which also has a somewhat different title page. In addition to her annotations, Carbery interleaves at the beginning her handwritten copy of 'The Author's Generall Censure' found in the manuscript of the genealogy now at the Bodleian.

[6] The microfilm of the register in the Westminster City Archives; also Arthur Meredyth Burke, ed., *Memorials of St. Margaret's Church Westminster Comprising the Parish Registers, 1539–1660, and the Churchwarden's Accounts, 1460–1603* (London, 1914), 175.

[7] The Funeral Book states she died at the age of seventy-three (*The Marriage, Baptismal, and Burial Registers of the Collegiate Church or Abbey of St. Peter, Westminster*, ed. Joseph Lemuel Chester, *Harleian Society*, 10 [1875], 279 n. 7).

of Maidstone. Before Cicely Freke died 'on the 6 Jan. 1650, of her age the 41st.', a memorial on the north side of the chapel door records, 'She bear her husband, who most derlie loved her, 2 Sonnes & 8 daughters of which 5 only survived her, Eli, Cice, Fran, Judeth and Phi'.[8] The parish register notes only the burial of the Frekes' first child, Thomas, a newborn interred on 25 June 1637, and the burials of two unnamed chrisoms, one on 25 August 1639 and the other on 14 October 1640. Elizabeth Freke never mentions her youngest sister Philippa, nor does this sibling appear in the Freke genealogy among the list of other sisters: Cicely, who was born in London in February 1642/3; Frances born in Oxford on 22 May 1644; and Judith, at Sarum in February 1646/7. The genealogy does spell out in considerable breadth the paternal ancestry of the Frekes.

Ralph or Raufe Freke was born the sixth of Thomas and Elizabeth Freke's ten children in the Dorset village of Iwerne Courtney, also known as Shroton, on 23 July 1596.[9] His paternal grandfather, Robert, had left an estate valued in the genealogy at one hundred thousand pounds; the father, eulogized on his Shroton church monument as 'magnificently bountiful, providently frugal',[10] ensured the family's substantial presence among the Dorset gentry. Ralph followed his older brothers John and Robert to Oxford, where he matriculated at Hart Hall in 1612, receiving a BA in 1615 and an MA in 1619. A year later he entered the Middle Temple, was called to the bar on 27 June 1628, and maintained his association with this inn of court. When the Brick Court chambers of Ralph Freke and William Nevile became a court of requests office in 1635, students at the Middle Temple continued to be bound over to him.[11] The births of children, first at Hollingbourne, then in London, Oxford, and Salisbury, suggest Freke did not reside solely in London, though his residence and life after his marriage are not clear. Presumably his wife and growing family lived much of the time near Hollingbourne at the Aldington West Court estate he had purchased from the heirs of Richard Smyth and held until his wife's

---

[8] Church Notes in Kent, BL, Add. MS. 11259, fol. 8v, attributed to Edward Hasted; Cave-Browne, 23–4. The burial date is old style or 1651, when she would have been in her forty-first year, having been baptized on 10 October 1610. The family name is spelled both Culpeper and Colepeper in the Hollingbourne parish register and on the church monuments. Culpeper, the name preferred in the Freke genealogy begun by Freke's father, will be used throughout this edition.

[9] SG, DO/R51, transcribed by P. J. Rives Harding.

[10] Erected in memory of their parents in 1654 by Ralph and William Freke as transcribed in John Hutchins, *The History and Antiquities of the County of Dorset*, 3rd edn., rev. William Shipp and James Whitworth Hodson, 4 vols. (Westminster, 1861–70), iv. 99.

[11] *Alumni Oxonienses, ... 1500–1714*, ed. Joseph Foster, 4 vols. (Oxford, 1891–2), ii. 534; *Middle Temple Register*, i. 111; *Middle Temple Records*, ii. 654, 733, 835; iii. 1,079.

death.[12] Another estate in north Wiltshire he and his younger brother William had inherited from their father, Thomas Freke, then became his principal residence. Completed in 1654, the manor of Hannington Hall appears to have embodied the Latin line from Psalm 133 etched on the house, 'Behold, how good and how pleasant it is for brethren, to dwell together in unity':[13] the two brothers and William's wife, Frances, the sister of Ralph's deceased spouse, Cicely, lived together at Hannington, where Frances continued to stay after her husband died on 18 September 1657.

Though Elizabeth Freke would fondly remember the aunt as a surrogate mother, other Culpepers were a significant force both in her life and in the nation. Cicely Culpeper was baptized in the Hollingbourne church on 10 October 1610, the sixth of eleven children born to Sir Thomas Culpeper (1575–1662) and his wife Elizabeth (1582–1638), the heir of John Cheney. Cicely's father, who inherited Greenway Court in Hollingbourne from his father, Francis Culpeper (1538–1591), had matriculated at Hart Hall in 1591 and three years later entered the Middle Temple. Knighted in 1619, Thomas Culpeper published *A Tract against Usurie* (1621) and served as a member of parliament; he also appears to have taken a limited role in the civil conflict of the 1640s, ultimately supporting the monarch.[14] His nephew and son-in-law Sir John Culpeper (1600–1660), the husband of Cicely Freke's older sister Judith, was more deeply committed to the royalist cause. Elected one of the Kent representatives in the Long Parliament, he later served as chancellor of the exchequer and master of the rolls, attaining the title of Baron Culpeper of Thoresway before seeking exile with Prince Charles in the civil war.[15] Among the Culpeper estates sequestered or confiscated in the conflict, the castle of Leeds purchased by Thomas Culpeper and given to his son Cheney concerned Elizabeth Freke, for the disputed mortgage on the estate would involve both her father, Ralph Freke, and her husband, Percy Freke, in a bitter legal dispute with the heirs of Thomas and John Culpeper.

---

[12] Hasted, v. 526–7; a memorial in the Hollingbourne church also notes Cicely's marriage to 'Radulpho Freke de Allington in Thornham Ar.' (BL, Add. MS. 11259, fol. 8r).

[13] Claude B. Fry, *Hannington. The Records of a Wiltshire Parish* (Gloucester, 1935), 35.

[14] Hasted, v. 466–7; Cave-Browne, 14–16; Fairfax Harrison, *The Proprietors of the Northern Neck: Chapters of Culpeper Genealogy* (Richmond, Va., 1926), 55–7; M. F. Lloyd Prichard, 'The Significant Background of the Stuart Culpepers', *Notes and Queries*, n.s., 7 (1960), 411. A 30 April 1646 entry in the *Calendar of the Proceedings of the Committee for Compounding, &c., 1643–1660*, ed. M. A. E. Green, 5 vols. (London, 1889–92) notes that he 'Never took up arms'; the fine of £1,318 was subsequently reduced to £844 (ii. 1,235).

[15] *CP*, iii. 363–4; Cave-Browne, 25–8; Harrison, *Proprietors of the Northern Neck*, 62–8; F. W. T. Attree and J. H. L. Booker, 'The Sussex Colepepers', *Sussex Archaeological Collections*, 47 (1904), 67–9.

Percy Freke was the grandson of William Freke, the brother of Elizabeth's grandfather Thomas Freke and her father's uncle. Arthur Freke, the heir of William and the father of Percy Freke, was born on 13 August 1604 in Sareen or Sarsen, Hampshire, matriculated at Wadham College, Oxford in 1623, and was admitted the next year to the Middle Temple.[16] Both registers indicate his father resided at the time near Shroton in Cerne Abbas; Richard Boyle, earl of Cork, would, however, eventually persuade his friend William Freke to join him in Ireland. There three of his children, Arthur, John, and Ann, would settle permanently. Through marriage to Dorothy Smith of Youghal, the daughter of Mary Boyle and niece of the earl of Cork, Arthur Freke strengthened the family relationship with the powerful Boyles.[17] From the earl's son-in-law David Fitzdavid, first earl of Barrymore, he rented the fortress of Rathbarry built in the fifteenth century on the coast of Cork, south of Clonakilty, by the Barrys, whose family possession was reconfirmed in the early seventeenth century.[18] Arthur Freke calls himself the 'owner of ye castle' in his manuscript account of the long siege of Rathbarry that one hundred people endured in 1642, but the civil war and the defeat of Charles I complicated his claims to any property.[19] Among the so-called Forty-nine Officers who served the king in Ireland before 1649, Arthur Freke sought through his relative the earl of Orrery one of the letters patent pardoning him under the declaration of 1660 that granted the restoration of the lands on the terms of possession held in October 1641.[20] A year later Orrery forwarded to Edward Hyde, first earl of Clarendon, a letter 'from a poor gentleman Ar. Freak' asking for 'the first vacant company or lieutenancy of horse'.[21] The characterization of Freke's financial straits may have been a rhetorical ploy, for 'Arthurus Freake Armiger' was at least in a position to represent Clonakilty in the Irish parliament that

[16] The Freke genealogy documents the birth; the Amport area registers for this period no longer exist. *The Registers of Wadham College, Oxford*, ed. Robert Barlow Gardiner, 2 vols. (London, 1889–1905), i. 67; *Middle Temple Register*, i. 115.

[17] Dorothea Townshend, 'Freke Pedigree', *CHAS*, 2nd ser., 11 (1905), 99, and *The Life and Letters of the Great Earl of Cork* (New York, 1904), 69, 298; *Burke's Irish Family Records*, 5th edn. (London, 1976), 1,039.

[18] On 22 October 1618 James I directed the lord deputy and chancellor 'to regrant to the Lord Barry, Lord Viscount Buttevant, all his estates', including Rathbarry (*CSPI*, 1615–25, 216).

[19] BL, Sloane 1008 describes the hardships those within the castle suffered from 12 January to 18 October, when they were relieved by Charles Vavasour and William Jephson and removed to Bandon. The castle was then set afire to thwart the Irish rebels (Herbert Webb Gillman, ed., 'Siege of Rathbarry Castle, 1642', *CHAS*, 2nd ser., 1 [1895], 1–20).

[20] *Fifteenth Annual Report*, iii. 623; *CSPI*, 1660–2, 316, 317, 319.

[21] Edward Hyde, first earl of Clarendon, *Calendar of the Clarendon State Papers Preserved in the Bodleian Library*, ed. F. J. Routledge et al., 5 vols. (Oxford, 1869–1970), v. 280.

began on 8 May 1661. Two years later he was listed as 'Arthur F., of Mogely, County Cork, Ireland, esq' in the entry recording his son Percy's admission to the Middle Temple.[22] The son ensured the Frekes' possession of Rathbarry and considerable further holdings in County Cork in large part through marriage to Elizabeth Freke.

The courtship of Elizabeth and Percy Freke is obscured by the lack of information about their early lives. The second of Arthur and Dorothy Freke's three children, Percy Freke was probably born in 1643 either in the nearby area of Bandon, where the commander of the besieged Rathbarry and his sick wife 'being wth child' found safety late the year before, or near her parents in Youghal, where a year later Arthur Freke was made a freeman.[23] Their son registered at the Middle Temple on 4 July 1663 without matriculating at a university. Despite a lengthy association with the London inn of court, he seems also to have left without being called to the bar. 'Peirce Freake' appears only in January 1670/1 minutes as one of several people threatened with expulsion if fines of twenty pounds were not paid 'for breaking open the doors of the Hall, Parliament Chamber, and kitchen at Christmas, and setting up a gaming Christmas, persisting after Mr. Treasurer's admonition, and continuing the disorders until a week after Twelfth day'.[24] By then he had already applied for the 23 June 1669 London marriage licence to 'Mrs Elizabeth Freke, of St Martin's in the Fields'.[25] Later, in her recollection of the wedding, which according to the registers of St Paul's Church Covent Garden took place on 14 November 1672, Freke recalls that she had been engaged for six or seven years; she also laments elsewhere the loss of the letters they wrote to each other over a period of seven years before they were married. Presumably the two met in London, though also possibly on a visit to Hannington, soon after Percy Freke entered Middle Temple. The registration of another marriage between them on 26 June 1673 at St Margaret's Church Westminster lends credence to her admission that the first marriage occurred privately without her father's knowledge or approval, prompting him to give his daughter away in a second, more suitable, ceremony. His new son-in-law, in any case, had considerably less prospect of providing for his daughter's material well-being than

[22] CJI, i. 589; 6 July 1663, Middle Temple Register, i. 168.

[23] 'Siege of Rathbarry Castle', 19; at his death in 1706, according to the remembrances, he was 'in the sixty third yeare of his age' (below, p. 253). Arthur Freke was among those who took the freemen's oath on 20 September 1644; he also became, according to C. M. Tenison, a lieutenant in the parliamentary army (The Council Book of the Corporation of Youghal, from 1610 to 1659, from 1666 to 1687, and from 1690 to 1800, ed. Richard Caulfield [Guildford, Surrey, 1878], 249; 'Cork M.P.'s, 1559–1800', CHAS, 2nd ser., 1 [1895], 378).

[24] Middle Temple Records, iii. 1,253.

[25] Allegations for Marriage Licences Issued by the Dean and Chapter of Westminster, 1558 to 1699, ed. Joseph Lemuel Chester and George J. Armytage, Harleian Society, 23 (1886), 165.

someone in Ralph Freke's position might have expected for each of his children.

Compared to her already-married sisters, Elizabeth Freke had, indeed, less assurance of economic prosperity. Ten years earlier, on 2 May 1661 at the Hannington church of St John the Baptist, her sister Cicely had married Sir George Choute or Chute, 'knight of Hinxhill in the County of Kent' and the heir to the Bethersden estate of Surrenden 'very much enhaunsed' by his ancestors, who 'improved the Beauty of the Ancient Structure, by additional Buildings'.[26] Though the marriage ended prematurely with the death of her husband in 1664, their son, Sir George Choute, succeeded his father, becoming a knight, a baronet, and a member of parliament. The next older sister, Frances, had also married a man who would receive a knighthood, George Norton of Abbots Leigh. The Norton family and their Somerset manor had gained some prominence in royalist history for the refuge provided for the disguised prince of Wales as he fled from England in 1651 after the battle of Worcester.[27] The manor house of Abbots Leigh, which was razed in the early nineteenth century, was 'a very large building situated on the brow of the hill northward' with commanding views of the Bristol Channel, the Welsh mountains, and the adjacent shires.[28] On the other side of England, an estate near the Kent village of Tenterden became the Heronden residence of the youngest sister, Judith, who on 14 October 1669 had married in Hannington Robert Austen, the second son of the baronet Sir Robert Austen. Her husband inherited their estate from his uncle John Austen. In his own right Robert Austen gained stature as a leader in the Kent militia, an administrator in local government, and a representative to parliament; the last five years of his life he was also a lord of the admiralty.[29] Neither Judith and Robert Austen nor the Nortons and Choutes had great wealth, yet the estates at Abbots Leigh and Tenterden in particular provided Elizabeth Freke throughout her life with a sense of place she struggled to find in her own marriage.

The brief entries recalling the Frekes' first married years in London underscore an insecurity measured in lost sums of money. The same year of their second wedding Percy Freke sold a mortgage in Epping

[26] John Philipot, *Villare Cantianum; Or, Kent Surveyed and Illustrated* (London, 1659), 72; Hasted, vii. 562, 488–9.

[27] Frances' father-in-law, George Norton, was knighted on 13 May 1660 'for his service in entertaining King Charles at his house & helping to convey him to Trent'; her husband was knighted on 14 December 1671 (*Le Neve's Pedigrees of the Knights*, ed. George W. Marshall, *Harleian Society*, 8 [1873], 58, 57).

[28] John Collinson, *The History and Antiquities of the County of Somerset*, 3 vols. (Bath, 1791), iii. 154.

[29] Hasted, vii. 206–7, ii. 174–5; *HC*, i. 573–4.

Forest valued at more than £5,000 that his wife had received from her father. Several months later her husband appears, at least in her accounting, to have unwisely invested money from her marriage portion in Hampshire real estate. Their fortunes turned out no better when three years later Percy Freke purchased from his father-in-law the right to a mortgage held on Leeds Castle. When Thomas, second Lord Culpeper, bought the castle from the estate of Cheney Culpeper, it was encumbered by a mortgage in Ralph Freke's name that Lord Culpeper failed to settle. The suit in chancery to recover the property moved towards the Frekes' advantage: a 29 November 1676 decree granted the plaintiff possession of the disputed property, and on 14 December the court ordered that 'a writt of Assistanse should be Awarded to the sherriffe of Kent to put the plt into the poss[essi]on of the lands'. Five days later, however, the court reversed itself, citing unspecified 'app[ar]ent irregularitys' and concluding 'that the sd Ld Culpeper & his Lady are not to be disturbed in or turned out of poss[essio]n of the Manision house of Leed & Castle' and that Ralph Freke should file an answer by the beginning of the next term.[30] A year later Percy Freke sold his right to the Culpepers, his wife claims without her knowledge.

The one financial transaction from the first years of marriage that would ultimately provide at least limited security was the purchase of the Norfolk manor of West Bilney in 1676. Located along the River Nar about seven miles south of King's Lynn, the West Bilney property had been mortgaged to Ralph Freke by Thomas Richardson, Baron Cramond. A chancery suit confirmed the Freke title to the manor, which Ralph Freke had given to Robert Austen as part of a marriage settlement. Austen sold the estate he considered too far from his Kent holdings to Percy Freke, who bestowed it in trust to his wife. At the time the manor of West Bilney had almost 2,700 acres, including common and warren, and a yearly rent of £413; the Frekes, however, did not have the immediate right to all the rent and holdings. Ralph Freke had confirmed in an indenture to Lord Richardson's widow a dower claim to the estate with a 'yearly value of one hundred thirty three pounds and five shillings being the third part of the said Mannor of Bilney'.[31] Until Lady Ann Richardson's death in 1698 the agreement prevented Elizabeth Freke from occupying the manor hall; for much of this time she would dwell in either Ireland, London, or Hannington.

The memoirs describe at some length only the last of the five times she lived in Ireland. The hope of recouping her diminishing fortune, she writes, prompted her to leave her newborn son at Hannington and

[30] PRO, C 33/247, fol. 140r; see also fols. 34r–v, 73r, and 202r.
[31] NRO, 19375 103X2. On the outside of the document, apparently in Freke's hand, is the notation, 'Deede of Dowre to the Lady Ann Richerson wch she Injoyed 27 Years'.

accompany her husband for an eight-month stay with her mother-in-law in Youghal and at Rostellan. When the Frekes returned a year later, in September 1677, she says nothing about where they lived during this period of seven months. Subsequent journeys back to Ireland, the first for almost two years and the second for a year, were spent at Rathbarry, which Percy Freke had purchased from the second earl of Barrymore. Neither memoir acknowledges the hospitality extended at Rostellan by the family of Lord Inchiquin or the welcome and support from other English settlers. Outside of the dangers encountered in sea voyages wracked by storms and plagued by pirates, Elizabeth Freke remembers most vividly the unkindness: the unspecified cruelty of her husband's mother, the grasping behaviour of his sister Mary Bernard, and the unjust demands of the Rathbarry tenant John Hull.

The death of her father on 24 April 1684 began a new stage of difficulties at West Bilney. News of Ralph Freke's imminent death prompted Percy Freke to lease Rathbarry to John Hull and return to Hannington, perhaps out of a desire to please his grieving wife and possibly in anticipation of her father's legacy. But the Hannington estate would go to none of the surviving daughters. Ralph and William Freke had promised their dying father 'that if they had no heirs male, they should let Hannington Estate come to their brother Thomas and his heirs', an agreement that the Freke genealogy states 'The 2 brothers, Rafe and William, made a settlement strait on'. The settlement was honoured, and their great-nephew Thomas Freke came into the property that might otherwise have descended to Ralph Freke's surviving children. Elizabeth Freke's only reaction to his death and the lost inheritance is the rueful comment that she was left 'his unhappy child, ever to lamentt him'. She was also left without the prospect of living at either Rathbarry or Hannington. While her husband went back to Ireland, leaving in all probability partly because of the discord acknowledged in the first manuscript, his wife stayed with her sister Frances Norton in London and her sister Judith Austen in Tenterden. By the end of 1685 and a year of dependence upon others, she left for King's Lynn resolved, as she notes, to find her fortunes anew at West Bilney and to resist her husband's efforts to make her sell the Norfolk estate and return to Ireland.

Until the conflicts that would lead to war in Ireland intensified, the Frekes remained separated for sixteen months and then again for seven months. The events in this period of the remembrances deal primarily with Elizabeth Freke's efforts to settle into the thatched house known as the Wassell Farm and to impose her will upon resentful tenants. Aside from mentioning the visit during which her husband took some of her money to buy a nearby property, the manuscripts ignore him and emphasize her own hardship and degradation. What little is known of Percy Freke during this period would suggest that he was serious and responsible in his commitment to Ireland. A letter from the earl of Longford to the duke of Ormonde in December 1685 recommends him as trustworthy and knowledgeable, 'a very honest gentleman of a good estate in the county of Cork'.[32] When his name appears on a list of Protestant families forced to flee the Catholic supporters of James II, the yearly value of £520 placed on his estate is considerably above the average.[33] He also was apparently actively involved in the militia, acquiring a knowledge of military affairs valued by the earl of Longford and the officer's rank Elizabeth Freke says was later taken from him by the Jacobites.

The tensions that led in 1689 to the armed conflict in Ireland between the forces of James II and William III brought the Frekes together for a considerable time in Bilney and, ironically, also determined Elizabeth Freke's return to Ireland for her last and longest stay. Having fled Ireland along with many other Protestants in 1688, Percy Freke was included the next year in an act of attainder against those who would lose their property and be considered traitors if they did not appear in court to answer charges of disloyalty and submit to James' authority. In his absence the Rathbarry estate was confiscated and given to the Catholic Jacobite Owen MacCarty. Several months before the July 1690 battle of the Boyne, while William III was gathering forces for the campaign he himself would lead, Freke returned to Ireland. He may himself have assumed an active leadership in the Cork military resistance to the Irish Jacobites, thereby justifying the title of colonel by which he was later known.[34] The defeat of James II and his supporters, in any case, led to the series of forfeitures that restored properties seized by the Jacobites. When two years later Percy Freke came back to Bilney, his repossession of the Rathbarry estate unencumbered by the former lease to Hull made it difficult for his wife to ignore his insistence that she return with him to Ireland. Together they lived from 1692 to 1696 in the place she had not seen for eight years and would never see again.

Despite her characterization of the four and a half years as a 'miserable life, and most of my time ther sick', the Frekes had a rather prominent position among their Cork neighbours. Percy Freke represented Clonakilty in the session of Irish parliament that began on 5 October 1692; and although he never assumes a significant role in

---

[32] *Historical Manuscripts Commission. Calendar of the Manuscripts of the Marquess of Ormonde, K. P.*, ed. F. Elrington Ball, n.s., 7 (London, 1912), 397.

[33] *Cork Remembrancer*, 330; transcribed from a Trinity College, Dublin manuscript.

[34] The parliamentary journals, for example, refer to him variously as Colonel and Mr Freake.

the journals of the House of Commons, he remained a member of parliament until his death. In 1693 he petitioned Whitehall 'to be tenant of wharfage, carriage and keyage' in Ireland as compensation for his 'great expense in the redemption of that kingdom'.[35] A year later he was high sheriff of County Cork, attending the assizes with a retinue his wife describes as 'two and twenty handsome proper men all in new liveryes'.[36] Their twenty-year-old son, Ralph, and his father further received considerable attention from Lord Drogheda, who saw the younger Freke as a suitable husband for his daughter. Other Cork families appear to have welcomed them into their homes. Percy Freke and his son rested on the way from Dublin at the Waterpark estate of Richard Pyne; Castle Mahon, the residence of the Bernards, afforded Elizabeth Freke a respite on another journey. Like the Powerscourts, who promoted the marriage suit on behalf of Earl and Lady Drogheda, the Pynes and Bernards were related in various degrees to the Frekes by marriage and birth, but the kinship shared among families bound together by their English heritage was not strong enough to overcome the isolation Elizabeth Freke felt.

She left her husband and son to reestablish her own life. Until Percy Freke came back to Bilney in late 1703, she was reunited with him in England only twice. Both times her husband left again, her memoirs stress, once he had obtained from her large sums of money. The remembrances do not describe, however, the extent to which Percy Freke used her resources to became a significant landholder in County Cork. The estate of Justin MacCarthy forfeited after the Irish war and granted to Henry Sidney became Percy Freke's in a 1698 transaction involving £1,031. When large quantities of forfeited land were sold in the government sales of 1702 and 1703, Freke was in a position to buy for £2,409 the forfeited Galway estates, including the town of Baltimore and lands of Bally Island; for another £700 he also purchased in 1703 the towns and lands lost by the attainted John Barry.[37] In all, these and a smaller acquisition for £98 in the barony of Ibane and Barryroe added more than 2,800 acres to holdings that included the Rathbarry estate, the unspecified amounts of land near Bantry and southwest of both Dunmanway and Skibbereen noted by Bishop Dive Downes in his 1700 visitation, and a £2,000 mortgage on Limerick property.[38]

In the meantime Elizabeth Freke re-established her former life in Bilney on a more modest scale. For two years she lived in the thatched

[35] Referred to the treasury on 4 June 1693 (*CSPD*, 1693, 169–70).

[36] *Cork Remembrancer*, 317.

[37] *Fifteenth Annual Report*, iii. 392, 393.

[38] 'Bishop Dive Downes' Visitation of his Diocese, 1699–1702', ed. T. A. Lunham, *CHAS*, 2nd ser., 15 (1909), 84, 86, 131; *The Manuscripts of the House of Lords, 1712–1714*, ed. Maurice F. Bond, n.s., 10 (London, 1953), 273–4.

house struggling to undo the alleged mismanagement of her property during four absent years, escaping the inhospitable Norfolk world only for long visits in London with her sister Judith Austen. When all the holdings of Bilney came into her possession on the death in 1698 of Lady Richardson, the 'empty' manor house and its 'bare walls' occupied her time. Entries in the memoirs describe the furnishings given to her by her sisters and purchased with her 'own mony'. They further emphasize the renovations she undertook on the neglected church. The management of the estate itself also now became her responsibility as she faced alone the domestic realities of arresting tenants and evicting families for unpaid rents. Adding to the burdens was the infirmity that increasingly preoccupies the pages of the memoirs.

Her physical and emotional well-being are not always easily distinguishable. The four and a half years she had spent in Ireland were, she insists, miserable years of unrelieved colic and vapours that kept her in her room virtually an invalid. Vapours were in the seventeenth century considered the 'most frequent of all Chronical Diseases'; their resemblance to 'almost all the Diseases poor Mortals are subject' also suggests that the illness has no apparent physical basis.[39] The phthisic or asthma that occurred in December 1700 following the visit of her husband and once again confined her as an invalid further strengthens the suspicion of hypochondria. A similar attack occurred following her husband's second visit in 1702: after he again took her money for his own property-buying ventures, she became unable to move across her chamber without assistance. An earlier description of a 'malignant fever' that affected her left side and turned her foot 'black as a cole' lends substance, however, to the gravity of another illness she claims left her bedridden and on the brink of death for five months. Like the graphic reconstruction of a fall in 1704 down a long flight of stairs into a stone wall, which left her 'allmost dead', the account of her affliction may exaggerate its seriousness, but the suffering had an undeniable physical basis.

Among the misfortunes and pain that marked the next years, the deaths of her grandson and husband affected her most deeply. In 1699 her son had married Elizabeth Meade, the daughter of a prominent lawyer and future baronet in Ireland, without the consent and probably the knowledge of his mother. Elizabeth Freke would not in fact meet her daughter-in-law until the autumn of 1704 when her son, his wife, and two of their three children came to Bilney. John, the three-year-old grandson she grew attached to during the visit, was accidentally shot in London with a pistol a servant had carelessly left loaded; three

---

[39] John Pechey, *A Plain and Short Treatise* (London, 1698), 10; *International Dictionary of Medicine and Biology*, ed. Sidney I. Landau, 3 vols. (New York, 1986), iii. 3,096, ii. 1,378.

days later, 13 June 1705, the little boy died. He was interred at West Bilney, the parish register notes, on 18 June after a large public funeral described in the remembrances. The unusual extent to which Elizabeth Freke commemorated the young boy reflects a sense of loss that later changes, it will become apparent, as she privately recounts the grandson's death in the two versions of her autobiography. In a different way the sickness and death of her husband also assumed, in time, a new meaning.

Shortly after Percy Freke had returned to Bilney in 1704 he survived a five-month bout of fever and gout that brought him, in his wife's view, beyond the care of physicians; in December of the next year the first symptoms of his fatal illness appeared. Five doctors, two surgeons, and three apothecaries tended with limited success to the asthma and dropsy that wracked and swelled his increasingly frail body. Throughout the ordeal that ended when he died on 2 June 1706, Elizabeth Freke appears in her narratives as the unstinting nurse who tended her husband through long days and nights at her own considerable emotional and physical expense. However self-serving this image may be, she undeniably spared little expense on medical care for her husband. Separate accounts compiled in 1709 and 1712 document with slight variations the daily sums of money expended over the fatal months. Hundreds of pounds were spent on the professional medical help Freke never trusted yet sought throughout her life; additional amounts detail the cost of the mourning rings, gloves, and hatbands; the wines, cakes, and ale; and the vault, leaded coffin, and pall befitting a 'gentlemans buriall'. While the versions of her husband's fatal illness, it will also be apparent, do not vary as strikingly as do those of her grandson's death, the loss significantly influenced the way in which Freke would later reinterpret the past.

Percy Freke's death left his widow once again alone and burdened with the responsibilities of her estate. Unlike the period in her life during which she struggled without him at Bilney, the years of widowhood intensified financial concerns paradoxically brought about by her prospect of greater wealth. In addition to those from the properties in West Bilney and Pentney, her husband's will bequeathed to his wife 'all the Rents and profitts ariseing out of all and every my Lands Tenements and hereditaments whatsoever in the Kingdome of Ireland not before setled upon my Sonn Ralph ffreke and his heires dureing the Terme of her naturall life'.[40] Elizabeth Freke values the Irish estate bequeathed to her at £850 a year not counting a further £1,200 in arrears; she stresses the difficulty, however, in realizing anything near this amount. Her cousin John Freke, the memoirs assert, had abused his power of

⁴⁰ PRO, PROB 11/489/145.

attorney by lowering the rents of the Irish properties and forgoing the arrears; her son, to his discredit, also failed to honour the rents he owed his mother. Besides the perceived mismanagement of the holdings in Ireland, the first years of widowhood were preoccupied with Norfolk tenants who took advantage of her failure to renegotiate the leases, cut trees from the properties for their own use, and ran away without paying rents long due. Charges and countercharges in the hundred court and assizes led to many small but expensive disputes.

Ill health exacerbated her difficulties. In the spring of 1707 the phthisic that had earlier incapacitated Freke prevented her from going to Ireland and asserting the legal rights of her husband's will; instead, she returned to Bilney, letting her cousin John Freke make the journey in her place and settle her affairs. Later that year, she contends, the cousin's handling of the business and her son's indifference to his mother aggravated the effects of an earlier fall and confined her once again to a chair for more than three months 'with such a violentt tissicke and shorttness of breath' that others 'thought itt imposyble for me to survive'. Freke attributes her failure to renew the leases following her husband's death to her invalid confinement; the trial in Norwich over the disputed trees left her, she writes, with a weariness and pain that defied conventional medical treatment. When she then consulted a well-known physician, the diagnosis was not encouraging: 'he told me twas too late: grife had brought me into the condition I were in; and thatt I were wasted all in my inward parts, both my kidnys and my back ullcerated with some fall I had lately had' (W, below, p. 98). His emphasis on both the physical as well as the emotional causes of her illness recognizes that the infirmity could not be attributed solely to hypochondria. The beleaguered widow, now in her sixties, suffered the accidents and chronic maladies of age tormented not only by 'rogues of all kinds' but by 'the wantt of health to supportt besids, and noe comfortt from any frind'.

The theft of her horse the next year added to the legal problems that unsettled the last years of her life; still more consuming was the protracted dispute with the Norwich ecclesiastical officials. At issue was Elizabeth Freke's fundamental effort to assert control over her Norfolk world. After her husband's death she sought to replace the minister who had served the parish for thirty-five years without seeking the bishop's licensing of her new choice. The long series of letters that ensued between her and the bishop and his chancellor raises a number of fine distinctions about governance that turn ultimately upon the bishop's insistence that 'you are both obliged to provide a curatte and allsoe to provide such a one as I shall approve' (W, below, p. 113). In response she pressed forcefully her conviction that her Bilney parish was not subject to the bishop's authority. Summoned to Norwich at the early stages of the dispute, she stressed the infirm condition that prevented her from appearing at the ecclesiastical court. The letters that remain her means of defence end in late 1710 on a grudging note of accommodation: she will accept a licensed minister 'dureing my pleasure'. But the basic conflict remained unresolved. Two other letters written three years later in response to the chancellor's warning of excommunication threaten in the end to tear down the church rather than acknowledge the Norwich authority. The sentence of excommunication issued by Thomas Tanner, chancellor of Norwich, on 18 November 1713 cites the refusal of Elizabeth Freke to appear when summoned three times to answer the matter pending before the court concerning the appointment of a suitable cleric.[41]

The intemperate tone of her last letters is perhaps more than the expression of a wilful woman intent upon protecting her threatened rights; the letters may well reflect in their irascibility and tenacity Freke's growing awareness that she is now a 'diseased criple' imprisoned in her confinement and 'used by every body'. Her fears that her tenants are scheming to cheat her and that her servants are plotting to murder her are not simply the paranoia of increasing age. Rheumatism, pleurisy, and colic compounded her phthisic and accentuated the loneliness, vulnerability, and virtual helplessness of the final years. At the age of sixty-eight her eyes also began to fail her; three years later she would tersely write, 'I am allmost tottally deprived of my eye sightt, an insuportable griefe to me' (B, below, p. 280). Her sister Frances Norton offered some support in London, and her other sister's daughter provided companionship in Bilney; the arrival of Ralph Freke and his family at the end of 1712 proved less comforting. During the four-month stay, her grandson's smallpox endangered her servants, and relations with her son and daughter-in-law were cold and occasionally hostile. Elizabeth Freke nevertheless purchased a baronetcy for her son before he returned to Ireland; she also appears to have derived some solace from contemplating the legacies waiting for each grandson. Like the series of extensive inventories undertaken the year before in the wallpaper-bound manuscript or the room-by-room list of her possessions included in the vellum-covered text, measuring or accounting may have provided both diversion and reassurance amidst the tedium and fear of pain and age. Near the end of her life the news items increasingly incorporated in her remembrances may have been a further attempt to break the confines of a Norfolk world of troublesome domestic concerns and the threats of the sheriff's bailiffs.

Two months after the last entry in her memoirs Elizabeth Freke died. The only evidence of the date is the inscription on the Westminster

[41] NRO, DN/CON/57.

Abbey monument: 'She dyed Aprill 7th 1714'. While her remembrances emphasize a desire to be buried with her husband in the West Bilney church of St Cecilia, her will states only that she be 'decently Interred in Westminster Abbey, If I shall happen to dye in or about London'.[42] Perhaps her sister Frances Norton arranged the Abbey burial; she was responsible, in any case, for the monument erected in 1718 to the memory of her sisters Elizabeth Freke and Judith Austen, who was interred on 24 May 1716. The marble monument in the south choir aisle not far from the Poets' Corner remains on the wall next to the elaborate one commemorating Lady Norton's daughter Grace Gethin, whose death in 1697 Elizabeth Freke mourns in her writing. An unmarked grave in the nave of Westminster Abbey contains the remains of all three sisters.[43]

At her death the rights to the Irish estates bequeathed in her husband's will went to her son and his heirs. When Ralph Freke died in 1717, his eldest son, Percy, succeeded to the baronetcy and the majority of the land in Ireland. Percy Freke never married; and at his death on 10 April 1728 his title and estate went to his youngest brother, John Redmond Freke, their brother Ralph having died unmarried the year before. The last of Elizabeth Freke's grandsons married Mary Brodrick, who died three years before her husband's death on 13 April 1764. Since they had no children, the baronetcy became extinct, and his sister, Grace, remained the chief beneficiary of his will.[44] She had married John Evans of Bulgaden Hall, the fourth and youngest son of George Evans, the first Baron Carbery. The second of their five sons, John, fulfilled his uncle John Redmond Freke's will by assuming the name and the arms of Freke; he was created a baronet in 1768. John Evans Freke, the first son of his marriage to Elizabeth Gore, succeeded his cousin on 4 March 1807 as the sixth Lord Carbery.[45] Algernon William George Evans-Freke, the ninth Lord Carbery, was the first husband of the woman who initially edited the remembrances, Lady Mary Carbery, the second daughter of Henry Joseph Toulmin. Their grandson, Peter Ralfe Harrington Evans-Freke, is the eleventh Lord Carbery.

The estates that Ralph and Elizabeth Freke had struggled to establish no longer remain in their descendants' possession. Their grandson John Redmond Freke sold the Norfolk property to Francis Dalton in 1750.[46] By the end of the next century the thatched house had been divided into three houses and the Hall bore little resemblance to the former

---

[42] PRO, PROB 11/539/67.
[43] Christine Reynolds, Assistant Keeper of the Muniments.
[44] *CB*, v. 15–16.
[45] *CB*, v. 378; *CP*, iii. 9–12.
[46] Blomefield, viii. 354.

residence. The church that Elizabeth Freke fought to control is now leased to the Norfolk Churches Trust, which offers services there only three times a year.[47] For two centuries the fate of Rathbarry Castle and its surrounding lands was quite different. A 1787 survey of the 15,276 acres in County Cork owned by Sir John Freke contains a detailed depiction of the 325-acre Castle Freke Domain, locating among the orchard, pastures, and deer park the castle overlooking the twenty-three acre lake, Lough Rahavarrig.[48] John Evans Freke, the sixth Lord Carbery, abandoned the old castle and commissioned Richard Morrison to build a castle in gothic style on another portion of the surrounding thousand acres. The new residence occupied a hill facing the south with views of the sea and coast. To the east were extensive plantations. 'When the view of the place first opens on the traveller', an 1820 description of Castle Freke observes, 'the whole has a grand and imposing appearance, presenting an extensive range of woodlands and undulating ground, with the fine turreted structure rising above it'.[49] The crenellated mansion remained in the nineteenth century the principal residence in County Cork of the Carbery-Freke family, major landholders of over 19,000 acres in Ireland valued in 1883 at £10,515 a year.[50] When fire destroyed much of the castle in 1910, insurance helped defray the expense of its rebuilding; the family fortune, however, was no longer what it had been. In 1919 the castle was sold to a consortium. The particulars of the sale listed in the illustrated catalogue describe the numerous rooms, the stables, cottages, and gardens on an estate 'extending to about 1,100 acres'.[51] For several decades Castle Freke was occupied; then in the 1950s it was stripped of everything that could be auctioned. Recently the son of Lord Peter Carbery bought Castle Freke, though there are no plans for extensive renovation. The many acres of the Carberys' Irish holdings now gone and the lake

[47] Mary Carbery noted some of the apparent changes during a visit in the first years of the twentieth century. Nicolaas Velzeboer, whose family owned the immediate property until he sold the uninhabited house 'in approximately 1985', has indicated in correspondence that the dwelling long known as the Manor House, and currently part of the Manor Farm owned by Stephen Fry, had been faced in yellow brick 'at some stage … as the home of a wealthy person'. Reverend Stuart Robert Nairn, The Rectory, Narborough, has also kindly provided the further information about the church.

[48] A Survey of the Estate of Sir John Freke Bart. in the County of Cork by Thomas Sherrard, 1787. Reverend C. L. Peters generously made available the survey, which is in his safekeeping at The Deanery, Rosscarbery.

[49] J. P. Neale, *Views of the Seats of Noblemen and Gentlemen, in England, Wales, Scotland and Ireland*, 6 vols. (London, 1818–23), iii. n.p. See also, for example, Samuel Lewis, *A Topographical Dictionary of Ireland*, 2 vols. (1837; reprinted Baltimore, 1984), ii. 488–9.

[50] *CP*, iii. 12.

[51] Peter Somerville-Large, *The Coast of West Cork* (London, 1974), 24–6; *Mary Carbery's West Cork Journal, 1898–1901*, ed. Jeremy Sandford (Dublin, 1998), 137–8, 153. Sandford reproduces the sale catalogue in an appendix to his edition, 155–8.

now a marsh, the ruins stand with their commanding views, a vestige of the past.

II

Part of that past is re-created in Elizabeth Freke's two distinct accounts of her misfortune. Though both begin with the same date and end within a year of each other, their differences are usually apparent despite the considerable duplication. The second remembrance begun in 1712 both retells and revises the earlier version, adding and deleting material to gain a tighter chronological continuity. Factual discrepancies that emerge in the later narrative, though they may raise questions of accuracy, do not compromise social and economic insights. Mundane details such as the cost of thatching a house, the furniture in various rooms, or the construction of a burial vault reinforce with unusual detail a rare picture of domestic life at this time. The value also lies in the implications of Elizabeth Freke's distinctly different representations of herself as a wife, mother, and widow.

The revision of the first entry reveals changes fundamental to a new self-portrait. Besides eliminating some of its awkward syntax, Freke expands the original version of the November wedding day twofold by adding information about immediate family members. The knowledge that her mother's death 'left me, the eldest of five daughters, aboutt six or seven years of age' and the description of the men her sisters had married may have been included simply to fill out the family background. Two shorter additions, however, suggest a further intention. The man she married is now described as 'my deer cosin Mr Percy Frek', not simply 'Mr Percy Freke'; the 'most grievous rainy, wett day' on which they were wed without her father's permission is remembered as 'a most dreadfull raynie day (a presager of all my sorrows and misfortunes to mee)'. The parenthetical emphasis underscores the event's ominousness, enhancing a melodrama intended to emphasize the disappointments of the ten years since the original entry. Over time Freke also comes to use the new endearment for her husband. In the context of her mother's death and sisters' marriages, her own wedding without the consent of the widowed father who had raised her may seem all the more defiantly unconventional because she now understands more fully the complexity and strength of the bonds of love and loyalty to both her father and husband.

Neither memoir ever explains why she married without her father's knowledge or consent, nor does either overtly admit guilt or regret for this parental disobedience; both manuscripts do convey the misery that stems in part from Freke's inability to end her dependency upon her father and commit herself completely to her husband. This failure to break the paternal bond may reflect the 'general genius of this family' recognized in the genealogy begun by her father. The headnote to the pages charting the Freke lineage from its sixteenth-century progenitor attributes the considerable prosperity and self-sufficiency to a 'frugall and judicious' nature. The monument in the Hannington church erected in memory of Ralph Freke similarly commemorates him as 'a wonderfull Example of Frugality & Liberality'.[52] Much the same phrase appears on the Westminster Abbey tribute to Elizabeth Freke: 'frugal to be Munificent'. The tacit link between father and daughter puts her preoccupation with money in a favourable perspective; its reminder of the Freke heritage might also account for some of her unhappiness. By nature frugal and strong willed, she married another strong-willed Freke who may have been frugal but not as liberal as her munificent father. Throughout her marriage and widowhood the struggle to achieve the self-sufficiency, if not the wealth, of her heritage compounded her misery.

An overprotective father may have ill-prepared Elizabeth Freke to endure adversity patiently. The man who cared for his young daughters after their mother died did so, both memoirs stress, with such kindness and indulgence that she 'was nott mised by us'. Until he died at the age of eighty-seven, almost thirteen years after his daughter's fateful marriage, the father's generous and loving nature did not lessen. He provided the newly married couple with a substantial estate, took them to his Hannington home for the birth of their son, and cared for the grandchild when the parents left for Ireland. Sensing his daughter's melancholy on a later occasion, he returned with bags containing £200 to be kept secret from her husband and to be used for 'pin money'. On the same visit he got her to promise that she would not leave him again while he lived in exchange for his promise that she would 'wantt for nothing his life'. She immediately wrote to her husband about the £200, 'hopeing', she says in the second manuscript, that 'itt might be a meanes for my continuance with him'. When 'with grief of hart' she left her father for the last time, his parting blessings cancelled a bond of £1,000. This and other sums of money that measure his continued care are tallied in the miscellaneous lists of both commonplace books. Throughout the narratives of the married years in which Elizabeth Freke moved by her reckoning seven times to empty houses and bare walls, the refrain 'nott a place to putt my unfortunatte head' underscores the deeply felt loss of the security and place provided by her nurturing father.

The failure of her husband to provide for her as her father had done

---

[52] Fry's transcription, *Hannington*, 74.

colours Freke's portrait of a troubled marriage. Both versions insist that
at least initially theirs was a marriage of love. Each entry describing
the first two years of married life attributes her unhappiness to the
absence of the husband she loved and not merely to the loss of much
that she associated with her father: 'And I never had of itt, to my
remembrance, five pound of itt and very little of my husbands company,
which was no small griefe to mee, I being governed in this my marriag
wholly by my affecttions' (B, below, p. 213). During the years Elizabeth
Freke and her husband lived sometimes together but often apart, as
Percy Freke continued to use her financial resources for his own
ventures, bitterness gradually displaced love. Neither account minimizes
the grief of a marriage that forced her 'to seek my fortune by
shiffting for my selfe'. The image of the husband, however, alters quite
significantly when the same years are recalled in the revision. His death
in the intervening decade seems to have contributed to the noticeable
change.

   The two accounts of his death reflect different emphases. Though
both describe the futile medical efforts to save his life, the second
version gives greater prominence to Elizabeth Freke's emotional reaction. Doctors and surgeons who earlier are said only to have ignored
her wishes now appear in their 'barbarity' to have 'murdered my deer
husband'. Before, others were rude to her; now, they are cruel. Her
leg that breaks into ulcers under the strain of continuous care becomes
in the retelling 'an aditionall misery to whatt I dayly laboured under I
dayly reckned would kill mee'. Entries found nowhere in the older
manuscript disclose that nights spent tending a husband wracked by
asthma and bloated with dropsy caused her to become, in the words
of others, a crazy woman, a characterization she admits was 'too true,
for my grife had made me very little better then crassed with seeing
him lye fowre monthes in thatt misery and my own legg broke in two
holes full of pains' (B, below, p. 250). The later passages also reveal
that the bedridden husband challenged his wife's detractors to a duel
at sunrise, 'Soe tender was my deer husband of my honour'. His death
in her arms befits the new portrayal. The trauma of the moment,
which in the first text frightened her so much that she was 'nott able
to hold him', vividly reappears in the later narrative: 'noe mortall was
with him butt my wretched selfe; [dying] in my armes, which quite
distracted me, [he] bid me nott stirr from him. But my amased
condition was such as my crying outt soon fill'd the house outt of the
church to be a wittness of my unhappy and deplorable fatte' (B, below,
p. 251). The cry seems one of grief as well as terror. The man willing
to challenge those who called her crazed became through their shared
suffering more nearly the husband she had married. In death he
becomes the 'deer husband' of the second manuscript.

The reconstructed remembrances often effect this transformation simply by omitting statements and actions that reflect a strained relationship. Most striking are two passages crossed out in the W text and absent from the B text. The first reveals the conflict caused by Elizabeth Freke's divided loyalties. Reluctant to leave Hannington and her father, Freke at first refused to go back to Ireland in 1683 with the husband she had left with considerable discord ten months earlier at Kinsale. 'His last parting wish' was, the deleted passage recalls, 'thatt he might never se my face more' (W, below, p. 49). The later version is more ambiguous: 'his parting with me last att Kingsaile stuck deep in my stomock' (B, below, p. 220). A year later another separation from her husband reveals the depth of her unhappiness during this troubled period. Percy Freke, who had reconciled with his wife and returned with her to England at the news of his father-in-law's imminent death, left once again for his Irish estates. While they were in England, he often was absent from his wife, 'which I cannott forgett', she confides only in the original narrative, 'itt was soe griveous to me' (W, below, p. 52). After his departure she does not restrain, in this version, her resentment at having been 'thrown off by my unkind husban; [who] never in his life took any care for me or whatt I did' (W, below, p. 53). Later Elizabeth Freke crossed out both passages from the vellum-bound account, perhaps because she recognized even as she entered them that they were emotional outbursts rather than considered reflection. They may also have appeared much too damaging for someone who insists in both narratives that she never revealed to others any differences she had with her husband.

Additional omissions made some years later in the rewriting further soften the conflict in the marriage. Thus two quite distinct versions describe the husband who returned the year after he had 'thrown off' his wife, hoping to convince her to sell the Bilney estate she held in trust for herself and her son. Originally Elizabeth Freke portrayed with less than fondness an ill-tempered, grasping husband bent upon having his will: 'he was very angry with me for being on this sid of the country, tho in all his tims of his being from me he never took care for a peny for my subsistance or his sons. For which God forgive him' (W, below, p. 55). The same entry rewritten after his death simply relates that he came from Dublin by post and 'was dayly importuneing of mee to sell my Billney to Sir Standish Harts Tongue for the like in Ireland; but my God gave me the resolution and courage to keep whatt I had rather then by parting with itt be keptt by my frinds' (B, below, p. 225). The statement, taken from the original, omits the final words in the W text, 'or trust to his or any ones kindness'. Also omitted is the reaction of her husband, who 'in a greatt anger' left his wife 'alone againe' and did not return from Ireland for almost two years. Other deletions

diminish Elizabeth Freke's pique at her husband's neglect and irresponsibility. Missing in the new entry about the £1,000 he had shifted
in 1702 to Ireland is the information 'given me by my deer father',
about which she wrote, 'This I thought very hard usage, butt tis true'
(W, below, p. 71). The later remembrance also overlooks her earlier
complaint that she had been 'cruly disgarded' by her husband and left
to the care of her sister, 'itt being more then Mr Frek has afforded me
this 17 yeare' (W, below, p. 72). Another entry for a period more than
a year later excises from the text a similar example of his selfishness:
'Mr Frek thus <deleted: barbarously> leaving of me to my shiffts
withoutt any pitty or comiseration two years' (W, below, p. 73). Her
complaint in a passage two years later about a lack of letters from
Ireland, 'which has much aded to my greatt misery and sickness' (W,
below, p. 76), becomes 'in all which time I never heard' (B, below,
p. 241). She is not as willing to forget her dismay and humiliation at a
later date when she waited fruitlessly for her husband to arrive at Bath
only to discover he had removed in her absence 'all I had'; she does
not, however, re-enter her comment, 'This is true. Which with many
more such triks I beg God to forgive him' (W, below, p. 78).

At the same time that she describes her husband less bitterly, years
of growing disillusionment seem to have strengthened her unwillingness
to sentimentalize the realities of a marriage whose unhappiness she
refuses to mitigate. While she omits her negative memory of her first
stay in Ireland – where she miscarried, 'my husbands mother being
very unkind to mee' (W, below, p. 42) – and says only in the second
narrative that the eight-year period at West Bilney was the most quiet
and comfortable of her life, she also accentuates her difficult fate. The
words 'miserable' and 'wretched' in the revision underscore her vivid
sense of the suffering she endured on their Irish estate, 'allmost frightned
outt of my witts', and emphasize the stress she felt without her husband
in England. Unappreciated is the extensive support she received from
her sisters, an omission all the more glaring in the self-characterization
added to the statement about her visit to Judith Austen preserved from
the initial text: 'And being very poore, I presented her in London with
six sillver plates cost me thirty six poundes' (B, below, p. 224). Though
able even then to afford a considerable gift of silver, Freke seems
compelled to exaggerate her misery in the revisions for reasons further
related to her plight after her husband died. The years of widowhood
that reshaped the memories of an unhappy marriage never altered,
however, her contention that his death was 'the dismalls and fattasst
day of my life' (B, below, p. 289).

Without her husband, the misfortunes of motherhood increasingly
assumed significance. Her son Ralph, born with such danger to his
mother, shared his father's interest in Ireland and settled there into a

distant, somewhat strained relationship with his mother. The death of the beloved grandchild and the fatal illness of her husband added considerable tension to her relationship with her son. Compounding the difficulties was the son's obligation in his father's will to settle with his mother the arrears on the family's Irish estates, an obligation that a December 1706 letter to her son included in the first remembrance admonished him to meet. Her son, she later notes in the second manuscript, 'had only as usuall a rude answer' (B, below, p. 254). His failure to pay the rents due to his mother each year increased her sense of his ingratitude. Another letter written four years later threatening legal action complains bitterly about the 'many slights and disrespectts' that have 'broke my hartt and brought mee to the condition I am in' (W, below, p. 132). By the time the son ended three years of silence with a letter and then returned to England in late 1712 to see his mother, her feelings of affliction and abandonment had deepened. The dismay and hurt she expresses in the original memoir are intensified in the revisions begun near of the end of her son's long absence.

Her reactions to Ralph Freke's marriage reflect the change. Both remembrances give less attention to the marriage than to her son's earlier effort to obtain the hand of Lord Drogheda's fifteen-year-old daughter Alice. While the accounts of this failure are substantially similar in detail, the second voices a hardened attitude. Where she first saw in the prospective bride 'nothing to be objected butt her quality, which I thought too much for a gentleman' (W, below, p. 62), Freke later comments, 'Butt I could nott think her <deleted: quality> proper for my son, clog'd with seven or 8 brothers and sisters'. She adds wryly, 'A fine lady she was, but I cared nott to be a servantt to any one in my old age' (B, below, p. 230). Whatever else she might have felt is lost in the rest of the sentence scratched out in the manuscript. A similar concern, however, is apparent in the further remark, 'I cared nott to bee frightnened outt of my mony nor my son too <deleted: several words>' (B, below, p. 231). Her complaint in the revised version that Lord and Lady Drogheda could have spared one of their many children to live near her conveys both affection and selfishness. She resists both the attempt of the prospective bride's parents 'to bring me to any tearms' as well as her husband Percy Freke's offer of better financial terms, thereby increasing the bitter anger of the son. Elizabeth Freke becomes spiteful when she recalls the son's later marriage without her consent to John Meade's daughter Elizabeth. Both versions ruefully wish him the good fortune she herself never had. In the second she records a cryptic, baleful thought: 'perhaps I mightt have opposed this match, I heering my son wish (to cross mee) thatt he mightt never prosper iff hee marryed there to thatt lady fifteen years of age. God forgive him' (B, below, p. 237).

Her complaints run through the rewriting of the memoirs. The birth of the first grandchild, for example, reminds Elizabeth Freke of her own motherhood, and she hopes 'thatt he may be a greatter comfortt to his parents then my son Frek has bin to mee, his mother' (B, below, p. 238). Long-suffering and self-sacrifice are an integral theme of another addition recalling the loan she secured two years later on her son's behalf. To the original complaint about his ingratitude she bitterly adds, 'This tis to have butt one child, and him none of the best to me neither. Butt God forgive him and give patience to me, his unhappy mother, Eliz Frek' (B, below, p. 242). Characteristic discontent reshapes her entry of 27 March 1704 on Ralph Freke's ill health. For almost a year, the mother originally wrote, she had received no news from her son; and her response at the receipt of a letter from his wife in March 1704 is to implore divine help 'to restore him to me and his children' (W, below, p. 78). Later she could write that he did recover from his illness, but by then the much longer anxious periods without news led her to decry the 'hard and uncomfortable fate of Eliza Freke' and to note that he had regained his health 'I hope to be a comfortt to mee, his unhappy mother' (B, below, p. 244). A year later the death of her grandchild occasioned much greater pain.

The original account of the three-year-old Jack Freke's tragic death is one of devastating loss. Elizabeth Freke loved him, she initially notes, with all her soul because he was an image of her own son; and she had begged her daughter-in-law to let him remain at West Bilney while the parents stayed at the Norfolk Street lodging, where the little boy was fatally shot. The grief-stricken grandmother is convinced that the child would be alive if the 'cruell' mother had left him in his grandmother's care; she is also certain 'I lost my child to show their undutifullness and cruellty to me, which God forgive' (W, below, p. 82). Originally Freke had wished divine forgiveness of 'her'; she changed the pronoun to 'them' as well as deleted two other references to her daughter as 'cruell'. Her need to grieve, however, is greater than her desire to blame. The grandmother writes that she 'shall ever lamentt' the child whose death broke her heart and took away 'any comfortt in this life'. Though she finds some solace in the large funeral she arranged, her sorrow remains unabated: 'Oh, my harde fatte; I am ruined and undone for my child, and I doubt shall never enjoy my self againe' (W, below, p. 82). When the daughter-in-law then refused to let her other child visit his sick grandfather while in London, Elizabeth Freke vowed never to see her again. Alone at West Bilney, she waited until her husband returned weakened by gout and consumed by 'extream malloncally for the fattall loss of this our deer babe, which he had too much as well as I sett his whole hart on' (W, below, p. 83).

Seven years later her husband's sorrow and not her own is central to her reconstruction of the tragedy. Time had lessened the pain that seemed so unbearable, and the troubled family relationship together with the death of her husband increased the need to reapportion responsibility. Once again Elizabeth Freke believes the grandchild 'must pay for all theire undutifullness and cruellty to me' (B, below, p. 247), but now she heightens the magnitude of her son and daughter-in-law's guilt. The revision emphasizes her warning against staying at the fatal Norfolk Street lodgings and her fears that the servant, who, she now stresses, had on an earlier occasion mishandled the pistols, would again be dangerously careless. Their dismissal of her wishes leads to the tragic consequences perceived as a direct and deliberate wrong to Elizabeth and her husband: 'Aboutt 5 a clock in the morning he gave up his soule to God for there undutifullness to mee, for elce my God would nott have taken from me roott and branch as hee did butt to show his judgments to them. Butt God forgive them both theire barbarity to the best of fathers and the indullgents of mothers' (B, below, p. 247). She considers this cruelty 'the most fattall'st thing that ever hapned to me' not because she had lost the lovely boy but because 'this same shott kild my deer husband' (B, below, p. 247). Her undutiful son, in effect, appears guilty of parricide, for Percy Freke's illness is now more emphatically a consequence of the shooting, a sickness aggravated by the daughter-in-law's refusal to let her older boy visit his namesake. 'Griefe for my child and his childrens cruell usage to him' now appear the cause of the 'extream malloncally' he suffered throughout the last months of his life. His death, Elizabeth Freke concludes, was 'to compleatt all my miseryes together' (B, below, p. 248).

The ungrateful behaviour of her son after the double tragedy exacerbates her misery. When she complains about his lack of correspondence in the months following the little boy's death, Elizabeth Freke omits in the revised account a probable cause of the silence – 'because I wrott him word of some mistaks he had commited' (W, below, p. 84) – and adds in the text the hope that God will forgive the son's 'crueltyes and undutiffullness' to her just as 'I, Elizabeth Frek, his unhappy mother, doe' (B, below, p. 248). Her contention that the year following her husband's death was as dreadful as any mortal had suffered now also ambiguously associates her son's behaviour with the loss of her husband: 'and those frinds I most trusted most deceived me, besids my own sons undutifullness to me, which affter the loss of Mr Frek was enough to have brok the hart of any mortall butt my wretched self' (B, below, p. 255). Whether she did in fact intend to suggest that the son's neglect of his mother was second in sorrow only to her husband's death, his growing silence continues to appear grievous from the perspective of later years. Ralph Freke's return to West Bilney after his long absence only confirms the tension. One of the last entries in the second manuscript records her attendance at a Sunday service where she had not been with him for seven years: 'My greatt and good God forgive him this and all his other mistaks to Elizabeth Freke' (B, below, p. 288). The narrative of her final months continued in the vellum-bound volume adds that her son frowned all the while they were in church 'for I know nott whatt (except itt were his feare of my coming alive home againe)' (W, below, pp. 197–8). Disagreements with her daughter-in-law and disappointment with their refusal to let her care for her grandchild prompted the familiar plea for divine forgiveness by 'unhappy mee, his wretched mother'. Yet Elizabeth Freke also writes in one of her last passages that for months after her son and family left she never went to bed dry-eyed: worried about reports of his death, 'I have paid those tears due to his death in his liffe to him' (W, below, p. 208).

Elizabeth Freke's troubled relationship with her son recalls her ambivalent feelings about her husband. The love she never expresses openly seems implicit in the reluctance to lose her only child in marriage and the desire to keep one of the grandchildren in his absence. Her close bond with young Jack Freke, the image of her son, suggests especially a maternal love, however much it is displaced; and her willingness later to hold her son responsible for the death of the boy implies a deep-seated feeling of betrayal. Like the decades of marriage, the years of troubled motherhood blurred love and blame.

Closely associated with her son's ingratitude during the years of widowhood is the irresponsibility of the other male figure who failed her, her cousin and attorney John Freke. Both narratives rue her decision to give him legal power, the later one adding bitterly, 'Lett me be a warning to trust friends with letters of aturny' (B, below, p. 256). Recalling in 1712 the cousin's willingness to renegotiate her son's lease, revised entries for 1707 complain that he 'ruiened me'. Her cousin, she asserts in retrospect, took advantage of her ill health and pressed her to sign the agreement; in his callous dealings he left her little recourse other than the prayer, 'From such friends and friendship, good Lord, deliver mee and forgive my son his undutifullness to mee, his poor unhappy mother, and grant his children may nott pay my debtt by their undutifullness to him' (B, below, p. 257). Over the years legal problems with local rents and debts increased her sense of grievance, exacerbating feelings of harassment as well as strengthening her resistance; and in the rewriting she expresses her growing belief that she cannot trust her attorney or any of her friends. By the end of 1711 both accounts of this period reflect Elizabeth Freke's conviction that she is being used by everyone. Weakened by attacks of asthma, plagued by diminishing eyesight, and confined largely to a chair, she found it easy to blame her cousin John Freke.

Accounts of earlier troubles reflect, paradoxically, in the rewriting feelings of vulnerability and tenacity. Returning to England in 1684 with her young son, Freke now appears especially isolated, having 'nott a place now to putt my unhappy head in either in England or Ireland' (B, below, p. 223). Alone in the sparsely furnished thatched house, she was forced 'to seek my fortune amongst a pack of bruite beast who endevered my rhuien as by their threats to me dayly, and my deer father dead, Mr Frek gone to sea, and my self quitt a stranger in this country. Leftt with nither mony or bed or the least of goods or credid' (B, below, p. 225). The new description of the final journey from Ireland in 1696 no longer blames her maid Margaret for the loss of her clothes: 'a roghy watterman stole every ragg of my clothes'. Freke was later denied her rightful place in the manor house, she now insists, because the death of Lady Richardson was 'concealed' from her; those who sought her ruin then subjected her to the 'shame' and further injustice of the courts. Yet the woman who was not above portraying herself as a weak and helpless widow in her protracted disagreement with the bishop of Norwich and in her refusal to appear before a drainage commission also appears assertive. She becomes the mother who now claims greater credit for the recovery of her crippled infant son and the wife who manages through her own 'care and skill' to relieve the suffering of her husband's life-threatening gout. With an independence missing from the earlier memoir, she refuses to accept at Bilney her sister Judith Austen's financial help: 'I thank God I had learned the way of shifting better then borrowing and ever esteemed itt more honorable to unhapy me' (B, below, p. 226). When her narrative later records that God had spared her to face the miseries and vexations of a return to Ireland, she projects courageous resolve, though she cannot resist further complaint about the four-and-a-half miserable years. 'I have undergone more then mortoll tongue can speak' is a claim that epitomizes her characteristic pattern of self-vindication. 'And tho seventeen year pastt', she continues, 'I have seen the fall of most of my enimise and am able to subsistt withoutt the help of my friends' (B, below, p. 229).

While Elizabeth Freke finds special pleasure in the misfortunes of specific enemies, dwelling in each manuscript on the just suffering of her antagonists, she obviously wants the support from others she claims not to need. Near the end of her life the troubled relationship with her sister Judith Austen described in the revised narrative especially reveals her ambivalence. An entry for 11 September 1710 recording the departure of her sister from West Bilney notes only the payment of £20 for the coach that 'I mightt receive noe further pitty or obligation on thatt accountte' (B, below, p. 266). Her resentment when she learns her sister left her not to return home but to visit others leads to the ironic remark,

'My God forgive her and raise her and hers upp better friends then I have bin to her and them' (B, below, p. 268). A lengthy itemized list of the money and gifts she had given her sister and niece adds bite to the prayer. The implicit rebuke was occasioned at least in part by a related disagreement a year later when her niece Betty Austen ended a three-month visit at West Bilney after her mother had written three letters requesting the daughter's return. Elizabeth Freke apparently did not want to lose the valued companionship, and she later notes in the revised manuscript that she gave her niece £50 for plate and £5 for expenses, but not before she complains about her sister's selfishness: 'affter my kind giveing her above fiffteen hundred pound, she might have spared this awhile to me, Eliz Frek; for I had deserved itt and more of her thatt have bin to her like a mother from her childhood. Butt my God forgive her and be my supportt' (B, below, p. 278). The falling out reflects a fear of being forsaken that prompts, almost reflexively, her defensive independence, and the dismay perhaps explains the deletion in the second memoir of a passage describing the kindness of her sister after the death of Percy Freke. Typical of the revision and her later years in general is the need to measure relationships in monetary terms.

From the earliest time in her marriage, money had been both a source of conflict and security, a preoccupation that increased with the years of widowhood. The value Elizabeth Freke places on wealth is clear at the beginning of the revision when she characterizes her first unhappy years in London 'wher I twice misscarryed, [and] where I lost two thousand five hundred pounds outt of my six thousand seven hundred sixty fowre pounds' (B, below, p. 213). The new collocation of miscarriages and money quantifies in remarkable terms what loss had come to mean near the end of her life. Money had become for her, quite simply, a measure of self-definition amidst isolation, sickness, and insecurity. Her awareness of the liberating power of money is even more noticeable in the relationship with her son. When her revised entry on the birth of his first child expresses the hope that the grandchild will be a better comfort to his mother than her son had been, she cannot resist adding that he 'was borne butt to two hundred pound a yeare and by Gods blesing on my industry has affter my death above two thousand pound a yeare. And I have provided for his two eldest sons' (B, below, p. 238). The desire and the failure to buy love appear again in her reaction to the naming of the grandson born after the accidental death of young Jack Freke. His parents gave their new infant the name of the dead son, resisting Percy Freke's desire to have the grandchild named in memory of his own father. 'Butt itt was deneyd him', the second manuscript observes with no apparent concession to the parents' feelings, 'and nott to bee purchased by me, his unhappy mother' (B, below, p. 250). Elizabeth Freke was able to acquire, however, the baronetcy for her son; and though the last visit ended with disagreements about unpaid debts and charges of ingratitude, she found some comfort in reviewing all the material wealth earned through her own efforts and to be left to her descendants. The list of expenditures dated 14 September 1712 and included in the second manuscript ends a detailed account of outlays for her husband's fatal illness and sums lost to unscrupulous tenants with the additional defiant note: 'Thus have I lived neer seven years in my widowhood in a continuall trouble and to see the fall of most of my enimies without the assistance, help, or comfortt of one friend' (B, below, p. 304).

Other lists compiled in 1712 complement the revision. Updated accounts of the West Bilney leases, the wealth she had brought her husband, and her own personal estate, along with records of the donative living and inventories of documents, are all part of a self-image reaffirmed in the expectation of death. From the need to count the bottles of wine in a closet to the detailing of every household furnishing, listing becomes a form of definition as well as a justification that reflects a fundamental desire to find order, control, and worth. Perhaps appropriately the last entry is a list of what she had given the West Bilney church but had taken away when she was excommunicated. This final act of repossession fittingly culminates Elizabeth Freke's desire to repossess the decades of her life. Together her manuscript narratives form a distinct and valuable attempt to refashion and perhaps reclaim the past. At times painfully defiant and obviously self-serving, their representation and re-creation nevertheless shape a self-portrayal of vivid individuality unusual among earlier domestic memoirs. Hers is a sensibility whose immediate counterpart may well be found in the fictional narratives shaped by the novels that later explore the central concerns of money, marriage, and family.

PROVENANCE   The British Library has no account of the manuscript acquisitions other than the fact that they were 'Presented by Mary, Lady Carbery', in 1941, two years after her death. The bequest also included a geographical survey of the British Isles and a list of dukes, marquesses, and earls Elizabeth Freke gathered in 1669 from William Camden's *Britannia* and Ralph Brooke's *A Catalogue and Succession ... of this Realme* (BL, Add. MS. 45720); miscellaneous Freke papers and Carbery correspondence (BL, Add. MS. 45721 A); and an annotated copy of the family genealogy begun by Ralph Freke and printed in 1825 (BL, Add. MS. 45721 B). The five volumes appear to be all the materials in Carbery's possession directly related to her edition. She provides no information about the provenance of the two immediately relevant manuscripts, mentioning in the edition only that Freke's 1669 geographical and historical compilation was at Castle Freke and that a manuscript by Grace Freke 'copied from a Diary of her Grandmother's' was at Hannington. The present resident of Hannington Hall, Mrs Mary Hussey-Freke, has no knowledge of Grace Freke's manuscript copy or its whereabouts. Like the Castle Freke manuscript, which has the bookplate of Elizabeth Freke's son Ralph, presumably many of her papers remained for generations in the Freke family. A major exception appears to be the vellum-bound manuscript. While Lady Mary Carbery may have come into possession of the later version of the autobiography through marriage, she bought the commonplace book containing the other account from a Norfolk resident.

An undated notation on a small piece of blue paper attached to its blank second folio identifies the previous owner: 'Diary ("White Vellum Book of Remembrances") of Mrs. Eliz. Freke bought by me, Mary Carbery, from Mr. Edmund Kent for £10'. A summary of the manuscript's contents written by G. G. Coulton and later interleaved establishes an approximate date of purchase and the identity of the owner. During one of his visits to the Coulton family house at Pentney, before he had begun to establish his reputation as a medieval scholar, Coulton was lent the manuscript by Edmund Kent, whom he acknowledges as the owner at the end of the summary written 'in this month of August 1890'.[53] A faded signature cut from the vellum cover and pasted to the back of the new cover when the British Library rebound the manuscript notes in an early hand 'Ed[ ]d Kent East Winch-Hall Lynn'. The identity of the signatory, whether Edward or Edmund, remains uncertain; no ambiguity exists, however, about the new owner, a retired gentleman farmer who was lord of the manors of East Winch and Carrow. Edmund Kent, his wife Anne, and their daughter Muriel are listed in the 1881 Census Index as the residents of East Winch Hall;[54] the East Winch parish register records his burial at All Saints on 24 March 1900. Lady Carbery would have purchased the manuscript from him, then, sometime during the 1890s, after she had married the ninth Lord Carbery.

How Edmund Kent came to possess the vellum-bound manuscript is unclear. East Winch Hall seems to provide the link with Elizabeth Freke and the means of possession; the provenance, unfortunately, cannot be traced through her association with the residents of the manor. The nearby neighbours mentioned quite often in her last years, the Edgworths and Langleys, were not in the end especially intimate

<hr />

[53] Coulton mentions none of the Kent family in his autobiographical account of his early life in King's Lynn, where he was born, and at the Pentney house his father later purchased (*Fourscore Years: An Autobiography* [Cambridge, 1943]).

[54] 1881 Census Index, PRO, RG 11/1995.

acquaintances; in any case, soon after her death the estate was lost to a London attorney who held a mortgage on the property. Only considerably later did the Kent family occupy East Winch Hall. Edmund Kent appears as a gentleman and freeholder of East Winch in the poll for knights of the shire in 1802; no Kent precedes him in the 1768 poll.[55] Originally a grocer and draper from Wereham, Edmund Kent married Charlotte Shene, the heir of Thomas Shene of Little Dunham; their son Edmund Kent (1800–1876) of Baron's Hall, Fakenham, a well-known solicitor who by 1864 had become lord of the manors of East Winch and Carrow, was the father of the Edmund Kent who sold the Freke manuscript to Lady Carbery.[56] His predecessor, George Edward Kent, had been vicar of East Winch from 1820 to 1842.[57] The Kents were therefore in a position to gain the manuscript, conceivably along with the other possessions of East Winch Hall or more probably in their roles as landholder or lawyer.

MANUSCRIPTS The folios of the vellum-bound commonplace book (BL, Add. MS. 45718), which measure eight inches wide and eleven and eight-tenth inches high, have more than one numbering. The verso of the initial folio's blank first side, numbered in ink ii, identifies the owner: 'Elizabeth Frek her book Given mee by my Cosen Sep. 1684'. Interleaved and numbered iii–v in pencil are the Carbery and Coulton additions. The commonplace book itself contains 245 folios numbered in pencil 1–245 on the recto sides. The first parts follow sequentially until the end of folio 103; subsequent entries begin with the last folio, continuing backward from folio 245v to folio 104r. The first several of

---

[55] *The Poll for Knights of the Shire for the County of Norfolk,* ... *July 20, 1802* (Norwich, 1802), 66. Edmund Kent, listed in the 1806 poll, appears as a freeholder in the 1817 *Norfolk Poll and Proceedings Relative to the Election* (Norwich, 1817), 91. 'Edmund Kent, sen., Esq.' is lord of the manor in William White, *History, Gazetteer and Directory of Norfolk* (Sheffield, 1836), 461.

[56] Rye, ii. 1,073; Carthew, iii. 95. Edmund Kent was buried in East Winch on 30 June 1839 at the age of eighty-three. The 1864 edition of White's Norfolk directory lists his son as lord of the manors of East Winch and Carrow. *The Poll for the Election of Two Knights of the Shire* ... *Taken July 22nd, 1865* (East Dereham, 1865), 139, also associates Edmund Kent of Fakenham with East Winch; the 1835, 1837, and 1852 polls note that Edmund and George Kent are eligible to vote from East Winch. Edmund Kent was buried in East Winch on 25 August 1876, three years before his wife Elizabeth, who was interred on 17 November 1879. The 1885–6 *Register of Persons Entitled to Vote* (Wisbech, n.d.) notes that Edmund, their son, has a 'Share of freehold house and land' (fol. N7); he is identified in White's 1883 Norfolk directory as lord of the manors of East Winch and Carrow.

[57] Reverend George Edward Kent is lord of the manor in the 1845 and 1854 editions of White's Norfolk directory. Educated at Corpus Christi and ordained in 1820, George Kent would become affiliated in 1848 with All Saints, St John's Wood, London (J. A. Venn, *Alumni Cantabrigienses. Part II: From 1752 to 1900,* 6 vols. [Cambridge, 1940–54], iv. 25).

these sections are paginated on each side in ink. The ink numbering is original to the manuscript; the pencil numbering is that of the British Library. Another pagination, however, also exists in red ink. With Edmund Kent's permission, G. G. Coulton renumbered both sides of the folios, completing the original ink pagination by numbering folios 35r to 103r (pages 63–200) and continuing from folios 244r–103v (pages 201–482). Thus the remembrances, which comprise the last of the sections starting from the manuscript's opening folios, begin on folio 46v or page 86 and end on folio 103v or page 200. The pencilled foliation rather than Coulton's pagination will be cited in the text.

The pagination of the other commonplace book is more straight-forward. The manuscript bound in the original brown wallpaper, patterned with a bird and a house with a clock at the top of its cupola, contains fifty-three folios numbered once again in pencil and measuring eight inches wide and twelve and eight-tenth inches high. The first two folios are blank except for the words 'A Letter' at the top of folio 1v; the remembrances begin on folio 3v, following another blank side. Freke paginated these memoirs 1–46 (folios 3v–26r). After two blank and unnumbered sides she then paginated a series of miscellaneous entries 2–31 (folios 27v–42r), the first of which is the ledger of expenses related to her husband's illness and death included in this edition. The remaining folios contain a number of blank sides interspersed among unpaginated entries. Once again the pencilled foliation done by the British Library will be cited in the text. The miscellaneous material taken from either this or the vellum-bound manuscript will be identified by folio numbers designated B or W.

The miscellaneous documents included in this edition complement the two versions of the remembrances. Like the ledger from B of the expenses incurred during Percy Freke's fatal illness, many of them are also accounts or assessments. Selections from the lists summarizing 'how West Billney stands' over the years have been limited to the time after Elizabeth Freke gained possession, excluding also the lengthy chancery decrees and legal agreements affecting the earlier estate but including one of her histories of the property. Audits and inventories chosen often from quite similar versions in both manuscripts recount funds given to her husband, received from her father, or acquired by herself and list documents, cordial waters, and household goods in her possession. The limited length of this edition prevents the inclusion of the Pentney land taxes, the fragment of her will, and the summaries of her protracted religious and legal disputes. Omitted too are the numer-ous recipes and the redactions of Gerard's and Culpeper's works, which are such a large part of the vellum manuscript, as well as from this manuscript a political song allegedly composed by her father-in-law Arthur Freke and the three anonymous poems, 'The Downefall of

Charing Cross by the Long Parliamt' (1648), 'The British Ambassadress Speech to the French Kinge' (1713), and an epitaph on William III.

EDITORIAL METHOD   The edited transcriptions of the manuscripts conform to the recommendations of the Camden Society and the principles established in R. F. Hunnisett, *Editing Records for Publication* (British Records Association, 1977). Capitalization has been modernized, and abbreviations other than those of signatures have been silently expanded; the ampersand has been replaced with the conjunction. Elided words have been separated and broken words have been joined according to the contemporary usage when Freke's intention is not clearly established among the textual variations. The original spelling has been retained; however, i and j, u and v have been modernized and to/too/two, of/off, and on/one silently emended. The punctuation has been modernized for greater clarity, though here too a sense of the original has been approximated. Possessives have not been changed, nor have numbers been hyphenated; apostrophes are original to the manuscript, and variants in the punctuation of Freke's abbreviated first name have been retained. The semicolon has at times been used for clarity when a comma might ordinarily be more appropriate.

The edited text of the remembrances reflects their chronological structure. Dates that Elizabeth Freke added in the margins to underscore her recollections have been printed where appropriate in bold type within the body of the text. The entries themselves, which often occur originally in longer passages or blocks of material, have been indented to reflect chronology. Occasionally Freke repeats with slight variations the end of the previous line when she begins a new folio side; these are retained and the preceding versions silently omitted. Editorial clarifications are included in square brackets, as are lacunae. The round brackets are original to the text; angle brackets indicate additions and deletions. Entries obviously out of place in the manuscripts have been moved only when noted; only the most obvious slips, such as the repetition of a word and transpositions, have been silently corrected. Unless designated as new style (NS) the dates reflect the English practice in force until 1752; those between 1 January and 24 March will be cited with both years, separated by a stroke (e.g., 1641/2).

DOCUMENTATION   *The Dictionary of National Biography, Alumni Cantabrigienses*, and *Alumni Oxonienses* are cited in the notes only when they provide the sole clarification or have not been superceded. Transcriptions of parish registers – usually held by the Society of Genealogists, London – are acknowledged; otherwise the specific local records and register bills of baptisms, marriages, and deaths are not noted. All unattributed definitions are based on the *Oxford English Dictionary*.

Variations in the spelling of proper nouns have been eliminated whenever possible in the notes to reflect those in works such as *Gazetteer of the British Isles* and *Cambridge Biographical Encyclopedia*; clarifications of titles as well as, in some instances, spellings are based whenever possible on the 106th edition of *Burke's Peerage & Baronetage* and the revised edition of *The Complete Peerage*. Gazettes are cited by the number of the issue rather than the date; along with clarification, they indicate implicitly possible sources of Freke's interests and information.

I. REMEMBRANCES, 1671–1714

[fol. 46v]

Some few remembrances of my misfortuns have attended me in my unhappy life since I were marryed, which was November the i4, i67i

i67i, Novembr i4 Thursday, Novembr i4, i67i, and Childermas Day, I was privatly marryed to Mr Percy Frek by Doctter Johnson in Coven Garden, my Lord Russells chaplin, in London, to my second cosin, eldest son to Captain Arthur Frek and grandson to Mr William Frek, the only brother of Sir Thomas Frek of Dorsettshiere, who was my grandfather, and his son Mr Ralph Frek [was] my own deer father.[1] And my mother was Sir Thomas Cullpepers daughter of Hollingburne in Kentt; her name was Cicelia Cullpeper. Affter being six or 7 years engaged to Mr Percy Freke, I was in a most grievous rainy, wett day marryed withoutt the knowledg or consentt of my father or any friend in London, as above.

i672, Jully 26 Being Thursday, I were againe remaried by my deer father by Doctter Uttram att St Margaretts Church in Westminster by a licence att least fowre years in Mr Freks pocttett and in a griveous tempestious, stormy day for wind as the above for raigne.[2] I were given by my deer father, Ralph Frek, Esqr, and the eldest of his fowre

[1] *The Registers of St. Paul's Church, Covent Garden, London*, ed. William H. Hunt, *Harleian Society*, 35 (1907), 49, indicates they were married on 14 November 1672. Freke confirms the 1671 date in an entry she adds to the West Bilney register and in her miscellaneous documents (below, p. 315). Childermas, the Feast of the Holy Innocents, commemorates on 28 December the young children Herod killed. Childermas was also, however, 'the day of the week throughout the year on which that feast fell, widely held to be a day of ill omen' (*ODCC*, 329). In 1671, 28 December was also a Thursday, so conceivably Freke intended the ominous association. See, however, her reference to Childermas, below, p. 75 n. 117. Samuel Johnson (1649–1703) became the chaplain of William Russell, Lord Russell, in 1679; he consoled his patron when Russell was executed for his alleged involvement in a plot against the king's life. See also below, p. 143 n. 256.

[2] *The Register of St. Margaret's Westminster London 1660–1675*, transc. Herbert F. Westlake and ed. Lawrence E. Tanner, *Harleian Society*, 64 (1935), 184, dates the marriage 26 June 1673. In her miscellaneous documents (below, p. 315), however, Freke dates the marriage 24 July 1672. William Owtram (1626–1679), archdeacon of Leicester and prebendary of Westminster, was rector of St Margaret's for the last fifteen years of his life. Two London marriage licences issued by the dean and chapter of Westminster contain different biographical information: '1669 June 23 Percy Freke [*sic* subs] of Middle Temple, Gent., Bachr, abt 24, and Mrs Elizabeth Freke, of St Martin's in the Fields, Spr, abt 22 & at own dispose'; '1672 Aug. 7 Percy Freake, of Middle Temple, Esq., Bachr, abt 27, & Mrs Elizabeth Freke, of Westminster, Spr, abt 22, her parents dead' (Chester and Armytage, eds., *Harleian Society*, 23 [1886], 165, 206).

daughters and the last marryed, being contracted to him by promise
for five years before, butt unwilling to give my sisters any presidentt of
my misfortunes prognosticated to mee by the two tempestious and
dreadfull days I were marryed on and which I looked on as fattall
emblems to me. Eliza. Freke

Agust 26 Mr Frek, Agust 26 coming over St James Parke aboutt i2
a clock att night, challenged my lord of Roscomon either to fight him
in St James Parke presently or to pay him downe a thousand pounds
my lord had long owed Mr Freke.[3] Butt the 26 of Agust att three a
clock in the morning ten men of the lifegard came and fetched Mr
Freke outt of his bed from me and immediatly hurryed him to Whit
Hall before Secetary Coventry, I nott knowing whatt itt was for more
then words spoken.[4] This was the begining of my troubles for my
disobedience in marrying as I did. Eliz Freke

i673, Febuary i4 My deer father was pleased to bestow on me as
a portion a mortgage on Sir Robertt Brooke estate of 500, five hundred,
pound a yeare neer the Green Man in Epping Forrest, five miles from
London, thatt I might nott bee disapoynted of a subsistance for my
life.[5] Which estate Mr Frek sudenly, unknown to me, contracted for to
sell to Sir Josias Child for five thousand six hundred sixty fowre pounds
or thereabouts, who was a greatt bruer in London; which niether my
deer father, my selfe, or my 5 trustees did know any thing of.[6] Soe off
itt was sould.

[fol. 47r]

i673, July 7 Aboutt the begining of Jully i673, to the best of my
memory, Mr Frek sold outtright my fortune given me by my deer
father, unknown to him or me or any of my fowre trustees, to Sir Josias
Childe for the sume of 5764 pounds, or 5664 l. This was nott kind, for

---

[3] Wentworth Dillon, fourth earl of Roscommon (1633?–1685), a poet, translator, and
essayist, had, like Percy Freke, ties to the Boyles: his first marriage was to Frances, the
daughter of Richard, first earl of Burlington and second earl of Cork.

[4] Henry Coventry (c. 1618–1686), a prominent member of parliament, became one of
the two secretaries of state in 1672, serving until 1680 (*HC*, ii. 148–54).

[5] The Green Man was in Epping Forest off Wall Wood Lane in the area of Waltham
Stow (John Rocque, *An Exact Survey of the Cities of London and Westminster . . . with the County
about It for Nineteen Miles* [London, 1747], plate 9). Robert Brooke's mother, Elizabeth, was
the sister-in-law of Judith, the sister of Ralph's wife; 'Lady Brook' and 'Lady Mary
Brooks', probably Robert's sister Mary, contributed to Freke's collections of recipes and
remedies.

[6] When Brooke (c. 1637–1669) died, his trustees sold his Wanstead estate in Essex to
Sir Josiah Child (c. 1630–1699) for £11,500. Child, the owner of a brewery in Southwark
and a prominent figure in London commerce and government, rebuilt Wanstead House
(*HC*, i. 726–7, ii. 57–9).

now I were by itt turned outt of doors and had nott a place to putt my unfortunate head in; and all my fortune, being in mony in a bankers hand, was in danger to be spentt by us or lost by him, which a little affter greatt part was to the vallue of i500, fiffteen hundred, pounds.

September i5 Aboutt the midle of September Mr Frek endeavouring to place my fortune on an estate in Hampshire of one Mr Coopers and trusting to one Mr Worldlige as his agentt in the purchas, wee weer cheated by them on a composition for aboutt fiffteen hundred pounds as the least loss; or elce Coopers cheatt was above two thousand (2000) pounds in fallce mortgages, he nott being worth any thing; and [we] had received att the first galle a thousand pounds in mony and three or 4 years law, butt to noe purpose.[7]

Thus was three of my unhappy years spentt in London in a marryed life, and I never had, as I remember, the command of five pounds of my fortune. Wher I miscaried twice and had very little of my husbands company, which was no small grife to me, I being only governed by my affecttions in this my marrying and withoutt the consentt of any of my frinds; and fearing all my fortune would be spentt, resolved with Mr Frek to goe for Ireland to his estat and try our fortuns there.

i674, Jully i4 Aboutt the midle of Jully my husband and my little familly wentt downe to Hanington to my deer fathers to take our leaves of him to goe for Ireland.

Agust 2 From thence I wentt to Leigh to Sir George Norton neer Bristoll to take leave of my sister Norton, who was then redy to lye in, as in two days affter she did.

4 My Lady Norton lay in of a daughter, a lovely fine child; **i2** which on my sisters desire I christned itt with the Lady Balldin, who was the grandmother, by the name of Grace.[8]

22 I, lyeing still for wind and shiping to goe for Ireland, wentt aboutt

[7] Thomas Freke of Shroton and John Cooper's son Sir Anthony Ashley Cooper were friends (K. H. D. Haley, *The First Earl of Shaftesbury* [Oxford, 1968], 626), but the transaction seems not to have involved the immediate family. The dispute concerns the 800–acre manor of Ditcham and Sunworth in the Hampshire parish of Buriton that Percy Freke had agreed to buy from a 'Richard Cooper esqr' for £7,300, the details of which are in Cooper's answer to a bill of complaint by 'Pearcy Freake esqr' (PRO, C 9/64/27). No relationship has been established between the agent and the only Hampshire Worldlige to have been identified, John Worlidge of Petersfield, an author of agricultural books (*The Victoria History of Hampshire and the Isle of Wight*, ed. William Page, 5 vols. [London, 1900–12], v. 425, 475). A composition is an agreement between a creditor and debtor in which the creditor settles for less than the original debt (Black, 259).

[8] Grace was born on 3 August and baptized on 10 August. Frances Norton's father-in-law, George Norton, died on 29 February 1667/8 and was buried at Holy Trinity Church in Abbots Leigh on 4 March; his wife, Ellen, who then married Sir Timothy Baldwin, was buried on 10 May 1677 in Abbots Leigh.

the two and twentieth of Agust to the Bath, wher with my husband I staid above a month.

Octtober 7 When my deer father heering I were with child sentt his coach and horses to fetch mee from the Bath to him to Hanington, wher I wentt aboutte the begining of Octtober. Mr Frek and I with my family went to my fathers to lye in att Hanington with him and my deer aunte Freke.[9]

[fol. 47v]

1674, Octtober 7 From Octtober the 7 to the Jully affter, I staid with my deer father and my auntt Frek thatt bred me up till the Midsomer affter, most kindly treated and used by both att Hanington till I were able to goe for Ireland.

1674/5, March 7 Sunday, March the 7, God took to himselfe my deer sister Sir George Chouts lady, who dyed of the small pox, as did Sir Georg Choutt, her husband, aboutt twelve years before of the small pox, which time she continued his widow from two and twenty years of age to her death.[10] My deer sister left behind her one son and one daughter, viz., Sir George Chout, a barranett now liveing (November 1702) and a batchaller, and her daughter, named Cicelia affter the name of her mother and my mothers—<dyed presently after of the small pox in London; both buryed att Hanington in Kent>.

1675, March 26 Aboutt the 26 of March my deer sister Choutt, being imbalmed in London where she dyed, was carryed downe to Hollingburne in Kentt and interred in my deer mothers grave in the chancell there, who dyed when I were butt seven years and a week old and the eldest of five daughters shee left behind her; who was nott mised by us, wee haveing soe good and kind a father and an aunt of my mothers sister.[11]

Aprill 5 God took to himselfe my deer neece Mrs Ciceally Choute of the small pox neer a month affter the death of my deer sister, which

[9] Frances Freke was baptized in Hollingbourne on 3 October 1613 and buried there on 19 December 1682.

[10] The date also on her monument in the Hollingbourne church of All Saints (BL, Add. MS. 11259, fol. 5v; Cave-Browne, 35). Cicely's husband was buried on 8 June 1664 at Bethersden. Her son, Sir George Choute/Chute, baptized in Bethersden on 10 February 1664/5, was buried there on 13 February 1721/2. The baronetcy he received on 17 September 1684 became extinct when he died without an heir, having never married. The estates then went to Edward Austen, the grandson of Judith Austen described in her will as his 'good ffriend and dear Relation' (CB, iv. 134; Hasted, vii. 488–9; PRO, PROB 11/587/177 and PROB 11/560/201).

[11] The Hollingbourne register records an earlier date of burial, 12 March; it and a church monument also date the burial of Cicely Freke 6 January 1650/1, two years later than Freke's age implies.

on her death bed request was buryed in her mothers grave in the chancell of Hollingburne in Kentt. Shee did dye in London, as did my sister, both to my greatt grife.[12]

June 2d Wensday, June the second, my deer son, Mr Ralph Freke, was borne aboutt three a clock in the affternoone att my fathers att Hanington, and by him with my aunte Frek and Sir George Norton hee was christned Ralph Frek of my deer fathers name.[13] I were 4 or 5, five, days in labour of him and had for him fowre midwifes aboutt me when he was borne, the man midwife afirming he had bin long dead in me to my husband and aunte [and] sister Norton with my Lady Thinn, all who were with mee severall days in this my extremity.[14] Att last the resullt was thatt he should be taken in peices from me or I should nott live one howre, which concideration of my life all consented to the takeing away my dead child from me in peices. Butt whilst the man midwife was putting on his butchers habitt to come aboutt me, my greatt and good God thatt never failed me (or deneyed my reasonable request) raised me up a good woman midwife who came in att this junture of time and for aboutt two or three howrs in her shift worked till by my Gods mercy and providence to me I was saffly delivered. [fol. 48r] And tho of a dead child hurt with severall greatt holes in his head, hurtt by midwiffes, my God raised him up to me thatt he was the same night christned by my deer fathers name, Ralph Frek. For which mercy to him and me I beg I may never forgett to be thankfull.

3d June I putt my son into the hand of a good surgion for att least six weeks, who came every day from Highworth, a mile from my deer fathers, to dress him, I being allmost all the time confined to my bed by the misfortune of this my hard laboure of him.[15]

Jully 7 In July my son was taken with a through thrush with which, and his head, he was againe given over for dead and carried away from me in order to a buriall.[16] Butt from this misfortune my God

[12] A monument now missing from the Hollingbourne church also states that she died on 5 April 1675 'in the 12th year of her age' (Cave-Browne, 35, 36; BL, Add. MS. 11259, fol. 5r). She was buried on 15 April.

[13] '1675. June 2nd. Ralph the sonn of Peircy Freke Esq & Madam Elizabeth his wife was borne & baptized'.

[14] Lady Thynne, who also contributed several of the recipes and remedies Freke collected, is either Mary, the wife of Sir Henry Frederick Thynne and the mother of Thomas Thynne, the future Viscount Weymouth who represented Oxford University in parliament and would inherit the Longleat estate in Wiltshire in 1682, or – less likely – his wife, Frances, the daughter of Heneage Finch, third earl of Winchilsea (HC, iii. 565–6; CP, xii, pt. 2. 585–8).

[15] No contemporary surgeon from Highworth appears in the Wiltshire Articles of Subscription (Wiltshire Record Office, D1/22/3–5).

[16] A mouth and throat infection, thrush was considered common among children; malign forms, however, were 'putrid, corrosive and spreading', covering 'the Roof of the

raised him up againe, I hope, to be his servantt and a comfortt to mee insteed of my deer sister Choutt, whom God took from me about two month before and who was to have binn with me in all this my troubles of lying in, wher my sister Norton and a greatt many of my frinds were mett together att my deer fathers to be merry. Which mirth my God soone turned to mourning <by the death of my sister and her daughter>.

December 14 Aboutt the midle of December whilst Mr Frek and I were in Ireland, my sons nurse by carelesness brok his legg shortt in the hackle bone.[17] Which she kept privatte for neer a quarter of a yeare till a jelley was grown between itt, she keeping him in his cradle and every body belived he was breeding of his teeth, hee haveing two att eighteen weeks old and att thatt age could stand allmost alone till this misfortune befell him.

1675/6, January 8 Aboutt the begining of January my deer father and deer sister the Lady Norton sentt and took my child away from nurse (Mr Freke and I being in Ireland knowing nothing of itt for troubling of us) and putt itt to a dry nurse close by my father att Hanington. Wher with nurse Deverall and in her lap affter the bone was sett, he lay in a sad condition for above half a yeare nott to stirr hand or foott, all dispaireing of his life.[18] Butt from this misfortun my God, I humbly thank him, recovered him with my poore, weak endeavours and his blesing on them thatt now, I thank God, he goes straight and well, and noe signe of these misfortunes, and the father of two lovely boys in Ireland, November 14, 1702.

1675, September 5 I wentt with Mr Frek for Ireland the first time and left my deer and only son aboutt a quarter [year] old att nurse att Hyworth. I landed att Youghhall in the county of Watterford, where when I came I had noe place fitt to putt my unfortunat head in. From whence Mr Frek and his mother carryed me to Rustillian, a house of the earls of Inchequeens,[19] where I staid neer eight months and miscaryed, my husbands mother being very unkind to mee – which

---

Mouth and Tongue', making 'deep Scabs', and affecting 'the internal Parts of the Throat' (John Pechey, *The Store-house of Physical Practice* [London, 1695], 432).

[17] Huckle-bone: hip bone.

[18] Anne, the wife of Samuel Deverell, gave birth to Jane in 1647; Jane Deverell married Daniel Bayly in Hannington on 6 November 1676. Either could have been the nurse.

[19] The estate of Rostellan, 'a noble seat, pleasantly situated' on the eastern side of Cork Harbour about two miles from Cloyne (Smith, i. 141). The second earl of Inchiquin, William O'Brien (c. 1640–1692), was married at the time to Margaret Boyle, the daughter of Roger Boyle, first earl of Orrery. Besides the family links with the Boyles, Arthur Freke and the first earl of Inchiquin had supported Charles I against the Irish insurgents; Percy Freke and the second earl traveled together from England to Ireland and were later attainted for their resistance to James II (Lodge, ii. 48–58; *CP*, vii. 52–3).

wentt very neer me, [fol. 48v] I never haveing had one unkind word from my father in all my whole life.

1676, Aprill 14 My deer fatther sentt for Mr Frek and me over from Ireland aboutt my deer son, whom all expectted hee would be a cripple or dye of his legg, he being given over by all.

May 7 Aboutt the begining of May or end of Aprill I landed att Bristoll, where Mr Frek sent to Abots Leigh to my Lady Norton to come to me. Butt my deer sister giveing me soe sad an accountt of my son, wee wentt away immediatly for London and sentt our servants to my deer fathers to bring him up with his nurse in a coach to us. Butt my child nott being able to stirr and my father every day, as he told mee, expectting his death, [he] would nott lett me goe downe into Hanington soe much as to see him, which was noe small grife to mee.

June 15 Aboutt the midle of June my deer father came up to London to me to satisfye me aboutt my son, of whose life he dispaired.

September 29 Aboutt the end of September, to my best remembrance, Mr Freke bought of my brother Austin with the consentt of my deer father West Billney in Norfolk, which he was pleased to bestow on mee and to settle itt on my son, now by Gods mercy to me in a faire way of recovery. He bought this estate of the Lord Richerson att the yearly rentt of 526 l. a yeare.[20] Butt Mr Frek nott being stronge enough with my mony to pay for itt, my deer father lentt me neer a thousand pounds to compleatt the purchas for mee on my husbands bond, which bond when I came over to see my own deer father the next springe he gave mee up withoutt paying him a peny of intrest for itt, to the greatt grife of my cosin Thom Frek, his executor.[21]

December 14 Aboutt the midle of December, to my best remembrance, Mr Freke sentt by my cosin Thom Frek to purchass outt my fathers right of Leeds Castle in Kentt. His arears on itt were, as to my best remembrance, two thousand five hundred pounds (2500), for which

---

[20] Thomas Richardson (1627–1674), second Baron Cramond, had inherited the manors of West Bilney and Pentney from his father, Thomas; his right to the Scottish peerage came from his father's stepmother, Elizabeth, baroness of Cramond. In 1647 he married Anne Gurney, the daughter of the lord mayor of London Sir Richard Gurney, and the title of Lord Cramond went first to Henry and then to William, their sons. Richardson represented Norfolk in the first two sessions of parliament to meet after the Restoration; he died on 16 May 1674 and was buried in Honingham (*Scots Peerage*, ii. 580–3; Blomefield, viii. 354, ii. 447; Rye, ii. 734; *HC*, iii, 330–2).

[21] Elizabeth's first cousin Thomas (c. 1638–1701), the son of John Freke of Cerne Abbas, Dorset and his second wife, Jane Shirley, had been educated at Middle Temple, where on 25 May 1655 he was 'bound with Messrs. Ralf Freake and John Rieves' (*Middle Temple Records*, iii. 1,079). A prominent Dorset official, he served as sheriff and high sheriff before his election in 1679 to the first of many parliaments. Luttrell notes his death in a 27 November diary entry for 1701 (v. 114); his will, however, was dated 29 November, and Iwerne Courtney parish records indicate he was buried on 12 December 1701 (PRO, PROB 11/463/5; SG, DO/R51, transcribed by P. J. Rives Harding; *HC*, ii. 365–6).

Mr Frek as earnest paid my deer father downe five hundred pounds (500 l.). The rest he was to pay when he had recovered itt of the Lord Cullpeper by law, and my master to sue in my fathers name for itt. Which he did and had a decree in chancery for 5750 pounds and the greatt guns of Rochester with the undershrife and 24 baylyes to give Mr Frek a quiett possesion.[22]

23 Which Mr Frek wentt downe into Kentt to take, where the tenants all aturned to him;[23] butt the Lady Cullpeper in with Alexander Cullpeper held outt the castle [fol. 49r] as the Lord Cullpepers right by the artt of a draw bridg in the mote and the fallcness of the shrifes and baylyes.[24]

1676, Decembr 24 Soe thatt affter the spending of five hundred pounds in law, and a hundred pound enroleing our decree, and a hundred and fiffty pound to the shrife and baylyes (I borrowed of my deer sister Choute), my deer cosin (Mr Frek) returned to London allmost dead of his jorney outt of Kentt Christmas Eve late att night. In which time the Lord Cullpeper privatly made his intrest with King James and with threats to the Lord Chancellor Finch, with threats of his futer rhuin iff he did nott revoke and reverse his decree given Mr Frek in Michellmas tearme.[25] Which was by these two greatt persons privatly done in the Candlemas tearme following and withoutt our

---

[22] Leeds Castle, a royal residence until Anthony St Leger gained possession in 1552, passed from his descendants into the hands of Sir Richard Smyth; his daughters and co-heirs sold the castle in 1632 to Sir Thomas Culpeper, who settled the property on his son Cheney (1601–1663), the oldest brother of Elizabeth Freke's mother, Cicely. Cheney mortgaged the castle to Ralph Freke in 1659; and when Cheney died intestate and in debt, his administrator John Colvert sold Leeds Castle to Thomas, second Lord Culpeper (1635–1689), the son of Cicely's sister Judith and John, first Lord Culpeper. The Frekes' suit in chancery claimed rightful ownership because the mortgage had not been paid (*Leeds Castle: Maidstone, Kent* [London, 1989]; David A. H. Cleggett, *History of Leeds Castle and Its Families*, 4th edn. [Maidstone, 1994]; Attree and Booker, 'The Sussex Colepepers', 67–8).

[23] Attornment is the tenants' formal recognition of a new landlord (Black, 119).

[24] Margaret, the wife of the second Lord Culpeper, was the daughter of Jean Van Hesse; Alexander Culpeper (1631?–1694), the son of Thomas Culpeper and Katherine St Leger, was a cousin and the secretary of the second Lord Culpeper (Attree and Booker, 'The Sussex Colepepers', 68–9, 71; Cleggett, *History of Leeds Castle*, 90).

[25] In a letter from Leeds Castle on 14 September 1675 to Secretary of State Joseph Williamson, Culpeper contends 'that some near relations of mine, who presented a petition to his Majesty against me', 'put in a bill against me in Hilary Term, and obtained a sequestration against me for not appearing'. The letter mentions that the king 'told me he was satisfied' with Culpeper's claim 'and would meddle no farther'; it concludes that the matter should be settled in court (*CSPD*, 1675–6, 294). The disputed issue may be that of Leeds Castle. James, duke of York, in any case, was not king. Heneage Finch (1621–1682), who began his public career in 1660 first in parliament and then as solicitor-general, rose to the position of lord chancellor in 1675. The year before his death he received the earldom of Nottingham (*HC*, ii. 317–22).

knowledge a month, tho we lived in London to atend this suitt and business.

1676/7, Febuary i2 Mr Frek pettitioned the lord chancellor and King Jams to have butt one heering of his cause more, tho they threw him outt thatt he might fall by law, and nott soe clandestinly, withoutt soe much as being favoured with a heering for itt. This was noe small loss and trouble to Mr Frek and me, butt nott to be holped butt by patience, our name being hatefull to King Jams for my cosin John Frek sake, whom he attempted to hang three severall times and once stood his tryall in the Old Bayly aboutt our time of being turned outt of our possesion of Leeds Castle.[26]

1677, May 2d I lay in of another son in Southhampton Square in London which by hard labour and severall frights was dead borne, which lyes buryed att the uper end of St Gilges chancell in London.[27]

Jully 20 I wentt with Mr Frek againe to my deer fathers in order to goe for Ireland, England being then full of plotts and troubles; where I staid for aboutt a month and wentt for Bristoll to gett a shipp for Ireland.[28]

---

[26] Elizabeth's second cousin, possibly once removed, was a descendant of her grandfather's brother John Freke. The Freke genealogy lists his father as Robert, but he is in fact the oldest of John and Margaret Freke's five children named in the father's will and residing at one time in the Dorset parish Winterbourne Strickland (PRO, PROB 11/278/360). Anthony à Wood's incomplete entry of 24 May 1676 seems relevant: 'In this month (May) ... Freake sent to the Tower for the ...; sometimes of Wadham. I have seen the libell, quaere' (*The Life and Times of Anthony Wood*, ed. Andrew Clark, 5 vols. [Oxford, 1891–1900], ii. 346). *The Registers of Wadham College*, ed. Gardiner, i. 279, indicates 'fil. Johannis Freke de Strickland, Dorcestr. gen. aet. 17' matriculated on 2 April 1669. John Freke, (1652–1717), who later handled Elizabeth Freke's legal business, was admitted to the Middle Temple on 30 June 1669 and was called to the bar on 5 May 1676 (*Middle Temple Register*, i. 179). A warrant issued on 28 May 1676 directed the constable of the Tower to hold John Freake 'for high treason, close prisoner' on undefined charges that seem connected to the publication of 'a scandalous paper of verses by one Belding *alias* Baldwin' of Gloucester (*CSPD*, 1676–7, 133; 1675–6, 567). On 6 June he was brought before the king's bench 'for high treason' but released on bail (*Historical Manuscripts Commission. The Manuscripts of S. H. Le Fleming, Esq., of Rydal Hall* [London, 1890], 127). An 11 September letter to Williamson notes 'We hear that Mr. Freke is also quitted'. On 10 July 1683 he was summoned in connection with Robert Ferguson, who was deeply implicated in the Rye House Plot to assassinate Charles II and the duke of York. Then on 19 May 1685 his name appeared among several sought, perhaps because of the threat posed by the supporters of the duke of Monmouth (*CSPD*, 1676–7, 318; 1683, 92; 1685, 157).

[27] Known by the eighteenth century as Bloomsbury Square, its three-and-one-half acres formed a 'pleasant, large, and beautiful Square' (Hatton, i. 9). The Church of St Giles in the Fields, St Giles's High Street, was razed and rebuilt in the 1730s. Its parish registers contain no entry of the burial.

[28] Charles II had adjourned parliament in May 1677, increasing the suspicions and fears of arbitrary government and popery raised by the king's dealing with France and Holland (David Ogg, *England in the Reign of Charles II*, 2nd edn., 2 vols. [Oxford, 1966], ii. 540–9).

Agust 25 An imbargoe being on all ships and all passengers nott to cross the seas withoutt a permitt, which we could nott procure, we wentt privatly off from Pill by boate to a shipp on Satterday, the 25 of Agust, and my second time of goeing for Ireland, when I left my deer son att Hanington with my deer father under his dry nurses care. Butt we were all like to be lost by most tempestyous winds and raine, butt by Gods mercy we putt in att Illford Combe.[29]

[fol. 49v]

i677, Agust 26 We putt in Sunday night att Illford Coomb, wher we stayed till Tuesday night.

28 A Wensday by two a clock in the morning, the 28 of Agust, wee wentt againe to sea and came thatt [night] within a watch of reaching Watterford, butt aboutt sun sett thatt night the wynd changed with the most hidious tempest of wynd and raine. **29** Which brought us back againe next day to Lundy, wher we lay with 4 ships more dispairing of life.[30]

30 With our mast all downe, our cabin shutt upp, wee lay roleing on an anker till nextt night; when being in a despratt condition, we atempted to shott the bay of Barstable, wher all thatt saw us on the hill gave us over for lost. When by Gods greatt mercy wee safe landed att Barstable.[31]

September 5th Wher we staid a weeke, till aboutt September 5, when we went to sea againe and by Gods mercy landed safe in Corke harbor the sixth of September. For which mercy the greatt God make me ever thankfull and grantt I may never forgett his goodness to me whilst I am Eliz Freke.

i678, May io I wentt againe for England with Mr Frek by the desire of my deer father, who sentt for me, and when I came to him to Hanington. Affter a little stay Mr Frek wentt for London, where unknowne to me or my father hee privattly sold outt his right in Leeds Castle to Allexander Cullpeper for the use of the Lord Cullpeper,[32] tho he had promised my deer father to settle itt as itt was on mee and mine – for which conciderattion my father gave my husband up a

---

[29] Pilots who navigated the Bristol waters lived in the village of Crockerne Pill on the River Avon approximately a mile from the coast. On the northern coast of Devon, Ilfracombe was also a port for those who guided ships up the Bristol Channel (Walter Minchinton, 'The Port of Bristol in the Eighteenth Century', in *Bristol in the Eighteenth Century*, ed. Patrick McGrath [Newton Abbot, Devon, 1972], 135).

[30] Lundy Island, eleven miles northwest of Hartland Point on the Devon coast.

[31] Barnstaple, a Devon seaport at the estuary of the River Taw.

[32] Lord Culpeper succeeded the governor of Virginia Sir William Berkeley, who died in 1677; although Culpeper did not leave for Virginia until 1680, he had given Alexander Culpeper power of attorney (Cleggett, *History of Leeds Castle*, 92, 93).

bond he owed him of eight hundred pounds (800 l.), as he did another nott long before of 760 l. due to him on our estatt in West Billney; which were then very wellcome to us and done by Gods derecttion.

1679, Aprill 3 Mr Freks mother dyed in Ireland whilst we were both in England att my fathers. On which news he wentt for London in order to goe for Ireland, wher he fell sick of an ague and feaver allmost to death thatt I were forced to returne againe to my deer fathers to Hanington. **June** Wher he lay sick of a plurisy and quinsy for neer six weeks.

Jully 23 Affter which we wentt to Bristoll, tho very ill.

1680, Agust 18 Butt my God had mercy on me, and with my deer sister Nortons kindness and care heer with my son [fol. 50r] endeavoured our jorney and took shipping aboutt the 18 of Agust.[33]

21 Where by Gods greatt mercy my husband, my selfe, and my son weere safe landed at the Cove in the Greatt Island neere Corke – my son being just five years of age the second of June before and his first coming for Ireland and my third time.[34] For which mercy God make me truly thankfull.

September 16 I came with my husband and son to Rath Barry, wher my husban sister Barnard had cleered my house of every thing good in itt, even to seven years letters which past between us before I were married and my cirtificate of my first mariag.[35] This I thought very hard to me. Besids she was pleased to take away all my plate to the vallue of neer two hundred pounds, tho I had itt before I married and itt was engraven with my own coat of arms in a losseng. And of two dosen of silver spoons of my own, I had nott one left or one scrip of my best linnen; all was conveyed away by my husbands sister Barnard, pretending itt was her mothers. And tho Mr Freke was her executor, neither hee nor my self had the vallue of five shillings (as I know of), butt a bill sentt in by my cosin Barnard of fowrescore pounds to pay for her buriall and doctters, and said I had bin her mothers death.

November But with much adoe and high words I gott my plate and for any thing elce thatt was taken away. This was very unkind usuage butt the best I have had in the family, as I am E Freke.

1681 However, I staid in Ireland allmost 22 month. In which time Mr Frek haveing before contracted with the earle of Barrimore for his

---

[33] Freke has no entries for the year between July 1679 and August 1680.

[34] Great Island, about five miles in length and three miles across, is located in the harbour of Cork. The port town of Cove on its southern shore is now known as Cobh.

[35] Percy's older sister, Mary, was married to Francis Bernard; their marriage settlement is dated 5 December 1661 (Bennett, 228). The oldest of their seven children, Francis (1663–1731), served with Percy Freke in the Irish parliament and became a judge of common pleas.

revertion of Rathbary affter our lease of 63 years, we were to pay for itt, as I remember, (i400) fowrteen hundred pounds, with some privileges on Allaglason and the royallties and court therto belonging.[36] This being concluded, Mr Frek made me write to my deerst father to lend him a thousand pounds on Billney security and the presentt settling of itt on me, which accordingly I did. And my deer father immediatly returned me a thousand pound (i000 l.) on Mr Freks bond rather then charge my Billney with itt, as he was pleased to say. This mony Mr Frek presently drue over, and with itt and some we had finished his purchas of Rathbarry, and has now, I thank him, settled itt on my son in the yeare i699 (on his mariage with Sir John Meads eldest daughter). And for a pull back, affter all our mony was paid on the Lady Barrys promise of her levying a fine on there son my Lord Buttivantt, neither of them would levy withoutt a hundred pound for there consents.[37] [fol. 50v] Which as itt was an unexpected disapoyntment to Mr Freke, soe itt was a greatter trouble to him then getting all the rest.

i68i, November 22 Aboutt November we paid of all to thatt familly; and I made all the hast I could for England, my deer fatther sending for me and my son to come and receive his last blessinge.

i682, Aprill 30 Soe thatt in Aprill I left Rathbary and wentt to Kingsale with my son to atend for a shipp for England.

May io Wher affter a fortnight weighting I had the oppertunity of a man of warr in which I putt my self and son, I haveing noe frind to take any care for me, and wentt outt to sea, as to my best remembrance, a Sunday, the io of May. **i7** Wher by Gods infinite mercy (affter striking three times on the sands), wee landed safly att the Pill att Bristoll the i7 of May with my son and 4 servants.

22 Att Bristoll I staide till I could send to my deer father, who aboutt the twenty second of May sentt his coach and horses to fetch me and my son safe to him to Hanington; **24** where wee came to my deer father about the 24 of May, and all my mony spentt in my travells.

Jully 7 Soe soon as I came to my deer father, he made me promise

---

[36] The legal agreement is with Richard, second earl of Barrymore (1630–1694), and his third wife, Dorothy Ferrer, the stepmother of Laurence, third earl of Barrymore (d. 1699), and mother of the fourth earl of Barrymore, James (1667–1748) (Lodge, i. 300–11; E. Barry, 'Barrymore', *CHAS*, 2nd ser., 6 [1900], 201–5). A reversion is the vested interest an owner retains in an estate upon termination of the grant (Jowitt, ii. 1,575). Allaglason, the land immediately to the west of the estate, is identified as Aghalasin on Smith's 1750 map, Aughaglaslin in Thomas Sherrard's 1787 survey of the estate then owned by Sir John Freke, and Ahaglaslin in the Ordnance Survey.

[37] Pull back: a draw back or hindrance (*EDD*). A fine is 'an amicable composition or agreement of a suit, either actual or fictitious', acknowledging ownership. The party who transferred the land 'was said to *levy* the fine'; the recipient had the land 'levied to him' (Black, 569). Before fines were abolished in 1833, a married woman thereby conveyed her land; entails on land could also be broken through a fine (Jowitt, i. 792).

him thatt I would nott leave him whilst I lived, which I redily and gladly did. And then he bid me take noe care for I should wantt for nothing his life, who made his words good with the greatest kindnes to me and my son. A greatt allterration itt was to whatt I found in Ireland from a husband.

Agust i5 And on my looking a little malloncally on some past reflecttions, he fancied itt was my wantt of mony; and my deer father, withoutt saying a word to me, went up into his closett and brought me downe presently in two baggs two hundred pounds, which 200 l. hee charged me to keep privatt from my husbands knowledge and buy needles and pins with itt. This was very kind in my father; and which the very next post I informed Mr Frek of, who presently found a use for itt. Butt I, thatt had nott had two and twenty shillings from my husband in the last two and twenty months I were in Ireland with my son, kept itt for my own use. Which with more my father had given me and the intrest, all which made up eight hundred pounds, [Mr Freke] took from me the year affter my son maryed and soe left me att Billny a beger againe.

i682/3, Febeary i8 Aboutt the midle of Febeary Mr Frek came to my fathers to Hanington unknown to me and to fetch me and my son over for Ireland. Butt on the ill usage I had there suffered from them, I positively refused ever more goeing with him, aleadging my promise to my deer father and ther <originally: his> unkindness to mee when ever I were in ther <originally: his> powre of command. Besides his last parting wish att Kingsaile (which was) <deleted: thatt he might never se my face more>; and this stuck deep in my stomack, tho [fol. 5ir] to this day (i7i2 <originally: i702>) I never lett my father know the least of difference between us or any unkind usage from the family I have received in thatt kingdome or elcewhere for feare of grieving of him, butt prepared to goe for Ireland with Mr Frek againe.

i683, Jully 24 When I takeing my last leave of my deerst father, hee gave me up the bond Mr Freke was bound for to him of a thousand pounds hee borrowed on the purchas of Rath Barry. For which he had only my thanks for thatt and all his other blesings to me since I maryed.

25 Thus haveing stayd aboutt thirteen months with my deerst father and the last time I ever saw him, I wentt Thursday, 25 of Jully, to Bristoll with Mr Frek and left my son att schoole att Sumerford with Mr Turner, aboutt 7 miles from Hanington.[38]

26 I took shiping att Pill, and by my Gods greatt goodness and

---

[38] The Turners were an established family in Somerford Keynes, since 1896 a part of Gloucestershire. John Turner, whose father had been the parish vicar, was its present minister; an Isaac Turner is identified as a schoolmaster at the time of his marriage on 18 December 1717 (Wiltshire Record Office, WL/R67). Thomas and William Freke, the subsequent owners of the Hannington estate, were also educated in Somerford Keynes.

mercy to me wee both came to Corke the Satterday following, being **29** of July. When itt being a troublesome time by plots in England, wee were both garded like prisoners before the maire of Cork to be searched, who being one Mr Covett was extreamly civell to us and treated us both like a gentleman, saying hee would and dared be securitty for us and our name.[39] And affter 3 or 4 botles of wyne drunk in his house, hee released us, giveing order for the presentt landing of our clothes and our other goods on ship board, to the amasementt of all beholders. Thus God provided for us when we had none to help us. And itt was the whole reportt of Cork thatt my husband was by the order of King James hanged up on ship board att Minhead for making his escap for Ireland withoutt his permitt (which we could nott gett).[40]

i683/4 January i My deer father sentt mee into Ireland a hundred pounds for a New Years guiftt, itt being my unhappy birth day, and ordered mee thatt iff Mr Frek medled with itt itt should be lost or he to answer itt with the Irish intrest to my son. Butt Mr Frek took itt from me; and I wer faine to make itt good to my son with the full Irish intrest the day affter he was of age, when I gave him two hundred pounds and five pound for a purse to putt itt in. Eliz. Frek, paid i696.

Febuary 24 Aboutt the 24 of Febuary and the dreadfull hard winter, my deer father sentt to me to come to him to Hanington with my husband and familly, wher I should meet my two sisters, the Lady Norton and my sister Austin, and be mery there together a little before he dyed, and thatt he would pay the charge of my jorney and give me his last blesing.

i684, March 26 In order to which aboutt the end of March Mr Frek, to my best remembrance, contractted with John Hull for the rentting of Rathbarry for a lease of one and forty years comenceing the May Day following att the yearly rentt of two hundred and fiffty pounds a yeare and, unknown to me, lett itt [to] Hull [fol. 51v] and took of John Hull twenty guinies as earnest, Mr Frek resolveing we should both goe and live with my deerst father as he desired me whilst he lived. In order to which hee signed this lease for one and forty years, to my greatt joy and satisfaction the liveing with my deer father.

i684, Aprill 24 Butt oh, the saddest of fattes thatt ever atended mortall was mine, for on the 24 of Aprill my God took to himselfe by death my deer, deerst father to my greatt loss, grife, and unspeakable sorrow before I could gett a ship to see him and receive his last blesing, which of all things in this world I desired. Butt my God knew whatt

[39] The Rye House Plot had been revealed in June. Richard Covett was mayor of Cork in 1682 (*Cork Remembrancer*, 309).

[40] Charles II was still king; Minehead: a Bristol Channel port in western Somerset, which Freke often mistakenly locates in Devon.

was best for me, for in the eighty ninth yeare of his age hee joyfully gave up his soule into the hand of his God and his body to be privatly inter'd in the chancell of Hanington;[41] and haveing noe son of his own, left his youngest brothers grandson Mr Thomas Frek his executtor to severall thousand of pounds personall estate and neer a thousand pounds a yeare land of inheritance lyeing round his house and mee, his unhappy child, ever to lamentt him, hee being known by noe other carractter then honest Mr Ralfe Frek.[42] I doe most humbly beg of God thatt as I have a blesing of a son thatt carries his name, may likewise his age [and] character follow his example in life and death. Eliza Frek

1684, May Day John Hull betims in the morning came to Rathbary when our house was full of company and with Sir Emanuell Moor, his unkle, demanded the posesion of the house, tho by his faithfull promise we had three weeks time to remove all our goods.[43] Butt nothing could prevaile butt they must bee immediattly thrown outt of doors and I with them. Butt the country heering of this inhumanity sent us in carts and horses to remove them as fast as we could (to Donowen) aboutt a mille from Rathbarry, wher by the way we lost neer halfe our goods, the whole country coming to see this cruellty to us. However, late att night I gott up behind Mr Freke and wentt thatt night to Cloghein, neer Clanikilty, to my cosin Hester Gookins, wher I staid three or 4 dayes and rested my selfe, leaveing my God to avenge my cause.[44] Which he did, for in 3 or 4 years King Jams came for Ireland and seised by the Irish all he had and gave away our estate to Owen

---

[41] His monument in the Hannington church erroneously indicates he 'died in the 88th year of his age Aprill the 23d 1683' (Fry's transcription, *Hannington*, 74). The register states that he was buried on 26 April 1684, 'aged 88 years & upwards'.

[42] Thomas Freke (1660–1721), the grandson of Ralph's brother Thomas and the son of Thomas Freke of Hinton St Mary, Dorset and his second wife, Elizabeth Clarke, inherited the Hannington estate. Neither he and his first wife, Elizabeth Pile, who died in 1714, nor his second wife, Mary Corbett, had children. He was buried in Hannington on 13 May 1721, leaving the Hannington property to his brother William (*HC*, ii. 366–7; PRO, PROB 11/580/129).

[43] Sir Emanuel Moore had married Martha, the daughter of William Hull and aunt of John Hull. Moore's wife was the granddaughter of Richard Boyle, the archbishop of Tuam; their son William's widow, Catherine, married in 1699 George Freke, the son of Elizabeth Freke's cousin Robert Freke of Upway, Dorset (*CB*, iv. 215; Ffolliott, 126).

[44] Donowen, located on Smith's eighteenth-century map to the east in the area of Ardfield; or perhaps Dunamore, on Smith's map to the northeast in the direction of Clonakilty. Hester Hodder, married Robert Gookin of Courtmacsherry in 1681 (*Marriage Licence Bonds*, 56); an uncle Thomas Gookin, identified in his brother Vincent's will as 'late of Clogheen', also had a wife named Hester who may well be the Hester Gookin, widow, buried at All Saints in Bandon on 21 June 1712. Unfortunately her maiden name is unknown, and the relationship implicit in 'cosin' is uncertain. The Gookins were, however, descendants of the Kent family from Ripple Court who controlled property in Hollingbourne and were long established in County Cork (Edward Elbridge Salisbury, *Family-Memorials*, 2 vols. [New Haven, 1885], ii. 414, 417; SG, IR/Reg/46762 in IR/R31).

Macarty, the loss of which with all his goods and his own estate brok his hartt, he haveing nothing left for his wife or family to subsist on butt with one of his children lies buryed in the open part of the church of Rathbary amongst the Irish.[45]

[fol. 52r]

1684, Jully 7 Being Monday and the 7 of Jully, Mr Frek and I took shipping att Kingsaile in a man of warr with Captaine Clemontt and came round to England by long sea.[46] Thatt night we were most griveously storm'd. **12** Butt by Gods greatt mercy (affter we were like to be lost on the Goodwin Sands neer Dover) wee were all safe landed att Billingsgatte in London the Satterday following.[47] For which greatt mercy I humbly thank my greatt and good God.

Agust 4 Mr Freke wentt into Norfolk, **17** and returned to London againe the seventeenth of Agust, leaving me a lodger in Brownlow Streett in the house with my cosin Clayton, wher I lay aboutt ten weeks and never had his company att diner with me ten tims.[48] Which I cannott forgett; itt was soe griveous to me.

September 17 Mr Freke wentt againe for Ireland with the Lord Inchequeen, unknown to me till the night before he wentt, and left me with my son and a man and maid att lodgings att Mrs Murrys in Brownlow Streett to shifftt for my selfe and family, declareing the morning he left me before his nephew Barnard and my cosin Clayton and the 3 Gookins with severall others thatt his estate in Norfolk would nott finde him in bread and cheese besids the charges of itt.[49] Which

[45] Owen MacCarty or Macartie represented Clonakilty in James' 1689 Irish parliament. A lieutenant-colonel in one of the infantry regiments raised for James II, he later served Louis XIV in continental military campaigns (John D'Alton, *Illustrations, Historical and Genealogical, of King James's Irish Army List, 1689*, 2nd edn., 2 vols. [London, 1861], ii. 99, 101; *English Army Lists*, i. 209; Charles Dalton, *Irish Army Lists, 1661–1685* [London, 1907], 118, 120 n. 5; Bennett, 276).

[46] Possibly John Clements, commissioned as a captain on 1 May 1667 and died on 10 June 1694; his name does not appear, however, among the officers listed in the sailing record of the royal fleet for 1684 (*Commissioned Sea Officers*, 85; PRO, ADM 8/1). 'Long sea' is a contemporary expression for the longer route around Land's End (Gordon Read, National Museums & Galleries on Merseyside).

[47] The Goodwin Sands, known in history as the 'shippe swalower', is an area some ten miles long by four miles wide, five miles off the Kent coast east of Deal.

[48] A 'pleasant and regular' street between Shorts Gardens and Castle Street off Drury Lane (Hatton, i. 12), Brownlow is now known as Betterton Street. Cousin Clayton is unidentified.

[49] The ratebooks and valuation lists that might identify residents of Holborn, which would include Brownlow Street, begin later. The nephew is his sister's son Francis or Arthur Bernard; the Gookins remain unidentified. The Gookins of Cork were, however, related to the Claytons: Augustine Gookin had married Ann Clayton in 1682; his aunt Dorothy, the widow of Captain Robert Gookin of Courtmacsherry, married Randal

estate is now lett for fowre hundred and fiffty pounds a yeare (1712 <originally: 1702>) and bought by my deer father for the yearly rentt of 526 pound a yeare <and in 1710 is lett for 500 l.>. Mr Frek staid aboutt Bristoll till the 8 of November following, neer 9, nine, weeks, before he took shipping.

September 28 Being thuss left by my husband to shifft for my self and familly and butt fiffteen pounds in the world, all which I laid outt the next day he wentt (butt three pound) in i suite of close of second morning (for my deer father) on his son and Own Killty, his man, and on a chest of drawers of aboutt fowre pounds, I were forced to try my fortune amongst my friends.

Octobr 15 And heering my deer sister Austin was very ill and brought to bed of a dead child, I wentt downe to Tenterden to my deer sister and brother aboutt the 15 of Octtober,[50] makeing a vertue of necesity by being thrown <deleted: off by my unkind husban; never in his life took any care for me or whatt I did>. Butt with my deer sister I staide with all the kindness imaginable till the 15 of June following.

June 15 When on my earnest request, thinking I had with my little familly bin troublesome longe enough, my sister brought me up with my son and servants in her own coach to London and on her own charge, I resolveing to try for a subsistance in Norfolk affter nine month stay with my deer sister Austin. <For which I presented her with six silver plats cost mee thirty six pounds (36). Eliz Freke>

[fol. 52v]

1685, Febuary 6 Febuary the 6 King Charls the Second dyed, being on Fryday, nott withoutt suspition of being poysoned by a French whore he kept, Madom Carrolus, whom he made a little before dutches of Portsmouth and her son duke of Richmond; and itt was talked this was done by the connivance of King Jams and his queene.[51]

Clayton of Mallow, County Cork. Gookins and Claytons were later among those who left the Jacobite-controlled Ireland (*Marriage Licence Bonds*, 56; Salisbury, *Family-Memorials*, ii. 413; *Cork Remembrancer*, 330).

[50] The residence of Judith and Robert Austen was located south of Tenterden, a Kent village ten miles north of Rye. Robert Austen had inherited the Heronden estate from his father's older brother John, who died without issue on 11 December 1655; their son Robert, in turn, lived there (Hasted, vii. 207; *Kentish Monumental Inscriptions ... Tenterden*, ed. Leland L. Duncan [London, 1919], 57).

[51] The *London Gazette*, which records that the king was 'seized with a violent Fit' on Monday, states on Friday, 6 February, that 'he expired this day about Noon' (2006). Gilbert Burnet mentions the 'many very apparent suspicions' that the king had not died of natural causes (ii. 473–8). The duchess was rumoured to have poisoned him with a cup of chocolate (Thomas Babington Macaulay, *The History of England from the Accession of James the Second*, ed. Charles Harding Firth, 6 vols. [London, 1913–14], i. 435). Supporters

1685, June 15 I came from my sister Austins att Tenterden, wher I had staid nine month. She brought me in her coach to London, the tims then being very troublesome and I had noe place to hid or putt my head in for my selfe and son and three servants. Butt the duke of Monmouth then landing att Lime in Dorsettshire, noe mortall could stirr and all roads were stoped, soe thatt I were faine to send downe my son againe into Kentt with my sister Austin and stay my selfe in London with my deer sister Nortton.[52] And I sent Richard Clark to Billney before me, nott being able to goe my selfe.[53]

July 10 The duke of Monmouth was brought to London for an insurrecttion in the west of England, being Fryday putt in the Towre; **15** and Wensday, the 15 of July, most barbarously beheaded on Towre Hill, choping his head, shoulders, and neck in five severall places.[54]

31 of July I sentt for my son from Tenterden to goe with me to Linn; who as soon as he came and I had given earnest for 4 places in the coach fell very sick att the Green Dragon in London, soe thatt I were faine to returne to my deer Lady Nortons againe.[55] Which sickness proved to be the small pox.

Agust 14 About the 14 of Agust I wentt with my deer sister Norton to Epsom for my son to drink the watters, where affter he had drunk them a forttnight, he fell sick of the small pox.[56] And like to dye hee was before they came outt to my greatt torture and distracttion, Mr

of the duke of Monmouth would also allege James II's complicity in the death of the king. Louise de Kéroualle (1649–1734), the mother of the king's illegitimate son Charles Lennox, first duke of Richmond (1672–1723), became in 1673 the duchess of Portsmouth. On his deathbed Charles, in the words of Burnet, assured the duke of York that 'he had always loved her, and he loved her now to the last' (ii. 473). She returned to France and her Aubigny estate.

[52] James Scott, first duke of Monmouth (1649–1685), the illegitimate son of Charles II and Lucy Walter, led an armed attempt in June 1685 to take the crown from James II. Monmouth landed in Dorset at Lyme Regis on 11 June; within a month the rebellion ended in defeat at Sedgemoor and the capture of Monmouth near Ringwood.

[53] Her servant.

[54] Monmouth was taken to Winchester on 10 July and then to London on 13 July, where he was beheaded on 15 July. Among the accounts of the execution, Luttrell (i. 353), Evelyn (iv. 456), and Burnet (iii. 55–6) all stress the ineptitude of the executioner, Jack Ketch. 'The wretch made five Chopps before he had his head off', Evelyn writes, 'which so incens'd the people, that had he not ben guarded & got away they would have torne him in pieces'.

[55] The Frekes travelling through London to Norfolk would have stayed most likely at the Green Dragon Inn off the west side of Bishopsgate Street near Gresham College, one of three 'great Inns' in the area 'of a considerable Trade, and resort for Waggons and Stage Coaches that go Northwards' (Strype, i. bk. 2, 107).

[56] Epsom's location only fifteen miles from London made it especially attractive to the city's citizens drawn to its mineral waters. The spa enjoyed greatest popularity around the turn of the century with its shops, walks, and four inns (Phyllis Hembry, *The English Spa, 1560–1815* [London, 1990], 104–10).

Frek being all the while in Ireland from me. Butt in the midst of all my dispairing, my God looked on me and brought them out most favourably on him and with less mallignity with drinking of the waters. For which mercy I am most humbly thankfull to my God for his mercy and my good sister Norton for her greatt kindness to me, I haveing bin now with her fiffteen weeks with all the kindness and pity immaginable. E Freke

[fol. 53r]

i685, September 29 Thus lefft by Mr Frek, I attempted againe to seek my fortune to Billney, to seek my bread. Wher on the 29 of Septembr I came with my son and three servants to Linn, wher I boarded in private lodgings till the eight of Febuary following.

December 24 Mr Frek came over by Dublin from Ireland, I haveing hardly heard of him or from him in three quarters of a yeare. As he came unlook'd for by me, soe he was very angry with me for being on this sid of the country, tho in all his tims of his being from me he never took care for a peny for my subsistance or his sons. For which God forgive him. My husbands erantt for England was to joyne with him in the sale of West Billney to Sir Standish Harts Tongue for the like in Ireland.[57] Butt I being left the only trusty for my self and my son, God gave me the courage to keep whatt I had rather then part with itt and be kept by the charity of my friends or trust to his or any ones kindness. Soe in a greatt anger Mr Frek lefft me alone againe and wentt for Ireland, wher he staid from me allmost two years.

Febuary 8 I came to my thacht house in West Billney, and the first time of my coming thither, to take a possesion of thatt estate for my self and son by the gift of my deer father. When I came I had neither a bed to lye on, chair to sett on, table to eat on, or dish, or spoon, or bread to eate. Butt by Gods goodness to mee I quickly gott all and my little house very well furnished, wher I lived by my selfe eight years in my thacht house, eight years with ease and comfortt, tho every day threatned by the neighbours thatt iff I thought to nest my self att Billny I should wash my dishes my self and milk my cows too. Butt when I gott footing, I soon evidenced my right to itt and as fast as I could removed those thatt thretned to turne me outt of doores and Billny

---

[57] Sir Standish Hartstonge (1627–1701), born in South Repps, Norfolk and heir to property in Ireland, represented Limerick in the Irish parliament from 1661 to 1666 and twice became a baron of the exchequer; he received a baronetcy in 1681. He, his son Standish, and Percy Freke were among those attainted in 1689; all three were later members of the Irish parliament, where in 1692 Hartstonge sat in the House of Lords (R. C. B. Oliver, 'The Hartstonges and Radnorshire: Part I', *The Radnorshire Society Transactions*, 43 [1973], 34–48; *CB*, iv. 213).

too. And being by Mr Frek thus thrown off with my son and my deer
father dead, I durst say nothing to them.

i3 Mr Frek wentt for London (and left me to seek my fortune) in
order to goe for Ireland, wher att sea he was twice like to be cast away;
butt by Gods greatt mercy to me he was saffly landed in Ireland Aprill
4th. For which mercy God make me thankfull. Wher he staid from me
till the i4 of June i687.

i687, Aprill 9 Goode Mamons house nextt to mine was aboutt ten
a clock att night burntt downe to the ground with heatting her oven
for Goody Saywells christning, and the poor woman burntt in itt on
Satterday night.[58] And tho I were up my self att the house calling of
the parrish, nott one would come to my help to save my house she
lived in or the poor woman in distress.

[fol. 53v]

i687, May 26 My deer sister Austin came to see me in my thacht
house with my deer neec and god-daughter Mrs Grace Norton, when
affter they had come from London in my sisters own coach. I were soe
ashamed thatt I would nott see them in my poor thacht house. Her
erantt was to fetch me up to London to live with her and to give me
her own and her husbands creditt in Mr Freks absence for any thing I
wanted.

June 6 My deerst sister Austen left me att Billney and wentt home
againe for London with my neece Norton.

i4 Mr Frek came againe from Ireland by Dublin to West Billney
affter he had left me sixteen months and three days.

September i9 Mr Frek wentt againe for Ireland affter he had staid
with mee aboute three months and five days to gett whatt mony he
could from mee, which he did att least five hundred pounds. With
which and some more aded to itt he bought six and forty pounds a
year att Pentney and putt in his own life into itt. Eliz Frek

i688, March 27 Mr Frek came againe to Billney affter he had staid
from mee and his only child neer nineteen months, he being prosecuted
by one of King Jams captains, one Buttler, to be shott to death for
refuseing to drink the Lord Tirconells health.[59] Which of two evills he
chose to come to Billney, Ireland being now very hott and unsafe for

---

[58] Mary Mammont, the widow of Thomas Mammont, was buried on 10 April 1687;
her husband had been buried on 12 January 1686/7. The West Bilney register also
records the 10 April christening of John, the son of James Sowell and Mary Scarning,
who were married on 28 April 1686.

[59] Among the many Butlers in the Irish army, two named Edward received commissions
as captains from Richard Talbot, lord deputy and later duke of Tyrconnell (D'Alton,
Illustrations, i. 10, 12).

any of the English, espeshally officesers – of which Buttler had Mr Freks company, affter he had on his own charge equipied itt by the desire of King Charls the second; wher he staid the heat of the Irish warrs till the 4 of March 1690.

Aprill 5 Richard Clark, my friend and servantt, dyed with me (aboutt a ten days affter Mr Frek came to Billney). He had lived with us neer eight years heer and in Ireland; and a good servant he was, just and faithfull, and dyed of a creek in his neck unexpected to mee.[60]

1688, November 5 The good King William the Third came in to Englands relife, he being then prince of Orange. He landed in the west of Dorsettshire neer Exetter. He had with him aboutt 12 saile of Dutch ships and aboutt 12 thousand men; against whom King James wentt with neer threescore thousand to oppose him. Butt for want of corrage he returned back to London and left his men to joyne with the prince of Orange, who came into London aboutt the end of November, when King James and his queen run away for France with her pretended prince of Walles.[61] The king was taken with Sir Edward Halles in a seamens habbitt att Feversham in Kentt and both brought to Rochester Casstle,[62] from whence affter aboutt three weeks stay King William lett him steale away into France to his queen to St Germans, wher he was by actt of parliament and the consent of the whole nation abdicatted.[63]

[fol. 54r]

1689, Febuary 13 King William and Queen Mary, the daughter of King James, were proclaimed king and queen of England, &c., and were both crowned the eleventh of Aprill 1689 in London.[64]

[60] Richard Clark was buried in West Bilney on 5 April 1688.

[61] Prince William of Orange landed at Torbay on 5 November and entered Exeter on 9 November. James soon abandoned attempts to resist invasion; by 24 November he decided to withdraw his forces to London.

[62] The sentence in the manuscript begins 'Affter a years reigne'.

[63] The queen and her son left for France on 9 December 1688; two days later James tried to follow. He was discovered in disguise at Faversham and brought back to London on 16 December. From there William permitted James to go to Rochester, where he was allowed to escape on 23 December. On Christmas Day James reached France and three days later was reunited with his wife and son. Edward Hales, the former governor of the Tower, was imprisoned for more than a year before he joined the exiled monarch in France (David Ogg, *England in the Reigns of James II and William III* [Oxford, 1957], 218–20; John Miller, *James II, a Study in Kingship* [London, 1991], 205–9).

[64] On 28 January 1688/9 the House of Commons resolved 'That King James the Second, having endeavoured to subvert the Constitution of this Kingdom; … having violated the fundamental Laws; and having withdrawn himself out of the Kingdom; has abdicated the Government; and that the Throne is thereby vacant'. At Whitehall on 13 February George Savile, marquess of Halifax, presented William and Mary with the Declaration of Rights drawn up by parliament; he then offered them the crown, and they were proclaimed king and queen (*CJ*, x. 14, 28–30). The *London Gazette* describes the

Octtober 25 I wentt to London to see my sisters and friends affter I had staid in my thacht house fowre years by my selfe dureing King Jams warrs, and staid ther with my two deer sisters about seven weeks and then returned home againe to Billney December the eighteenth.

Aprill 29 My cosin Percy Crossby, my husbands nephew, came downe from London to me to Billney like to dye of a consumtion. He dyed a marter to King James the 19 of May following and lyes buried in the chancell of Billney.[65]

1690, March 4 March 4 Mr Frek left me and wentt away againe for Ireland, I nott knowing of itt above two days before, to endeavour the getting of his estat, tho given away by King James to Ower Maccarty. My husband being then outtlawed for an absentee had all his estate of above 700 pound a yeare with all his stock and good given away by the said kinge and his greatt house att Rathbarry burnt downe by the Irish to preventt its being made a garrison, as itt had held outt on nine months for King Charls the First by Captaine Arthur Frek, my husbands father.[66]

1690, June 4 King William came over for Ireland to the conquest of itt, and he had putt itt againe into the posesion of the English.

Jully 1 The greatt fight of the Boyn was fought by King William and King James army. King William was shott through his hatt and in his shoulder as he pased the Boyn with all the English army, the sight of which made King Jams with his Irish army run away to Dublin to gett for France.[67]

3 After this greatt fight att the Boyne, King William posest himself of Dublin, King Jams and his deputty Tirconell being both shipt off for France the night before to save themsselves being taken by the English.[68] Then wentt King William to raise the seig of Limbrick, the only place which held outt against the Irish in Ireland, wher ther was neer six thousand, as said. They were soe straitly beseiged by the Irish army thatt when our good king came there was nott, as said, a thousand left in the towne (most starved).[69] After which our Protestant king

---

13 February ceremony at Whitehall; it also recounts at length the coronation ceremonies on 11 April (2427, 2444), which Luttrell (i. 520–1) and Evelyn (iv. 632–3) also describe.

[65] Patrick Crosby, the second son of Colonel David Crosbie, married Percy's sister Agnes in 1664. Percy or Pierce Crosby, the eldest of their seven sons and two daughters, was among the absentees who were attainted. He was buried in West Bilney on 20 May 1690 (Lodge, iii. 329–30; *Marriage Licence Bonds*, 51).

[66] At the time the loss was set at £520 (above, p. 12 and n. 33); her later remembrances value the estate at £800. The castle was regained the next year and served as a garrison until 1650, when Cromwell's forces took control. See also p. 7 and n. 19.

[67] See Freke's history of the Irish war below, pp. 145–6.

[68] Tyrconnell did not flee with James II to France.

[69] Freke confuses the siege of Limerick with that of Londonderry, where those loyal to William earlier had withstood a long, bitter siege.

returned for England with greatt glory and tryumph to London, wher he was joyfuly received. Eliza Freke

[fol. 54v]

1691, Jully My servant Henry Crutland shott off his hand with my sons gun a shoutting of a pigion and lay in a sad condition fowre month under the surgions hand. And then I took itt to cure, which with Gods blesing I effecttually did. He was the most patient creture I ever saw.[70]

Jully 21 I had my last tryall with Captaine Spillman of Norbrow aboutt inhabitting of Doching. He wentt to the sesions of Linn through Billney against me with his two Norwich lawyers and aboutt sixteen behind him, horsemen of his own parish, against me in Mr Freks absence, all of them calling to mee to come and justifye my cause. And I had nott one to appeare for me of my side butt my greatt God and my son, aboutt 17 years of age, with his man. And God gave itt of my side thatt I cast him in the publick courte.[71] Eliz Freke

1692, March 30 Mr Frek, haveing now left me to shifft for my selfe above two years, never lett me have any quiett butt commanded me to leave all my affairs att Billney and come over to Ireland. Wher affter halfe a years concideration I forced my selfe to undertak againe a jorney for Ireland, and in order to itt wentt with my son and servants to London in my deer sister Nortons coach and left my house and goods in the care of Jams Wallbutt, then my servantt and affter my cheating tenant.[72]

Aprill 2 I came to my deer sister Austins, who lived then in St Jams Sttreett in London (my brother Austin being then one of the lords of the admirallty); wher by reason of the French invation I

---

[70] Henry Cruckland was buried in West Bilney on 9 November 1693.

[71] The Spelmans of Narburgh Hall were a long-established family in Narborough with links to both Westacre and Grace's Manors. Mundeford, the son of John and Ann Spelman, resided at the Hall with his wife Ann, who died in September 1691. He is not listed at this time, however, as a member of the Norfolk militia or among the regular commissioned officers (Blomefield, vi. 150–4; *The Visitation of Norfolk Anno Domini 1664 Made by Sir Edward Bysshe, Knt.*, ed. A. W. Hughes Clarke and Arthur Campling, *Norfolk Record Society*, 5 [1934], 204–5). John and Mary Dochin had apparently been living in West Bilney, where their son was born and buried earlier that year. The Norfolk quarter sessions at King's Lynn on 28 April 1691 decided that the order of two justices of peace for settling the Dochins at Narborough 'be respited til the next general quarter session of the year to be held for this division' (NRO, C/S2/4). The next record of a Lynn session is 3 October 1691; the disposition of the case is not mentioned in the NRO records of this or other Norfolk quarter sessions that year. Cast him out: 'defeated at law, condemned in costs or damages' (Jowitt, i. 292).

[72] James Wallbut and Martha Mee, who were married in West Bilney on 1 January 1692/3, lived in the dwelling known as the Ale House.

staid till aboutt the twentieth of July following with all the kindness immaginable.[73]

May 24 I putt my son, Mr Ralph Frek, being within one week of seventeen years of age (viz., 2d of June), to Mr Du Veales, a French Hugonett, to learne French and all other quallifications of a gentleman; wher I paid for his dyett and chamber forty fowre pounds a yeare.[74] And when I had seen my son settled, I endeavoured for Ireland.

Jully 25 Aboutt the 25 of Jully I wentt to the Bath, wher I rested my self neer a month for shiping.

Agust 14 From Bath I wentt to Bristoll to be neerer the shiping aboutt the midle of Agust, wher I took me a lodging on Bristoll Green neer the cathedrall church; where I staid (for feare) and ship till the 2d of Octtober following.

Octtober 2d When in Captain Poole ship I went to sea;[75] 5 and the 5 of Octtober, Thursday, I safe by Gods mercy landed att the Cove in Cork, wher the day before the French privatteers had taken two ships outt of the harbor and kild the captaine, &c., and stript all the pasengers, setting them on the shore. From whom God did preserve me to be thankfull. E Freke

[fol. 55r]

1692, October 26 I came into Cork late att night, wher in a boatt wee were all like to be lost on the key by the ships and boys which we cold nott see, itt was soe darke. And with much adoe I landed. And when I came, the day before Mr Frek was gone to the parliamentt of Dublin; and I knew noe Christian in the towne, nor could I gett a

[73] Austen was commissioned a lord of the admiralty on 23 January 1690/1, a position he held until his death in 1696 (John Ehrman, *The Navy in the War of William III, 1689–1697* [Cambridge, 1953], 639–40). Thomas Freke of Hannington also had a residence on St James Street, a 'spacious Street, with very good Houses well inhabited by Gentry' (Strype, ii. bk. 6, 78). Evelyn notes in April 1692 the 'Greate talke of the French Invading; & of an universal rising'; on 5 May he writes that the fears of invasion 'alarmed the Citty, Court & People exceedingly' (v. 97, 99). The defeat of the French in the naval battle of the Hogue (May 19–24), however, ended the threatened invasion of 20,000 French and Jacobite supporters of James.

[74] No Du Veales appear in *Letters of Denization and Acts of Naturalization in England and Ireland, Publications of the Huguenot Society of London*, 18 (1911), 27 (1923), and 35 (1932). A Charles Marie Du Veil who emigrated in 1677 and became a minister and a Hans De Veille who was later a library keeper at Lambeth appear in a list compiled by Samuel Smiles, *The Huguenots: Their Settlements, Churches, and Industries in England and Ireland* (London, 1876), 392, 386.

[75] Two Pooles, both named William, were captains by 1672; Benjamin Poole was commissioned a captain on 20 December 1680. None of these officers, however, appears as a captain in the records of sailings by ships in the royal fleet for this period (*Commissioned Sea Officers*, 362–3; PRO, ADM 8/8).

lodging in the whole city till Doctter Edwards in pitty took me into his house.[76] Wher affter I had bin two days, I fell sick with the hardness of my jorney and the coldness of the watter thatt the docter and every body thought I would dye. Butt my God spared my life to know more misery.

November 12 For aboutt the midst of November I came a horse back to Rathbary, from whence I had bin absentt eight years. Where when I came, I found the house burnt downe: neither a bed, table, or chair, or stool fitt for a Christion to sett on, dish or plat to eate outt of, or meat or drink fitt to suffise natture; and on the land, to the best of my remembrance, only two sheep and two lambs and three or 4 garron horses worth about ten shillings a peice. And this was the fiffth time I came to bare walls and a naked house since I were married.

December 2i In this most deplorable condition I staid till neer Chrismas the Irish parliamentt adjorned, when Mr Frek came home affter hee had left me thus shifting aboutt from place to place for three years and a quarter or more.[77] However, in this miserable place I staid for fowre years and a halfe and sick all the whole time thatt I hardly wentt downe stairs butt as I were carryed to the garden.

1693, March 27 Att the asises of Cork Mr Frek had a letter to goe for England againe for my son to come over for Ireland.

Aprill i7 When on Easter Munday, Aprill i7, he left me att Rathbary and wentt to Kingsaile for a shipp.

May i5 And he landed in England aboutt the midle of May. From thence he went to London and suprised my son and my friends; wher he staid aboutt a month and went with my son to Billney, wher they staid aboutt a fortnight. And they fetched all my plate, linnen, thre of my best beds, and all I had worth carraige or removeing and brought itt away for Ireland to furnish Rathbary – and, which was most my concerne, my downe fether bed I allwaise lay in. Soe thatt of my eight years industry heer att Billney I had nothing good now leftt mee. This is my true and miserable hart fate. Eliz Frek

Agust i6 However, Agust the i6 the greatt and good God brought both my husband and son safe home to me to Rathbarry when I did nott the least look for either of them. For which mercy the Lord make me for ever most humbly thankfull. Eliz. Freke

---

[76] 'Mr Edwards' in the other remembrance; no Dr Edwards, in any case, has been identified as the Cork physician.

[77] Percy Freke and his nephew Francis Bernard represented Clonakilty in the parliament that convened in Dublin on 5 October 1692 and adjourned on 3 November. He remained one of its representatives until 1699; when parliament next met on 21 September 1703, he represented Baltimore and his son, Ralph, served Clonakilty (*CJI*, ii. 568, 634; iii. 4).

[fol. 55v]

1693, November 2d A greatt Dutch ship was lost on Rathbary strand. By a mistak of the Old Head of Kingsaile [it] overshott his course and was staved all to peices, and every creature in itt drowned with all the goods in itt butt fowre men Mr Frek took upp amongst the rocks and buried them in Rathbary church.[78] This sad prospectt happned in little more then two months affter my deer cosin and son landed saffe. For which mercy to mee the great God grant I may never forgett and make me thankfull. Eliz Frek

1694, November 3d Mr Frek was made shriff of the county of Corke in Ireland. He kept his first asises in Cork, wher I were with him, and did putt against the asises two and twenty handsome proper men all in new liveryes to attend him. Sir Richard Pyne and Sir Richard Cox being the two judges, wher thatt asises were condemned eight and twenty to be hanged and burned – and one young English man, an only son whose life I begged, itt nott being for murder.[79] I concidered my own condition thatt have butt one child and his father an estated gentleman in Devonshire. E Frek

1695, March 2d Mr Frek went to Dublin to give up his shrifes accounts, wher was by the Lord Drohedea a match proposed to him for my son and his eldest daughter, the Lady Ealce Moore, with a portion of three thousand pounds presently laid downe.[80] She was a very handsome, fine lady and nothing to be objected butt her quality, which I thought too much for a gentleman.

May 28 Mr Frek returned from Dublin from gieving up his shrifs accounts.

Agust 22 Mr Frek wentt againe to Dubblin to the parliament, where he staid for three months, and had againe the match earnestly renewed

---

[78] Old Head juts into the ocean west of Kinsale Harbour, rising to 265 feet. It was still 'sometimes fatally mistaken' by eighteenth-century sailors for the promontory near Rathbarry Castle known as Galley Head (Smith, i. 249).

[79] Richard Cox (1650–1733), later chief justice of the common pleas, lord high chancellor, and chief justice of the queen's bench, would receive a knighthood in 1692 and a baronetcy in 1706. Richard Pyne (1644–1709) also became a chief justice of both the common pleas and the king's bench; he too was knighted in 1692. Appointed first commissioner of the great seal, he would sit in the Irish House of Lords (F. Elrington Ball, *The Judges in Ireland, 1221–1921*, 2 vols. [New York, 1927], ii. 51–6, 59–60; *CB*, iv. 237).

[80] Henry Moore, third earl of Drogheda (d. 1714), was with Percy Freke attainted in 1689; both were members of the Irish parliament, where in 1692 Moore assumed a seat in the House of Lords. Moore and his wife Mary, the daughter of John Cole, first baronet of Newland, had eight sons and two daughters. Fifteen-year-old Alice was baptized on 29 December 1679 (Lodge, ii. 109–12; *CP*, iv. 464).

for his son with the Lord Droghedas daughter the Lady Ealce Drogheday <Moore>.

Octtober 22 Mr Frek sentt for my son to see this young lady
(aboutt fiffteen years of age), wher he was very kindly received by my
Lord and Lady Drogheday. Wher he staid till the 2d of December
following, all the while kindly received.

December 20 Mr Frek and my son came from Dublin mightilly
fancing the young lady and brought me letters from the Lady Poorscortt
and others to expediatt the match presently.[81]

i696, Aprill i4 Mr Frek and my son wentt againe to Dublin to
finish the match or break itt quitt off. Which affter aboutt three weeks
stay and atendance was brok off. My son was to be wholy tyed to live
in thatt partt of the country, which I thought very hard to loose my
only child when they had ten chilldren [fol. 56r] might as well have
trusted mee with their daughter or att least to have lived within twenty
miles of me. Which nott being alowed of, I resolved to be indiffirentt
in itt. Besides they found my son soe taken with the young lady thatt
they would have made us their servants in being paymasters to the
young cupple, tho my husband offered the earle of Drogheda as much
mony as would buy six hundred pounds a yeare for the ladys joynter
to be laid outt any where (by her frinds) in the county of Cork, wher
all Mr Freks estate lay. Besides which I promised to settle all my estate
in West Billney in the county of Norfolk on them to oblige my only
son. Butt they thought my sons affecttions engaged. Yett to my greatt
concerne and my sons trouble, off wentt this greatt match, which I
foresaw would elce be rhuinous to us, tho my son was most bitterly
angry with me for itt. And home both father and son came in aboutt
the midle of May.[82]

May 28 In their jorney from Dublin home my son was taken most
dangerously ill, when he was nott able to reach further then Watter
Parke, Sir Richard Pines house, where he lay six weeks of a voylentt
feaver like to dye and given over by all the phisitions. Butt my greatt
God had mercy on me and restored him to me againe (with the good
Lady Pins care), I hope to be his humble servantt and a comfortt to
me, Eliz Freke.[83]

---

[81] The wife of Folliott Wingfield, Viscount Powerscourt, Lady Elizabeth was the elder
daughter of Roger Boyle, first earl of Orrery; two of her recipes are among those Freke
collected. Lady Powerscourt died on 17 October 1709 without children (Lodge, v. 274–6;
CP, x. 636–7).

[82] A year later on 11 September 1697 Alice married Sir Gustavus Hume; she died on
13 April 1750 (*CB*, ii. 443).

[83] Waterpark was on the River Blackwater. Sir Richard Pyne, the son of Nicholas of
Mogeely, inherited the estate in 1674 from his brother Henry, who had gained title to
Waterpark under the Act of Settlement. His third wife, Catherine (1664–1732), the

June 2d My son, Mr Ralph Frek, was of age of one and twenty years when I gave him for a New Years guift two hundred pounds (200 l.) and five pounds for a purse to putt itt in <of my fathers>.

5 June 5 I left Rathbary in order to goe for England affter I had staid ther 4 years and a halfe, most of the time very sick (being frighted att my first coming to see whatt a place I weere come to). I rested my self a week or more att Castle Mahon;[84] from thence I wentt to Corke to try for shipping by my selfe.

25 Wher the 25 of June i696, I came on ship board of Captain Townsend with a maid and another woman, a man and a boy, and my husbands nephew Thom Crosby, for whom I were to gett a place in a shipp to serve the king as a vollenteere.[85]

Jully i I landed att Plymouth, wher I mett Collonel Robert Frek, then haveing his company ther, [who] was govener of [the] towne.[86] Who was most extreamly kind and civill to mee: who offered 20 l., twenty pounds, for a coach to carry mee to Portsmouth rather then I should goe againe to sea and thatt he would goe with me thither to putt me in a coach for London. [fol. 56v] Butt I could gett none excep I would borrow Madam Found, who very kindly offered her coach to me; which I thought nott proper to accept on the little acquaintance I had.[87]

i696, Jully 6 Soe thatt Sunday, July 6, wee wentt againe to sea, where we lay beating up and downe the sea till Thursday in a tempest and mists, nott knowing where we were. **io** This forced us to an anker

---

daughter of Sir Christopher Wandesford, was the hostess (H. F. Morris, 'The Pynes of Co. Cork', *The Irish Genealogist*, 6 [1985], 696–710).

[84] Castle Mahon, which dates from the reign of John I, came through the Beecher family into the possession of the Bernards. The 1657 will of Francis Bernard describes an estate of '357 acres English'. In the eighteenth century, when it was renamed Castle Bernard, the residence underwent a series of major changes. A fire in 1921 gutted the castle; its once extensive lands of 60,000 acres are now less than 300 (Ffolliott, 34; Smith, i. 240–1; Bennett, 241–2, 245–6; Paddy Connolly, 'Castlemahon/Castle Bernard', *Bandon Historical Journal*, 12 [1996], 27–34).

[85] If her ship were among those of the royal navy, its captain might have been Sir Isaac Townshend, commissioned a captain in 1690 and commander of the seventy-gun *Ipswich* and its 446 men 'With the Fleet' in July 1696 (*Commissioned Sea Officers*, 442; PRO, ADM 8/4). Percy Freke's nephew Thomas Crosby, the son of Patrick Crosby and Agnes Freke, is said to have become a colonel in the army (Lodge, iii. 330), but his name does not appear in *English Army Lists* or in Charles Dalton, *George the First's Army, 1714–1727*, 2 vols. (London, 1910–12).

[86] Robert Freke (1655–1709) was the oldest son of Elizabeth's cousin Robert Freke of Upway. A career officer who rose to the rank of colonel, he was appointed deputy governor of Plymouth in 1696 (*English Army Lists*, iii. 317, 397; v. 281).

[87] One of the Fownes of Plymouth, she was probably Petronell Fownes, the daughter of Oliver Edgecumbe of Ugborough and the husband of Richard Fownes of Ugborough, or possibly Anne Fownes, daughter of Edward Yard and wife of John Fownes of Kittery Court (J. L. Vivian, *The Visitations of the County of Devon* [Exeter, 1895], 372–3).

for two days more in a tirrible storme, our shipp soe crasy itt durst nott stirr again any more to sea and our boatt nott worth a crowne. Thuss were I sentt outt of Ireland by long sea, or round the whole Lands End.

i2 And in this storme we att last ankered on the Goodwin Sands i2 of July, wher a shipp was lost a little before of 300 tun by shiping her anker with all their crue, when my God preserved me round the world in a leaky shipp and boatt.[88] However, I being tired att sea took the costom boatt to land me att Deal. Wher when we came to the beech, the boattmen and all belonging to me jumpt on the shore; butt I nott beeing able to stirr with my sickness and jorney were by a greatt wave carried away againe to sea and expectted to be lost, when by another greatt wave the boatt was thrown on the beech and I in itt. When severall men with iron graples pull'd itt soe farr on the shore as to take mee out, butt I am insencible how; till they demanded five guinyes for bringing five of us from the Goodwin Sands. Butt outt of all my troubles and from all these my misfortuns my greatt and mercifull God has delivered mee and brought me safe into my own country againe. Eliz Frek

Jully i3 We landed at Deall, wher I hired a coach for London and a horse for my cosin Crosby. **i4** Wher att Maudlin in Kentt I were besett by five highwaymen, one of which told mee I would never reach Cittingburne and bid my boy behind my coach drinke hartily for itt was the last he would ever drink.[89] From these blads they rid, and wee drove for itt and reached the towns end just before them.

i6 I came from Cittingburn to Rochester and soe to Gravs End.

i7 Latte att nightt I landed att Billingsgate, wher my maide Margarett lost every ragg of my clothes and a mantue and petticoatt I would nott have taken thirtty pounds for, nor shall I ever be mistress of the like againe.[90] Butt withoutt a ragg to my back I came aboutt midnight to my deer sisters [fol. 57r] the Lady Nortons att her house in Brownloe Street in Drurey Lane.

1696, Jully i8 And the next day my deer sister Austin came in her coach and fetch'd me to her house in Soho Square, where I staid aboutt a week and wentt to lodgings of my own neer Soho Square.[91]

---

[88] No shipwrecks for 1696 appear in the list Richard Larn compiles in *Goodwin Sands Shipwrecks* (Newton Abbot, Devon, 1977), 165–74, though he documents three in 1697.

[89] Maudlin does not appear on contemporary maps or among the placenames of Kent. A. C. Entwistle, Centre for Kentish Studies, has suggested Maudlin may refer to one of the parish churches dedicated to Mary Magdalene; if so, the nearest to Sittingbourne would be in Davington, a village about six miles away.

[90] Mantua: a loose gown; see below, p. 166 n. 323.

[91] Originally known as King's Square, in the first decades of the eighteenth century Soho was a 'fine large square' 'near 3 Acres' (Hatton, i. 43) with 'very good Buildings

Thiss, the loss of all my cloths, was my first wellcome into England.

August 18 By the favour of my brother Austin, who was one of the lords of the admirallty, I gott my nephew Crosby a comision to serve the king in a man of warr, which he as carelesly lost, spending his mony in coach hire and sights which should have supplyed his occasions att sea. Affter which I offered my cosin Thomas Crosby, iff he would goe to sea, to fitt him with all conveniency on my charge before my brother and sister Austin. Butt hee ungrattfully refused itt, saing he was nothing beholding to me (tho then I had bore all his charges from Plimouth), and said iff I had nothing elce to doe I might send his unkle, my husband, word of itt and his mother too, to whome he would returne on purpose to vex his friends in Kerry.

20 Soe I gave him five pounds to carry him to Bristoll for him to returne againe.

2i I gott my usquabath on shore I still'd for my deer fatther, all which was by bringing in vessells forffitted to the kinge; and I were faine to pay to the customers above six pound.[92] Besids they had soe mingled itt thatt itt was good for nothing.

22 Agust the 22 itt pleased God to take to himselfe my deer brother Austin a Satterday aboutt two a clock in the afternoon, just entered the 56 year of his age the 6 of Agust. He was a very good friend of mine. He left my sister 450 pound a yeare rentt charge on his estatt, and the rest of his estate to his son Collonel Robert Austin and three thousand pounds debt to pay, and his three younger chilldren never a cross for ther fortuns.[93]

i696, September 5 I came againe to West Billney, againe to bare walls and every thing elce wantting, Mr Frek haveing taken away all I left good behind mee. Wher when I came, by the managementt of Jams Wallbutt I found allmost the whole estatt in my hand and the tennants run away with my rentt and every thing in a disorder. Where I lost by the tenants and the calling in of all the mony of the nation to new quine itt twas above 500 pounds outt of Mr Frek way and loss to him.[94] E Frek

---

on all Sides, especially the East and South, which are well inhabited by Nobility and Gentry' (Strype, ii. bk. 6, 87).

[92] Usquebaugh: aqua vitae; often a mixture of herbs, raisins, and aqua vitae.

[93] Robert Austen was buried at St Mary's Church in Bexley on 23 August 1696 (SG, KE/R19, fol. 206, transcribed by Thomas Colyer-Fergusson). Besides his son Robert, a lieutenant at the time of his father's death, were Judith, Elizabeth, and Thomas.

[94] An act passed by parliament in January limited the circulation of clipped or debased silver coins to the payment of taxes made before 4 May and of government loans before 24 June. Milled coins newly minted from the debased silver coinage began to circulate in February, but Evelyn's complaint about 'Money still continuing exceedingly scarse' was not eased until the end of the year (v. 242). Left with money no longer legal except in the discharge of taxes or loans, the inhabitants of Norwich complained to the

[fol. 57v]

1696, Decembr 2i I left Billney and wentt to Lin Regis to Mr Benetts, an aturney, to finish my accounts and leases there made fallen by the managementt of Jams Wallbutt neer fiffty pounds a yeare (and this in fowre years time) besids the loss of neer 500 pounds.[95] This is to trust stuards.

3i of Decembr I came with my two servants to my deer sister Nortons in Covent Garden.

January i, 1696/7 I came to my own lodgings in Red Lyon Streett over against my deer sister Austins very sick and ill, and in the doctters hands there I staid for fowre or five months sick.[96]

Febuary i6 Shrove Tusday, February i6 (I take itt), my deer neece and god-daughter was privatly marryed to Sir Richard Gettings, an Irish barronett, and dyed the eleventh of Octtober following to the unspeakable grife and loss of my deer sister the Lady Norton, her mother, she being her only child.[97] And iff she had lived butt to have bin blest with a child, itt might have enjoyed an estatt of neer fiffteen hundred pounds a yeare of Sir George Nortons. This Lady Grace Gettings was a lovely, fine woman; and as she lived good to all thatt knew her and in the schoole of afflicttions all her life, soe shee evidenced itt signally att her deatth like a saintt or angell. She manifested itt att her death to the admyration of all beholders and the unspeakable grife of me, whom I loved as my own life.[98] Eliz Frek

1697, Aprill i7 I came againe to Billney with my deer sister Austin, being encouraged by letters from the Lady Richerson on security for her rentt for the Hall, which she had then keptt from me twenty seven years for her thirds of her dowre given her by my deer father frely when she stood suitt for all the rest of her dowre. However, I brought

government about the hardships of a devalued coinage (Albert Feavearyear, *The Pound Sterling*, 2nd edn., rev. E. Victor Morgan [Oxford, 1963], 136–49).

[95] No Benett is identified as an attorney in the King's Lynn poll and land taxes for the period; the 1689 poll tax does, however, list a William Bennett, gentleman.

[96] Red Lion Street: a 'spacious' street on the east side of Red Lion Square 'betn *High holbourn S.* and the Fields' (Hatton, i. 68).

[97] According to the marriage licence issued on 15 February 1696/7 Grace married Richard Gethin (1674–1709) of Gethins Grot, County Cork at St Mary Magdalen in London (*Allegations for Marriage Licences Issued by the Bishop of London, 1611 to 1828*, ed. Joseph Lemuel Chester and George J. Armytage, *Harleian Society*, 26 [1887], 320; *CB*, iv. 201). She died within the year, on 11 October 1697, in St Martin in the Fields and was buried in Hollingbourne on 15 October.

[98] A commemoration of Elizabeth's mother in the Hollingbourne church of All Saints recalls the last hours of her granddaughter 'ye Lady Gething who lay 12 hours in a trance, which when she came out of, she often repeated these words, Glory be to God who has chose me for his own, and thus resigned her pious soul to God' (BL, Add. MS. 11259, fol. 7v; Cave-Brown, 35).

downe my security, viz., a bond of Sir George Chouts with Collonel Robert Austins, both of them my nephew and which she knew, for ten thousand pounds and my sister Austin, a widow with five hundred pound a yeare charged on her husbands estate.[99] Butt when I came to treatt with her, she prefer'd a little Shepherd beffore mee, soe thatt still I were destitutt of a place to putt my head in.[100] Therfor [I] resolved to returne to London againe, which I did very ill.

May i8 Aboutt the midle of May I heard of my deer sons, Mr Ralph Frek, being like to dye of a malignantt feaver in Ireland, which soe terryfied and frightned me thatt I had noe rest in me. And affter a eleven weeks stay there I leftt Billney and with my deer sister Austin came to London. Eliz Frek

[fol. 58r]

i697, June 29 The greatt God haveing recovered my son, for which I most humbly thank him, I left Billney June 29. I came to London againe in order to goe to Tunbrige to drink those watters for my health.

July i I rested my selfe att my sister Austins house in Red Loyon Streett till July twentieth.

20 I wentt with my deer sister Austin to Tunbrige very ill, wher with her I staid three weeks oppositt in a fine house on the walks, butt growing worse were forced to remove more to the country att Rust Hall.[101]

August 24 Butt still continueing very ill, affter five weeks stay I wentt back to London with my deer sister to her house in Red Loyon

---

[99] The letter from the nephews George Choute and Robert Austen dated 2 April 1697 is in BL, Add. MS. 45721 A: 'Madam, We are both of us extreamly glad that we can in any thing be serviceable to you, and should have been obleig'd to the lady who hath put us into a possibility of being so if itt had not given you so great a trouble as you have been att to inform us how itt lay in our power to do you any. But if her ladyship thinks her security sufficient to give her that satisfaction she desires, we shall both of us be ready to enter into itt when she pleaseth, that we may in some measure be instrumentall in making you easy upon your own estate. And we heartily wish itt lay more in our power to testify to you how much we are, dear madam, your most affectionate nephews and humble servants. Geo. Choute, Robt. Austen' (fol. 3r).

[100] A member of the Shepherd family, perhaps one of the children of Thomas and Mary Shepherd, who both died in early 1679. He had been a tenant at West Bilney. Ambrose Shepherd, the miscellaneous documents claim, had purchased the West Bilney manor along with Edward Richardson, holding it in trust for Thomas Richardson.

[101] By the end of the seventeenth century, Tunbridge Wells was a popular and fashionable summer spa. Daily coach service from London eased the thirty-six-mile journey, and the many shops along the upper and lower walks together with the greens for bowling and dancing catered to those who sought more than medical benefit. The lodgings and spacious greens at Rusthall and Southborough, about a mile from the wells, were especially attractive (Hembry, *The English Spa*, 45, 79-85; Alan Savidge, *Royal Tunbridge Wells* [Tunbridge Wells, 1975]).

Street, being Barthollmew Day; wher I staid very ill, nothing better butt worse with the fright of my deer sons sickness, till September i5.

September i5 I fell downe quite sick att my deer sister Austins of a malignant feaver (of which my deer Lady Gettings dyed) and of which I kept my bed like to dye for neer two month under the hand of the doctters, apothicarys, and surgions.[102] Affter two month this feaver fell into my left side and settled in my foott and ankle as black as a cole; wher ill I lay of itt nott able to stirr in my bed for neer three month more, all concluding itt would kill mee (of which feaver my maid lay sick for half a year, given over by all the doctters and apothycarys; hers settled in her back). Butt outt of this and all my other afflictions (and my husband neer three year frome me), my greatt and good God delivered mee and raised mee up againe to know more of his mercyes; and for which I am most thankfull for all those I have received. Eliz. Freke

i697, Octtober ii My deerst neece Norton (now Lady Grace Gettings) gave up her pious soule to God on Tuesday, as I take itt; shee dyed of this mallignantt feaver, of which my God raised me up off, and made a saintlike end to the presidentt of all thatt knew her and the perpetuall sorrow and grife of her deer mother, my sister, and my selfe. She lyes buryed and interded in my own deer mothers grave in Hollingburne church in Kentt amongst all our relations. Wher there lyes neer threescore of them in Hollingburn chancell, amongst which is my deer mother and seven brothers and sisters of my own besids my grandfather and grandmother with their ten children, all butt one maried. And all their posterity of ther chilldren lye in the said chancell; and in which my deer sister the Lady Norton has erectted a very fine monumentt in the memory of her of black and whitt marble to the vallue of aboutt two hundred pounds, as she has another in the south side of Westminster Abby with a sermon for ever to be preached in memory.[103] [fol. 58v] And my sister has given fiffty pounds to the

---

[102] Ague and fever are listed in the London Bills of Mortality as the third greatest cause of death in both 1697 and 1698 (Thomas Birch, *A Collection of the Yearly Bills of Mortality, From 1657 to 1758* [London, 1759], sigs. P4r, Q1r). Contemporaries categorized fevers by severity: putrid, malignant, and pestilential (Charles Creighton, *A History of Epidemics in Britain*, 2 vols. [1891–4; reprinted with additional material, New York, 1965], ii. 16). The later remembrances call it plague fever. It is also an obsolete term for an intense form of autumnal fever.

[103] A monument on the north wall of the chancel in All Saints Church and a gravestone mark her remains. An engraving of the monument in the south choir aisle of Westminster Abbey appears in the third edition of *Misery is Virtues Whetstone. Reliquiae Gethinianae* (London, 1703) along with two poems by William Congreve. The poet was not alone in the praise he bestowed upon the posthumously published collection of Grace's writing: 'so compleat the finish'd piece appears, / That Learning seems combin'd with length of Years' (4); a century later Isaac Disraeli pointed out in the seventh edition of *Curiosities of Literature* (London, 1823), v. 117–24, that she had done little more than transcribe passages from a number of

presentt bishop of Rochester, Dr Spratt, for this sermon and bread to the poor to be given every Ash Wensday for ever to continue her memory. The like has my deer sister given of a hundred pounds to Hallingburne church, wher she lyes inter'd.[104]

1697/8, Febuary 16 February 16 I left my deer sister Austins house, being just recovered of my malignantt feaver; and I came a Satterday, the 19, to Billney to take in Mr Freks name posesion of the Lady Richersons dowre, who was in her closett burntt to death the Christmas before.[105]

21 I took by Gods leave posesion of West Billney Hall and with itt a house to putt my poor unfortunatt head in, I haveing bin marryed above six and twenty years and have had noe place to rest my wearyed carkas in butt troubling my frinds. This was, as I remember, the seventh time since I were an unfortunatt wiffe thatt I have come to an empty house with nothing in itt butt bare walls and just redy to fall on my head, as was the chancell with the rest of the houses in the possesion of the Lady Richerson. Eliza Freke

1698, Aprill 8 My husband and son (affter leaveing of me to seek my fortune by shifting for my selfe above three years all alone) both landed safe att Minhead in Devonshire aboutt two howrs before a most grievouss storme hapned.

13 They came both to London safe, which was a greatt mercy to mee, **23** and the three and twentyeth saffe to West Billney. For which the greatt God make me for ever most thankfull. Eliz Frek

May 30 My husban and my son wentt both to London aboutt a greatt match for my son, which he would nott be perswaded to see.

31 May 31 my cosin Bradrup, the prebend of Norwich, with his wife and neece came to see me and staid with me till the third of June following.[106]

seventeenth-century essayists, especially those of Francis Bacon. Freke's copy of the third edition of her niece's work, now at the Beinecke Library, is signed 'Elizabeth Frek her Book Given me by my Deer Sister the Lady Nortton, June 21 1703'.

[104] Thomas Sprat (1635–1713), who wrote the history of the Royal Society, was both dean of Westminster and bishop of Rochester. After the sermon on the morning of each Ash Wednesday, loaves of bread were distributed to forty poor men and women; ceremonial shillings were also bestowed upon widows (J. Jancar, 'The Gethin Shilling', *Bristol Medico-Chirurgical Journal*, 89 [1974], 1–3). The Gethin legacy is now part of the Dean's Gift; the last commemorative Ash Wednesday sermon was in 1990 (Christine Reynolds, Assistant Keeper of the Muniments). No Gethin commemoration is observed at All Saints Church, Hollingbourne.

[105] Anne Richardson died in Honingham on 31 January 1697/8 and was buried there (Blomefield, ii. 447).

[106] Richard Broadrepp (d. 1717), the son of John and Elizabeth Broadrepp of Shroton, Dorset, was installed a prebend of the Norwich cathedral on 11 August 1697 (*Fasti Ecclesiae Anglicanae*, 56). From 1681 to 1685 he had been the vicar at Hannington, presumably through the influence of Ralph Freke, a signatory in the parish register to his possession

July i6 My husband and son retturned from London withoutt the sight of any good fortune, tho he had severall greatt ones made him. Butt I suppose he was before fixtt in Ireland on Sir John Meads eldest daughter, wher he soon affter marryed, unknown to mee.

July 23 My deer sister Norton sentt me towards furnishing my bare house a large, fine tortershelld cabinett, which now stands in my best chamber, vallued att neer a hundred pounds, with some china for the top of itt.

[fol. 59r]

1698, Jully 23 Jully 23 my deer sister Austin sentt me towards my house five greatt china jarrs for my best chamber with a new cane squab now stands in the greatt parlor.[107]

29 Aboutt the same time I bought for my self a new green damask bed with tapstry hangings for the parlor and two chambers with two greatt glasses and a new damask coach for my self with severall other things to aboutt the vallue of thre <originally: two> hundrid and fiffty pounds.[108] All which I bought outt of my own mony, which was neer a thousand pounds given me by my deer father the last time I saw him to buy pins with, with 8 or 9 years intrist.

1698, Agust the io Mr Frek and my son Frek left mee all alone att West [Bilney] with two maids and a man and a hundred pounds a year in my hand and nott one peny to stock itt, he haveing before he left me took from mee my thousand pounds given me by my deer father and putt itt in his own name in the East Indy Company in order to remove itt for Ireland, which he did in Agust i8, i702, with the intrest.[109] This I thought very hard usage, butt tis true. E Frek

Agust i5 They both came safe to Chester and took shipping the nextt day, butt were tost up and downe by storms and tempest till the 25 of September and putt in to five severall harbours. **Octtober i** Att last in an open boatt withoutt the least of shellter or subsistance, every day expectting the fate of a mercyless sea, the greatt and the good God of his infinitt mercy landed them both safe in Dublin affter haveing bin neer seven week cast up and downe to my unspeakable torture and

---

of the vicarage on ii October i681. Broadrepp was married to Ann Freke, the daughter of John and Margaret Freke of Winterbourne Strickland and the sister of John Freke of Middle Temple, the cousin to whom Elizabeth Freke entrusted legal and financial concerns.

[107] A couch or sofa.

[108] Damask: silk or linen fabric with a figured or patterned weave; glasses: mirrors.

[109] The stock ledgers, transfer books, and lists of shareholders in the British Library Oriental and India Office Collections (L/AG/i4 and H/2–3) contain various transactions by John Freke, Esquire, as well as John Freke of Change Alley, none of which can be linked specifically to Elizabeth and Percy Freke.

the infinitte mercy of God to me. For which mercy I humbly [beg] I may never forgett to be thankfull. Eliz Frek

Novembr 3d Affter this greatt fright I could nott stay any longer att West Billny nor have any rest night or day in my mind; **6** therfor left my house and servants and came up to London to try my frinds kindnes of being heer with mee.

30 When on the 30 of November my deer sister Austin, commiseratting my deplorable condition to be thiss cruly disgarded by both my son and my husband, was soe kind to come downe with me, which I shall never forgett itt; wher she staid with me confined to my chamber in bare walls and hardly a bed for her to lye in till the fourth of Aprill following, full fowre month. For which I am thankfull to her, itt being more then Mr Frek has afforded me this i7 yeare. Eliz Freke

[fol. 59v]

i699, March 5 My son Freke was marryed to Sir John Meads eldest daughter.[110] He had with her three hundred pounds a yeare land in Ireland; or iff Mr Frek liked to sell the land, hee would give with his daughter fowre thousand pounds. My deer and only son never soe much as asked my blesing or consentt in this match. For which I have and doe forgive him and wish him better fortune then I, who marryed withoutt my deer fathers knowledg or consentt. E Frek

Aprill 4 My deer sister Austin left me affter she had done penance with me aboutt fowre month, a greatt kindness indeed. Shee then returned home againe to her house in Plumbtree Streett.[111]

June i3 I wentt with Prebend Bradrapp and his wife to London affter they had staid neer a week with me heer att Billney. Wee hired a coach to our selves att Linn to travill att ease.

Jully i I came home by my selfe from London to West Billney, when aboutt this month I new slatted and lathed and made the whole chancell of Billney church, left redy to fall by the Lady Richerson.

Aprill 23 And aboutt the Easter before, being in Aprill, I gave to

[110] Freke also enters in the West Bilney register her son's marriage 'in the County of Corke in Ireland'. Elizabeth was the daughter of John Meade (1642–1707) of Ballintubber, near Kinsale, and Elizabeth Redman, the second of his three wives. Both Meade and Percy Freke were representatives in the Irish House of Commons, where the prominent lawyer and future baronet was a significant presence. Elizabeth, who married on i January 1717/8 the fourth Baron Kingston, James King, died on 6 October 1750 (*CB*, iv. 232–3; Lodge, iii. 233; *CP*, vii. 298–9; *The Register of the Parish of S. Peter and S. Kevin Dublin. 1669–1761*, preface James Mills [Exeter, 1911], 236).

[111] Between Great Russell Street and St Giles's High Street, Plumbtree Street was 'a new built Street, with pretty good Houses, runs up to the back side of great *Russel Street*' (Strype, ii. bk. 4, 84).

the chancell of West Billney a handsome table cloth of my own and my deer mothers worke embrodered on purple cloth as likewise a pullpitt cloth of my own work embrodered and pullpitt cushion to itt.

1700, Aprill 30 My son Freks eldest son was borne the thirttieth of Aprill and christned by the name of Percy Frek, my husbands name.[112] Hee was borne two days before the last quarter chang of the moone; whom I humbly begg of God to bless and to preserve with his grace, long life, and health. E Frek

June i9 I wentt to London to see my deer sister the Lady Norton, wher att her house in Brownloe Streett I staid till the 3i July.

July 3i I came from London with my neece Judith Austin and Mrs Willis, where att Billney we all staide till December 2d.

December 2 I wentt to London with my neece Judith Austin and Mrs Willis, I haveing lett outt part of my house with all the land to Harry Fish the Michellmas before and given away all my stock, &c.[113] Mr Frek thus <deleted: barbarously> leaving of me to my shiffts without any pitty or comiseration two years. E Frek

[fol. 6or]

1700, December 5 I came to London December the 5 to my deer sister Austins, where the very nextt day I fell down right sick and soe stufft up with a tissick thatt I could hardly fetch my breath in the doctters and surgions hands or goe cross my chamber or downe a paire of staires till aboutt the midle of Febury 1700/i.[114]

i7oi, May io I came home to Billney with my two maids and a boy. And aboutt the end of May I had a letter from Bristoll from Mr Frek of his saffe landing the twentieth of May butt very like to dye of a dropsey and scurvy – distempers he purchased in Ireland rather then to live with me, he haveing bin now within three months three years from me. Eliz Frek

June i7 Tuesday, I heering Mr Frek was like to dye att the Bath, tho nott well able, left my house and servants att Billney and came to London and soe as fast as I could to the Bath; **2i** wher I came the 2i

---

[112] Freke wrote in the parish register that her grandson Percy 'was borne Aprill 28, i700 att Castle Mahon', a date later confirmed in the first remembrance (below, p. 199). The entry in the Bandon church register of St Peter is incomplete: '1700 May ... Frake Piersey, son of Mr Ralph' (SG, IR/Reg/28087 in IR/R31).

[113] Judith was the older daughter of Judith and Robert Austen; Mrs Willis was Freke's maid. Henry Fish, the husband of Margaret, was buried in West Bilney on 23 May 1702.

[114] Tisick or tissick, an obsolete and dialect form of phthisic: chronic cough, asthma, or tuberculosis.

of June, above two hundred milles in fowre days.[115] Wher tho I found him very ill, yett I humbly thank my good God hee was well enough to chid mee, tho nott seen me in neer three years before. This, tho itt was nott kind, I expected itt. EF

Jully 9 I left the Bath and with Mr Frek came to London the i2, twellf, of Jully; **25** and I came home by my self to Billney the 25 of Jully.

30 And Mr Frek, his man, and my maid Mrs Evans came home to Billney the 30 of Jully, where and in England Mr Frek staid till Agust i8, i702.

i7oi, Jully i8 My son Frek had his second son borne, which was christned by the name of John, the grandfathers name of the mothers side.[116] To whom God Allmighty give his grace and blesing too, and make him an honest, good man as my deer father was, and thatt they may both live to be as old and as healthy and fortunat is the dayly prayer of Eli. Frek. <Butt he now lies buryed in the vault of Billney, shott to death in London.>

i7oi, September 30 On the 30 of September my deer and only child left Ireland with sickness and given over, as I was told, by six phisitions, and by my Gods greatt mercy to him and mee landed safe att Minhead, a seaportt in Devonshire, just before a most greviouss storme.

October 6 He came to the Bath aboutt the sixth of October, wher he staid and drunk the Bathe watters and bathed for aboute five weeks, by which he found greatt good. For which mercy my God make me ever thankfull. Eli. Frek

[fol. 6ov]

i7oi, November 8 November the 8 I thank God my son was soe well recovered as to come to London with my deer Lady Norton in the stage coach, where they both stayed nigh a fortnight.

22 And both my son and my deer sister Norton came to Billney the 22 of November and staid both with mee till the i9 of January following.

January i9 God be praised my son was finly recovered when both my son and sister left Mr Freke sick in bed of an ague and goute. **2i** And my self was taken with a voylentt ague for aboutt a fortnight too.

---

[115] Without the turnpike system developed in the eighteenth century, travelling this distance in four days would have been very difficult. By 1700 the fastest journey between London and Bath, almost 110 miles, took fifty hours (Eric Pawson, *Transport and Economy* [London, 1977], 288).

[116] In the parish register Freke adds that her grandson was born 'in the Parrish of Rathbarry neer Ross Carberry'. The Rathbarry church is now in ruins and its register lost; none of the Frekes of this period appears in the Rosscarbery register.

Thus when wee most wantted a friend, we had none butt my great and good God, which never yett left me. E Frek

29 Aboutt this time my son leftt London with my Lady Norton and wentt to Bristoll for a shipp for Ireland. Where att Sir George Nortons att Abotts Leigh my son lay wind-bound till the eight of March, most remarkable for the death of our good King William.

1701/2, March 8 Hee dyed on Sunday aboutt ten a clock and on Innocentt Day, as his good Queen Mary did aboutt five years before him. Our good Protestant King William dyed to the loss of the whole nation. He was kild by falling from his horse, which brok his coller bone; which being ill handled by his surgions kild him.[117]

13 Fryday my deer son landed att Balltimoor on his own land in Ireland and continued his health well recovered, and came the next day to Rath Barry; **15** and Sunday wentt to Kingsaile to his wife, being the 15 of March.[118] For this greatt mercy God make me thankfull.

March 25 Thom White run away from me with neer threescore pound; carried away all his goods and stock, and I never knew itt, tho he lived nextt doore to mee, and left his wife and three children to be keptt by the parrish.[119] E Frek

1702, June 9 Mr Frek and I wentt to London to my deer sister Austins, where my husband took up of my mony in Irish debenters outt of the East Indy Company a thousand and fowre pounds to buy more Irish land with.[120] Att my sister Austins I staid a full month very ill with my tissick, nott able to fetch my breath or stirr cross the room butt as I were led by two people, tho I were blouded twenty ounces for itt till I were laid for dead.

Jully 9 Then by advice I wentt into the country. I wentt to my deer sister Nortons to Abotts Leigh neer Bristoll to accompany Mr Frek to

---

[117] On 21 February near Hampton Court William was thrown from his horse. The *London Gazette* (3788) reports he fell while hunting, as do both Evelyn (v. 491) and Luttrell (v. 145), though another tradition states his horse stumbled in a molehill while he was riding. Debilitated by earlier infirmities, he died on Sunday morning, 8 March 1701/2. Mary did, in fact, die on Innocents Day, 28 December 1694; in 1702 that day fell on a Monday, the day of ill omen throughout the year (above, p. 37 n. 1). Asterisks in the margins indicate Freke intended to shift the account of the king's accident and the 25 March entry from their original positions in the manuscript on fol. 61r.

[118] The small village of Baltimore, twenty miles southwest of Rosscarbery, is located on a harbour sheltered by Sherkin Island. On 31 May 1703 Percy Freke paid £1,809 for the forfeited estate of Edmond Galway, including the town of Baltimore (266 acres), Cony Island and Harbour's Mouth (51 acres), and Rathmore (404 acres) (*Fifteenth Annual Report*, iii. 393).

[119] Thomas and Anne White apparently lived in the White House, later occupied by Henry Cross. Their daughter Elizabeth was baptized in West Bilney on 16 March 1700/1.

[120] Government debentures issued by the Forfeitures Act on estates lost by James II's supporters; see P. G. M. Dickson, *The Financial Revolution in England* (London, 1967), 393–6.

his shipp, wher Mr Frek staid with mee till the eighteen of Agust.

Agust i8 On which day, being Tuesday, hee took shiping att the Pill to goe for Ireland and caried with him above a thousand pounds of mine given me by my deer father, Mr Ralph Freke. **20** By Gods mercy Mr Frek landed safe and well att Watterford in Ireland; wher affter resting himself he went to Cork, and soe to Rathbarry, wher I humbly thank God he found his young familly well. E Freke

[fol. 6ir]

1702, September 9 September the Ninth, Wensday, I left Abotts Leigh and my deer sister Norton, wher I had bin kindly treated by her and Sir George for two months.

i2 I left my deer sister att the Bath and my cosin Betty Austin, whom I brought to Leigh to her; and I came to London from Bath the i2 of September.[121]

i9 of September I came to West Billney home very ill affter I had bin abroad aboutt i3 or i4 weeks, and where I have kept my chamber till this end of November. In all which time neither my husband or son have binn soe kind to lett me heer a word from either of them, which has much aded to my greatt misery and sickness. Only my cosin John Frek sentt me word thatt aboutt the 25 of September Mr Frek was goeing to Dublin and thatt I must immediatly retturne him more for his Irish purchas above fowre hundred pounds, which I desired my cosin to doe on my creditt to give my son. The which my cosin Frek writt me word he had done the i5 of Octtober last. All which has nott deserved a letter of thanks from either of them, tho now the end of November. Eliz Frek

Octtober 3i I arested Goode Fish, who was endeavouring to show mee such another trick.[122] Which by doeing, tho I have gott noe mony, yett I have gott the trouble of three farms into my hand and her raged regimentt outt of my house November i6. Which by the help of God I will never partt with my house againe for any welth in this world; I have soe suffered for this two years parting with itt. Which being larg and my husband allwais liveing from mee and I all alone encouraged me to actt this folly, which I have deerly paid for. Eli. Freke, i702

November 2i I had a letter from Mr Frek datted then thatt he had finshed his purchas of my Lord Sidnyes land, which he said cost him

---

[121] Elizabeth, the younger daughter of Judith and Robert Austen.
[122] Margaret Fish, whose husband, Henry, had died earlier that year.

three thousand pounds.[123] Of which he took frome me of itt this sumer a thousand pound, viz., last Jully, and fowre hundred pounds the last Octtober, all in Irish debenters, two hundred of which I sentt my son Frek, and had thanks from nither of them. E Frek

[fol. 61v]

1702, Novembr 28 I made an end of new laying the court before the house, which was 5 weeks adoeing and took upp aboutt twenty fowre load of green flaggs.[124]

December 2d I had a letter from Mr Frek outt of Ireland from Dublin, and the first I had in three month of him since the last of Agust. EF

22 I levied a ffine for to pass away all my right of thirds to my son outt of Rathbarry, &c., to the vallue of three hundred pounds a yeare and gave him fowr hundred pounds besids towards his purchas of Dirriloan, for which I never had his thanks.[125] I passed this fine before Sir John Turner and Allderman Turner.[126] E Freke

1703, May 8 May the eight my deerst sister the Lady Norton came downe to mee to West Billney outt of her greatt pitty and charraty; left Sir George and her fine house and came to doe pennance with mee, who had kept my bed and chamber for seven month before. The very sight of my deer sister revived me and restor'd me againe. EF

1703, June the first My deerst sister Nortton left Billney and wentt to London affter she had done pennance with me heer three weeks, when she took the trouble of carring me with her to the Bath. This kind visett God grantt I may never forgett in her whillst I beare the name of Eliz Frek; itt did soe revive ye soule.

May 7, 1703 I had a letter from Mr Frek outt of Ireland to desire me to meett him att the Bath and thatt hee would then come home and live with me comfortably att Billney. Which, tho I had kept my

---

[123] Among the estates of Justin MacCarthy forfeited after James II's ill-fated Irish campaign were those 'granted to Henry Viscount Sydney, ... by deeds of lease and release dated 2nd and 3rd November, 1698, for the sum of 1,031 *l.* 1 *s.* 6 *d.* conveyed to the said Freake. – *Inrolled 10th March, 1702* [/3]' (*Fifteenth Annual Report*, iii. 386).

[124] Flagstones.

[125] On 31 May 1703 Percy Freke paid £700 for the forfeited land of 'Colonel John Berry and his sons', including 'The towns and lands of Derrylone and Knock, 164 A. & 8 P[erch]' in the parish of Kilkerranmore, near Clonakilty (*Fifteenth Annual Report*, iii. 393; Books of Survey and Distribution, Lisle Parish, County Cork, fol. 66).

[126] John Turner (c. 1632–1712), the oldest son of Charles and Elizabeth Turner of North Elmham, was mayor of King's Lynn. Knighted in 1684, Turner also represented Lynn in many sessions of parliament. His youngest brother, Charles (c. 1648–1711), a merchant and lawyer, also served as mayor in 1694 and 1706 (*HC*, iii. 613; Carthew, iii. 129; Hamon Le Strange, *Norfolk Official Lists* [Norwich, 1890], 195).

bed and chamber neer seven months, I made a hard shift to doe. Wher and att Abots Leigh I impatienttly atended his promise, tho very ill; butt from thatt day to this, being the fourteenth of September, I never heard one word of him or from him whether live or dead. This is true. Which with many more such triks I beg God to forgive him. Eliz Frek

June the 3d I wentt to London to meett Mr Frek and make up all accounts with my cosin John Freke. Wher outt of five hundred pound bank in the stock of mine I paid him for Mr Frek debt due to him three hundred eighty six pounds, eleven shillings, and fowr pence (the rest I took for my own use, being ii3–9–0 and the use from last June i702,) and which was all I ever gott of my own fifteen hundred pounds given me by my deer father and my improvementt of itt for i8 years. E Freke

Jully i I wentt to Bath of a fools errantt to meett Mr Frek, wher I stayed ten days, viz., till the i3 of July.

[fol. 62r]

i703/4, March i4 I bought my son Freks youngest son call'd Mr Ralph Frek, my deer father and deer sons name, an estate in the parliamentt funds of the exchecker of above a hundred pounds a yeare for ninety nine years from this our Lady Day i704 commenceing, which cost me above fiffteen hundred pounds; which I doe give to my deer grandchild as a mite of the much I have received of my deer father, Mr Ralph Frek, who bears his name.[127]

i6 I left my two sisters in London and came home for West Billney with Mr Freke. **i8** Wher we came a Saterday, being the eighteenth of March, affter he had leftt me and this place for neer two years; and for neer a twellve month of the time I never heard of him or from him, he being in Ireland. E Frek

i704, March 25 I received a letter from my daughter outt of Ireland how ill my son was of a dropsey and thatt his leggs pitted very much.

27 I writt to them both to hasten over to me to seek for help in England, being his own native country, wher I beg of my God to restore him to me and his children. E Frek

Jully 25, i704, St James Day, Tuesday I wentt up into my uper closett of an errantt; when coming downe the second paire of staires, my head was taken, and I fell from the topp allmost to the bottom, neer twenty high stairs. Which as itt stund me soe, for a time I were

---

[127] On 24 February 1703/4 royal assent was given to a Loan Act administered by the exchequer; the bulk of the loan was to be raised through the sale of ninety-nine year annuities paying an interest of 6.6 per cent from 25 March 1704 (Dickson, *Financial Revolution*, 60). Freke indicates in the parish register that Ralph, her third grandson, was born 'in the parrish of Rathbarry' on 20 July 1703.

as dead till Mr Freke (heering the noise of my fall and noe complaintt) came outt of his bed in his shirtt (aboutt nine a clock in the morning); and calling company to him, I were by fowre men taken up allmost dead – my head and face against the wall bruised to peices, my back to all judgmentt allmost brok, and the cupp of my leftt knee brok. The voylence of this my fall struck outt my check teeth – 9, thatt strong as they were fell outt of my mouth, roots and all, into my hand – and brok outt my other teeth <in margin: eight teeth>. The second day affter I was lett bloud, when I were struck five or six times in severall places before I could bleed a dropp. Itt was above a fortnight before I had this dreadfull fall, butt I were forewarn'd of itt in my dreame and told Mr Frek and my maid of itt, [fol. 62v] viz., thatt I were in my uper closett on a high lader wher, turning aboutt to call my maid for something, the lader and I fell downe; and I were taken up dead; and tho I came to my selfe, I should live miserably till I dyed. Which I truly fear will likwise prove true to me, I being tho a fortnight since my fall soe very ill in my head and back as thatt I am a sad prospectt to behold. And tho my good and mercyfull God has restored me againe to liffe, for which mercy I am most humbly thankfull, yett the effects of itt I expect to carry with me to my grave when ever my God shall make me soe happy to take me to himselfe and release me of my miseryes. Eliz. Freke

1704, May i8–i9 Mr Frek was taken violenttly ill of a sore throatt which turned him into a violentt feaver; when I watched with him eight nights together, expectting for above a month every day his death; the violence of which turn'd him into the goutt for another month affter itt broke in one of his feett. Wher for above three monthes he was confined to his bed and chaire, butt by Gods mercy to him and me hee is now restored, and this day, being the sixth of Agust, is able to goe to church to thank my God for his greatt mercy to him.

I fell downe the greatt stairs, as above mention'd, and am still very ill with this my fall Agust ye i8. EF

July 26 My son, Mr Ralph Freke, with his wife and his two sons Percy and John Frek took shiping att the Cove in Cork in the Shoram friggatt, a man of warr; the captains name was Pasenger.[128] They sett saile a Wensday in the evening and landed att Minhead.

Agust 3d From thence took a marchantt and came to the Pill neer

---

[128] William Passenger, commissioned a captain on 20 May 1695, is listed in 1704 as commander of HMS *Shoreham*, a rate 5 ship of 145 men and thirty-two guns stationed during this period on the 'Coast of Ireland' (*Commissioned Sea Officers*, 349; PRO, ADM 8/9). The log of the *Shoreham* indicates the ship was in Waterford about this time but not in Bristol. The entry for 21 July 1704 does mention, however, 'haveing under our Convoy a sloope bound for Bristoll'; on August 2 the log notes eleven sails 'under our convoy' and bound for Bristol (PRO, ADM 52/287/5).

Bristoll, wher by Gods mercy and goodness to me they safe landed the Thursday sennight affter. From whence my deerst sister the Lady Norton fetched them in her [fol. 63r] coach to her with her chilldren and servants, wher they all staied att Sir George Nortons att Abots Leigh and rested themselvs for aboute six weeks – my deer son, and his wife, and my two deer grandchilldren Percy Freke and John Frek, with their three servants.

8 The eight of Agust my deer sister Norton presented my daughter in law with a necklace of a hundred pounds to be kept affter her use for a Grace or Ralph, her godson and my deer sons third son, whom I beg God to bless with long life and make him as good and as old as my own deer father.

30 Mr Frek (Agust the thirtyeth, Wensday,) sitting in a chaire a little off from the greatt barne doore whilst they putt in a load of barley, the cart unloaded withoutt any provocation to the horses; they run the cartt in the twinkling of an eye to the very chaire Mr Frek sate in, who very hardly gott off from itt butt itt was broke all to little peices, and a new chaire. This was a greatt deliverance and mercy to him and me. God grantt I may be thankfull for itt my whole life. Eliz Frek

1704, Septembr 6 Wensday, September the sixth, aboutt twelve or one a clock one of my best houses in the parish, in which Jams Wallbutt lived and sold alle, by some accidentt of carlesness was in aboutt three howres time burnt downe to the ground. Tho aboundance of people endeavering to squench itt, yett the wind being soe high and the fire soe firce, ther was nott saved the vallue of twenty shillings by the man and his wife with eight small children, which I fear must all come to the parish; and my loss in the house easylye vallued att two hundred pounds. The last year I lost neer a hundred pounds by this same man and now must, I feare, loose a great deale more due to us.

18 September the 18, Monday, my deer sister the Lady Norton with my son, and daughter, and my two deer grandchildren Mr Percy and Mr John Frek went to the Bath, where they staide till the twentieth sixth of October.

October 28 Saterday, Octobr 28, my deer son and all his familly came up to London, wher in the fattall lodgings of Mr Mosson they staid in till the sixteenth of November.

Novembr 18 Satterday, November the 18, my deer son, his wife, and my two deer grandchildren, and their three servants came to Billney affter they had bin neer fowre months in England, my deer son loaded with his dropsicall humor and grown soe big and fatt with itt I hardly knew him.

[fol. 63v]

1704/5, January 1 January the first I beged of Mr Frek to give my deerst son fiffty pounds and a years intrest for a New Years guift, which he gave him; and I gave him ten pounds for a New Years guift. EF

2d The nextt day Mr Frek and I in my chamber speaking of itt by our selves, only my maide who had lived a greatt while with mee, my daughter in her own chamber stood harkning att the doore, flew into the chamber to us, and told Mr Freke, her father in law, hee might be asshamed to speake of such a triffell as thatt guift before my servantt; and she said she had a good mind to kick her downe staires and said she would be gone iff I did not turne her outt of doors. Soe affter I were forced to discharge her and take a stranger aboutt my selfe affter she had lived three tims with me, and the last time two years want one month. My daughter was neer two month and never said to her father or me good night or good morrow.

1705, May the 7 Munday, the 7 of May, my deer son, his wife, and my two deer grandchilldren left me allone att Billney and wentt away for London, Mr Frek carring them all up att his charge, as he did eight of [them] heer half a yeare; in which time I offten beged of my daughter the youngst child, her son John,[129] finding him noe favourite, and I loved him to my soule because he was the pictture of my deerst son. Butt shee as cruelly deneyed him to me and caryed him away from me, which turned me to a violentt sickness for above six week I thought would have binn my last.

May 10 Nottwithstanding this and severall other cruelltys to me, I sent my daughter up to London (paid on sight by my cosin John Frek) a hundred pounds to ease ther expences in London. For which and ther half year being with me att Billney, eight of them, servants, and horses, and all maner [fol. 64r] of bills, pothocarys, letters, smiths, neer twenty pound in corde, &c., 5 asses, and a horse to drive them to Bristoll – all which never deserved thanks from them.

1705, May 27 While Munday, the 27 of May, I writt to this my said daughter for God sake to carry my two deer grandchildren outt of London, for elce there I should loose them, since she would nott be soe kind to trust me with either of them (soe longe as till she went for Ireland). Butt weer never thought fitt to be answered by letter or other ways, itt being neer two month since.

June 10 June the tenth, Sunday, aboutt two a clock my deerest grandchild I had soe offten beged for, being like my own deer son, neer fowre years old (and in my eyes the lovelyest child was ever seen by mee), by name Mr John Frek, he [was] with his brother Mr Percy

---

[129] John was two years older than Ralph.

Frek and Mr Molson ther landlord two sons wher they lodged.[130] Wher
Thom Molson found my sons pockett pistolls charged and primed and
soe left by his man Perryman.[131] Which pistoll the lad took and
discharged by accident in the head of my deerst and best beloved
grandchild Mr John Frek. The bullett wentt in att the eye; and tho all
the means of London was used, yett noe help.

June 13 Soe thatt on Wensday, the thirteenth of June, aboutt 5 a
clock in the morning my deer babe gave up his soule to my God, who
would nott have taken root and branch from me had itt bin left by my
cruell <deleted: daughter>. Butt God forgive them <originally: her>.
And I shall ever lamentt itt, for I had sett my whole hartt on itt, which
itt has brok thatt and me for any comfortt in this life. E Frek

June 18 Munday, June the eighteenth, my deerst grandchild Mr
John Frek was brought downe from London in a herse to me to be
heer intered in Billney chancell, wher he lyes att the uper end, and
where, God willing, I will lye by him as fast as I can gett to him.[132] I
lost my child to show their undutifullness and cruellty to me, which
God forgive them <originally: her>. E Frek

[fol. 64v]

1705, June 18 My deerst grandchild Mr John Frek thatt day hee
was inter'd in Billny chancell, being June the eighteenth, a Munday
nightt, was three yeare and eleven months old. Hee had an apeerance
of above two hundred of my neighbours att his funerall, all which
attended from Sunday one a clock till ten att night. And soe from
Munday ten a clock till eight att nightt I kept his passing bell goeing
them two days till he was enter'd. Oh, my harde fatte; I am ruined
and undone for my child, and I doubt shall never enjoy my self againe.
E Freke

June 21 Thursday, June 21, my deer son and his son Percy Frek and
his <deleted: cruell> wife (affter the murder of my deer child) left
London and wentt to the Bath to divertt themselves. Shee staid with
her chilldren six week in London against my consentt or all I could

---

[130] The fatal lodgings were at Norfolk Street, which is not included in the rates of the
Dutchy Liberty Royall Ward from 25 May 1705 to 24 May 1706; the name Molson does
not appear among the residents listed in the area next to the church that would include
the unnamed street located between Arundel and Surrey Streets.

[131] The will Ralph Freke drew up in September 1715 gave his 'Trusty Old Servant'
Richard Perryman £100 and a suit of mourning 'for his long and faithful service done
me and his indefatigable care and diligence in his tendance of me in this long time of
Sicknesse' (PRO, PROB 11/563/100).

[132] 1705 Johanes filius Radolphi Freke Armig: sepultus erat Juny 18'. Elsewhere in the
register Freke adds that he 'was most unfortunatly shott in the head' and 'kild Sunday
the 10 of June and was heer att Billney buryed the 18 of June just 4 years of Age'.

writt or say. In all which time Mr Frek, her husbands father (who lay very ill of the goutt just by her), my daughter never soe much as sentt or came to see him, tho she had bin, I think, very kindly used in his house half a year just before and all her familly till the night before she left London. Nor did she permitt his surviving grandchild to see him or ask his blesing before she carryed him away to the Bath for Ireland. For which with all her other inhumanityes to me I begg God to forgive her, butt I will never see her more.

Jully 7 Satterday, Jully the 7, Mr Frek returned from London, wher he staied above two months. He came home much swell'd with his gout and dropsey and in an extream malloncally for the fattall loss of this our deer babe, which he had too much as well as I sett his whole hartt on itt.

(May 7) Memorandum. I forgott thatt May the seventh to enter heer Gods greatt mercy to me, which was my sons cook man Mr Peryman, thatt morning they weare all goeing for London, as on the other side. The said servant man took one of my sons pockett pistolls charged with a brace of bulletts which went off in his hand amongst a room full of people who came to take their leaves of his master and Mr Frek. He was standing att the kiching table whilst the rest of the servants and tenants were ther att breakfast. Itt gras'd on one of ther ears, the iron scowring rod like to kill his, my sons, groom. The room was full of smoak, and the bulletts rebound all aboutt and hurtt noe body. My God gave them this signall warning before they weere charged to shout my deerst grandchild Mr John Freke, whose hard fate I shall ever lamentt and his death, and, I hope, [be] thankfull to God for the first – above – deliverance. Eliz Freke

[fol. 65r]

1705, September 19 My son Frek and his wife, son, and servants took shiping in a man of warr (Sunday morning), Sir Charls Rich master of itt, [and] came back againe to Pill on Monday.[133] From whence my Lady Norton fetch'd them to Leigh. They tooke shiping againe on Wensday in the same ship and by Gods blesing arived safe in Cork or Kingsaile on Fryday nightt, **24**. For which mercy the great God make me ever thankfull.

My son has nott bin soe dutyfull to writt to me one word since I buryed his child the 18 of June, and itt is now the fifth of December,

---

[133] Sir Charles Rich, the son of Robert Rich, baronet of Rose Hall, Beccles, Suffolk, was commissioned a captain on 12 January 1702/3. In September 1705 he was the commander of 155 men on the thirty-six gun *Feversham*, which 'Attends on ye Coast of Ireland' (*Commissioned Sea Officers*, 377; John Charnock, *Biographia Navalis*, 6 vols. [London, 1794–8], iii. 280–1; PRO, ADM 8/9).

because I wrott him word of some mistaks he had commited. Tho I gave him a hundred pounds in May together, and he and his familly were wellcom to me halfe a yeare together att Billney; wher Mr Frek gave him fiffty pounds for a New Years guiftt, and I supplyed him with whatt ever mony he or his familly of eight persons had occation for whilst with mee; and Mr Frek discharged all his bills for doctters, apothycary, letters, horse meat and on my desire carryed them all up to London on his own charge and sett them all in their lodgings. For all which neither hee nor my self have had soe much as thanks from him or his wife. This is true. Eliz Frek

1705, Decembr 25 December the 25 Mr Frek goeing to church to the sacramentt with me complained of a shortness of his breath. **January i, 1705/6** Which soe increased on him by New Years Day (when he had all his tenants att Billney Hall to dine with him) thatt he could butt just goe downe to them and up stairs againe with a violentt astma, every howre like to be choack'd.

Febuary 2i And thus he lay under Docter Shorts hand of Berry, Doctter Barkers hand of Lin, and Mr Goodwins,[134] with there apothycarys, till the one and twentyeth of Febuary, Thursday, sitting up in a chaire day and night for above two months, and never hardly wentt into a bed or gott the least of sleep butt two or three a night to watch with him, holding his head behind his chair in a fine hancher or napkin for feare of his being choaked. The Docter Thomas Shortt had then given him over as past all cure, when I sentt for them againe to as little purpose, he being with neer ten weeks setting up and noe sleep all the whille was soe swell'd up with his belly, stomack, and leggs thatt I every day expectted when he should break with this timpany, as did all the docters.[135]

Thursday, 2i of Febuary In the evening Mr Frek wentt, contrary to my will, soe latte to Saffum in a sad condition with his astma

<hr/>

[134] Several generations of the Short family practised medicine in Bury St Edmunds. Thomas Short could be the son of the physician Peregrine Short, who died in 1679, or of his brother Thomas, a Bury St Edmunds physician who died in 1688; he may also have been a son of William Short, the MD who had matriculated at St John's College in 1650, or related to the physician Henry Short (S. H. A. Hervey, *Biographical List of Boys Educated at King Edward VI. Free Grammar School, Bury St. Edmunds. From 1550 to 1900*, Suffolk Green Books, 13 [Bury St Edmunds, 1908], 350, 351; Venn, iv. 68; Wallis, 541). Robert Barker, an MD educated at Cambridge and Leyden, is listed in the King's Lynn land tax of 1703 as a physician dwelling in the Sedgeford Lane Ward. He was made a freeman of Lynn in 1710–11 and died on 3 April 1717 at the age of fifty-three in Middleton (NRO, KL/C47/26–34, 45; *Freemen of Lynn*, 218; Blomefield, ix. 30). John Goodwyn, a surgeon with property in Chequer Ward, became in 1702–3 a freeman of Lynn 'In respect of several cures of poor people which he had affected'. Later a mayor and alderman, he remained a surgeon there in the 1720s (NRO, KL/C47/26–34, 45; *Freemen of Lynn*, 210, 226, 228; Le Strange, *Norfolk Official Lists*, 195–6).

[135] Tympany: swelling or tumour.

and dropsey and putt himself into Mr Shelldrick hand and Doctter Ducketts.[136]

23 Febuary Where Satteday, Febuary the 23, I came to him, where I found him in a most sad condition by takeing a most violent purge the night before perscribed him by Doctter Barker.

Febuary 25 Sunday night or Munday morning his dropsey brok in his right legg with a continuall droping, when itt run for above a month cleer water, judged by the doctters and a apothycary to be aboutt nine gallons.

Saterday, Febuary 30 Febuary the thirtyeth[137] I sentt againe to Bery to Docter Thomas Shortt and to Doctter Duckett and to [fol. 65v] Doctter Cosins and Mr Shelldrick, all which judged itt (by sight of him and the violentt humour to his legg) imposible for Mr Frek to live a week in March, viz., to the equanoction.[138] In all which time he never wentt into a bed or sleptt butt sett up in his chaire. All which time I sett up with him till I brought my self in a very ill condition; and my left legg swell'd and broke likewise, butt nott as my deer cosins did.

Thursday, March 14 Thursday, March 14, I wentt to Mr Lifs with Mr Frek for ayre for him, wher he was soe rude: tho he had severall beds in his house, [he] lett us all sett up for fowr nights and never soe much as offered me a bed to rest my selfe upon.[139]

March 18 Soe thatt on Monday, the eighteenth of March, I came to Mr Ibotts to board with the minester of the parish att ten shillings per week our selves and five our 4 servants.[140] In all which time Mr Frek never wentt into a bed to sleep till the day I came to Mr Ebots, viz., the 18 of March. Wher with the mortification of his legg he never rose outt of itt butt with the help of 4 men to make his bed for neer five

---

[136] Tobias Sheldrake, licensed to practice medicine in Norfolk, signed the Articles of Subscription on 13 June 1692 (NRO, DN/Sub 1/1). The first account of expenditures related to Percy Freke's sickness and death states Ducket was 'a minister who practised in phisick' (W, fol. 36v); either Nathaniel or Peter Ducket, who were both educated at Cambridge, would have most likely provided care. As rector of nearby Tittleshall and Wellingham, Nathaniel was more accessible than his brother Peter, rector of the Suffolk parish of Huntingfield (Venn, ii. 71).

[137] An obvious instance of Freke's occasional misdating; both her previous entry and the calendar confirm that Saturday was 2 March.

[138] Henry Cozens was a surgeon in Swaffham, where the parish register indicates he lived with his wife Mary until his death in 1720; notices in 1712 promoting his practice appear in the *Norwich Gazette*.

[139] The only Lifs in the Swaffham parish register are Nathaniel and his wife, Mary; he was at the time twenty-one, having matriculated three years earlier at Pembroke, and would be high sheriff of Norfolk in 1721 (Venn, iii. 84; Mason, i. 536).

[140] Thomas Ibbot, educated at Clare Hall, Cambridge, became vicar of Swaffham in 1696; earlier he had received the rectorship of Beechamwell (NRO, DN/Sub 4/1 and DN/Sub 4/4; Blomefield, vi. 225).

weeks together; and every howre I expected his last, as did all his docters, surgion, and apothycary.

Munday, March 25, 1706 Mr Frek in all hast had his vault in the church under the chancell begun by Mr Towrs order with all hands and carts could be gott for himself to be inter'd in and att the same time order'd Mr Towrs to writ to his son to come over to him.[141] Who immediattly did on the third of Aprill 1706 leave his own house att Rathbarry and by Gods greatt mercy to me came safe to Saffum on Sunday night late with my cosin Thomas Crosby; **Sunday, April 18** when, I thank God, he found his father alive tho very ill. In this vault I have inter'd my little, deer grandchild John Frek, who was the tenth of June last murder'd in London by a pistoll shott into his head.

Aprill the My daughter was brought to bed of another lusty boy in the room of thatt which God took from me, and he is named John Redman Freke. He was borne att Rathbary.[142]

May the 9 I being in greatt tormentt with my legg brok in two places with six month attendance and watching with my deer husband, I with his leave wentt to Billney to rest and ease my legg and left Mr Frek att Mr Ebbott with my son; my cossin Crosby; Mr Freks two men, viz., Petter Good and James Minican; and my sons man; and a woman. All to attend my deer husband whilst I wentt the ninth of May, Thursday, with my maid home butt sentt or heard from him every day. Wher I staid, my deer cosin being tolarable well when I left him, till Satterday, the twentieth fifth of May. In which time of my unfortunatt absence I found att my returne (I fear by neglectt) his legg mortifyed and perished. For which God forgive the acttors of itt. And of which he dyed in a momentt Sunday, the second of June, and none by him butt mee, wretched E Freke.[143]

1706, June the second The second of June 1706 my deere husband departed this life, being Sunday aboutt three a clock in the affternoone, in a fitt of the astma. And tho I had my son and cosin Crosby and fowre servants in the house constantly attending him, yett att the fattall houre of my life and his death, I had nott one to help me in the house butt were frightned outt of my life, his soe suden leaving of me and I nott able to hold him.

June 7 Fryday, June the seventh, I buried my deer husband in the vault under the chancell in Billney, which vault hee dereicted the

---

[141] Henry Towers of North Runcton, one of the three witnesses of Percy Freke's will and later Elizabeth Freke's bitter enemy; he had married Mary Spelman in Narborough on 23 August 1670.

[142] In the West Bilney register Freke dates the birth 14 April.

[143] Asterisks in the margins and the marginal notes 'heer to bee inserted but forgott by me' and 'to bee inserted three leavs backward' (fol. 68r) indicate Freke intended the 9 May entry to be placed here.

makeing in his longe sickness;[144] and itt was begun the 25 of March, expectting the presentt use of itt. I being distractted for my loss, my <deleted: good> cosin Mr John Frek, one of my testators, with mee came from London to doe this kind and charitable office for mee. I gave him a gentlemans buriall, and I had all the [fol. 66r] gentry and neighbours in the country of my 25 years <originally: 20> acquaintance to atend it and severall hundreds I did nott know. Itt cost me with the makeing of his vaultt he lyes in neer eightt <originally: fowr> hundred pounds. And ther lyes inter'd in double lead, and wher, God willing, I will lay my unhapy and miserable carcass by him when God please to call mee to himselfe. Eliz Freke

June 24 Midsomer Day I wentt to London in my own coach with my son (and cosin Crosby), wher I seldom saw him, tho I gave him a hundred pounds to buy him mourning and three of my best horses I had; and I sentt my sons wife a gound and peticoatt cost me neer thirty pounds, as my sister who paid for itt can tell. And I bore all their charges both att Saffum and att Billny and till they came to London with my cosin Crosbys, to whom I gave likewise mourning to the vallue of fourteen pounds and ten guinies in mony. For all which I never had from my son soe much as thanks or to take his leave of me when he left London.

Jully 4th I wentt the 4th of Jully, being Thursday, with my cosin John Frek, Mr Freks executor, to prove my deer husbands last will in which he left me all his estate unsettled for my life in England, and in Ireland, and in the bank exchecker and gave me att my own disposall all his personall estate. And with itt twelve hundred pounds fell to me undisposed of in London, which I am putting more to itt to buy an anuity of a hundred pounds a year for the youngest of my grandchildren, as I have now done for my second grandchild named Ralph Frek.[145] Both which I beg of God to spare their lives and make them his servants.

Jully 22 I left London, being Munday, and with my deer sister Austen in my own coach came downe to Billney affter I had staid almost a month att her house in London. **24** Shee was soe good and kind to commisratt my condition and come downe with me to Billney

---

[144] Freke added later in the parish register, 'My deer Husband Percy Freke Esqr departed this life June the second 1706 att Saffum and was Interr'd in the vaultt under the Chancell in Lead June the 7 and left wretched me his unhappy widdow Elizabeth Freke to survive him and ever to Lamentt him'.

[145] Annuities for ninety-nine years were offered in February 1705/6 for 25 March 1706; another offering was authorized for 25 March 1707 (Dickson, *Financial Revolution*, 60–1). The miscellaneous documents note that Freke bought an annuity in 1706 for £1,500 (below, p. 318); on 31 March 1707 she also paid her cousin £100 for transacting exchequer business (below, p. 94).

Wensday, the 24 of July, tho she had hardly bin to venter her self in a coach for 7 years beffore. This was an unexpected kindness received by EF.

*1704, July Now to sume up my two years misfortunes since St Jams Day, Jully 25, 1704, which day I fell down the greatt staires and were taken up allmost dead. With which fall I were forced to keep my bed and chamber severall monthes, and then with which fall I knock'd outt eight or nine of my best teeth, viz., all butt three in the upper sid of my mouth.

June 10, 1705 Then June the tenth my deer grandchild Mr John Frek was murdered in London by one of my sons pockett pistols which his cook Peryman left charged. He was sentt downe to Billney and lyes entered in the vault under the chancell. EF

[fol. 66v]

June 2d, 1706 Then June 2d, my sons birth day, I lost my deer husband affter he had laine above six month under the hands of doctters and surgions in a dropsey brok in his legg and mortifyed, which with a violentt astma carryed him off and left miserable me allways to lamentt him affter I have lived his wife thirty three years. I buryed him in the vault under Billny chancell, caryed by eight gen-tellmen, as on the other back side of this leafe.

1706, Agust 6 I wentt up to my closett for a bottle of wyne and fell downe my closett stairs; wher iff my deer sister Austin had not bin by accidentt att the foot of the stairs to brek my fall, I had bin kild or ruined for ever. For which great mercy the greatt God make me ever thankfull to him for this and all his other mercys to mee, Eliza. Freke.

Octtber 10 Fryday, Octtober the tenth, Jams Wallbutt dyed of a bruse received by a cow at Winch. He was a bitter underhand enimy to me; and affter hee had the cheating of mee for neer fourteen years, in which time I lost by him above five hundred pounds, he himselfe dyed and left his eight children to be provided for and keptt by the parrish, and himself was by the parrish buryed in Billny church yard.[146] Eliz. Freke

1706, November 14 November the 14 (and my fattall weding day) I renewed my coppy hold att Pentney given by Mr Freks will to mee. The present maire of Linn came to my house at Billney (Mr Charls Turner), wher he kept court; for and when in payment I paid him

---

[146] He was buried on 13 October 1706; his wife Martha, on 20 July 1706. The West Bilney register includes the baptisms of nine children and the burials of two. ˙

downe for itt neer fourteen pounds as by aquitance.[147] EF

November 23 I had a letter thatt my son Frek was in Dorsettshire affter I had bin for neer two month frightned allmost outt of my sences fearing he had bin lost att sea. Neither my sister Norton or any friend could give me any account of him till my good cosin John Frek heard the day before he writt to me he was safe in England. The great and good God forgive him and lay nott this sin to his charge.

November 25 He left London the ninthteen of Jully in all hast for Ireland to his familly ther; and from thatt time hee has spentt in runing aboutt the country by the opertunity of three of my best horses I gave him, which with a 100 l., hundred pounds, I gave him to buy mourning for himselfe and sent his wife a new coulered suitt cost mee neer thirty pounds. I paid all his charges for himself and man and Thom Crosby, his wicked companyon, to whom I likewise [fol. 67r] gave mourning and ten guinyes in his pockett; and carryed them all to London on my own charge; and paid my sons bills heer he and his companyon had taken up att Saffum, butt one of my Lord Iccarons.[148] For all this I never had soe much as thankes or heard from my son or his companyon in above fowr month whether alive or dead. God forgive him and lay nott this sin to his charge or make his child deale by him in the like sort. Eliz. Frek

1706, Decembr 23 December the 23, 1706, a letter I wrott to my son Frek and sent my cosin Frek:

By a letter my sister Austen received from my cosin John Freke, I understand you are still in England and, to my greatt supprise, with Collonel Frek att Upway affter this tempestious season which for severall months has kept me in a continuall fears for you, never heering from you since Jully last. For which God forgive you.

Your hast outt of London in July last, when you did nott afford your selfe time to ask my blesing before you went for Ireland, enclined me to beleive your stay in England had binn limmitted. Butt since I am convinced to the contrary, I must and doe tell you with griefe of harte I am troubled thatt your unkindness should add to the afflicttions of my unfortunate condittion. However, itt is my comfortt thatt by Gods

---

[147] A copyhold estate was subject to the custom of the manor and the will of its lord. Copyholders held copies of the rolls recording the terms or customs of the manor established in the manorial customary court. Acquittance: a written release or discharge from a debt or obligation (*Oxford Law*, 289–90; Jowitt, i. 463–4, ii. 1,488). Freke explains the relationship of her copyhold to the lord of Pentney's Ashwood Manor in a letter to the chancellor of Norwich (below, p. 126).

[148] Pierce Butler, fourth Viscount Ikerrin (1679–1711), was the cousin of Ralph Freke's wife: Lord Ikerrin's mother, Eleanor, was the daughter of Daniel Redman and the sister of Elizabeth, the mother of Elizabeth Meade Freke. He died at Rathbarry Castle (Lodge, ii. 316–17; *CB*, iv. 233; *CP*, vii. 44–5).

blessing on your deer fathers and my industry you are left in soe ample a condition as nott to wantt or vallue the kindness of your poor distractted mother.

However, deer son, itt is my dutty to convince you as farr as I am able in all your mistakes, which are to God and mee many, greatt, and grievouss and nott lesened to see you rather expose your selfe and mee to the kindness of distantt relations whilst in England rather then to comply and submitt to a mother wher you may have a wellcome and a home when ever you please to exceptt itt. I confess myne is nott soe divertive butt, I think, mightt have binn as proper affter your loss of such a father and I such a husband, wher wee might have joyn'd together in the managementt of whatt God has bles'd me with by the justice and kindness of my deer husband. For a threefold cord [fol. 67v] is nott easily broken, butt single is subjectt to all maner of accidents. Nor is itt below the carractor of a Christian or reflection of a gentleman to help supportt the infirmityes of a diseased, malloncolly, aged mother (66 years of age). To which mercy I pray God open your eyes to see your errors and mollyfye your hartt and forgive you all your unduttyfullness to mee in all kinds thatt you may bee cappable of Gods blesing to your self and posterytye, for itt does more grive me the injury done to them then the slights and disrespectts show'd to mee.

Therefore, since you have stayed soe long from Ireland, I doe advise you iff itt suits your inclinattion to spend the rest of your time till spring with me att Billney, where your selfe and man shall be wellcome to mee. I designeing, God willing, to goe in March for Ireland my selfe, and then we may posible goe together, and hope by the kindness of my good cosin Freks company to see there whatt can be done for your better ease. Pray seriously concyder whatt I write and from whome itt is that your days may be longe (as I thanke God myne have bin) to enjoy those blesings God and your parrents have given you. For I never knew sorrow till the loss of your deer father the second of last June he dyed <deleted: and your birth day>. I shall nott further trouble you att presentt butt yett will on your reformation continue your affecttionate mother,

Eliz. Freke

This letter I writt to my son Frek by my cosin John Frek affter hee had bin six months in England unknown to mee wher he was. Who when I parted with him, I gave him a hundred pound to buy him mourning and my three best horses I had and then last July sent my daughter a new suite of cloths costt me in London neer thirty pounds, bought by my sister Austen. Besids I cann say thatt in little more then three years I have given my son and his wife neer eight hundred pounds and yett never had soe much as thanks from either, as wittness Eliz Frek.

i706/7, Febuary 4 I had a letter from Leigh from my son, then att Sir George Nortons, who lay for to goe with the first wind and shipping for Ireland withoutt ever soe much as coming to see me. The great God bless and goe with him and give patience to his afflicted mother. Eliz Frek

[fol. 68r]

i706/7, Febuary i2* I had a letter from my deer sister Norton thatt thatt very evening my deer son sett saile for Ireland from Sir George Nortons att Abbots Leigh withoutt ever sending to mee or wrighting to me to ask my blesing. God of his mercy goe with him and lay none of my miseryes to his charge.[149] E Frek

January ii dyed Sir John Mead of an appoplexy sudenly; a greatt loss to me he is. Dyed the ii of January, and Mr Robert Mead gave me an account of itt the forth of Febuary.[150]

Febuary 24 I wentt with my deer sister Austen and her maid in my own coach up to London – ther to settle my business in order for my jorney and voyage for Ireland, where I humbly beg of my God to goe with me and bless me, his unworthy servant, Eliz Freke. Affter she had done penance heer att Billney with me seven monthes. EF

i707, Aprill i5 I came outt of London, being Easter Tuesday, and nott any way able to goe for Ireland with my griveous tisick, [which] forced me affter I had there made my will and putt outt in the tax of England a thousand pounds for my grandchilld. I gott my <deleted: good> cosin John Frek to take this jorney and voyage for me to Ireland, ther to settle my concerns and prove my deer husbands will, &c. EF

i6 I had a griveous fall or two by the turne over of my coach att sixty six years of age which, though much bruised me, I thank God has nott broke any of my limbs.

i9 I came home to Billney in a new coach I bought in second mourning for my deer husband, which cost me allmost fiffty pound, viz., forty fowre pounds to Mr Sheppherd, the coach maker, for his payment of work. Eliz Freke

[149] Asterisks in the margins of this and the 15 February entry imply Freke intended some rearrangement; the passages remain here in their original positions.

[150] *Burke's Peerage & Baronetage*, ed. Charles Mosley, 106th edn., 2 vols. (Crans, Switzerland, 1999), i. 580, states John Meade died on 12 January 1706/7, the day he was succeeded by his son Pierce. Robert Meade of Kinsale (b. 1645), John Meade's second youngest brother and the husband of Frances Courthope, was designated in his brother's will the beneficiary of considerable land in the absence of male heirs (Ffolliott, 143, 152).

[fol. 68v]

1706/7, Febuary i5* Febuary the i5 my son landed safe in Cork by Gods great blesing to me, for which I am most thankfull to God, Eliz Freke. Tho I have nott heard from him since July he left mee in a most distracted condition in London, nor since he wentt for Ireland, or butt once since my deer husband, his father, dyed, now just upon a twelve month. God forgive him. EF

1707, Aprill 2i My cosin John Frek wentt for Chester for me to goe with himself and man for Ireland, there to prove my deer husbands will and to settle my accounts there, I nott being able (tho I went to London on purpose the 24 of Febuary, wher I staid till the i5 of Aprill,) to undertake the jorney. My tisick was soe violentt I were faine to hasten home againe to my Billney. The seventh of March before, I gave my cosin Frek a hundred pound in payment and am to pay his charges home againe and then give him another, E Frek. I likewise paid him Mr Freks legasy of a hundred pound. EF

May ii I had a letter from my deer son Frek dated att Rathbary outt of Ireland, and the second letter I received since I buryed his son John kild in London, being the i8 of June i705. I bless and humbly thank God he safe landed the i5 of Aprill. My son says he found his wife ill, and his eldest son was given over by the doctters 4 or 5 days butt, I thank God, was then on the mending hand. For which I am ever most thankfull to my good God. E Frek

Saterday, May io My cosin John Frek landed saffe att Dublin affter he had bin fowre days att sea in the packett boatt from Chester. He wrott me word thatt Wensday and Thursday whilst he was crosing the sea were eleven ships taken by privatteers from Hollyhead and from which, I most humbly thank God, he escaped.[151] E Frek

May i9 I received this accountt from [him] and of his kind care of my business in Ireland. EF

Agust 2 My Cosin John Frek left Ireland and in the paquett boat from Dublin and landed safe, I thank God, att Chester and from thenc to London. **i9** And he came to London Tusday, the i9 of Agust, from whence he gave me a most sad accountt of all my affairs in Ireland, and all by my sons unkindness to me. I am cheated of above fowre thousand pounds by Joseph Jerrvice, &c.[152] E Frek

Sunday, Agust 3i Sunday about ten a clock, Agust the last day, I were goeing downe staires to goe to church when by my hard fate thatt

---

[151] Holyhead, off the Isle of Anglesey, sixty miles from Dublin.

[152] Percy Freke's cousin Elizabeth, the daughter of Captain John Freke, married Joseph Jervois in 1680; her sister Alice married Samuel Jervois in 1683 (*Marriage Licence Bonds*, 51). Percy bequeathed £50 to Captain Joseph Jarvois.

allwayes attends me I fell downe allmost all the greate stayers and were by three or fowre taken up allmost dead and carryed to my chamber, when [fol. 69r] immediatly I sentt for two surgions to Saffum. Butt they nott being att home, being Sunday, I thank God he raised mee up thatt cast me downe without the help of any mortall man or friend neer mee. Which mercy God grant I may never forgett.

September 30 September 29, Sunday, I discharged Mr Addams from ever supplying my church of Billney more (and then I paid him downe ten pounds) for his quarrellsome drinking and debauched life he ledd, affter I had borne with him above thirty years for the sake of his wife and 4 children and my offten writing to him to perswad his amendmentt.[153]

Octtober i3 All was to noe purpose, soe thatt Munday, Octtobr i3, I left my church of Billney in Mr Smith care, the minester of Winch, for burialls and for christtnings till I came from London, where I were forced upp by my cosin John Frek to receive from him the fatte of his ill jorney from Ireland and my sons follyes.[154]

i5 Wensday, the i5 of Octtober, I came into London late att nightt; wher with my ill jorney, the vexeation of my bussiness from Ireland, my sons unkind behaivour to mee, and the effects of my fall six weeks before, I were the nextt day, being Thursday, taken with such a violentt tissicke and shorttness of breath thatt I were confined to a greatt chaire for neer sixteen weeks together and nott able to goe to my bed butt as I was carried, when all my relations and friends in London thought itt imposyble for me to survive this longe fitt of tissick with a most violentt cough. And for fourteen weeks of this my miserable time I lay ill at my cosin Herlackendane in Devenshire Streett neer the fields; when I paid her for my lodging, &c., forty shillings per week, and for her kindness and care of me I gave her daughter fiffty pounds above all charges.[155]

---

[153] William Adams indicates in the parish register that he is a Balliol MA. He is probably the William Adams from Herefordshire who matriculated in 1663 and received his BA in 1667 and MA in 1670 (*Alumni Oxonienses*, ed. Foster, i. 7). Adams became the West Bilney vicar in 1675, signing the Articles of Subscription in March 1675/6 (NRO, DN/Sub 1/1). Bilney and Pentney register bills indicate he later served as the minister until his burial in Pentney on 15 January 1730/1.

[154] Edward Smith received a Cambridge MA in 1674 and became the East Winch vicar in October 1691; in June 1706 he was also 'licenced to practise phisick & chyrurgery' (NRO, DN/Sub 3/6 and DN/Sub 4/3). His wife, Catherine, was later interred at East Winch, where according to the parish register he was buried on 19 June 1716 – a date at odds with the inscription on a gravestone in the East Winch church of All Saints: 'Mr. Edward Smith, vicar 24 years, who died 16 June 1715 A°. aetat. 66' (Blomefield, ix. 152).

[155] Katherine Harlackenden was the daughter of Walter Harlackenden and Paulina Culpeper, the sister of Elizabeth Freke's mother. Freke bequeathed £50 to her cousin Katherine Harlackenden and £50 to her daughter Mary. Katherine was also a beneficiary of her aunt Frances Freke's will (PRO, PROB 11/539/67 and PROB 11/373/83). Devonshire Street was 'a spacious new str. on the N. side of *Red lion square*' (Hatton, i.

And three weeks more I lay in this sad condition in St Jams Streett, butt att last by my Gods greatt mercy and goodness to me I grew something better and made a hard shift to compas my own deer home.

Febuary 14 Febuary the fowrteenth, Satterday, I came to my beloved Billney all alone withoutt any friend with mee affter I had given away and spentt (in thatt eighteen weeks I were in London) above five, 500, hundred pounds besids my guiftt to my son, Ralph Frek, of five hundred pounds a yeare and three or fowre years arrears of my Irish estate to pay his debts thatt none myght be a looser by hime butt wretched Eliz Frek.

26 I paid Mr Smith for burring of 5 corps and christning two children in my eighteen weeks absence whilst in London. EF

28 And I gave the parish forty shillings more for Wallbuts child that Richard Cross keeps.[156] Eliz Freke

[fol. 69v]

In July 1706 I paid my deer husbands lagasy of a hundred pounds to my Cosin John Freke.[157] Eliz Frek

1707, March 3i And in March 3i, 1707, I gave my cosin John Frek a hundred pounds in gold for tranceactting in my exchecker business, and then he promised me to goe for Ireland to settle my affairs in thatt kingdome.

Aprill i6 He wentt the i6 of Aprill following; wher he staid three month to little or noe purposs more then to tell me Joseph Jervoyce, Mr Freks stuard, the imprudence of [my] son, and the tennants were run away with all my rents and arrears, and the estatts left in that kingdom in my hand.

Agust 2 My cosin John Freke left Dublin and came for England. **i9** And he arived safe att Chester and came to London Agust i9, 1707.

November i8 November the i8, 1707, my cosin John Freke informed me of my sons condition and of his greatt debts and thatt iff I did nott now help him outt my familly must undoubtedly sinke, for which I had bin soe long aworking for them. I made up my cosin John Freks accounts, and then I paid him all due to him, and then I gave him

24) with 'good Houses' on its west side 'but the East side lieth yet open' (Strype, i. bk. 3, 254).

156 Richard and Elizabeth Cross, probably the Elizabeth Croxson and Richard Cross married in East Walton on 18 December 1694, had buried two sons in Bilney within the previous two years.

157 Elizabeth Freke and her cousin John Freke were the executors of her husband's will, which left John Freke £100 to be paid by Elizabeth six months after her husband's death (PRO, PROB 11/489/145).

two hundred pounds in conciderration of his jorney for Ireland. Eliz. Freke

Febuary i2 And when I came away, I gave him aboutt threescore pounds, the intrest of a thousand pounds of mine in the land tax which was <originally: will be> due to me next Midsomer 1708.[158] EF   460 l.

And I lentt my cosin Giells, my cosin John Frekes neece, fiffty pound three year to trade with.[159] And when he said he took the kindness as to himselfe, I then affter three years profitt of itt gave her the fiffty pounds.   50–0–0

Then in December when I made up my last account with him (i7ii), I then gave him a years intrest of aboutt a thousand pound.   40–0–0

And when I sent for him downe to Billney to returne me some mony up to London for me, I gave him for his jorney thirty guinyes, viz., thirtty two pounds, as wittnes my hand Eliz Frek.   32–5–0

Soe thatt my cosin John Freke has had of me this six yeare in guift above (590) five hundred and ninety odd pounds besids my barbar[ous] lease hee made to my sone and still deneys my exchecker orders, EF. Tho bought with my own money, Jully i7i2.[160]

i708/7, January 3d I gave my deer sister Austen for a New Years guiftt a ioo l., hundred pounds.

Febuary i2 And when I came from London Febuary i2, I gave my deer sister a bond of fiffty pounds. Eliz Freke.

I gave my neece Austen, her daughter in law, a silver bason and a sutte of laced head dress cost me both about thirtty six pounds. Eliz Frek

I gave my two neece Austens ten pound a peice to buy them whatt they had a mind to. E Freke

I gave to my cosin Lackendens familly six pound for a New Years guiftt her daughter, and son a scarlett coat. EF

Besids I gave my cosin Herlackenden when I came away fiffty pounds to be putt outt for her daughters portion as her first begining.[161] Eliz Frek

In all is 262–0–0.

[158] In 1692 a land tax deducted from the tenants' rent was set at four shillings in the pound 'to be levied on all real estate, offices, and personal property'. Percy Freke was among the local commissioners charged to collect the tax (Stephen Dowell, *A History of Taxation and Taxes in England*, 3rd edn., 4 vols. [New York, 1965], iii. 81; Mason, i. 433–4).

[159] Elizabeth, the daughter of John Freke's sister Elizabeth and her husband, Richard Gyles. In his will John Freke gave his niece Elizabeth and her sister Anne 'Lottery Orders' worth £350 and £500 respectively; he gave their brother Richard £100 (PRO, PROB 11/559/154).

[160] The different handwriting and colour of the ink suggest that the previous four entries were made at another time, presumably in 1712.

[161] Katherine and Mary Harlackenden; see above, p. 93 and n. 155.

[fol. 70r]

1708, July 20 The quarter sesions was held att Saffum, wher were eight justices of peace; when Thom Garrett my tennantt came before them all and laid assalt, battry, and royatt to my charge and swore itt before the grand jury, who brought itt in ignaramus.[162] And well they might when I had nott gone hardly cross my chamber by my selfe since the death of my deer husband or bin butt twice in my parlor. This he did because I threatned Thom Garrett for cutting downe sixteen greatt elmes while I were in London last winter and conveyed away all the wood of them, as hee did seven and twenty ashes the year Mr Freke dyed. E Freke

Jully 22 Mr Towres and Charles Turner of Linn putt into the hundred courte for five and thirty shillings, unknown to me, which cost me above six pounds to his carpenter Marshall and his baylyes.[163] And itt is the thyrd time he has thus roged mee by his tricks since my deer husband dyed above two hundred pound.

Jully 22 I wentt in my own coach to Norwich, ther to atend a tryall with Towrs for he and his carpender cutting me downe five and twenty growing oakes in Pryers Close while I were last winter in London, besids ashes and elmes.[164] All which wood and trees were conveyed away before I came home except the setting of a hundred of boards for pails and rails.

26 My wittness came affter me to Norwich, being John Bonion, Luke Wingfield, Richard Cross, John Dawson, William Kirke, and William Johnson; all which I keptt neer a week drinking – cost me above ten pounds them, ther horses, and supenas that part of the week.

27 Then came against me Mr Towers and his carpenter Marshall and young Danell Coats. Charls Turner was Towrs atturney; and Selfe was mine, who kept all my wittneses drunk att the Angell in Norwich whilst my cause was tryed, and I nott able to goe or stirr cross my chamber.[165]

---

[162] Neither Freke's nor Garrett's name appears in the records for the sessions held at Swaffham on the twentieth and twenty-second of July 1708 (NRO, C/S2/6). Thomas Garrett or Garrat, who married Jane Wood in East Winch on 29 November 1700, rented Paws Farm. Ignoramus (we are ignorant or do not know) written on bills of indictment indicated a lack of sufficient evidence to support the charges (Black, 672).

[163] Contemporary records for the Freebridge Lynn hundred, in which West Bilney is located, no longer exist.

[164] The quarter sessions were held at Norwich Castle on 13 July 1708; Lord Chief Justice Thomas Trevor and Justice Robert Dormer were scheduled to hold summer assizes on Tuesday, 27 July 1708, in Norwich (*London Gazette* [4446]).

[165] Daniel and Anne Coats rented the Common Farm, remaining its tenants in 1712; he was buried in Bilney on 7 May 1731; Thomas Selfe is identified in the 1690 Lynn poll tax as an attorney residing in New Conduit Ward; the 1703 land tax lists his property in

29 Thursday Towrs swore with his bayly before the Lord Cheife Justice Trevors thatt the trees were all cutt by my order and the wood delivered to me.[166] Hee likewise then swore in the courtt with Charls Turner and his bayly thatt I never sued any one butt I ruyened them and made there famillyes begers. And tho I sent fowre times the morning my cause was tryed to know when itt should bee, yett Towrs and Turner and his bayly and carpenter jugelled soe as thatt I could have noe notice of itt, tho eight witteses in the towne, till I were cast thatt Squire Barnish came to my chamber and told me of itt.[167] This tryall with my own charges a fortnight in Norwich costt me above sixty pounds, and itt is the fourth peice of rogery I have received from Towrs since my deer husband dyed, as wittness my hand E Freke.

30–3i, Jully 30 Towrs sentt me word as soon as he had cast me thatt he had putt into my house for a tennantt the greatest rogue in the county of Norfolk and thatt he would undoe him. Besids this, Towrs and Charls Turner made Grigry Rusell run away, which was above a hundred pound to my loss, E Freke, last yeare when I were in London, and his fifth peice of rogery to E Frek.[168]

[fol. 70v]

1708, Agust io Agust the tenth, Tuesday, I came home weary and very ill to Billney, wher as soon allmost as I came I sentt to Mr Smith of Winch to lett me bloude and to cutt off all my haire, both for my head and tissick. Butt for little ease.

i4 The bayly of the hundred courtt (Spice by name) came and warned mee in to apeer against Thom Garrett in the acttions hee laid in against me, E Frek. Thus am I tormented by rogues of all kind in

Paradise Ward (NRO, KL/C47/12–15 and KL/C47/2–34, 45). The Angel, a long-established inn located in the Marketplace, remained popular into the nineteenth century when it became first the Royal Hotel, then in 1899 the site of the Norwich Opera House and Theatre of Varieties (*Norwich Gazette* [ii. 80]; Leonard P. Thompson, *Norwich Inns* [Ipswich, 1947], 55–8).

[166] Thomas Trevor (1658–1730), knighted in 1692, was appointed lord chief justice of the common pleas in 1701 and later first commissioner of the great seal and lord privy seal. He became in 1712 Baron Trevor of Bromham (*CP*, xii, pt. 2. 30–1; Edward Foss, *The Judges of England*, 9 vols. [London, 1848–64], viii. 71–6). The later remembrances, however, identify the judge as Sir John Trevor, who was master of the rolls, not lord chief justice (below, p. 258).

[167] The remembrances also identify Squire Barnish as Barnish of St Mary's, Squire Berners, and Barnes from St Mary's. None by this name has been located in the registers of the church by this name in nearby Narford; and Freke appears to have in mind the Berners family from Wiggenhall St Mary the Virgin, specifically Hatton Berners whose 21 November 1709 letter to her Freke copied and included in the miscellaneous documents (W, fol. 39r). See also below, p. 99 n. 173.

[168] Gregory and Mary Russell rented Wassell Farm.

this my unhappy condition, and the wantt of health to supportt besids, and noe comfortt from any frind like the civillity I found from meer strangers in Norwich.

22 Besids these troubles and disapoyntments, I have this yeare lostt five fine coach horses soe thatt now nesesitty will oblige me to stay att home since I cannott walke a foott, I haveing butt one left, which since I came home from Norwich is fallen blinde. This is my hard ffate of Eliz Frek.

7 As itt was to heer my tenantt Richard Cross the seventh of Agust this presentt month swere before a greatt company att Norwich, drunk as he was, thatt I had murdered his onlly child and thatt his wife was stark madd ever since; which I knew nothing of till told me by all the gentry in the house I lodged in, [who] asked me by whatt accidentt itt was done. On which I call'd Cross to me, who owned the same words before my face, tho I were in London last Octtober when his child was killd by his own cartt carring flaggs for Thom Davys wife.[169] And this was one of my wittneses; the rest I beleive nott better, tho cast by a foulle tryall of knaves of all sorts.

7 I paid att Norwich all the quitt rents due for 8 years past to last Michellmas i707: first the arch deacon for 7 years, and Mr Thimblethorp for 9 years past, and Lord Oswellston, and recttory, &c. All which came to with lapst time and acquitances neer twenty pound.[170] I likewise wentt to Doctter Jeffrys, aboutt eight miles from Norwich, the most excelentt doctter of this country.[171] As soon as he saw mee, he told me twas too late: grife had brought me into the condition I were in; and thatt I were wasted all in my inward parts, both my kidnys and my back ullcerated with some fall I had lately had, which on the least stoppages of flew up to my unhapy head and caused my greatt shortness of breath, which would sudenly take me off. Therfore [he] advised me nott to be alone or expectt ever to be cured of my missery, which he said must bee very greatt by my watter. Which in Gods good time I

---

[169] Richard and Elizabeth Cross' son Francis was buried in West Bilney on 16 October 1707; Thomas Davy and Diana Thomson were married in Bilney on 29 January 1701/2.

[170] Quit rent: a small fee or rent freeholders and copyholders of manors paid annually, 'so called because thereby the tenant goes quit and free of all other services' (Jowitt, i. 32). Among the many Themelthorpes or Thymblethorps in Norfolk, Edmund Themilthorpe was, along with Percy Freke, a tax commissioner in 1696 (Mason, i. 434). Themilthorps had also long held property from the prior of Pentney (Blomefield, xi. 86). Lord Oswellston may be Charles Bennet, Baron Ossulston, who was created earl of Tankerville in 1714 (CP, xii, pt. 1, 633).

[171] John Jefferie of Neatishead (ten miles northeast of Norwich) was 'a local quack doctor of great repute' who died in 1714 (Rye, i. 401); presumably he is the Dr Jefferies who in 1711 advertised in the *Norwich Gazette* (v. 237). In her husband's sickness Freke also sent for a Doctor Jefferys from Norwich, perhaps the John Jefferys, Norfolk doctor of physick, who was buried in Neatishead in May 1706.

should bee eased of, butt nott by doctters, who could doe me noe good.

November 25 Charles Turner of Lin sentt two baylyes up to my chamber with an execution to seise me body and goods for eight pounds awarded him, &c., for his Agust perjury, when I knew nott thatt I owed him one farthing butt thought I had paid him and the rest all charges due to them; and att the same time I had above eight hundred pounds in mony in my house, as wittnes Eliz Freke.[172]

1708/9, March 10 I had two very rough letters from my cosin John Frek from London, affter I have given him above 590 l. in little more then two years, by way of threats <deleted: iff I altered my presentt condition> (above 590 l.).

ii March I had a refference with Robin Good (before Squir Berners) for rentt due to me from John Fish, who dyed the 29 of January last, and hee being his executor has yett dealt by me as the rest of this country doe now I am confined to a chaire and helpless, May 22.[173]

Aprill 25 I had a letter from Mr North of Ruffum to give me nottice thatt Thom Garrett had chose him a refferee in Garrets behalfe to compremise the suite then depending between us.[174] In which letter of Mr North hee inclosed to mee a letter he wrott to Mr Barnish to stand with him a refferree for mee, which letter I sentt to St Marrys the nextt day, being Easter Eve.

27 And on the 27 of Aprill, being Wensday, the said Mr North with Mr Barnish and me, Mrs Eliz Frek, wentt to Middletowne, a publick house, the apoynted place [fol. 71r] of our meeting.[175] Wher affter two

---

[172] Writs of execution are court directives carried out by the sheriff or bailiff. A writ of *fieri facias* authorizes seizure of goods or chattels; a writ of *capias ad satisfaciendum* could bring about imprisonment (*Oxford Law*, 448).

[173] Other references in this remembrance and in miscellaneous documents emphasizing the obligation John Fish left his son Thomas to fulfil by 1710 identify the squire as Barnish (below, p. 104; W, fol. 40r) as well as Berners (below, p. 261; B, fol. 41r). Fish's death is not recorded in the remaining records of West Bilney, Pentney, and East Winch. Robert Good, his executor, was taxed in 1704 for the Pentney properties of Mill and Bush Fenn; the assessment appears in lists of the 1692 and 1704 Pentney land tax Freke copied at least in part from James Hoste and included among the miscellaneous documents in W, fols. 44v–45r.

[174] Roger North (1651–1734), the youngest of Dudley Lord North's six sons, bought the estate of Yelverton Peyton in Rougham in 1690, where the successful London attorney was an integral part of Norfolk country life. Unlike the biographies he wrote of his brothers, his autobiography was never finished, and his life at Rougham remained untold (F. J. M. Korsten, *Roger North, 1651–1734, Virtuoso and Essayist* [Amsterdam, 1981]; Carthew, ii. 495).

[175] The B text names Hatton Berners, not Barnish, at the meeting (below, p. 261). Hatton Berners, the son of Hatton and Anne Berners of Wiggenhall St Mary, was a justice of the peace and a freeman of Lynn. He died on 23 November 1713 at the age of seventy-three and was buried three days later in Wiggenhall St Mary the Virgin (Clarke and Campling, eds., *Visitation of Norfolk*, 4 [1934], 22–3; *Register of Gray's Inn*, 292; *Norfolk Lieutenancy*, 115; *Freemen of Lynn*, 213; Blomefield, ix. 181). The Crown, listed by name in

howrs stay Thom Garrett came, butt nothing was done more then that I paid twenty fowr shillings for my diner and witneses with atendance. Soe wee all parted, Garrett haveing affronted Mr North by delays and mee and att last cheated me of all rent, charges, covenants, repairs, &c., to above seventy pounds or eighty pounds loss to me.

And by his example, i709, John Dawson, another tennantt, did on Sunday night, the i5 of May, run away with all my stock, and three half years rentt, and one and fifty pounds in arrears, both to the vallue of a hundred twenty six pounds.[176] And both these tennants were taken by my deer husband, nott with my approbation. Eliz Frek

i709, Aprill 27, Wensday Aprill the 25, i709, my charge I laide against Thom Garrett when Mr North wrott to me for a refference for him and when Mr North wrott to Mr Barnish to stand with him, both unknown to mee. Mr North appoynted Middletowne at the Crowne, wher I and Mr Barnish attended on him att ten a clock to noe purpose, as wittness Eliza Freke.

Imprymus – Thatt there is due to me from Thom Garrett thirtty pounds for halfe a years rentt for his farme last Michellmas i708.

Item – Thatt there is likewise due from Thom Garrett to me for rentt of the parrish house which he received as overseer of the poore two pounds or forty shillings, which he received as mine last Michellmass was twelve month, i707.

Item – Thatt the said Thom Garrett or his order did cutt downe unknowne to mee in or aboutt the time of my deer husbands sickness or when I were away 27 fine young ashes, all timber trees in Cappon Wood belonging to his farme.[177] Which my son missing in my deer husband sickness desired me I would sue the said Thomas Garrett for them, butt the death of Mr Frek soe mortifyed me I knew nott whatt I did. He, Thomas Garrett, pleads my acquittance of discharge for this and other his rogerys.

Item – Thatt since, viz., last winter was twelve month, i707, when I were in London, the said Thom Garrett did by himselfe or his order cutt downe unknowne to me eighteen greatt elmes, all timber trees, as is now to be seen, i709, on the place. He carryed away the timber butt the stumps; out of which he made above twenty new cow bins, ten of which I took up by Mr Host warrantt Jully the 20, i708, on susspision till proofe was made of the wood (tho he threatned me iff I came in

the Alehouse Recognizances of 1789 (NRO, C/Sch 1/16), can still be found on Lynn Road in Middleton.

[176] John Dawson, a witness to Percy Freak's will, rented Manor Farm; he was buried in Pentney on 26 March 1713.

[177] Cappon Wood appears on neither Faden's 1797 map of Norfolk nor on the earliest of the Ordnance Survey maps.

his yard he would shoutt me).[178] Then he pretended Mr Noes gave him the wood; which I convinced him the contrary, under Mr Noes own hand, he never gave him a stick.[179] And fourteen of these bins were made by Thom Johnson, my carpenters brother.

Item – Thatt the hedges and fences and drains were soe left by Thomas Garrett contrary to the covenants of his lease thatt of three tennants I had lett itt to all refused the entry except I alowed them ten pounds towards the makeing up the fences and wood; which I were forcst to, as Mr Smith, minester of Winch, can testifye thatt Robertt Coe and Allin Mils said it was the least itt could cost, and so they left itt affter bringing twenty load of hay.[180]

[fol. 71v]

Item – Thatt the said Thomas Garrett contrary to the covenants of his lease has carryed away from off my land all his hay, straw, stover, and muck from my said farme to aboutt twenty pound damage, as my now tennantt Knopwood demanded butt last week.[181] For which I were forst to aloow him his conciderration in the leiw of itt.

Item – Thatt contrary to the covenants of his lease thatt there was noe sumertill left wheras ther ought to have bin ten akers with fowre earth plowing left me, &c.; of which none butt a few akers of turnups nott worth howing, the disapoyntmentt of which is greatly to my loss. For which I am faine likewise to alow my tennantt for in his rentt, or could nott lett my farme.

Item – Thatt of 25 gates belonging to the said Garretts farme weere all broke to peices and carryed away with hooks and henges and their verdalls, exceptt fowre old ones withoutt hook or henge and a few old spars nott worth carring away wher the old gats were, as on Johnson the carpenters veiw; butt all there hooks and henges of the whole 25 quite gone.[182]

---

[178] The son of James and Elizabeth Hoste of Sandringham, James Hoste (d. 1729) had been a captain of a troop of Norfolk militia and a high sheriff of Norfolk. He was also a justice of the peace and a freeman of King's Lynn (Mason, i. 436, 536; Blomefield, ix. 69, 71; *Freemen of Lynn*, 208; *Norfolk Lieutenancy*, 100, 148).

[179] Charles Nowyes of Wood Ditton in Cambridgeshire, lord of Ashwood Manor in Pentney.

[180] Robert Coe is listed in the 1692 Pentney land tax; he and his wife Mary had a daughter baptized in West Bilney on 26 July 1695. Allin Mils' name appears in neither the local tax lists nor parish registers.

[181] Stover: fodder; often made from clover, straw, and reeds. William Knopwood rented Paws Farm in 1708, remaining its tenant in 1712; he was buried on 21 October 1721 in West Bilney.

[182] Verdall, among various dialect spellings, is the half of the hinge that pivots; also 'the bottom hinge of a gate' (*EDD*). Spars are wooden bars used to fasten gates.

Item – Thatt all the bricks in the parlor and kiching, both well paved, are all by the said Garrett or his order taken up and conveyned away, as I my selfe saw, and only a rough flowre left useless for a tennantt till I have new laide itt for them.

Item – Thatt aboutt the 20 of Jully last, 1708, I wentt downe in my coach with my servantt maid and one of my tenants wives, viz., Goody Cross, and the constable with Mr Host warrantt to enter upon one of the barns in the said Garretts occupation due to me the May Day before by a covennant in his lease.[183] In which barne I have locked up the bins made outt of my wood by Thom Johnson, partt of them, viz., ten, which I secured; on which Garrett abused me in the most scerulous language never before I think given to a Xtian, threatning to be even with mee.

Item – The nextt day or the day affter was Saffum sessions, wher the said Thomas Garrett wentt to the sesions and did there before nine or ten justices of peace indite me of a royatt, assault, and battry and there offered before the jury to swere I came downe on purpose to murder his wife and children. Whilst I knew nothing of these my crimes laid against me till the next day the grand jury were so civill to me as to send me word thatt they had brought itt in ignoramus and thatt they were glad they could serve me against such a rogue as Garrett was.

Item – Thatt aboutt the midle of Agust following the said Garrett sentt Spice the bayly (Mr Smith, minester of Winch, being then in my house) to warne me into the hundred courte of Goward in severall infamous actions, amongst which he putt in againe the aforesaid royatt, assault, and battry.[184] His 2d acttion was for stealing of ten akers of his grass, more or less; and his 3d action for eateing up ten load of his hay, more or less. His 4th acttion was for falce poundage when he owed me nothing, tho yett he owes me the rentt May 3d, 1709, for Michellmas 1707. With severall other acttions of infamy on me.

Item – Thatt the said Thom Garrett brought his repleven outt of Goward courte and aboutt eleven a clock att night brok up my courte gates and sentt severall rude fellows up to my chamber att that time of the nightt, who with ther rude, threatning language soe affrighted mee I could hardly compose my self affter itt for severall days.[185]

Item – Affter this said Garretts usage thus of me, I arrested him for

---

[183] Elizabeth, the wife of Richard Cross, the tenant who left in October 1708.

[184] Goward: perhaps Gaywood, the village near King's Lynn where the Freebridge Lynn hundred court had been held (Blomefield, viii. 328). The few remaining records from the hundred court indicate it was still a meeting place in 1637 (NRO, BL VIb[1]); no final date has been established.

[185] Replevin: an owner's action to recover goods or chattels wrongfully held or detained (Black, 1,168).

my halfe years rentt, viz., thirty pounds, and for breach of covenants, &c. And I did by Mr Carter remove my selfe outt of Goward courte all my said acttions, which with the tryall and removall from Goward fiffteen pounds, as I have to show by their acquitances.[186]

Item – Thatt the second of March last, being Wensday, I had my tryall att Norwich against Garrett, who loaded a cart load of wittness [fol. 72r] against my two wittneses; and when he was come as far as Gyton, heering the pasing bell of Billny tole, Garrett came back (neer three miles) to know iff I were dead because of right placeing his charges. Butt by Gods providence I recovered; and by the favour and civillity of the gentry and jury added to the justness of my cause, I cast him in every one of his infamous acttions, tho a stranger.

Item – Affter this tryall on a months petition of Garrett and Mr North letter to mee and Mr Berners, I did Aprill the 27, 1709, permitt of an arbitration att the Crowne att Midletowne, where I did waite on Mr North and Mr Berners. Wher affter two howrs attendance on Garrett, he vouchsaffed his company; butt nothing was done, only I paid ther 1-4-6 for my diner and servants, &c.

Item – Being thus disapoynted I resolved, God willing, to renew my tryall againe, iff posible to try itt in London, and wrott to the gentlemen these ensueing words, viz., I humbly desire you will both be pleased to concider with the loss of my reputation in the abusses placed on me, which has bin and is an extreame afflicttion to me. And therfore I doe intreate thatt there may be a suiteable sattisfacttion made me thatt itt may nott be a president to my other tennants soe to use me in this kind and thatt iff any thing be done the said Garrett and Woods may give you and me such a security in whatt you shall think fitt to award me both for my rents, breach of covenants, charges, &c. Thatt I may nott be putt to a further trouble againe and charge for itt is the desire of your most humble servantt. Eliz Freke

1709, May 13 May the 13, Fryday, I sentt to Dawson, being to goe the 15 of May to London, to pay me som rentt, I haveing three half years rentt in arrears due to me of fiffty pounds a yeare besids his note for fiffty one pounds, three shillings. John Dawson sentt me word he had nott yett sold his sheep, &c.; soe affter haveing received a hundred such mesages withoutt one peny of mony, on Fryday, the thirteenth day of May, Mr Buck, the minisster, being with me, I sentt my servantt to the constable to make a seisure for mee for entry.[187] Butt Dawson had information whilst he was coming and carried off all my distress

---

[186] Perhaps a lawyer or official, he has not been associated with the Carters of Pentney.

[187] Charles Buck matriculated at Trinity College, Cambridge in 1684, receiving an MA in 1691. He was ordained a priest in 1698 and signed the Articles of Subscription as vicar of Gayton in September 1705 (Venn, i. 245; NRO, DN/Sub 4/2).

from my land except fowre or five horses which I destrained with a little lumber and a few shotts.[188]

i4 Satteday, the fowrthteen of May, Luke Wingfield and severall of the tennants came beging and perswading mee with Knopwood, the constable, perswading of his honest paymentt.[189]

i5 I did on Sunday, the i5 of May, release his stock, cartt horses, &c., forty cows, sheep, and other stock. **i6** And the same nightt, being Sunday night, nottwithstanding his hand and promise to the contrary he conveyed away all my distreess stock, goods, &c., by three a clock Munday morning and sentt me word itt was to show me hee could carry away his stock and goods when I weere heer as well as iff I had bin absentt.

i7, i8 Hee then lodged his stock and goods att one Nettles of Winch,[190] wher the i7 and i8 of May by two days of sale the said John Dawson run away from me with three half years rentt and fiffty one pound, three shillings in mony, which with taxess and all allowed him coms to a hundred twenty six pounds. And this is my fiffth loss in a year and half by my inabillity of goeing outt of my chamber, viz., their severall nams are as followeth:

Xmas i707 First att Candlemas Gregory Rusell with sixty pounds in mony and half a years rentt, besids all the fences downe and gone, and till the nextt Michellmas the farme in my hand unstocked of fiffty seven pounds a yeare. E Freke

September i708 Then rogue Garrett run withe the above charge away from me, to my charge and loss above a hundred pounds and all the inhumanity, as wittness E Freke.

January 29 John Fish dyed; when Robin Good adminestered, who before Mr Barnish allowed my demands of io9 pounds.[191] I gott butt forty and am faine to alow Luke Wingfield twenty pounds to make up my fence, viz., a years rentt. E Frek

Octtobr i708 Then Richard Cross wentt from me with aboutt sixty pounds, carried off all his stock to Mr Norths.

May i3, i709 This rogue John Dawson cheatted me, as above, of i26 pound, all the fences down, and the land on my hand, as wittness Eliz Frek.

---

[188] Distress: a landlord's common law right to distrain or take the goods or chattels of a tenant delinquent in his rent (Black, 426). Shotts: shoats.

[189] Luke Wingfield rented Parsonage Farm as well as land in Billney Closes and Pryers Close. He and his wife Judith baptized and buried several children in East Walton, where he was later a church warden. The constable was probably Freke's Paws Farm tenant.

[190] Humphrey and Ann Nettle, the widow of Francis Ouldman, who were married in East Winch in 1705.

[191] In B it is Berners.

[fol. 72v]

May 1709 Which iff right reckned by me, Eliz Frek,
coms to aboutt   505–0–0
Besids the loss and falls of my rents the severall half years   125–0–0
And the repairs of every farme in gates, fences, and
workmen, and for nails <in margin: cost me 12 l. in nails,
&c.>   42–0–0
And the falls of my rentt for ever coms to aboutt heer and
att Pentny sixteen pounds a yeare.   16–0–0
And this all by my inabillity of being able to goe outt of
my chamber soe farr as the parlor this three years or since
the death of my deer husband, as wittness Eliz Freke.   688–0–0

1709, March 25 Being to goe for London to ease my cosin Frek of
his troubles in being a truste for my grandchildren, affter I had lost all
the above sums by my inabillity, I did putt Mr Buck, the minester of
this parrish, to the care and looking affter my estate heer in Billney
and Pentny. For which I promised him ten pounds a year and his
charges and twenty pound a year I allow him for the serveing my
church att Billney. E Frek

And besids this above loss by five tenants, I have spentt in law and
charges belonging to itt with lawyer fees and councell and wittneses
and tryalls of causes and travailling aboutt these five villians and in the
hundred courte att the least seventy pounds.   70–0–0
And all in the compass of a year and halfe have done it to
crase mee.   758–0–0

1708, March 26 I gave Mr Taffe warning by Mr Smith for my house,
who told me itt was a day affter the faire [warning], soe he would hold
itt on.[192] E Frek.

Michellmas, September 29 I then gave Taff my selfe warning for my
house persuantt to the covenants of my lease, who still insistted on a
more faire warning from me. E Frek

1709, March 25 I then the third time gave Richard Taff warning
thatt I would enter on itt as att nextt Michellmas 1709, who still insisted
on the errors of his lease and told me I had a much better house
provided and redy furnished for me att St Marys and thatt he was
promised to hold outt his lease heer by Mr Barnish. Which much
moved my pattion, and I swore I would nott keep a pimp in my house
any longer and bid him soe tell his benefactor. E Freke

Aprill 21 Aboutt the 20, 21 of Aprill Mr North of Ruffum sentt me
word by Mr Buck, the minester of the parrish, thatt the whole country

---

[192] Richard Taff (Tafft, Tofts) rented 176 acres, including Hall Farm, Dyes Close, and
the Ale House land; in 1712 he was the Manor Farm tenant.

had sold and given me up to Mr Barnish and did writt 2 or 3 very handsom letters to mee, &c. All which I answered him in. E Freke

i709, May i3 As I said before, John Dawson run away from me with his year and half rent and one and fiffty pounds in mony and bidd me make the best of my deer husbands lease, for he would performe none of itt, either rents or covenants, tho itt was three years affter his death. And with this villian ends all the leases made by my deer husband. Which iff I have right reckned coms to 758–0–0, as above, besids above threescore timber trees cutt downe and carryed away unknown to mee, the houses pull'd down and the flowrs up, and all the fence to be new made by me, [and] the first years rentt for allowances in the new letting the land rather then to fall the rents too much. And all this by my cosin John Freks nott letting me know I ought to have made new leases att my deer husbands death and my ignorance and inabillity of being able to stirr further then my chamber or chaire. E Freke

May i9 Mr Buck, the minester, came to me from Mr Barnish of St Marys and told mee thatt iff I would persue my health in London and devirt my self with my frinds this sumer he would assist Mr Buck in the management of all my affaiers in my absence. The like has bin sent me from other of my neighbours to see my usuage and noe friend to my helpe of my own or relations. E Frek

i709, May the 24 The tennants names thatt have run from me by my deer husbands leases since his death, now three years wanting one fortnight, are as followth:

Gregory Russell, the Wassell Farme	i707, Candlemas	lett att 57–0–0
Sam Brett, my Pentny farme	i707, Michellmas	lett att 46–0–0
Thom Garrett, Paws Farme	i708, Michellmas	lett att 60–0–0
John Fish, Billney Closes	i708, January 29	lett att 32–0–0
Richard Cross, the White House	i708, Michellmas	lett att 43–0–0
John Dawson, the Maner Farme	i709, May i3	lett att 50–0–0
		288–0–0

All these butt Brett run away with my arrears and rentt due to me. And by Brett I lost very considerably, and I were faine to make greatt abatments and alowances to Englebright, his successour. Besids I were forst to keep ther farmes in my hand the yeare withoutt stock and new make up all their drains and fences and gats. Eliz Freke

[fol. 73r]

i709, May the 24 And in all these my troubles and losses before mentioned my cosin John Frek, my pretended truste (who gave away from me to my son my deer husbands estate in Ireland hee gave me of 750 pounds a year), never did concerne himself more then iff I had bin a stranger to him or in the least ever assisted me, tho I had given him in the compass of two years time fowre hundred and fowrescore pounds outt of my own pockett from my children and grandchildren. Nor did he ever informe me thatt I should have new leased my land affter my deer husbands death till I had lost above 758 l. (seven hundred fiffty and eight pounds). Persuantt to the same has binn my sisters and other relations call'd friends since I have bin a widdow, which is now neer fowr years. In which station I humbly begg Gods blesing on me and thatt I never may trust such frinds or relations more, I haveing found more kindness and favour in my unhappy state by three of my neighbours heer then all my own relations, as wittness my hand Eliz Frek.

About the end of Agust 1708 Charles Turner of Linn, thatt arrested me with two baylies in my chaire on body and goods for eight pounds and with Mr Towrs both swore against me att the last asises att Norwich Jully 29 – thatt to compass there cause swore I never sued any one butt I cast them and affter brought them and their whole familyes to be parish charge – before the Lord Cheif Justice Trevours and a whole country, and tho my self and eight wittneses were in town with three servants. Thess villians Turner and Towrs, whose constant oath was to me he knew nott any thing of the cutting of 2i oaks in Pryers Close (by the liveing God), yet affter att the asise bench saidd itt was by my order to him hee did itt, and soe with the above expretions cast me and arrested me when I thought I had paid all maner of charges – seised me body and goods for 8 l., when I had in my closett att the same time 850 l. This is true. And my God has soe farr espoused my cause as a widow and helpless thatt in less then a month affter this oath one of Turners eyes dropt outt of his head; and aboutt three month affter his wiffe dyed raveing, the best part of him; and his son in law Captain Asdall (Turners son in law), thatt maryed his only daughter, run away to the West Indies with another wife.[193] And all this in the compass of little more then half a yeare, as I foretold him by my letter itt was revealed to me from above.

1709, May 25 And Towres, my other perjuered oath man, dyed sudenly and sencelessly on the 25 of May 1709 and [was] privatly putt in the ground for fear of a worse accident to him by nine a clock in the morning, 26.[194] And these things looked to me like somthing of a judgmentt on him. Besids Mr Towrs eldest sone, a liuetenantt, poysoned

[193] Charles Turner's wife, Mary, the daughter of Edward Allen, died on 28 December 1708 at the age of forty-eight. In 1699 their daughter Jane married Thomas Archdale of Stanhoe, possibly the Archdale commissioned a captain in 1706 but no longer in regimental service by 1711, the year his will was proved (Carthew, iii. 129; *English Army Lists*, v. 198, vi. 73; PRO, PROB 11/522/159).
[194] Henry Towers was buried in North Runcton on 27 May 1709.

himself to avoid the justice of the law when he was arained and condemned by a courtt marshall for selling his souldiers to France with Captin Somes and Dashwood. All three poysoned themselves.[195] If this does nott look like a judgmentt, &c., I know nott whatt does; and I humbly thank God I am still alive and see justice from the hand of God to my enimies. And nottwithstanding all the abuses and loses placed this year on me, I am still able by Gods mercy to me to goe through all my troubles withoutt the kindness or countenance of any of my friends or humanity of either of my two sisters, tho both in London.

May 25 I bought me a paire of good coach horses cost me above three and thirty, 33, pounds of Captaine Berney of Weesnam (affter haveing lost 5 very good coach mares this yeare), aded to my other losses, to goe for London.[196] Eliz Freke

June 2i Tuesday, June 2i, I took my jorney for London with these two coach horses, which I humbly thank God brought mee safe to London in fowre dayes, viz., Midsomer Day, being Fryday and the 24th of June. E Frek

30 Thursday, June the thirtyeth, my greatt coach maire was stole from mee in London by one George Morlly, who was taken on his back att Barnard.[197] Wher nottwithstanding all my favours to my cosin John Freke and guifts to him since my widowhood of neer 400 pound in three yeare, I was faine to goe my selfe in person to Barnard, ten miles [fol. 73v] from London, in a hired hackny coach in quest of my coach maire stole from me (tho Mr Berners in pitty to mee offered me to ease me of this cruell jorney, as itt was to me).

Jully i Jully the first I took itt up by my coachman att Barnard and by him made my challenge to itt by Mr Robison, tho secured and challenged by the lord of the maner.[198]

---

[195] In miscellaneous documents Freke identifies Towers' son as Arthur, who is not mentioned in his father's will (B, fol. 41v; NRO, 346 Famm). 'Arthur Towers, gent., eldest son of Henry T. of North Runcton, Norfolk, gent.', entered Gray's Inn on 3 June 1697, possibly after he had matriculated at Queens' College on 5 July 1693 (*Register of Gray's Inn*, 349; Venn, iv. 256). An Arthur Towers was commissioned in 1705 a lieutenant in Colonel Edmund Soame's regiment; George Dashwood was a lieutenant-colonel in the same unit. Soame and Dashwood died on board the fleet at Torbay in September 1706 (*English Army Lists*, v. 190, 176; iii. 69; Luttrell, vi. 84, 85). Their names do not appear in the courts martial preserved in PRO, WO 71/13 (1692–1710) and 71/1 (1706–11).

[196] John Berney, the son of Thomas and Sarah Berney, was married to Philippa Browne; their son Thomas became a recorder of Lynn. Probably one of the two captains listed by this name in the 1697 Norfolk militia, he is identified as a voter from Weasenham in the 18 February 1714/15 *Poll for the Knights of the Shire* (Norwich, 1715), 235 (Carthew, ii. 465; *Norfolk Lieutenancy*, 123; Mason, i. 435).

[197] High Barnet or Chipping Barnet, eleven miles from London on the North Road.

[198] Robison has not been linked with William Robison, whose name appears on the 1692 tax rate, or William Robinson from nearby Narford, listed on the 1715 *Poll for the*

2d I, Eliz Frek, wentt and hired a coach and wentt againe my selfe and made my second challenge to my coach maire beffore Justice Haddly, swore to itt to be mine, [and] paid all itts charges att Barrnard.[199] I were bound over to the said Justice Haddly in a bond of forty pound to the queen to prosecute the rogue att St Allbons sessions (and there to hange him or loose my maire, which cost me neer twenty guinyes but a month before).

Jully 13 Wensday, Jully 13, I wentt in my own coach againe to St Allbons and tooke my cosin Herlackendane with me to the quarter sesions (twenty miles from London) to the tryall and execution of this rogue George Marlow. **14** Where on the fowrtenth I satte on the justices bench by the justysies, maire, and recorder; where I had the greatest hardship ever forcest on a gentlewoman by their forceing me to hange this rogue, he being taken on her back.[200] And when the justices and jury saw I would nott hange him, nothing would sattisfye them butt she then belonged to the lord of the manner. Which I told the bench possesion beeing nineteen parts of the law I would nott easilly part with her, butt I would pay whatt ever fees and charges they pleased to impose on me besids my charge and trouble past. Soe after aboutt two howrs dispute of the whole bench of justices, maire, recorder, lord of the maner, and the jury, itt was agreed I should then prosecute him att the Old Bayly sessions in London the Fryday senight affter. Which I positively reffused, as likewise the generall quarter sessions thatt month att St Allbons. Affter which I were by the justices and gentlemen handsomly dismist, affter itt had cost me neer ten pounds besids my troublesom jorneys for aboutt five severall days.

15 The fiffteenth day, being St Swithings, I returned againe home to London to my sister Austens house in Ormand Streett very ill of my tissick.[201] A very fine day. Eliz. Freke

25 Jully the 25 I wentt from London, being Monday, to the Bath in

---

Knights of the Shire, 148. The lord of the Barnet manor was Thomas Cooke (*The Victoria History of Hertfordshire*, ed. William Page, 4 vols. [London, 1902–14], ii. 331).

[199] George Hadley, the justice of peace, matriculated at Trinity College, Oxford in 1666 (*Hertfordshire County Records*, ed. William Le Hardy, 10 vols. [Hertford, 1905–57], vii. 376; Foster, *Alumni Oxonienses*, ii. 627). Prosecutions for the loss of personal property were still the responsibility of the victims, who also bore the expenses (J. M. Beattie, *Crime and Courts in England, 1660–1800* [Princeton, 1986], 36).

[200] The mayor of St Albans was Matthew Hubbard (A. E. Gibbs, *The Corporation Records of St. Albans* [St Albans, 1890], 105). No mention of Freke or the charge appears in the Hertfordshire County Records Calendar. The records of St Albans Liberty quarter sessions and St Albans Borough quarter sessions for this period do not exist at the Hertfordshire Record Office.

[201] Ormond Street, 'a str. of fine New Buildings' on the north side of Red Lion Square between Red Lion Street and Devonshire Street (Hatton, i. 61).

my own coach with my sister Austen and her maide.[202] **29** Where in fowre days I thank God I came safe and easy with my two horses, butt my selfe soe ill with my tissick and astma that I durst nott [fol. 74r] use the Bath, the doctters telling mee iff I wentt in I would never come outt alive againe. And the watters which I drunke 5 or six days soe swell'd me I were forcst to leave them. Doctter Baynard was my doctter there.[203] Soe affter a fortnight stay att Bath, Sir Georg Norton and my deer sister Norton sentt there horses and servants to mee to Bath for to bring me to Leigh.

Agust ii or i2 Where affter i4 miles of very bad way, I came Thursday, Agustt the eleventh, to Sir George Nortons to Abbotts Leigh in order to goe for Ireland; wher I staide by theire perswasions with my Lord Chiefe Justice Pine to goe with me over and his further service there for me till the i2 of September.[204]

September i2 And noe man of warr being to be had in thatt my month stay with my deer sister and Sir George Norton, Monday, the twelfe of September, I were forcst by my own businiss to goe home. When the first day I had Sir Georg Nortons horses and servants, three of them, goe with mee, being very ill. **i9** Yett in five days misserable high watter, bad wayes, and weather, I humbly thank God I compased London, itt being Fryday, the i9 of September.

26 Att London I rested my selfe in lodgings very ill for one week till the Fryday affter, being 26 of September, when I attempted in my own coach to come home for Billny. Wher by Gods greatt mercy to me I compassed home in five days and time enough to seaise my house and take me a sett of new servants. And in the compass of i4, fourteen, weeks I have bin with these my two horses above five hundred miles and I think never once whiptt, butt by Gods mercy brought me safe and well home to my deerly beloved Billney, and brought with me a large sillver flagan for the communion table cost me aboutt i3 or fowrteen pounds, which I intend to presentt to the church.[205] Eliz Freke

---

[202] By the beginning of the eighteenth century Bath had between two and three thousand permanent residents; another 8,000 came to drink the water and bathe in the hot springs. Two theatres, two coffee houses, and a pump room offered by 1710 a growing challenge to the amenities of the other major spa, Tunbridge Wells (Sylvia McIntyre, 'Bath: the Rise of a Resort Town, 1660–1800', in *Country Towns in Pre-industrial England*, ed. Peter Clark [Leicester, 1981], 198–249; Hembry, *The English Spa*, 85–93, 111–20).

[203] Edward Baynard (c. 1640–1717) practised medicine in Bath as well as in London. A fellow of the Royal College of Physicians of London, he was the author of *Health, a Poem*, which went through numerous eighteenth-century editions (William Munk, *The Roll of the Royal College of Physicians of London*, 2nd edn., 3 vols. [London, 1878], i. 451; Wallis, 39).

[204] Pyne's second wife was Catherine Norton, the sister of Elizabeth Freke's brother-in-law George Norton to whom Sir Richard bequeathed £20 in his will (Morris, 'The Pynes of Co. Cork', 708; PRO, PROB 11/513/24).

[205] Freke notes in the parish register the 21 September 1709 purchase of the silver flagon in London for £12. Thirteen inches in height, it is inscribed 'The gift of Mrs.

September 29 I discharged Mr Buck, the minester of Billny church, the bishop of Norwich haveing sentt me word by him he would force my takeing a lycence under him. Which as itt will lessen my intrest there, I haveing never yett bin threatned with the like in forty years neer in possesion of itt, I am resolved to try itts right. And in all which time I have never received two pence in tiths this forty years, tho I have kept a minester to itt outt of my own generossity att above twenty pounds a yeare. Yett I will nott be forcst to itt, butt I will try my right with the bishops of Norwich, to whome I writt the following letter and sentt att his vissettatyon, being Octtober the 20, 1709.

[fol. 74v]

1709, Octtobr 20 A letter I wrott to the bishop of Norwich, Doctter Charles Trimnell, from Billney when hee suspended Mr Buck, then minester of the parrish (by my guift), because he officiated withoutt his lycence,[206] Eliz Freke:

My Lorde,
     Att my returne from the west last week, Mr Buck came to me and informed me thatt your lordship had forbid his further attendance on my church att Billney without your licence, and in obedience to your command I have this day discharged him. I should have thoughtt itt a presumtion in me to have asked a licence where I knew there was noe tithes or indowments butt whatt my generosyty bestows or deserved from me. And I have bin oner of this place neer forty years and never had by these severall bishops, Doctter Moore, Doctter Floyde, and Doctter Sparrow, your predessours, ever any trouble from them or the least tittle of my rightt questioned in this kind.[207] Nor did I ever receive to my knowledg a peny tithe from this place [in] my life. I dispurte nott your lordships rightt, and farr be itt from me to intrench on your

Eliz. Freke to her Church of West Bilney, owner of the Parish and relict of Percy Freke, Esq. September 21st, 1709, there interred June 7th, 1706' (H. S. Radcliffe, 'Church Plate in Norfolk – Deanery of Lynn Norfolk', *Norfolk Archaeology*, 18 [1914], 265).
     [206] Charles Trimnell (1663–1723), prebend of Norwich and archdeacon of Norfolk, succeeded John Moore as bishop of Norwich in February 1707/8. He remained its bishop until August 1721, when he assumed the see of Winchester (Blomefield, iii. 592–3; *Fasti Ecclesiae Anglicanae*, 60, 47, 39).
     [207] A marginal note states 'From the yeare 1672'. Anthony Sparrow (1612–1685), bishop of Exeter, was appointed to the see of Norwich in August 1676, where he remained bishop until his death on 19 May 1685. William Lloyd (1637–1710), who succeeded Sparrow as bishop of Norwich in July 1685, lost this position in February 1690/1 after he refused to swear his allegiance to William III. John Moore (1647–1714), consecrated bishop of Norwich in July 1691, held this position until 1707, when he became bishop of Ely (Blomefield, iii. 586–90; Mason, i. 422, 424–5; *Fasti Ecclesiae Anglicanae*, 39).

prerogitives, butt I begg you will nott putt me to any trouble to defend my just rightt to this soe small a place consisting butt of six little tennaments besids my own house. Yett I have hitherto by my greatt veneration to the church and my own honour ecliptt my selfe to allow a small matter to a neighbour minster to officyatt in itt once every Sunday my whole time, a greatt partt of which Mr Adams of Pentney did serve in itt till his notorious life was soe unsupportable to me thatt I rather chose to displace him then complaine on him. Affter which I fixtt my self on Mr Buck, which I conceived more perticulerly under your lordships favour and protecttion by your presenting him with Gyton a marke of itt. My lord, I doe nott feare your justice and favour to mee or conciderattion of my condition as a woman and an unhapy widow. Nor would I desire a better judg then your selfe in this case, or with your leave or refusal I will reffer my selfe and itt to the arch bishop of Canterbury by waiteing on him. For I cannott affter forty years exceptt of new conditions [that] may prejudice my rightt and and be injurious to my children and familly. Butt if your lordship will be pleased to endow [fol. 75r] this little chappell of mine, I shall take itt for a greatt honour to have such a patron to itt; and then to presentt to itt will be a greatt charity to the poore widow and to this little village to be soe eased of my further trouble in itt. I doe most humbly beg your lordships pardon for this forced trouble and leave to tender you my most humble dutty and service. Begging your blessing, doe subscribe my selfe

Your most humble servant,
Eliza. Freke

Superscribed: For the Right Reverend Charles, lord bishop of Norwich, humbly presentt

The lord bishops answer to this my letter from London datted the 29 of November 1709 came nott to me till the 7 of December:

Madam,

I was in soe much hurry the rest of the time thatt I stayed in Norfolk affter the receitt of your letter thatt I had nott time to answer itt there; nor can I answer itt soe perticulerly from hence as I could doe from Norwich, from whence you might and may still receive an accountt thatt the curattes of your parish ought to have a licence from the bishops for the discharge of thatt office. Your nomination of him does nott exempt him from my jurisdicttion. And tho I have no exception to the person himselfe, haveing collated him to a liveing in my dispossall, yett I had soe much the more reason to expectt that he would nott take upon him the service of another cure under my jurisdicttion withoutt my authority, which I doe insist on as nessesary. Tho rather

then the service should be neglected, I consentt for the presentt that itt
should be in your own way till I am able to convince you thatt you
are both obliged to provide a curatte and allsoe to provide such a one
as I shall approve. I desire, iff possible, to have noe difference with you
or with any one elce, butt this is a poyntt upon which the good order
thatt the dioceses dos soe much depend [fol. 75v] thatt I cannott departt
from itt. And I hope thatt when you have more fully concidered itt
you will nott dispute itt with, madam,

> Your very faithfull,
> humble servantt,
> Charles Norwich[208]

This letter, tho dated the 29 of November in London, I did nott receive
itt till the seventh of December 1709. Eliz Freke

1709, September 29 I haveing discharged Mr Buck by the bishops
order from his further attendance on my church heer att Billney
withoutt his lycence, which I refused, haveing bin in the posesion of itt
neer forty years and in all thatt time never yett had my right questioned
either by Docter Sparrow, Doctter Floyde, and Doctter Moore, your
predicessours, I could nott give up my right withoutt its tryall. Which
has occationed my inspecttion into the old records.

Octtobr 20, 1620 Where I find thatt the state of this place and
church with the donative of Pentney are both parts and parcells of the
late desolved monastary there of Pentney and that in 1620, in an old
maniscript of the church, thatt affter thatt desolution of the monastray
of Pentney, when Thomas Windam, Esqr, was then lord of the maner,
thatt West Billney and Pentney was then an impropiation and stipendery
and thatt then in the yeare 1620 was likewise stipendery with this
difference only, thatt Pentny payes tributt or takes wages (and tithes).[209]

1675 And in the yeare 1675 my deer father did permitt Mr Adams
to the service of Pentney and Billney church, now six and thirty years
agoe, being December 7, 1709, dureing his pleasure and did allow him
a salary for itt. In the same manascrip I find neither Billney or Pentney
subjectt or liable to institution or induction butt both stipendary

---

[208] The original letter is in BL, Add. MS. 45721 A, fols. 5r-v, 6v. Aside from some
variations in spelling, Freke's transcription is accurate.

[209] Francis Wyndham gained possession of the West Bilney and Pentney property from
Sir Thomas Mildmay. His descendants Thomas and Henry Windham sold the holding
to Sir Edward Bullock, who conveyed it to Sir Thomas Richardson (Blomefield, ix. 40,
viii. 354). Donative: a benefice bestowed by the patron without the bishop's presentation
or authorization. Impropriation: granting a lay person or corporation, known as an
impropriator, a benefice or the right to its revenues. Stipendiary: a clergyman who
receives a stipend or salary.

donatives – both which my father, Ralph Frek, Esqr, did then presentt to both churches (Mr Adams).[210]

1620 And in the same maniscrip I find thatt to make an appropiation licence itt must be obtained of the kinge in chancery, and the consentt of the dyocesan pattron and incumbantt are nessesary iff the church be full. Butt iff the church be voyde, the diocesan and the patron upon the kings licence may conclude itt.

1620 In the same maniscrip I find an appropriation is thus described: itt is a terme [in] our law (or the church law) when any corparett body or pryvatte person hath the right and converts the proffitts of an ecclesiasticall liveing to his or theire own use, only mainetaineing a vicker or curatte to serve the cure.

1709, November 7 This I took outt of a maniscrip [fol. 76r] of the church of Padors Winch by Mr Edward Smith, vicker of thatt place, who has held thatt church about twenty years neer.[211] Taken outt of the maniscript November the 7, 1709, by Eliza. Freke.

14 Aboutt November the 14 I writt to my Lord William Richerson to know iff his lordship laid any claime or challenge to the donative of Pentney church, my deer father Ralph, Esqr, presentting last to itt and to West Billney in the yeare 1675; and iff he challenged noe right to itt, hee would give me leave to try mine with the lord of the manor.[212] In which I desired the Lord Richersons answer and to these ensueing querryes, who very honorably did the same day.[213]

Query 1 Whether the donative of Pentney be depending upon the maner, or whether itt be a rightt singly and sepratly by itts selfe.

Query 2 Whether itt be paide outt of any perticuler estate or outt of the whole estate, and in whatt proportions.

Query 3 Who hath the right and tittle to nominatt to this donative, and by whatt intrest they have a nomination.

Query 4 Whether the presenttation or nomination to a single life may bee vallued, and att whatt purchase [if] more then a year and a halfe.

Query 5 Whether the perpettuall advowson to a liveing is offten vallued att three years purchas.[214]

---

[210] Institution: the bishop's granting of a parish to a cleric. Induction is the last and ceremonial step in the appointment of an incumbent, confirming his authority in the parish (*ODCC*, 839, 829).

[211] Pedders Winch is an older variant of East Winch (Blomefield, ix. 152).

[212] William Richardson (1654–1719), the third son of Thomas Richardson, became Lord Cramond on the death of his brother Henry in 1702. He and the wife of his second marriage, Elizabeth Daniel of Norwich, had a son, William, with whom the title ended on his death in 1735 (*Scots Peerage*, ii. 583–4; Rye, ii. 734).

[213] These queries and an often similar summary account of her church conflict also appear in miscellaneous documents, B, fols. 33r–34r, and W, fols. 115r–113r.

[214] Presentative advowsons are held by individuals or patrons with the power to

Query 6 Whether there be an institution or inducttion to the church of Pentney or only a donattive. Eliza Freke

To which answer thatt by the maniscrip of 1620 sayes thatt there is nither institution or inducttion requisite to Billney or Pentney church. Mr Edward Smith, vicker of Winch, has the book from whence I took out these informations to the justifyecation of Eliza Freke.

December 14 14 of December 1709 I took outt of the same manascrip att Padors Winch by Mr Smith, vicker of thatt place: a donative benyficio is thatt which is meerly given and collatted to a man by the pattron withoutt either presentation to or institution by the ordinary or induction by his commandementt – see the stattute ano. 8 of Richard the 2d, Second, chapter the 4th.[215] Eliza Freke

1709/10, Febuary 13 On examination of [the] Winch manyscrip in Mr Edward Smiths hand, vicker of Paders Winch, I find Billney and Pentny churches are both of them peculers and impropiations, neither subjectt to institution, or induction, or lapsing to or licence of the bishop, butt both donatives in which my deer father did place Mr Adams, 1675, dureing his pleasure and mine and my heirs, &c.; and thatt Billney has nott a foott of gleab butt is stipendry; Pentney pays tythes and recieves wages, and has soe continued since the desolution of thatt monastry, about a hundred and fiffty years since.[216] Eliza Freke

[fol. 76v]

1709, Decembr 14 Another letter I writt to the lord bishop of Norwich of thanks in answer to his of the 29 of November 1709, and itt was written by me to him December the 14, 1709, Eliz Freke:

I doe returne to your lordship all the gratfull thanks I am culpable of acknowledging for the honour of your letter and your goodness and justice in condesending to my just rightt in my little chapple, in which I shall observe my dutty and your commands in placing in itt one your lordshipp may approve of and as soon as posible I can provide my self. In the intrim I have with your leave taken care for a sacramentt att Xmas and for christnings and buryalls on my accountt, Mr Buck now nott being in this country, whose good carractor amongst his neighbours and your lordships patronise of him in Gyton was my error and nott

nominate a clergyman to a living or benefice; collative advowsons are controlled by the bishop, who appoints clergy to these positions (*ODCC*, 21).

[215] No relevant statute appears among those listed for the reign of Richard II in *The Statutes of the Realm*, 12 vols. (London, 1810–28).

[216] A peculiar parish is not under the jurisdiction of the diocesan bishop or ordinary. Glebe is the land set aside for the support of the incumbent, who has the right to lease it (*ODCC*, 681).

his. Butt since your lordship does nott approve of him, I am in treaty
with another for itt, which is pritty hard to doe or gett where there is
nott one peny settlementt on itt for encouragementt of a curratt to
serve itt. For tho [in] my greatt veneration to the church as the house
of God and my own property I give to itt whatt I please, yett I feare
they thatt survive me will nott doe as I have done. For, my lord, on
my examination of this register datted 1560, I find 8 severall curatts (to
the year 1675 my deer father pressented Mr Adams with my consentt);
I cannott find one shilling allowed for their subsistance to Billney butt
the duttys of the church and charrityes of good people. Be pleased to
concider who will serve itt on unsertaintys; for my life itt shall nott
want bread, I love itt soe well – iff I may enjoy itt with ease and quiett.
I need nott informe your lordship thatt the donative of this little
chappell with Pentney are both stipendry impropryations and parcell
of thatt dissolveed monastry, both these donatives in my property. Butt
Pentney pays tithes and receives wages (and is licenced), as the church
records mention. Butt Billney has nought to depend on. And both
peculers. My lord, I never were a beger in my life; butt might I presume
to be a pettitioner to your lordship, itt would bee to putt me in a way
this church mightt pertake in a small pention of her majesties bounty
settled on such vacancies to the encouragementt of a curratt for itt
when I am dead.[217] I doe most humbly intreatt your good lordship to
concider of this charitty to a small church in your own dioces to which
I have lately laid outt above a hundred pounds in the inside of itt and
the outt partt, and itt was butt last Michellmas [fol. 77r] I gave to the
comunion table a silver flagon cost me allmost fiffteen pounds. Besids
itt is a greatt generosity to the poore widdow thatt owns itt. Butt iff
this may nott suitt your conveniency, I humbly begg you will pardon
this, my presumtion, giveing me leave to tender you my most humble
dutty and service, and craving your blesing doe ever subscribe my
selfe your most obedientt, humble servantt,

Eliza. Freke

Superscrightt: For the Reverend Charls Trimnell, lord bishop of
Norwich, humbly present

1709/10, January first Sunday, New Years Day and my unhappy
birth day, the church being vacantt by the bishop suspending Mr Buck
for preaching att Billney withoutt his lycence, I gott Mr Smith, vicker
of Winch, to preach for me there and to give the sacramentt in the

---

[217] Queen Anne's Bounty. In 1704 a corporation was established to augment the
incomes of needy clergy by dispensing the revenues raised from first fruits and tenths,
'royal taxes on ecclesiastical dignities and benefices' (G. F. A. Best, *Temporal Pillars*
[Cambridge, 1964], 21, 31).

church and to me, of whome I took itt, the church being thatt day vacantt a quarter of a yeare. I paid Mr Smith for his sermon and service that day twenty shillings and to his son 5 shillings and to the two clarks more five shillings.[218]

3d And more, I gave poor Thom Betts chilldren, three of them, new cloths outt of this mony I saved of the church. Cost mee, both soms, above fiffty shillings.[219]

4 And to poore Mary Frek, come to me to crave my assistance and help to her, to whome I gave in charity five pounds and sentt to her sister Ann twenty shillings by her.[220] Which I take to bee more charity then to be drunk outt by Mr Adams, &c. And both these sums come to aboutt 8–io–o. In payment of the next quarter ending nextt Lady Day will be thirty shillings more. E Frek

5 Mr Smith came and cristned Goode Croses child and did then church the woman for mee.[221] EF

i709/io, Febuary i3 I wer Febuary the i3 citted to apeer att the bishops of Norwich courte ther to be held Febeuary the one and twenty, i709, by the chancellour, Doctter Thomas Taner, with his cittation underwriten, Eliz Frek.[222] By him dereictted to Elizabeth Freke of West Bilney in the county of Norfolk and dioces of Norwich, widdow, propryetory of the parish church there.

February i3, i709

Madam,

By vertue of a process under seale to you heerwith shown, I cite you to appeer (iff you think itt your intrest soe to doe) att the lord bishop of Norwich his consistory courte, holden in the cathedrall church in Norwich upon Tuesday, the one and twentieth day of Febuary in the yeare of our Lord Christ i709 att the howre accustomed for heering

---

[218] Smith's son Thomas was baptized in East Winch on 18 May 1695.

[219] Thomas Betts' first wife, Alice, was buried on 8 August 1697; his second wife, Mary, whom he married on 13 February 1697/8, was buried on 15 November 1707. Five children were also baptized and one buried in West Bilney.

[220] Mary and Ann Freke are not in the local parish registers, nor have these sisters been identified among the siblings of the same names in the Freke genealogy.

[221] Freke records in the parish register, 'Sarah Cross daughter of Henry Cross and Frances his wife was Baptized by Mr Smith Vicker of Winch Dec 7, 1709, Eliz Curatt'. The Crosses were married in Pentney on 20 August 1704; Frances was buried there on 10 April 1711. 'The Thanksgiving of Women after Childbirth, Commonly Called the Churching of Women' (Book of Common Prayer), usually occurred a month after childbirth, marking the end of the period in which the mother traditionally kept to her house and did not participate in church services.

[222] Thomas Tanner (i674–1735) became the chaplain of the bishop of Norwich John Moore, who appointed him chancellor of the diocese in 1701. Later a canon at Ely and at Christ Church, Oxford, Tanner became archdeacon of Norfolk in 1721 and bishop of St Asaph in 1732 (Mason, i. 566; Blomefield, iii. 636–7).

causes there.[223] Then and there good and sufficientt cause, iff any such you be able in due forme of law, to shew why the tithes and proffitts belonging to the appropryatt parrish church of West Billney, afforesaid, or a ssufficyentt portion thereof should nott be sequestered and keptt under sequestration for and towards the sallary or stippentt of an able curratt to be licensed and appoynted dully to serve the cure of souls of the parishoners of West Billney, afforesaide, (which as the said court is credibly informed hath bin neglected and unserved for severall [fol. 77v] months past nor is att presentt provided for with any settled curratt) and further to doe and receive as to law and justice shall appertaine. And further, I doe heerby intimatt to you thatt iff you doe nott appeer att the said time and place or, appeering, iff you doe nott shew good cause and suffycientt to the contrary, the judg of the saide consistory courte or his lawfull surrogate will sequester and keep or cause to bee keptt under sequestration the said tithes and profits or a ssufficentt portion thereof for and towards the use above mentioned, your absence or rather contumacy affter service heerwith in any wise nottwithstanding.

Supperscribed: For Madam Freke this

My answer to this summons in a letter Febuary the 20, 1709[/10], dereicted to the chanceller:

Sir,

I were honoured by your parritor to appeer att your courte on my pyrrill the one and twentyeth instantt;[224] where I wish I coulde come, butt I have nott bin cross my chamber since last November. Therfore I canott come; nor doe I know whatt business I have there except to answer for my extravagencys to the church in supporting a minester six and thirty years as I have done Mr Adams, and Mr Buck neer two years, and need nott have done itt, and paid them outt of my own pockett. Which could nott have bin forced on me or a penny from mee for itt butt in respectt to my deer father, who placed him heer and att Pentney, and some pitty to his family with a due respectt for my selfe.

Butt since I find my generositty and extravagency in this kind is endeavouread to make me a property, itt is high time for me to concider thatt my imprudence may nott exceed my justice to my children and

---

[223] Consistory courts conducted by chancellors heard ecclesiastical cases within the dioceses on nondoctrinal issues involving charges against ministers and financial affairs. The court of appeal from the diocesan consistory court was the archbishop's court; the London court of the archbishop of Canterbury was held at the court of the Arches (*Oxford Law*, 274–5).

[224] Parritor, an obsolete form of paritor: a summary officer of an ecclesiastical court.

grandchildren and be injurious to them in placeing an unjust charge on them they are nott liable to.

In my deer husbands time I had enough to be generous with; now only my joynter to depend on for my life, which must force me to retrench my extravagencys to nesesarys. And I greatly lamentt thatt the bishop in his whole dioces cannot find a more worthy person to evidence his displeasure to then an unhappy widdow loaded with years and burdened with infirmityes. And I am grived to be a mark of his lordships displeasure, butt I must submitt to itt amongst my other misfortunes. And being a weak woman, helpless and noe friend in this country, I begg his lordships leave I may deffend my right under the queen in the arch bishops courte in London, wher I have severall friends and relations will appeer for me who better understand this business then I doe. For I humbly conceive thatt the bishop and your selfe may bee both under a mistake as to my church; which is a peculer, and mine, and an impryation neither subjectt to institution or inducttion or lapsing or licence from the bishop butt only in the queen and my disposall, as is under the same circumstances Pentney church, and in my nomination only, by my register I find, thatt pays tithes and receives wages. Both churches [are] stipendery and peculliers, and both my father placed Mr Adams inn dureing his and my pleasure.

Nor need I informe you, sir, who keep the register, thatt Mr Perce, who officioeted heer as curratt for neer forty years, viz., from 1636 to 1673, aboutt which yeare I did in pitty to him give him with my sister Austen a guiny.[225] He then lived in a little thacht house of mine of forty shillings a yeare and drew alle for his subsistance, which had there bin either gleab or tithes he need nott have done. And iff his lordship can find any gleab heer or tithes, I shall nott detaine itt from the church.

Nor could I have displaced Mr Adams and putt Mr Buck in his room had nott my powre by my register warrented mee – a man thatt was coallated by the bishop to Gyton, therfore I presumed unobjecttable as to his person, as I have under the bishop hand to show in his letter to me; and hee offichyetter for me a year and a half, for which I paide him. Yett he was by you and the bishop in my absence last Agust [fol. 78r] forbid his further service heer on my pirrill withoutt his further licence, soe att Michellmas I paid him off. Sir, this I thinke very hard thatt my selfe and my familly and my little parrish should be forced to seek shellter in other churches and have one of my own. Butt loveing quiett, I must submitt to authority and shall as to my contience in the further ease of thatt charge for the time to come. And since this my church cannott be lapst to his lordship, itt being a peculer and mine, I

[225] Arthur Peirse/Pierce, educated at Caius and ordained a priest in 1625, became curate of Pentney and West Bilney in 1636 (Venn, iii. 328).

will in humanity and charity allow for my life three sermons a yeare
with sacraments, xings, and burialls att the usuall times att my own
charge. As I had on last Xmass, soe I have taken care for one att
Easter with the sacramentt. Sir, I have lived to above sixty years of age
withoutt the infamy of a bishops courte, which to me, I hope, will
prove the court of honour by evidenceing of my generossitty to itt and
my charrity to this church and the sopportt of itt for soe many years
thatt were nott obliged to itt, or can any thing be forced from me for
itt or my children. Therfore I hope when my lord bishop has more
seariously concidered itt and my generossitty soe longe he will be soe
good, generous, and charitable as to settle a subsistance for a currate
on itt. In which iff his lordship please butt to deposite one hundred
and fiffty pounds, which is nothing to him, I will make a hard shift to
putt as much more presently to itt to be laid outt for a curratt for ever
for this church rather then one in his diocess shall wantt the service of
God in itt. Butt iff what I offer cannott bee obtained, I must rest
sattisfyed I have done my best endeavours and nott shewed my self
mercinary to the church or injurious to my honour. This long scrole
craves itts pardon and leave to subscribe,

Your unknown servantt,
Eliza. Freke

Superscribed: For Doctter Thomas Tanner, chancellour of Norwich

The chancellour of Norwich letter to me, Eliz Freke, aboutt my
church datted Febuary 28, i709[/io], in answer to the above:

Madam,

I had the favour of yours of the i6 instantt, butt nott till some time
affter the datte; and I give you the trouble of this to sett you, iff posible,
right in this affaire of Billney, which is nott nor ever was a peculiar
butt subjectt in every thing to the lord bishop visitation and other
jurysdiction as much as any other parish in the diocess. Tis true of late
years thatt there has bin noe institution and induction, tho we have
ten or eleven upon our booke. Yett iff itt was a meer impropiation, noe
body will informe you thatt thatt makes itt exempt. Itt was an institutive
recttory in the patronage of the pryer and conventt of Pentney, who
gott itt appropiated to them aboutte the yeare i350 and for severall
years affter presented an institutive vicker. Butt some time beefore the
desolution the vickerage seems to have binn desolved; and the cure
was taken care by them to have gott and regullerly served by some
stipendury curratt or one of ther own cannons, which they were obliged
to doe upon the appropiation of the greatt tithes. Upon the desolution
this impropiatt came into the crowne butt expressly by actt of parliamentt charged with the same burdens, payments, &c., as when in

the posession of the pryer and conventt. And you thatt have itt by purchas or otherwise from the crowne enjoy itt upon the same conditions: the reppaires of the chancell; and the providing a conformable curratte to be approved of by the bishop; the paying of procurations, sinodalls, and such other eccleasticall dues which are by the law of the land [fol. 78v] annexed to the possesion of tythes, whether in clergy or lay hands.[226] Soe thatt I crave leave to differ from you in my sentyments aboutt the allowance of twenty pound per anum by your self and father and predycessours to the curratt of Billney which you say has bin of pure charrity. I think you are of rightt obliged to itt by the laws of God and man. And I am aptt to think itt must concerne a lady of your sence and edication in contience to receive the whole tithes and gleab which were dedicated to the service of God, and take noe further care of itt then thatt itt be performed three times in a yeare. You are sencible thatt you are in the eyes of our law parson, tho you cannott officiatt your selfe; yett seeing you enjoy the revenues, you should outt of them find some clergyman to take care of the souls of the parishoners and thatt this may be reguler done. The excleasticall law of this realme provids thatt none shall bee admitted to officiatt as currate in any church without quallifyeing themselves by subscribbing the Articles, declarations of conformitty, takeing the oathes, &c., before the ordynary, who is thereupon to lycense him under seale. In this manner I can assure you the curatts of Billney have acknowledged the episcopal jurisdiction for above a hundred years past (Mr Howling, Mr Browne, Mr Dey, Mr Perce, and Mr Adams).[227] The same thing was expected of Mr Buck, who, refuseing itt by your express command under the notion of being a peculiar and exempt, was inhibbitting from officiatting in thatt church whereunto he had noe legall addmission by institution of lycence from the ordinary. Iff you please to send him to my lord bishop or me to doe those things which the queens excleasticall law requirs of every clergyman before he presume to undertake a cure of soules, or any other to be curratt there before our Lady Day nextt, there will be an end of this controversy. Iff nott, you must nott blame my lord for takeing such meassuers as by law he may to provide for the due service of the church, which I dare be positive will fall upon

---

[226] Procurations and synodals: fees paid to the archdeacon or bishop for his visitations; procurations, which were paid annually, were also subsidies supporting the poor.

[227] Bartholomew Howlinge was admitted to Caius in 1580 and ordained a priest in 1583; the next year he became curate of Pentney. John Browne, a curate in 1562, is not listed among those entering either Oxford or Cambridge. Oliver Day or Dey, educated at Caius and ordained a priest in 1609, was curate of West Bilney from 1620 to 1633 (Venn, ii. 420, 23). Separate lists of curates in the miscellaneous documents (B, fol. 34r; W, fols. 113r, 110r) also include Clemont Bacon (1612–), Robert Powis (1616–), William Pewlax/Pontax/Powtack (1620–) and Thomas Hudson (1631–); none appears among those educated at Oxford and Cambridge.

you att last. Butt, madam, doe nott take my word (tho iff itt was the case of my own mother, I must bee of the same oppinion), butt consult any doctter or proctter in the arch bishops courte (whether you must appeale iff any wrong be attempted to be done you heer), and tell them your own state of the case and whatt I tell you of the other side. And further, iff you please, thatt itt can be proved thatt this parish church of Billney has binn subjectt to the ordinary of the bishop of Norwich; thatt the church has bin constantly vissetted by the arch deacons of Norwich in thatt respectt; and on thatt accountt procurations and sinnadalls are paide, the church wardens annually sworne and admitted by the ordinary, the currats appeer att the visitation and have bin till this last licensed by the lord bishop or his vicker generall; and thatt the parishoners have had from time immemoriall service performed every Lords Day by such curratt, to whome has binn paid twenty pound perr anum by your selfe and ancestors. And I scarce think any person thatt understands the eccleasticall laws of this realme will give itt as his oppinion thatt Billney is an exemptt peculiar, and thatt the parisheners have nott a rightt to have devine service and sermons every Lords Day, and the bishop has nott a rightt to licence the curratte there nor powre to oblige you to find such. Itt is, I assure you, grievous to me to doe any thing uneasy to any body, espeshally to a gentlewoman of your quallitty, soe thatt I hope you will concider better of this matter and send Mr Buck or other fitt person to be licensed withoutt more trouble to your selfe or me. For withoutt your submision of your curratt to my lords authority, the proceedings begun canott be stoptt unless by breach of thatt trust my lord reposes in. Madam,

Your most humble servantt,
Thomas Tanner

Transcribed by me, Eliz Freke, March 5, i709[/io].

[fol. 79r]

My answer I wrott to the chancellours letter datted the 28 of Febuary and answered by me, Eliza Frek, March the 7, i709[/io]; to Doctter Thomas Taner, chancellour of Norwich, superscribed:

Sir,

I am obliged to you for the favour of your letter and the kind information in itt you are pleased to give me aboutt my church and your further permision in asking advice of my friends before I actt any thing in this matter, tho I dare as much depend on your justice as there frindship. Yett being a widdow and, I hope, mother of fowre chilldren and grandchildren and a party of executor to my deer deceased husband, I canott with justice actt in any thing withoutt my partner executor; which now I have your permission, I shall write up to London aboutt itt. And in the meantime I intreat you will heer my weak defence I shall offer to your more serious concidecation.

First, as to Mr Adams haveing a licence, I never knew itt till last Agust, nor did my father, who placed him in Billney and Pentney. Whose notorious life was soe offencive to my age I were nott able longer to bear itt, and butt last week I sentt him word I would ejectt him outt of Pentney and putt in a currate to serve both these churches iff he were nott better then hee is. Sir, you need nott question my contience when I have in honour to my deer father for above six and thirty years supported with twenty pounds a yeare the most ungratefull and worst of his function, butt I concider his age.

Then for Mr Perce, hee served this place for many years to my knowledg withoutt a peny sallary, tho promised itt. And for the greatt tithes which your letter mentions I receive in this place, give mee leave to tell you thatt ther is nott one aker of land thatt my father has nott purchased att itts full vallue, and every aker specifyed in my deeds and inrolled by a decree in chancery which, iff I may nott be beleft, may there be seen for half a crown. Affter which my father in generosity permitted my Lady Richerson withoutt trouble to enjoy the thirds of this my estate for 28 years for her life, hee makeing up itts vallue to me outt of his own.

Then as to my owning of tithes by paying of procrations and sinadalls, how could I help itt when aboutt two yeares agoe one Clark, a proctter in your courte, came up to my bed chamber and threatned me [that] for aboutt fowre or five years he said was behind I should be made by him an example in the bishop courte, with such language as did nott become him to give a meaner person then my selfe.[228] When att the same time, I saw by the book Pentney was three and twenty years in arrears. On which I wrott and complained to the arch deacon, who presently returned me his answer offering me to turne him outt. Which letter I keep in honour to him.

Butt, sir, iff you can find any gleabe or tithes on this estate, I shall bee most glad to have itt restored to the church with as much justice and honour as you can desire itt. Butt for me to make a settlementt on this church of twenty pounds a yeare and my youngest grandchild nott a groatt settled seems to me very unnaturall and which St Paule

---

[228] Proctors, the equivalent of solicitors in the bishop's diocesan consistory court, were trained in Roman and canon law (*Oxford Law*, 1,004). No Clarks appear among the proctors listed in E. H. Carter, *The Norwich Subscription Books* (London, 1937), 70. Conceivably he could have been one of the several Clarks at Middle Temple called to the bar in the preceding decades (*Middle Temple Register*, i. 178, 230, 225, 226).

informes me is worse then an infidell.[229] Besids, sir, give me leave to informe you as this estate is settled (itt is outt of my powre) by my father and my husband, my selfe and son being only tennants for life, affter which itt is fixtt on my grandson aboutt eight years of age. Therfore [it is] beyound my comprehention how you can affix a settlementt by me to this church except you can find any gleab or tithes. And itt is beyound my expresion and trouble to me thatt I have laid my deer husband in the chancell wher I expectt soon to goe to him my selfe and noe scertainty for a curratt to the church. And I doe, sir, with you in my contience think that this church oughtt to have an able curratt fitt to undertake the care of soules and twenty pounds a yeare settled for his maintenance. Butt itt is outt of my powre or possibility to doe itt, and whatt signifyes my few days continuance (thatt have nott gone the length of my chamber allmost this half yeare), exceptt you find outt a metthod for a scartainty to the church. Which iff such a one proper for Mr Freks executor to grantt and me nott to deny, I shall most gladly imbrace itt; and itt will be the joy of my soule to see a good one settled heer.

Sir, this time you perfix is much too shortt for me, a stranger in this country, [fol. 79v] to gett a curratt in. And iff I must lye under the sensure of your courte, tis hard affter haveing latly lost above ten thousand pounds for my religion I should receive a second excominycation from a Protestantt bishop and in England. And affter I have lived neer twenty years in Ireland under the shellter and favour of the arch bishop and all the Protestantt bishops there, to be made an example heer seems to me somewhatt cruell. Butt I must be att your mercy. Sir, this longe scrole must begg itts pardon and a continuance of your further favour to

Your humble servantt,
Eliza. Freke

A letter I received from the chancellour of Norwich September the eight, 1710:

Madam,

Haveing had the misfortune for some time the papers of your queryes which was some time since left with me from you, I hope youl pardon my nott answering them sooner, this being the first returne of the wagon since they came to my hand.

Whatt ceremony or forme the church of Pentny is to be possesion of or entred upon in Mrs Freks right.

---

[229] 'But if any provide not for his own, and specially for those of his own house, he hath denied the faith, and is worse than an infidel' (1 Timothy 5:8).

If the tithes and prophits belong to the church and rectory be demanded and received by Mrs Freke or her agents, iff they occupy the gleabe or receive rent for the same or hinder any person from being burryed in the chancell or the like, itt will be sufficientt. And further then thatt, you may appoynt some proctor to appeere judycially before my lord bishop or my selfe, and alleage and prove your right to the church, and nominate a fitt, conformable clergyman to bee your curatte there. Att his admision upon, your tittle will then be recorded in the actts of the lordd bishops consisttory courte, and you may have an exemplyfycation of itt under seale when ever you please.

Outt of regard to your worth and quallity, madam, I have stopt all proceedings with regard to West Billney above this halfe yeare in expecttation of Mr Smith, whom you promised should quallifye himselfe as by law required before my lord bishop or selfe. Butt this week Mr Buck [came] to offer himselfe as curratt. Butt because you had never mentioned him as such, I was nott willing any thing should be done in prejudice to your rightt and therfore stopt his licence for the presentt. For tho I don't beleive Mr Buck would applye withoutt your consentt, yett your right and tittle to the nomination and donation of thatt curracy would be better secured by two or three lines to thatt purpose under your hand. Which, when you please to favour me with, shall be dispatched; and soon Ile send Mr Buck his licence, and then there will be an end of thatt affaire. I am, madam,

Your most humble servantt,
Thom Tanner

September the 15, 1710. My answer to the above letter to the chancellour of Norwich, E Frek:

Sir,

I am obliged by the favour of yours of the 8 instantt, for which I returne you my thanks, and for your information as to Pentney church; and on the receitt of itt I did impart the heads of itt to Mr Adams and sent and demanded of him the key of thatt church by way of possesion.[230] Butt this day he wrott me word the church warden had itt and would nott parte with itt (a pittyfull poor fellow in the parrish) [fol. 80r] nottwithstanding his severall letters of giveing me a quiett posesion when ever I please. Soe thatt I doubt I must ejectt him for itt, which I have bin tender in doeing because of his age and irreguler life and my deer fathers placeing of him there and in my Lord Thomas

---

[230] Adams' resignation is included in BL, Add. MS. 45721 A: 'I doe hereby resigne my right and title to Pentney church into the hands of Madam Freke of Bilney. Witnesse my hand, Wm Adams June 5th 1710' (fol. 7r).

Richersons life time, 1675, with this of Billney. Both which have continued together under the same circumstances and nomination since 1562 in the donation of my Lord Richerson and under eight severall curratts, as I find by my register book. And since you have given your selfe this trouble, bee pleased to give me leave to state the thing to you of this my demand, fearing Mr Buck might mistake itt. Billney and Pentney being both impropiations and both under the same circumstancys in all their priviledges, only Pentney has some small tithes towards the supportt of itts curratt, and Billney has none. And both in the donation of the Lord Thomas Richerson, Baron Gramond, who sold the maner of Pentney to Thomas Windham, Esqr, of Ashwood, reserveing to himselfe some royalltyes as the church, &c., and then turned his estate in Pentney into coppy holds renewable every life, amongst which I have there forty five pounds a yeare, all which pay tithes [and] quitt rents to thatt courte of Ashwood. Butt the lord of thatt maner being lately dead, his executors pretend to dispute my right and tittle to the nomination of a minester to Pentney church as likewise its seats therto belonging. Butt I challanging my right from my Lord Richerson as well by the presentt presentation of Mr Adams as neer forty years injoymentt of itt and never seprated from Billney till aboutt three years agoe I parted itt, they seem now to oppose my tittle in itt. Which tho I gett nott a peny by itt, I will nott loose the priviledg of, and have writt to Mrs Noes my resolution of ejectting Mr Adams and desired them to oppose my right and defend ther own tittle or elce I will engrose itt with Billney in your courte.[231] Butt I can heer nothing from them or ther agents.

I am now, sir, to appoligyse as to Mr Smith, who promised me severall times and did endeavour itt to oblige me in serveing the cure of my parish. Butt his weakness was such as I were convincst he could nott undertak itt either to the preaching partt or the diffycullty of rideing. And knowing noe greatt faultt in Mr Buck, I were perswaded to except of him; he being coalated by the bishop, I beleft [he] might be exceptable to both. Butt my nott giveing you an account was a mistake in me, which I beleft would be easyer pardoned then the troublesome impertinance of womens letters. And I doe likewise acknowledg my perticuler thanks for your carefull caution as to Mr Buck and my intrest and right heere as to my nomination and donation of this curacy, and am willing to have itt secured to my self and my heires. Mr Buck will nott, I suppose, deney your licence when ever demanded, butt I except of him noe longer then his good behaivour to the church

[231] Charles Nowyes, the lord of Ashwood Manor, had died earlier that year and was buried in Wood Ditton, Cambridgeshire on 17 April 1710 (SG, CA/R73, transcribed by T. P. R. Layng).

and dureing my pleasure (for I will not be plagued with noe more drunken, debauched currats). And for his salary I will be att noe certainty butt whatt I please, and this I told him att his entrance. And soe I am offered others will supply itt, tho justice inclined me to give him the first offer of itt.

And now, sir, since I have condesended to the bishop and your desire in placeing a minester heer to six or 7 houses, my request to you both is thatt you will bee pleased afix a subsistance for his maintenance, towards which I am most desyrouss to submitt to the strictest serch and enquiry you can make as to tithes and gleabe on this estate soe thatt this church may have somthing to support itt affter my death (for, sir, presidents are noe payments). And iff my Lord Richerson who had neer three thousand pound a yeare outt of his generosity and charity did give the minester twenty, butt for me thatt have little more then two hundred pound a year cleer, I cannott doe itt; and I should think itt as imprudent as prodygall in me. Pray therfore be pleased to concider of itt and interceed to the bishop for his bounty and charyty to itt, which favour will oblig your humble servantt.

Eliz Frek

[fol. 8ov]

i709, September 29 I discharged Mr Buck from attending my curacy of West Billney for his dareing to take a licence from the bishope of Norwich for my church withoutt my leave (Docter Trimnell), who had suspended him in my absence last Agust i709 from officiating in my church till licensed. Soe I kept the church in my hand and the key in my closett till the thirttyth of Aprill i7io, imploying Mr Smith, vicker of Winch, for sacraments, barryalls, and christning for thatt halfe year. In which time I wrott to the bishop the foregoeing letters and to the chancellour.

Octtobr 20 I wrott to the bishop my positive resolution of nott excepting his licence to my church.

November 29 The 29 of November I had a very civill letter from him thatt rather then the church should be vacantt I should dispose of it. E Freke

December i9 I wrott the bishop my foregoeing letter of thanks, and I promised him to fill up the vacancy, allowing me my wright of nott bringing my church under his jurisdiction by his licence.

i709/io, January first The first of January and my unhapy birth day, being Sunday I ordered a sermon and sacramentt att Billny church; which was given by Mr Smith of Winch, tho Mr Edgworth forbid him thatt day – for which I gave him five and twenty shillings.[232]

Febuary ii The chancellour of Norwich sent me his process to t[
courte for my lapsing the church and detaining itts tithes, a coppy
which I have before this inserted with my answer to itt. EF

20 My answer to the chancellours letter of process and my positi
denyall of putting one in the church under the bishops licence; b[
bid him take his tithes wher ever he found them butt thatt I wou[
nott be tyed to a peny charge for the church, as may be seen by n
letter foregoeing, fur[ther] then for three sacraments a year, christning
and buryalls which I would doe in charyty. EF

Febuary 28 The chancellour, Doctter Thomas Tanner, wrott
me another very civill letter to beg and perswade me to settle and ke[
as I have for this six and thirty yeare a minester to the church and
alow him twenty pounds a yeare, which letter I sentt up to London
my cosin John Frek to be examined in the arch bishops court. [N
church of Billney being a peculer and an impropiation, I looked up[
under the queen and nott the bishop.

i709/io, Febuary 2 My honoured good cosin Hammillton dy[
of an appoplexy. Shee was taken speechless the Sunday and dyed
Tuesday night – lyes buryed by her father, the Lord John Cullpep[
att Hollingburne in Kentt – in the seventy second yeare of her age a[
aboutt the 38 year of her widowhood. She had butt two sons: Jam[
Hamillton, now Lord Abercorne, and William Hambleton, who mary[
Sir Thomas Cullpepers second daughter.[233] She dyed vastly rich a[
handsomly provided for twelve of her grandchildren and her two so[
Eliz Frek

March i I sentt my coach and two horses with my two men a[
my maid to New Markett [to] fetch my deer sister Austin to me, bei[
very ill.

2d Thursday, the second of March, my sister Austin came to Billn[

---

[232] Robert Edgworth, from Longwood, County Meath, Ireland, was the third husba[
of Isabella Barnes of East Winch Hall. The date of a lease signed by them indicates th[
were married by 8 March 1708/9 (NRO, 12395 30C6).

[233] Elizabeth Hamilton (1638–1710) was the daughter of Judith Culpeper, the sister
Elizabeth Freke's mother. The monument in the Hollingbourne church states s[
'departed this life Feb ye 1st 1709 aged 72' (BL, Add. MS. 11259, fol. 6v); the par[
register notes she was buried on 6 February 1709/10. Her husband, James Hamilt[
who served Charles II as a groom of the bedchamber and a regimental colonel, died
1673 from wounds suffered in a campaign against the Dutch. Their son James (166[
1734) also commanded a regiment, coming to the aid of those besieged by the Jacob[
forces at Londonderry; he gained in 1701 a Scottish peerage as the sixth earl of Aberc[
and received the Irish titles baron of Mountcastle and viscount of Strabane. His broth[
William Hamilton of Chilston Park, married Margaret, the second daughter of Cic[
Freke's brother Thomas and his wife, Alicia Culpeper. Before his death in 1737 he v[
in Kent a justice of peace and a regimental leader in the militia (*Scots Peerage*, i. 56–
CP, i. 6; Lodge, v. 120–3).

[fol. 81r] safe and well, I humbly thank my God, butt a cold in her eyes of rhume which fircly followed her eyes for above i4 weeks. She found mee very ill, haveing hardly gone cross my chamber since last November butt with the help of two for to lead and help me and in continuall misery, laboureing under the hand of a mercyfull God ever since my widowhood, now allmost fowre years, and have hardly known one days ease or quiett.

i4 March the i4 I had another very civill letter from the chancellour to perswad me to settle a minester there in my church att Billney and to except the bishops licence, which tho to him I still refused, affter haveing tryed all ways with me by faire means and some threats of the bishops being bound to fill the vacancy iff I did nott in half a yeare place in a minester. I being very ill sent him word itt was thatt I waited for, thatt he would place in one and pay him; however, fearing I should dye before the church was provided and haveing keptt itt vacantt for neer seven month butt as I supplyed itt some times by Mr Smith, vicker of Winch, whom for xings and buryalls and sacramentt att Easter I paid him for itt, and I gave the ballance of my halfe year to cloth Betts chilldren, and poor Mary F[reke] five pounds, and her sister twenty shillings.

i7io, Aprill i6 Mr Smith gave the sacrament att Billney, when I consecratted my sillver flagon I bought last Michellmas for to give to the chancell wher my deer husband lyes intered.

25 And affter Mr Smith had preached two sermons heer as my curratt, he fell soe ill that he came to me the Tuesday aftter and said he was nott able to supply my place and church. For which two sermons I gave him twenty shillings and his daughter thatt came with him five shillings.[234] Eliz Frek

30 Aprill the 30 by the perswasion of my deer sister Austen I was by her prevailed with to exceptt of Mr Buck againe, which I did to oblige the bishop dureing my pleasure and his good behaivour; and I did enter him in Sunday, the thirtyeth of Aprill. Eliz Freke

30 And then I paid Mr Smith of Winch cleer off for his officiating in my church, and then I entered Mr Buck as curratte againe and gave him the register.

May io My son wrott to my cosin John Frek, my executor and trustte, the following letter, over leafe, which my cosin sentt downe to me to Billney.

i4 Sunday Mr Berrners made me a vissitt heer againe att Billney. E Frek

i7 I destrained Thomas Pallmer Wensday, and I took a bill of sale

---

[234] Joyce was baptized in East Winch on 23 December 1698; her sisters Katherine and Mary had died in July 1709.

of him on his stock and corne for his year and halfs rentt which will be due nextt Michellmas to mee, and I marked his stock by the constable William Knopwood.[235]

22 Monday, the two and twentyeth, I marked his stock, &c., according to law.

23 Tuesday, 23, I received the letter, over leafe, of my sons from my cosin John Frek enclosed in a letter to mee dated May the 20 on the other side.

24 I answered this letter of my sons to my cosin John Frek, as over leafe. E Frek.

28 Whitson Tuesay sitting in my chamber with my sister Austen, I weer taken aboutt noon allmost blind with mulltitude of blaks before my eyes, which I never had one in my life before, I being neer 68 years of age. And iff this be vapours in my head, from them deliver me, good Lord. E Freke

[fol. 81v]

1710, May 23 A coppy of a letter I received from my son dated May 10, 1710, wrott to my cosin John Frek, Mr Freks executor with me, and one of mine, transcribed by me, Elizabeth Frek, and by me answered May 24, 1710:

Deer Cosin,

I owne my greatt faultt in nott wrighting to you lately, butt I hope you will excuse and pardon itt when I tell you itt was my reall conscearne and trouble for nott being abble to remitt my mothers mony to you has hindred me. And I have now enclosed, sentt you, a bill on Mr Thomas Clark for a hundred and seventy pounds and payable att sight <in margin: never received by EF, 1713>. And I will use all my endeavours to remitt you more as soone as posible I can. And I must likewise own to you thatt I would have retturned over more to you of my mothers rentt before this butt thatt I had two bonds and judgmentts of mine of above six hundred pounds, for which I paid eight pounds in the hundred percent intrest ever since, has call'd in my mony thatt I was obliged to pay them of. And besids this I have paide the commisioners of the Sowrde Blads two hundred thirtty two pounds in partt of severall peices of land I boughtt of them aboutt Agust last, and most of the arrears thatt was leftt are remaineing still

---

[235] Freke had let Wassell Farm to Palmer and his wife Mary, reserving three rooms for herself.

due.[236] Therfore I begg, deer cosin, thatt you will excuse my nott wrighting to you all this while, for there is noe body has a greatter reliance on your favour and frindship then my selfe. Nor has nothing hindred the two little boys goeing over to you butt the wantt of an oppertunitty to send and land them carefully, which I hope will offer by a man of warr before the sumer is past. Butt iff you think itt nott fitt they should stay soe long, lett mee know itt, and they shall goe the very first man of warr thatt leaves Corke or Kingsale affter I receive your letter. For my wife and I both wish them very hartilly with you and are uneasy till they are under your kind care, knowing they can be noe where better.

My wife gives you her very hartty service, and I still begg of you to beleive I am, deer cosin,

Your most obliged kinsman
and humble servantt,
Ralph Freke

Mine and my wives duty to my mother. I am plagued with thatt rogue Kelly, and I begg your assistance and advice against him, for whom I have had two comissions against; and now my sixt clark, Mr Ludloe, says they are good for nothing for want of my mothers answer to him, &c.

Transcribed by me May 23, i7io, Eliza Frek, and answered by me May 24, i7io.

i7io, May 20 A letter my cosin John Freke wrott to me May 20, i7io, when hee sentt mee the above letter from my son, Ralph Freke:

Madam,

I should nott have bin soe long sillentt had nott your sons conductt made me asshamed to appeer in your presence tho butt in a letter. Butt now thatt I have received one from him late this evening, I cannott forbeare testifyeing my joy thatt he begins to be sencible of his faults towards you, which I look on as an earnest of his amendment. I have sentt you his letter and begg your dereicttion whatt I shall doe aboutt his two sons, intending nott to answer his letter till you returne itt me; by which time I hope his bill will be paid, which I shall charge my

---

[236] The Sword Blade Company was incorporated on 15 September 1691 for the purpose of making hollow-ground sword blades; in the eighteenth century it entered the realm of finance, challenging the Bank of England. When the forfeited Irish lands were sold in 1702 and 1703, this company became a major landholder, purchasing estates with army debentures it had received in exchange for stock (W. R. Scott, *The Constitution and Finance of English, Scottish and Irish Joint-Stock Companies to 1720*, 3 vols. [Cambridge, 1910–12], iii. 435–40).

selfe debter to you for in my accounts and give him notice of itt. An
iff in any thing I cann be serviceable to you, pray freely command.

Your humble servan
John Frek

[fol. 82r]

i710, May 24 My answer to this letter of my sons sentt me by m
cosin John Frek from London May 23 and by me answered May th
24, i710, Eliz. Frek:

Deer Cosin,

I am obliged to you for the favour of yours I yesterday received, a
I were for one from you of a former date, for both which pray b
pleased to exceptt my thanks. Inclosed in yours yesterday came on
from my unduttyfull and ungratefull son to the best of fathers an
mothers. However, I am glad to heer of his and his childrens goo
health and thatt he has a rightt and true sence of your kindness an
favours to him. And as to my selfe, I pray God to forgive him and la
nott these his sins to his charge, which has broke my hartt and brougl
mee to the condition I am in and laubour under.

And as to my deer grandchildren, sir, my son has most sencibl
convincst mee of my errors by his long sillence, which has given me
more serrious time of conciceration of the trouble and the severa
accidents thatt may happen to the eddication of them in Englan
Which being better concidered by there neerer and more indullgen
parrentts, I doe freely accquitt my selfe (and you) from all furth
trouble of soe valluable a charge as they are to mee. For since my so
has thoght fitt to place on me soe many slights and disrespectts as h
has done and to forfitt his lease by nonpaymentt to me, I will with i
take thatt advantage of thatt covenantt in itt of the care, trouble, an
charge of other peoples chilldren in my old age. My prayers are fo
them, and lett him disspose of them as he thinks fitt.

Butt, deer sir, give me leave to tell you thatt tho I am nott unsencebl
of your kindness and friendshipp to my familly, yett I cannott boast o
itt to my selfe to engage me in a very foollish lease which you kno
and can nott butt remember how offten you engaged your word an
honour to me to be my paymaster your selfe of my rentt and of m
sons good usuage and grattitude to me before I would signe this leas
and nott be brought in a fools trapp to seale away eight hundred an
fiffty pounds a yeare for three hundred and fiffty, and thatt never pai
me. Butt I doe nott questtion butt your sencesibillity of my usuage w
oblige you in justice to my deer father and deer husband, both whic
thought I merritted whatt they gave me, will convince you, as being

parttner with me in Mr Freks will, to receive thatt justice and honour from you as for their saks to place me in my right againe and to see me justly paid all my arrears of fowr years due from Mr Freks death and for three years rentt due to me before of neer 2000 l. All which I have by my will secured on thatt estate and this to my grandson for an additionall portion to him affter my death by my executors persuantt to the seddulle you last brought over with you, viz., 664 l. a yeare besids Garren James lease.[237] This letter, pray sir, be pleased to send my son with my blessing and service.

Deer cosin, being dayly summoned by the infirmityes I labour under, I doe think itt butt prudentt in me thatt all my small abbillityes now loose should be more properly and sattissfacttory now settled by you in my owne name and to my own disposall – as well whatt is in your hands as my years funds with this returne of my sons, paying your self whatt is laid outt for mee, and thatt as soon as you can. Nott being att all sattisfyed (finding your partiallitye soe great against me) and you being my husbands and my executor, you may find or make a law affter my death to disspose of itt contrary to my intention is the true reason I ask this justice and favour of you, which kindness added to all your others will oblige, deer sir, your obliged kinswoman and humble servant.

Eliz. Freke

[fol. 82v]

1710, June 22 Some emblems for my own reading.[238] Text is Psallm 6, verse 2d:
Have mercy upon me, Lord, for I am weak;
O Lord, heale me, for my bones are sore vexed. Eliz Frek

A Diologue betwen the Soule and Jesus

Soule – Ah, son of David help.
Jesus –   Whatt sinfull cry
    Implowrs the son of David?
Soule –   Itt is I.
Jesus – Who artt thou?
Soule –   Oh, a deeply wounded breast
    Thats heavy laden and would faine have rest.

---

[237] Garrane James, lying between Mogeely and Killeagh in County Cork, was leased from Charles Boyle, second earl of Burlington, for 21 years; Ralph Freke bequeathed to his son John Redmond 'all my right Title and Interest that I have unto the Lands of Garrane James scituate in the Barony of Imokilly' (PRO, PROB 11/563/100).

[238] With the exception of the third piece, which is originally in verse, the manuscript preserves no poetic form; the edited poems reflect their pentameter lines.

Jesus – I have noe scraps, and dogs must nott be fed
  Like houshold chilldren with the chilldrens bread.
Soule – True, Lord, yett to larate[239] a hungry whelp
  To lick their crums, oh, son of David helpe.
Jesus – Poore soule, whatt aylest thoue?
Soule –   O, I burne, I fry,
  I cannott rest; I know nott where to fly.
  To find some ease I turne my blubbred face
  From man to man; I role from place to place
  To avoid my torturs, to obtaine releife,
  Butt still am dogged and hanted with my grifes.
  My midnight torments call the slugish lightt;
  And when the morning comes, they woo the nightt.
Jesus – Surcease thy tears and speak thy free desires.
Soule – Then squench my flames and swage these scorching fires.
Jesus – Canst thou beleive my hand can cure thy griefe?
Soule – I beleive, Lord; help my unbeleife.
Jesus – Hold forth thy arme and lett my fingers try
  Thy pulce. Where cheifly does thy tormentt lye?
Soule – From head to foott itt raigns in every partt
  Butt plays the self-lawed tyrantt in my hartt.
Jesus – Canst thou dygest, canst relish wholsome food?
  How stands thy tastt?
Soule –   To nothing thatt is good.
  All sinfull trash and earths unsavory stuff
  I can dygest and rellish well enough.
Jesus – Is nott thy bloud as cold as hott by turns?
Soule – Cold to what is good; to whatt is bad itt burnes.
Jesus – How old is thy griefe.
Soule –   I took it at the fall
  With eateing fruite.
Jesus –   'Tis epydemicall:
  Thy bloud is infected, and the infection sprung
  From a bad liver; tis a feavor strong
  And full of death unless with present speed
  A veine be oppened. Thou must dye or bleed.
Soule – Oh, I am faintt and spentt. Thatt lance thatt shall
  Lett forth my bloud letts forth my life withall.
  My soule wants cordialls and has greater need
  Of bloud (then being spentt soe farr) to bleed.
  I faintt allredy; if I bleed, I dye.
Jessus – Tis either thou must bleed, sick soule, or I.

---

[239] Undefined; Freke seems to mean 'to allow' and not 'allatrate': to bark.

My bloude is a cordiall: hee thatt sucks my veins
Shall clense his own and conquer paines
Then these. Cheer up. This pretious bloud of mine
Shall cure thy griefs; my hart shall bleed for thine.
Believe and veiw me with a faithfull eye;
Thy soule shall nither languish, bleed, or dye.
Canst thou be sick and such a doctter by?
Thou canst nott live unless thy doctter dye!
Strang kind of griefe that finds no medicyne good
To swage her pains butt the phisitions bloude.

                              Eliza. Freke

Psalm the 143, verse the 2d:
Enter nott into judgmentt with me, thy servantt,
for in thy sight shall noe man liveing be justifyed. Eliz Frek

A Diologue between Jesus, a Sinner, and Justice

Jesus – Bring forth the prisoner sinner.
Justice –   Thy commands
    Are done, just judge; see, heer the prisoner stands.
Jesus – Whatt has the prisoner done? Say whatt is the cause
    Of his committment.
Justice –   Hee has broke thy laws
    Of his too gratious God, conspired the death
    Of thatt greatt majesty that gave him breath,
    And heapes transgretion, Lord, upon transgretion.
Jesus – How know'st thou this?
Justice –   Even by his own confession.
    His sins are crying, and they cry aloud:
    They cryed to heaven; they cryed to heaven for blood.
Jesus – Whatt sayst thou, sinner; hast thou ought to plead
    Thatt sentence should nott pass? Hold up thy head
    And show thy brazen, thy rebellious face.
Sinner – Ah mee, I dare nott; I am too vile and base
    To tread upon the earth, much more to lift
    Myne eyes to heaven. I need noe other shifftt
    Then mine own contience. Lord, I must confess
    I am noe more then dust and noe whitt less
    Then my indittement stiles me. Ah, iff thou
    Search too severe with too severe a brow,
    Whatt flesh can stand? I have transgrest thy laws.
    My merrits pleads thy vengance, nott my cause.
Justice – Lord shall I strike the blow?

Jesus –   Hold, Justice, stay.
   Sinner, speak on; whatt hast thou more to say?
Sinner – Vile as I am and of my self abhor'd,
   I am thy handy work, thy creture, Lord,
   Stampt with thy gloryous image, [fol. 83r] and att first
   Most like to thee though now am poore, accurst,
   Convicted cative and degeneratt creture
   Heer trembling att thy barr.
Justice –   Thy fault is the greater.
   Lord, shall I strike the blow?
Jesus –   Hold, Justice, stay.
   Speak, sinner; hast thou nothing more to say
   (For thy self)?
Sinner – Nothing butt mercy, mercy, Lord. My state
   Is miserable, poor, and despratte.
   I quite renounce my self, the world, and flee
   From Lord to Jesus, from thy selfe to thee.
Justice – Cease thy vaine hopes; my angry God has vowed
   Abused mercy must have bloud for blood.
   Shall I yett strike the blow?
Jessus –   Stay, Justice, hold.
   My bowels yearn, my fainting blood grows cold
   To veiw the trembling wretch; me thinks I spye
   My fathers image in the prisoners eye.
Justice – I cannot hold.
Jesus –   Then turne thy thirsty blade
   Into my side; lett there the wound be made.
   Cheer up, deer soule; redeem thy life with mine.
   My soule shall smartt, my hartt shall bleed for thine.
Sinner – O groundless deeps! Oh love beyound degree!
   The offended dyes to sett the offender free.
         Is Eliza. Frek.
   Mercyes of mercyes. Hee thatt was my drudge
   Is now my advocate, is now my judg.
   He suffers, pleads, and sentences alone.
   Three I adore and yett adore but one.
         Eliz Frek

Ecclesiasticus the 2d, verse i7: All is vanity and vexation of spiritt.

         i
How is the soule of man befooled with his desire
Thatt thinks a hectick feaver may be cool'd in flams of fire
Or hoop's to rake full heaps of burnish'd gold from nasty mire.

A whining lover may as well request a scornfull breast
To melt in tears as woo the world for restt.

2

Lett witt and all her studied plotts effectt the best they can.
Lett smiling fortune prosper and perfectt what witt began.
Lett earth advise with both and soe projectt a happy man.
Lett witt or fawning fortune vye their best. He may bee blest
With all that earth can give,
Butt earth can give noe rest.

3

Whose gold is double, with a carefull hand, his cares are double.
The pleasure, honour, wealth of sea
And land bring butt a trouble.
The world itt selfe and all the worlds comand is butt a buble.
The strong desirs of mans insatiate breast may stand possest
Off all thatt earth can give,
Butt earth can give noe rest.

4

The worlds a seeming parrydice butt her own
    And mans tormenter,
    Appeering fixtt butt yett a roleing stone without a tentter.
Itt is a vast circumfrance wher none can find a centure.
Of more then earth, can earth make none possestt.
And hee that least regards this restless world
Shall in this world find restt.

5

True rest consists nott in the oft revying of worldly drosse.
Earth mirry purchas is not worth the buying: her gaine is loss;
Her rest butt giddy toyle iff nott relyeing
Uppon her cross. How wordlings broyle for trouble!
Thatt fond breast thatt is possest of earth withoutt
A crosse has earth withoutt a restt.

6

Worldlings, whose whimpering folly holds the losses
Of honour, pleasure, health, and wealth such crosses,
Look heer and tell me what your arms engrosse
When the best end of whatt ye hugg's a crosse.
                              Eliza. Freke

[fol. 83v]

1710, June 23 A Diologue between the Serpentt and Eve. The textt is Jams i, &c: Every man is tempted when he is drawn away of his own lusts and enticed.

Serpentt – Nott eate, nott tast, nott touch, nor cast an eye
    Upon the fruite of this faire tree? And why?
    Why eatest thou nott what heaven ordained for foode?
    Or canst thou think thatt bad which heaven calls good?
    Why was itt made iff nott to bee enjoyed?
    Neglectt of favours maks a favour voyde.
    Blessings unused pervert into a wast
    As well as surfeitts. Woman, doe butt tast.
    See how the laden boughs make sillentt suite
    To bee enjoyed; looke how there bending fruite
    Meetts thee half way; observe butt how they crouch
    To kis thy hand. Coy woman, do but touch.
    Mark whatt a pure virmillion blush has dyed
    There swelling cheeks and how for shame they hide
    Thier palsy heads to see themselves stand by
    Neglectted. Woman, do butt cast an eye.
    Whatt bounteous heaven ordained for use reffuse nott.
    Come pull and eatte! You abuse the things yee use nott.
Eve – Wisest of beast, our great creator did
    Reserve this tree and this allone forbid;
    The rest are freely ours, which doubtless are
    As pleasing to the tast and to the eye as faire.
    Butt touching this, his strictt commands are such
    Tis death to tast and noe less then death to touch.
Serpentt – Pish, death's a fable. Did nott heaven inspire
    Your equall ellements with liveing fire
    Blown from the spring of life? Is nott thatt breath
    Immortall? Come, ye are as free from death
    As he thatt made you. Can the flams expire
    Which hee has kindled? Can ye quench his fire?
    Did nott the greatt creators voyce proclaime
    Whatt ere he made (from the blue spangl'd frame
    To the poore leafe thatt trembles) very good?
    Blest he nott both the feeder and the food?
    Tell, Tell me, then, whatt danger can accrue
    From such blest food to such halfe gods as you?
    Curbe needless fears and lett noe fond conceitt
    Abuse your freedom, woman; take and eate.

Eve – Tis true we are imortall; death is yett
  Unborne; and till rebellion make itt, debtt
  Undue. I know the fruite is good untill
  Presumtious disobedience make itt ill.
  The lips thatt open to this fruit's a porttall
  To lett in death and make immortall mortall.
Serpentt – You cannot dye; come, woman, tast and feare nott.
Eve – Shall Eve transgress? I dare nott. Oh, oh, I dare nott.
Serpent – Afraid? Why drawest thou back thy timmorous arme?
  Harme only falls on such as feare a harme.
  Heaven knows and fears the virtue of this tree
  Twill make you perfectt gods as well as hee.
  Strech forth thy hand and lett thy fondness never
  Feare death; do pull and eatte and live for ever.
Eve – Tis butt an apple, and itt is as good
  To doe as to desire fruites made for food.
  I'll pull and taste and tempt my Adam too
  To know the [   ] of this dainty.
Serpentt –   Doe, doe.
                     Eliza Freke

Some remembrances convenyentt for me to think on in which I were
a deep sufferer with my deer husband, Percy Frek, Esqr, to the loss of
all we had by King Jams and excominycated by him and outtlawed
for an absentee in 1689

1689, March 12 King James took shipping att Brest in Franc for
Ireland with aboutt 1500 French, Scotch, and Irish officers and saffly
landed att Kingsaile the next day, being March 12, with his numarous
attendance; **24** and was by the earle of Tirconell March the 24 receiv'd
into Dublin tryumpantly; and next morning call'd a cowncell and
published five proclamations.[240] **1689, May 7** And King James created
the earle of Tirconnell a duke and lord liuetenantt of Ireland insteed

[240] Freke's account of the Irish war draws upon George Story, *A True and Impartial
History of the Most Material Occurrences in the Kingdom of Ireland during the Last Two Years*
(London, 1691), at times following the text closely. Story states James' force numbered
1,800. Dublin welcomed James on 24 March with a celebration; the next day he issued
five proclamations: besides summoning a parliament for 7 May, the king established a
new currency based on brass coinage, encouraged the return of subjects who had left
Ireland, provided for supplying the army, and urged the suppression of theft and violence
on the local level (Thomas Davis, *The Patriot Parliament of 1689*, 3rd edn. [London, 1893],
11).

of the duke of Ormond he displac'd.[241] And the 29 of Aprill the kir wentt to meet his Irish parliamt att Dublin, wher were all maner crully actts made against the poor English Protestants, all now utter ruined; 7020 of which shelltered themselves in London Derry ond the govermentt of Mr Walker and Major Baker, which garryson an regymentt of 7020 Protestants were under eightt collenolls and 3 inferiour officers – a bold undertakeing thus naked withoutt arms mony or any sort of ammonition.[242] **1689, Aprill io** This was don Aprill io, i689, only with ten days provission. The 20 of Aprill Kir Jams invested this place and begun to batter itt, of which the govenou sent an account of itt to England by Mr Bennett and thatt they wou [defend] themselves to the last man.[243] Wher att London Derry severa attacks were made by the beseigers, wher the beseiged had allways th advantage had nott famine and sickness within discouraged them. **2** The king returned to his Dublin parliamentt and left the beseige before London Derry, [fol. 84r] who were againe repullced with grea slaughter, tho all this while the beseiged lay sorely weakned by the rag of famin. **i689, June i5** And aboutt this time Mr Baker was take very ill when Conrad de Rose, the French generall, swore he wou levell the place to the ground and bury those thatt deffended itt in i ruiens and putt all to the sword of whatt sex or age whatt ever, bu the poor beseiged of London Dery absolutely defend themselves an their religion against all the mallice of King Jams and his assistance.[2]

---

[241] Richard Talbot, duke of Tyrconnell (1630–1691), had been commissioned lo general in June 1686 and became lord deputy in February 1686/7, displacing Lor Lieutenant Henry Hyde, second earl of Clarendon (1638–1709). Talbot had earlie influenced the decision to remove James Butler, first duke of Ormonde (1610–1688), fro his position as lord lieutenant (Simms, 17–18). The appointment of the new lord deput John Reresby notes in his memoirs, 'made a great many people that were Protestan leave or sell their estates and come over for England' (*Memoirs of Sir John Reresby*, e Andrew Browning [Glasgow, 1936], 445; see also Luttrell, i. 386). On 30 March 168 Talbot became duke of Tyrconnell and in 1691 lord lieutenant (*CP*, xii, pt. 2. 119).

[242] Freke's recollection of the siege of Londonderry is indebted to George Walker, *True Account of the Siege of London-Derry*, 3rd edn. (London, 1689); his figures, however, li 341 officers (20). George Walker (1646?–1690), rector of Donoughmore in County Tyron and Major Henry Baker (c. 1647–1689), the son of an established English family i Dumaghan, County Louth, became the governors of Londonderry in April 1689. Bak died of illness during the siege on 30 June; after the city successfully withstood the Iris Walker received considerable acclaim, including the prospect of becoming bishop Derry. Three editions of *True Account* were published before he died in the battle of th Boyne, 1 July 1690 (Patrick Macrory, *The Siege of Derry* [1980], reprinted Oxford, 1988]).

[243] Joseph Bennett escaped to Scotland and from there went to London, where h appeared before a parliamentary committee 'appointed to inquire who has been th Occasion of the Delays in sending Relief over into *Ireland*, and particularly into *Londonderr* (*CJ*, x. 162), and published *A True and Impartial Account Of the most Material Passages in Irelan Since December 1688* (London, 1689).

[244] Lieutenant-General Conrad de Rosen (1628–1715), a soldier of fortune born i

20 Dyed Governor Baker to the greatt loss and affliction of the beseig'd; and tho they were reduced to the nesesity of horses, doggs, catts, ratts, and mice, salted hids – all lothsome things for there subsistance – rather then surrender itt. **Jully 30** Sunday, affter sermon when they could hold outt noe longer, Doctter Walker, the governour, espyed three ships with Major Generall Kirk with provision from England when they had butt 2 days provision left. **31** Soe thatt on the last of July the seige was raised.[245] By this example the Innyskillin held outt against King James, headed by Liuetenentt Collonell Loyde with 200 men in the castle, wher the Inniskillenors signilysed their vallour and allwayes come off with advantage.[246] Butt none of those acttions was soe remarkable as thatt which happened by a perticuler appoyntment of providence on the same day London Derry was releived wherein 2000 Inniskelloners fought and routted 6000 Irish att Newton Buttler and took there Commander Maccarty with the loss only of 20 men kill'd and 50 wounded.[247]

1689, May 7 King James mett his Irish parliamentt att Dublin, **12** where he made his proclamation which ended the 12 of May. Hee repealed the Actt of Settlementt, the forfitted estates of the Roman Catholicks in 1641;[248] and to give itt a more fattall blow, ther was then an actt of attainder past in parlyamentt thatt all Protestants thatt appeer'd nott to there names in person when this bill was presented were attainted and the rest upon common fame. In this black actt there were noe fewer attainted then 2 arch bishops, 1 duke, 17 earles, 7 countesses, 28 vicounts, 2 vicountes, 7 bishops, 18 barrons, 33 barronetts,

Alsace and with long service in the French army, was senior commander of the French forces in Ireland (Edward B. Powley, *The Naval Side of King William's War* [London, 1972], 50 n. 19; *La Grande Encyclopédie*, 31 vols. [Paris, 1886–1902], xxviii. 944). Walker says that Rosen threatened the inhabitants on 24 June 'or thereabouts', but the copy of the ultimatum Walker included in an appendix concludes, 'Given under my hand this *30th* of *June*' (50).

[245] Major-General Percy Kirke (1646?–1691) brought the relief that ended the siege of 105 days. The *Mountjoy* from Derry attempted on 28 July to break through the boom erected across the River Foyle; accounts disagree whether it, the *Phoenix*, or the *Dartmouth* first completed the breach (Walker, 40–2).

[246] Enniskillen, the other Ulster place of Protestant defiance, held out under the leadership of Lieutenant-Colonel Thomas Lloyd of Roscommon, known among the Jacobites as 'little Cromwell' (Simms, 114).

[247] On 31 July at the battle of Newtownbutler, some fifteen miles from Enniskillen, the forces of Colonel William Wolseley (1640?–1697) defeated those of Lieutenant-Colonel Justin MacCarthy, Viscount Mountcashel (c. 1643–1694), who was wounded and captured. MacCarthy escaped to the continent, where he commanded the Irish Brigade in the service of Louis XIV; Wolseley became in 1696 a lord chief justice of Ireland (John A. Murphy, *Justin MacCarthy, Lord Mountcashel* [Cork, 1959]; *English Army Lists*, ii. 32, i. 259).

[248] A court of claims was to hear suits for the restoration of property forfeited by landholders involved in the 1641 uprising. Outlawries from this period were also voided, and the property of those who resisted James was to be seized (Simms, 81–4).

5i knights, 83 clargymen, 2i82 esqres and gentlemen – of which my deer husband was one and lost all ever wee had of estate, mony, and goods affter an excomunycation for an absentee.[249] Our house and castle att Rathbarry was burntt downe to the ground by the Irish and my deer husband Mr Percy Freks estatt in Ireland given by King James to Maccartty, a poor rogue worth nothing, and with itt he made him his collenell. And all of the above persons of 243i were unheard, declared traitors, and ajudged to suffer the pains of death and forfitture of all there estats. In which I lost above a thousand pounds a year and with much adoe saved my deer husbands life. The famous proscriptions of Room, the last tryumpant, came nott up to the horrour of this, ther being more then double the number condemned in this little kingdome. And to make this of Ireland yett the more terrible and unavoidable, the actt itt self was concealed and noe Protestantt allowed a coppy of itt till fowre monthes past, wheras in thatt of Room the names of the persons proscribed was decreed and therby oppertunity was given to many to preserve themselvs by flightt.[250] **Jully 20** Soe affter this the 20 of Jully this parlament was prorogued to the i2 of January ensueing. In which time King Jams and Tirconell, his deputy liuetenantt, turn'd outt all the fellows and scollers of the colledg of Dublin; seiesed on ther furniture, library, and plate; and every thing belonging to the colledg or scollers were taken away; and turned the chappell to a magasine and the chambers into prisons for Protestants; and all the Protestantt churches shutt up throwoutt the whole kingdome.[251]

King William May 7, i689, declares war with France by the Lord Sumers;[252] before which, hee fought the French att Bantry Bay May

[249] Freke relies on William King, *The State of the Protestants of Ireland Under the Late King James's Government* (London, 1691) for the numbers and names of those affected by the act of attainder. Her figures, however, do not always agree with King's. The name '*Piercy Freak of Rathbarry*' appears along with '*Pierce Crosby*, Son and Heir apparent of *Patrick Crosby*' (250–1), among those required to appear before judicial authorities by 10 August 1689. Freke's name also appears in *A List Of such of the Names of the Nobility, Gentry and Commonalty … attainted of High Treason* (London, 1690), 15.

[250] Freke follows closely King's contention that the act was perhaps 'never equall'd in any Nation since the time of the Proscription in *Rome*' (182). He asserts that those attainted were 'not suffer'd to know one word of it, till the time allow'd them to come in was past at least three Months' (159).

[251] Freke's account reproduces almost verbatim that of King (194). On 6 September soldiers following James' orders turned the college into a garrison; on 11 September it became a prison, and on 16 September the fellows and scholars were forced to leave. The chapel plate along with the mace was seized on 28 September; Catholic mass was celebrated in the chapel on 21 October, and later powder was stored there (The College Register, in John William Stubbs, *The History of the University of Dublin* [Dublin, 1889], 127–31).

[252] The *London Gazette* (2452) prints 'Their Majesties Declaration Against the French King'. John Somers, Lord Somers (1651–1716), was solicitor-general when he penned the

the first under Admirall Herbertt, now made earle of Torrington June
the first, 1689.[253] Affter this the king, William, goes to Portsmouth to
reward those souldeirs and officers who had distingushed themselves in
this late engagementt. To all the officers hee gave honour and to each
souldier and seaman ten shillings a peice, which came to above 26000
pounds besids the provision for the widows of those thatt lost their
lives.[254] And affter the kings returne from Portsmouth, he and the queen
purchased the Earle of Nottinghams house att Kensington for twenty
thousand pounds.[255]

[fol. 84v]

Aprill the 22, 1689, attainders were reversed by actt of parliamentt as
the Lord Russells, Allicia Lisle, Allgernoon Sidney, earle of Devonshiere,
Tittas Oats, Mr Johnsons [were] all annull'd with severall others, and
Oats allowed 5 l. a week.[256]

declaration; he subsequently became lord chancellor (William L. Sachse, *Lord Somers: A
Political Portrait* [Manchester, 1975]).

[253] Arthur Herbert (c. 1648–1716), first lord of the admiralty and commander of the
fleet off Ireland, encountered the French admiral François Louis de Rousselet, marquis
of Chateaurenault, on the west coast of Cork. The smaller English fleet lost ninety-six
men; the French forty. Though John Evelyn wrote in his diary, 'we came off with greate
slaughter, & little honor' (iv. 639), Herbert became first earl of Torrington on 29 May.
His career in the navy ended, however, when he was court-martialled, though acquitted,
for his alleged failure to confront the French fleet in the major naval loss in the Channel
off Beachy Head in June 1690 (*HC*, ii. 526–8; *London Gazette* [2451]; Powley, *The Naval
Side of King William's War*, 134–43, 166–8).

[254] The *London Gazette* (2454) reports that on 16 May in Portsmouth aboard the *Elizabeth*
King William knighted two captains and gave 'a Donative of Ten Shillings a Man, which
was distributed accordingly, amounting to about 2600 l.', not the £26,000 Freke notes.

[255] The sentence concludes, 'and paid for itt for the reliefe of maimed seamen and
souldiers to which they gave itt, both King William and Queen Mary'. The conclusion,
omitted in this edition, must refer to the ship-board grant and not to Kensington. In an
18 June 1689 entry Luttrell notes, 'The king hath bought the earl of Nottinghams house
at Kensington for 18,000 guineas, and designs it for his seat in winter, being near
Whitehall' (i. 549). The court began residing at Kensington on 24 December 1689; during
the next years the first stages of an extensive renovation of the house and gardens began.
Both the king and queen were often at the London residence, where Mary died in 1694
(Arthur T. Bolton and H. Duncan Hendry, eds., *The Royal Palaces of Winchester, Whitehall*[,]
Kensington, and St. James's, Wren Society, 7 [Oxford, 1930]).

[256] William Russell, Lord Russell (1639–1683), accused of complicity in the Rye House
Plot, stood trial for treason at the Old Bailey in July 1683, was condemned to death, and
was executed on 21 July. A petition by his wife, Lady Rachel Russell, and his father, the
fifth earl of Bedford, led to the parliamentary reversal of attainder in March 1688/9 (*HC*,
iii. 365–8; Lois G. Schwoerer, *Lady Rachel Russell: 'One of the Best of Women'* [Baltimore,
1988], 103–36, 187–8; *CJ*, x. 45–6, 50). A bill from the House of Lords was first read in
the House of Commons on 9 May 1689 to reverse the attainder of Alice Lisle, who had
been executed on 2 September 1685 for her alleged complicity in sheltering John Hickes
after he had supported Monmouth's unsuccessful military efforts at Sedgemoor. The

1689, July 24 The duke of Gloster was born by the princes of Denmark, sister to the queen of England, and baptised by the name of William, his majesty and the king of Danmark being his godfathers; whom presenttly the king crated duke of Gloster.[257]

1690, Febuary 6 Aprill the 2d his majesty thought fitt to putt an end to this sesions of parliamt, which was prorog'd to the 2d of Aprill, and by proclamation was desolved the 6 of Febuary and att the same time another call'd the 20 of March. Which they mett accordingly and chose Sir John Trevor speaker of the House of Comons;[258] when his majesty acquainted them he thought itt convenientt to leav the govermen of the kingdome and the affairs of itt in the queens hand, which was confirm'd by an actt of parliamentt to her, whilst the king went to the redduceing and settling the goverment in Ireland.

1690, May 20 The king gave the royall assent to an actt of parliamentt of putting the adminstration of the govermentt into the queens hand when ever his occasions call'd him outt of England or outt of any part of the kingdom.[259] Affter which the 7 of July the

reversal received royal assent on 24 May 1689 (*CJ*, x. 126, 151). Algernon Sidney (1622–1683) had been found guilty of treason for his involvement in the Rye House Plot and executed on 7 December 1683. A bill sent to the House of Commons on 26 April 1689 'annulling, and making void, the Attainder' received royal assent on 11 May (*CJ*, x. 105, 130). William Cavendish, first duke of Devonshire (1641–1707), had been fined £30,000 and imprisoned for physically assaulting Thomas Culpeper in July 1685. The House of Lords considered in May 1689 whether the judgment violated the peer's privilege of parliament and reversed the judgment (*Journals of the House of Lords*, xiv. 201–3, 211; *HC*, ii. 35–9). Titus Oates (1649–1705) was tried for perjury in 1685, whipped, and imprisoned until 1688 for alleging in 1678 the existence of the Popish Plot to assassinate Charles II and establish the duke of York on the throne. A resolution to reverse the judgment as 'cruel and illegal' was introduced in the House of Commons on 31 May 1689 and debated without final resolution; a warrant pardoning him of perjury was issued on 23 July and on 19 September the king ordered 'that 10l. a week be paid to Dr. Oats' (*CJ*, x. 177; *CSPD*, 1689–90, 197; William A. Shaw, ed., *Calendar of Treasury Books, 1689–1692* [London, 1931], ix, pt. 1. 53). Samuel Johnson was 'whipt by the common Hangman from *Newgate* to *Tyburn*' in November 1686 for publishing a tract allegedly encouraging revolution. A parliamentary resolution initiated on 11 June 1689 overturned the second conviction as 'illegal and cruel' (*CJ*, x. 177, 193–4).

[257] The son of Princess Anne was born at Hampton Court on Wednesday, 24 July, at 4.00 a.m. The bishop of London, Henry Compton, christened him William Henry on Saturday evening, 27 July, 'the King and the Earl of *Dorset*, Lord Chamberlain of His Majesty's Houshold, being Godfathers, and the Lady Marchioness of *Hallifax* Godmother' (*London Gazette* [2473, 2475]). Anne's only surviving child died of smallpox on 30 July 1700, ending the hopes of the Stuart succession.

[258] The proclamation to prorogue parliament appears in the *London Gazette* (2530). John Trevor (c. 1637–1717), a speaker of the House of Commons in the reigns of James and William, was expelled for corruption on 16 March 1694/5. As a master of the rolls, Trevor continued to occupy a prominent judicial position (*HC*, iii. 604–7; Foss, *Judges of England*, viii. 64–71).

[259] The *London Gazette* (2559) records the royal assent on 20 May to 'An Act for the Exercise of the Government by her Majesty, during his Majesty's Absence' (*CJ*, x. 422).

parliamt was adjorned to thatt day when the king begun his jorney for Ireland.[260] **June 14** Then King William lands att Carrickfergus with Prince George of Danmark and many other persons of distintion and thatt evening in the duke of Schomberg's coach wentt to Bellfast.[261] **26** Hee veiwes the army the 26 of June, which he found to consist of 36000 of English, Dutch, French, Danes, and Germons all well appoynted in every respectt. **27** From thence he march'd to Dundalke the 27 of June and was soe pleased with the prospectt of the country as he rid along thatt King William said thatt itt was highly worth fighting for to those aboutt him.

30 As soon as King William heard thatt the enymye had repased the Boyne, hee ordered his whole army to move by break of day [to] thatt river, hee marching in the frontt of them with the prince of Denmark, duke of Schomberg, duke of Ormond, &c. **June 30** Wher on takeing a veiw of the enimy, King William was shott by them on his right shoulder, which took away a peice of his coat and wounded him. Which affter he had dressed, he mounted his horse againe and show'd himself to the enimy and his whole army, where he rod aboutt till 12 a clock att night with torches quitt throw itt in person and gave the word (Westminster) and the signall, sprigs of green in their hatts.[262] **Jully 1** Jully 1 both kings mett, viz., King William and King Jams, when aboutt six a clock in the morn they drue up for battle, when the Dutch foott first enter'd the watter, [and] when the duke of Schamburg, the kings generall, was shott through the neck and kild immediattly. Nott long affter Docter Walker, soe famouss for the defence of London Derry, was shott in the belly and presently dyed.[263] Dureing all these acttions King William might be said to be every wher by his corrage and conductt and must have his honour of the day; for tho wounded,

---

[260] The *London Gazette* (2573) reports that on 7 July parliament was 'Prorogued to the 28th of this Month' (*CJ*, x. 424). William left Whitehall the morning of 4 June; the gazette (2563–6) chronicles his journey to Chester, where he arrived on 7 June. He embarked from nearby Hoylake on 11 June with a fleet of some 300 ships.

[261] Prince George of Denmark (1653–1708), the husband of the future queen Anne and the brother of Christian V, had defected to William's side in November 1688. Made the duke of Cumberland in March 1689, he fought at the Boyne and became in Anne's reign generalissimo and lord high admiral (Edward Gregg, *Queen Anne* [London, 1980]). The Heidelberg-born Frederick Herman (1615–1690) distinguished himself in a number of continental armies before he supported William militarily in the November 1688 landing in England. The new king gave him the title of duke of Schomberg and the position as commander-in-chief of the English army in Ireland (*CP*, xi. 522–6). Story reports that the duke and king stayed in Belfast the evening of 14 June at Sir William Franklin's house (66).

[262] Story, 75, 78. The *London Gazette* (2572) also relates in detail the wounding of the king and his evening ride.

[263] Story states only that Walker was fatally shot and his body stripped (82); modern accounts document a mortal stomach wound.

his sword hee drew and rod att the head of his army with itt naked and drawn to the enymy, who were coming towards him. Butt with the loss of aboutt i500 men, King Jams hastned off and went away for Dublin; and King Williams loss was aboutt 500, an inconcidrable loss for such a battle iff the renown'd duke of Schamberg had nott bin one, who was eighty two years of age when he was killed.[264]

King James, haveing staid att Dublin one night, the nextt morning attended by the duke of Berwick, Tirconell, [and] Lord Powis posted away for Watterford. He broke down all the bridges for fear of being persued.[265] There he went abourd a vessell redy to receive him. And King William upon this defeat of the Irish att the Boyne rested the next day. **3** And on the 3d of Jully went to secure the citty of Dublin. **6** When att Finglass he heard the late king was imbarked, the sixth of Jully, being Sunday, King William rod in tryumpphantt maner into Dublin and wentt dereictly to St Patricks church, the cathedrall of thatt metropillis, to pay God Allmighty his pious acknowledgments for his late victtory.[266] **7** The 7 of July the king publishes his declaration of protection to all the English and Irish with their pardon iff by their submision and resignation of ther arms they relyed on him, and **27** supprest all the coper mony made currant by the late King James the Second.[267]

[fol. 85r]

The 27 of Jully i690 King William left the campp att Carrick and wentt to Dublin in order to embark for England; before which hee ordained a weekly fast and published his severall declaritions of grace

[264] According to Story the Irish suffered between 1,000 and 1,500 casualties; 'on our side were killed nigh four hundred' (85). Other contemporary accounts disagree about the number killed (Simms, 151 n. 66). Schomberg was seventy-four at his death – not eighty-two, as Story reports.

[265] James stayed the night of 1 July at the castle in Dublin with Lady Tyrconnell; from Waterford he sailed on 3 July to Kinsale, where he left on 4 July for France, never to return. James Fitzjames, first duke of Berwick (1670–1734), the illegitimate son of James II and Arabella Churchill, rose among James' military leaders to the position of commander-in-chief in Ireland before he left for France following the loss of Limerick. His death on the battlefield ended a long military career with the French. William Herbert, duke of Powis (c. 1626–1696), served James in Ireland as a privy counsellor and lord chamberlain of the household; he died an exile in France (CP, ii. 162–4, x. 646–8).

[266] 'This day being Sunday, His Majesty rode in great Splendor to the Cathedral at *Dublin*, where all the Services of the Church were Solemnly performed' (*London Gazette* [2574]).

[267] Both Story (93–4) and the *London Gazette* (2574) reprint the declaration, which promised to pardon the common people – soldiers and civilians – who surrendered their arms and returned to their homes by 1 August. They also note the royal proclamation prohibiting the circulation of brass money (106–7, 2576).

and favour Agust the first.[268] **1690, August 4** Butt heering the French had only burnt a village in the west of England and were returned off againe, King William returned againe to his army the 4 of Agust, which he found encamped att Golden Bridge. The army being posted, the king sentt his trumpentt into Limbrick to summon the towne, which was opposed by the duke of Berwick and Sarsfield for King James.[269] **30** Att last affter greatt opposition the seige of Limbrick was raised Agust 30. **31** And King William entered itt the next day and sent away all bag and bagage, leaveing itt in the care of Liuetenant Generall Ginckle.[270] **September 7** And then his majesty embarked att Duncanon Fort with Prince George of Danmark and some others of quallity; and arrived safe the nextt day in King Road neer Bristoll; and on the 9 of September came to Windsor, wher he was received by the queen.[271]

Affter this Cork was beseiged by the duke of Wittingberg and the duke of Marlbrow and duke of Graffton for King William and opposed by Collonell Makillicute for King James. **September 28** And the garrison consisting of 4000 men all made prisoners of war and surrendered 28 of September.[272] The same day the king took Cork, he

[268] The second declaration published on 1 August extended the promise of leniency to officers who surrendered; foreign troops who submitted would receive passes to leave. A general fast was also proclaimed for each Friday 'imploring a Blessing upon Their Majesties Forces' (Story, 111; *London Gazette* [2583]).

[269] Story, 111–15. Patrick Sarsfield, first earl of Lucan (1665?–1693), returned to Ireland in March 1689 with James. As a major-general he played a central role in withstanding the first siege of Limerick. Sarsfield later led Irish forces for the French until mortally wounded two years later on the battlefield of Landen (Piers Wauchope, *Patrick Sarsfield and the Williamite War* [Dublin, 1992]).

[270] William did not enter Limerick; bad weather and unbroken resistance forced the English besiegers to withdraw, and on the last day of August 'all the Army drew off' (Story, 133). Godert or Godard van Reede, baron de Ginkel (1644–1703), a career officer from Utrecht, came to England with the prince of Orange in November 1688. After the Irish campaigns of 1690, he commanded the English forces throughout the rest of the war. In 1692 he became the first earl of Athlone (*CP*, i. 300).

[271] William sailed from Duncannon Fort, near Waterford, on 5 September, landed near Bristol the next day at seven in the evening, and arrived at Windsor the evening of 9 September (*London Gazette* [2590, 2591]; Luttrell, ii. 102–3).

[272] Ferdinand Wilhelm, duke of Würtemberg-Neustadt (1659–1701), a lieutenant-general in Austria and Hungary, was commander-in-chief of the Danish force in Ireland. Later he supported William in the military campaigns of the Low Countries, becoming the governor of Dutch Flanders (*The Danish Force in Ireland, 1690–1691*, ed. K. Danaher and J. G. Simms [Dublin, 1962], 141–2). John Churchill, first duke of Marlborough (1650–1722), entered the Irish war at the head of forces sent into southern Ireland following the siege of Limerick. After his success at Cork and Kinsale he was not involved in the later Irish battles; he would distinguish himself in the War of the Spanish Succession. Colonel Roger MacElligott (c. 1650–1702), earlier with the earl of Pembroke's regiment in Holland, was captured at the fall of Cork and imprisoned in the Tower until 1697, when he went to France as a colonel in the Clancarty regiment (*English Army Lists*, ii. 150, 155). Henry Fitzroy, first duke of Grafton (1663–1690), the illegitimate son of Charles II and Barbara Villiers, countess of Castlemaine, was a naval officer in the 30 June 1690

sentt his summons to the towne and fortt of Kingsaile by the earle of
Marlbrow, Octtober the first, and the prince of Wirtemberge; **Octtobr
i6** to whome itt was dellivered up the i6. And the garrison conssisting
of aboutt iioo men marched the next day, bagg and baggage; the loss
of English before this place was little less then 300 kild and wounded.[273]
And affter haveing settled Ireland returns for England to the k[ingdom]
and parliament.

i69i, January i6 The king, haveing settled his affairs att home and
in Ireland, imbarked for Hollond att Graves End with a numerous
rettinue January i6; **i9** and affter severall fatigus hee arrives att The
Hague January i9 to the unexpressable joy of the Hollonder;[274] and
wher hee received all the complements of all persons of distintion and
the conferrats by there personall attendance on him: as the electtors of
Brandenburge and Bavaria; the dukes of Luxenburge; the landgrave of
Hess; the dukes of Zell; the duke of Wolffenbattle; the prince of
Cremercy; the prince of Wyrtemburge; Prince Walldeck; the marquis
of Gastanaga, govener of Flanders; the countt de Windittsgratz, the
emperrors plenypotentiary; the counte de Prela Dorya from the duke
of Savoy; the minesters of the ellector Pallatine, of the electtors of
Sexony, Mentzs, Tryers, and Collogne and of severall other princes.[275]
All came to The Hague to King William to conscert measurs to
preserve the libertys of Europe; wher the king made them a speech
which soe took with these princes thatt itt was imediatly resolved thatt
two hundred twenty two thousand pounds should be by him imploy'd
against France by them given and subscribed to.[276] Affter which the

battle at Beachy Head, then joined the forces Marlborough led into Ireland. Grafton
died on 9 October of wounds suffered in the engagement at Cork (*CP*, vi. 43–5; *London
Gazette* [2598]).

[273] Story estimates that the garrison at Kinsale had 1,200 men and that the English
lost 200 killed and wounded (145). The *London Gazette* (2604) reports the Irish surrender
on 15 October.

[274] The king sailed from Gravesend at around four on the afternoon of 16 January
'with divers of the Nobility, and other Persons of Quality' (*London Gazette* [2628]); he
arrived in The Hague on 20 January, after having landed the day before on the fog- and
ice-bound coast.

[275] The *London Gazette* describes the joy and celebration as well as lists some of the
many dignitaries (2631–3, 2636–8); some are also listed in *The History of the Royal Congress
at The Hague* (London, 1691). Frederick III was the elector of Brandenburg; Maximilian
II Emanuel, the elector of Bavaria. Others in Freke's list include François Henri de
Montmorency-Bouteville, duke of Luxembourg; Charles, landgrave of Hesse-Cassel;
Georg Wilhelm, duke of Celle; Anton Ulrich, duke of Wolfenbüttel; Charles, prince of
Württemberg; Georg Friedrich, prince of Waldeck; Don Francisco Antonio Agurto,
marquess of Gastañaga; Gottlieb Amadeus von Windischgrätz, representing Emperor
Leopold I; Count de Prela Doria, envoy from the duke of Savoy, Victor Amadeus II;
Count d'Autel, from the Palatine elector John William Joseph; Sieur d'Haxhuysen, from
the elector of Saxony, John George III.

[276] A 27 February (NS) report from The Hague in the *London Gazette* (2638) says the

King returned for England the 2i of March. **May 3** And resolveing to head the Confederate army himselfe, goes for Hollond May the 3d.[277] Wher haveing settled the state of the warr for the year ensueing, returned to England, wher he mett thatt agreeable news, the surrender of Limbrick to Generall Ginckle (wher Tirrcollnell dyed of a broken hartt). And with the conquest of this place ended the Irish warrs Octtober 3d, i69i.[278]

Occtober i9 King William arrives att Kensington, when the parliamts meets Octtober 22.

i692, June 7 And on the 7 of June i692 following was a most tirrible earthquake which shook the island of Jamaica as allmost entirely ruined the towne of Portt Royall, thatt besids damages was noe less then fifteen hundred persons perished in itt.[279] And aboutt two months affter, viz., September the 8, perticulerly in London was there another earthquak. The king was then att diner in his camp, which shook soe much thatt all people apprehended the fall of the house before he could gett outt of itt.[280]

Aboutt the begining of this year dyed Robertt Boyle, Esqr, a man exemplary for his pyety, goodness, and experymentall philosopher these latter ages ever produced. His life was a continued example of goodness and pyety.[281]

i692 This year the duke of Hannover, a Protestantt prince, was through King William intrest advanst to be an electtor of the empire; and therby a ninth electturatte was constittuted, which never before exceeded eightt.[282]

Confederation agreed to commit 220,000 men, not pounds; England pledged a force of 20,000.

[277] William arrived in London on 13 April; he sailed from Harwich on the morning of 2 May for Holland (*London Gazette* [2653, 2658]; Luttrell, ii. 208, 219).

[278] The king landed at Margate on 19 October and arrived that evening at Kensington. Tyrconnell died of a stroke on 14 August, though it was rumoured that he had been poisoned. Articles for the surrender of Limerick were signed on 3 October (*London Gazette* [2707, 2705]; Luttrell, ii. 296).

[279] News of the 7 June Jamaican earthquake reached London in August and appeared in the *London Gazette* (2791); Evelyn (v. 115–16) and Luttrell (ii. 533–4) also record the event. *The Truest and Largest Account of the Late Earthquake in Jamaica, June the 7th. 1692* (London, 1693) says the number of dead 'is commonly reckoned at fifteen hundred persons, besides Blacks' (4–5).

[280] An earthquake that occurred on Thursday, 8 September, lasted, the *London Gazette* notes, about a minute 'and was felt very sensibly', though no damage occurred (2800; Evelyn, v. 115). A report in the next issue of the gazette 'From His Majesty's Camp at Grammen' (2801) describes the threat to the house in which the king was dining.

[281] Robert Boyle (1627–1691) died on 30 December. The son of the first earl of Cork, Boyle was among the founders of the Royal Society and an important natural philosopher who made significant contributions to physics and chemistry.

[282] The *London Gazette* (2811) carries a report from Ratisbon that Ernst August, duke of Hanover, was to become 'one of the Princes Electors of the *Empire*'. The Electoral College

Scottland being now in perfectt quiett and the govermentt of Ireland settled, [fol. 85v] the king imbarks for England to meett his parliament the i8 of Octtober i692 affter having settled his affaiers in Hollond and saffly landed att Yarmouth the 29 of Octtober. The queen mett him att New Hall and went to Kensington through the city, wher the lord maire, alldermen, and recorder, [and] shrieffs attended their majestyes to honour their citty with his presence att a dinner with all the acclamation of joy could be made for his hapy returne from those hassards hee had encountred.[283]

i692, November 4 The parliamentt mett, when the king made them a most ellegantt speech and proclaimed a day of thanksgiveing. **i4** The Commons address to the king with their thanks for his judicyous speech November i4, wher they satt till the i4 of March and the king had passed 2i actts; the parliamt was prorogued till the 2d of May.[284]

i694, Febuary i8 Towards the end of Febuary a fleett of marchants ships under the convey of men of warr commanded by Sir Francis Wheeler, haveing sailed on the i7 of thatt month [for] Gybralltar, towards the straits mett the next day with soe violent a storme which continued all that day and the night following thatt on the i9 day about five a clock in the morning Sir Francis Wheelers own ship, the Sussex, was foundred; and himself with all his men (being aboutt 800), in which was my sister Austins son Captain John Austen, were all drowned and lost except two Moores; as was the Cambrige, and Lumly Castle, the Serpentt Bomb ketch, and the Mary ketch together with the Ittalian Marchantt, the Alleppo Facttor, the Great George, and the Barkshiere bound for Turky, the William for Venice, and the Golden Marchant for Legorne – all English ships driven ashore on the east sid of Gibralter and most of there men lost. The same fate attended ships richly laden: all lost.[285]

---

had expanded from seven to eight electors in 1648; a March 1693 ceremony in Hanover celebrated the election of the ninth electorate, whose candidacy King William actively supported (Ragnhild Hatton, *George I: Elector and King* [Cambridge, Mass., 1978], 15, 46).

[283] William landed at Yarmouth on 18 October and came to Kensington the evening of 20 October. The *London Gazette* (2811–12) notes the arrival and celebration.

[284] The *London Gazette* includes the king's 'most gracious speech' (2816), lists the twenty-one public acts, and reproduces the speech William gave to the members of parliament assembled together in the House of Lords (2853). Parliament was then prorogued until May but did not meet until November (*CJ*, x. 850–1).

[285] Men of war under the command of Admiral Francis Wheeler (1656?–1694) had been sent to Cadiz at the end of 1693 to thwart Turkish attacks on Spanish shipping in the Mediterranean. The fleet encountered a severe storm on 18 February in the strait between Spain and Africa, losing by the end of the next day over 800 lives (Ehrman, *The Navy in the War of William III*, 509–10). The *London Gazette* (2961) lists the ships lost. Luttrell describes further the specific losses (iii. 287); Evelyn notes the 'dismal newes' of 'so vast a losse as had hardly ever been known' (v. 169). John Austen was one of three lieutenants on the *Sussex*, an eighty-gun ship of 490 men (PRO, ADM 8/3); he was baptized in Tenterden on 21 July 1676.

1694, June 8 The Bank of England was formed by the corporation
June 8 and signed by her majesty Queen Mary (the king being in Hollond)
and the charter, which was to pas under the great seale of England affter
the first day of Agust iff the sum of i200000 l. should be subscribed by
thatt time; which the comissioners haveing taken subscriptions, which
was fill'd the whole sume by the 5th of thatt month.[286]

November 8 The King embark'd for England and landed the 9;
and on the i2 the parliamt mett, wher affter the kings speech he
confirmed the actt for a treniall parliamentt, &c.[287]

22 The bishop of Canterbury dyed, Dr John Tillottson, in the 65
yeare of his age; a man of greatt piety, learning, and moderration – his
death much lamented by all lovers of unity and peace – whose sermons
will be a standing patern to posterityе.[288]

Decembr 2i On Fryday, the 2i of December, the good Queen
Mary was taken ill att Kenssington, which proved to be the small pox.
28 Which grew in few days soe violentt thatt her majesty expired in
the armes of a loveing husband the 28 and amidst a courtt drowned
in teares.[289] And December 3i the lords in parliamentt send an adress
of condoleance to the kinge; to which the king thanked them for their
kindnes butt much more for there sence they shewed of there great
loss, which was above whatt he could express.

3i Att the same time the House of Commons presented there adress
to the kinge to condole the irrepairrable loss of thatt most exelent
princess and thatt they would stand by him with their lives and fortunes
to supportt him [against] all his enimies both att home and abroad. To
which the king answered that hee took very kindly their care of him
and the publick espeshally att this time when he was able to think of

---

[286] Parliament authorized the establishment of the Bank of England, and it passed on
8 June 'under the Great Seal' and 'is to pass in like manner immediately after the first
day of August next, if [half] the Sum of Twelve Hundred Thousand Pounds' is subscribed
(*London Gazette* [2982]). Subscriptions began on 21 June, and the entire sum was subscribed
by 2 July (John Clapham, *The Bank of England, A History*, 2 vols. [Cambridge, 1944], i. 18–
19).

[287] The *London Gazette* describes the celebration at the king's return and prints his
address to parliament (3026, 3027); 'the Bill for the frequent Meeting and Calling of
Parliaments' received royal assent on 22 December (*CJ*, xi. 182, 193).

[288] The announcement of the archbishop's death and the characterization of his life
follow closely the *London Gazette* (3030). John Tillotson (1630–1694), who suffered a stroke
several days before his death on 22 November, had been consecrated the archbishop of
Canterbury on 31 May 1691.

[289] The *London Gazette* (3039, 3040) as well as Luttrell (iii. 416–19) records the course of
Queen Mary's illness. Burnet, who was called to the king during this crisis, is especially
noteworthy in his recollection of William's sorrow (iv. 246–7, 249–50), though neither his
nor the other accounts of the final hours mention that the queen died in her husband's
arms.

nothing butt his great loss.[290] Affter which the citty of London and all other parts addresed there condoleance of her to the king. She was a perfectt example of humility and piety, wise and prudent and charitable beyound whatt can be spok of her. Both publick and privatte shee was a perfictt example of conjucall love, chastity, and obedience. And itt is remarkable thatt when Docter Tennison, arch bishop of Canterbery, went to comfort the king his majesty answered he could nott butt griefe since he had lost a wife who in seventeen years had never bin guilty of an indiscretion. She maintain'd sincirity intirely and had an avertion to any slanderour or any evill speaker and was as free from scensures as deserveing them. And when she received the intimation of aproaching death, itt was with an entire resignation to Gods will. To sum up all, she was a tender, respectfull wife, a kind friend, a gentle mistress, a good Christian, a dobonair queen, and the best of women, and the glory and delight of this happy island.[291] E Frek

[fol. 86r]

1710, Aprill 30 I paid Mr Smith, vicker of Winch, for officiating in my parish church att Billny; and by my sister Austen and his perswation were prevailed with to except Mr Buck againe, whom I putt by for taking a licence from the bishop of Norwich. Heer being noe tithes on this place, I stood outt all his and the chancellors threats before I fill'd this vacancy of Billney; and had nott then done itt butt the apprehention of my death, being very ill, and I were nott willing iff I dyed to leave my church wher I hope to lye withoutt a minester.

May i Soe thatt May the first I entered Mr Buck my currate to my church of Billney.

28 May the twenty eight, Whitson Tuesday, sitting in the chamber with my deer sister Austen (who came to see me the 2d of March last past), I were taken aboutt noone allmost blind with a mulltitude of black flyes before my eyes, of which I never had one in my life before, I being neer sixty eight years of age. And iff this be vapours in my head, from them, good Lord, deliver mee, Eliz Frek, thatt have and doe labour under them above three months allredy.

May the first I entered Mr Buck my curratt att Billney for feare I

---

[290] Parliament resolved on 29 December to express its sorrow to the king through the speaker; their condolences and the king's response, which was read to the members on 1 January (*CJ*, xi. 194), appear in the *London Gazette* (3040).

[291] Some of the unparalleled 'universal sorrow' seen in both court and town (Burnet, iv. 247) is apparent in the issues of the *London Gazette* relating the kingdom's tributes (3041, 3043–6, among others). Thomas Tenison (1636–1715), who was at the queen's deathbed, praises her wisdom, prudence, piety, charity, and humility in *A Sermon Preached at the Funeral Of Her Late Majesty Queen Mary ... March 5, 1695* (London, 1695).

hould dye and noe minester in the parish affter I had three quarters
)f a yeare contended with the bishop and chancellour of Norwich. To
)oth which I wrott word when I permitted him to take their licence,
vhich was September 15, 1710, thatt I excepted him butt dureing his
;ood behaivoure to the church and to mee dureing my pleasure. Both
is to his time and his sallary I would nott be tyed to butt whatt I
hought fitt or he deserved, and soe I told him att his entrance; and
hatt I would never more be plagued with a drunken, debauched priest
is I have binn with Mr Adams for aboutt thirty eight yeare; and iff he
lid nott like itt, I was offered another would soe take itt on these
.earms. I wrott the chancellour word I placed him in Billney September
,5, Docter Thomas Tanner, as witness Eliz Freke.

28 of May, Whittson Tuesday, sitting in my chamber with my deer
;ister Austen aboutt noon, I were taken with a mulltitude of black flyes
n my eyes, which I never had before in my life, did almost quite take
iway my sight; which has now continued soe to me neer 4 month to
ny greatt grief and torture, and for my comfort I am told itt is
vappours. From which, good Lord, deliver Eliz Frek.

Agust 9 Mr Edgworth of Winch was arested for a hundred pounds
)y nine baylyes who brok up as many locks to take him, who was att
.ast found run up two mens length in his chamber chimney with a
)istoll charged. This 100 l. was given his servant towards the purchas
)f his wife, which afferwards (shee the maid) was amongst them
)oysoned to save thatt mony, which was first 200 l. And itt was butt
just before Edgworth had the impadence to writt me word Mrs Barns,
his wife, was worth him twelve thousand pounds.[292] In answer to which
I writt him word when hers and his debts were paid they would have
little enough.

10 Mr Edgworth and his man stole away for feare of further trouble
in thatt, and I had writt to him before he went 6 or 7 letters for aboutt
fowre pound rentt they owed me for my 5 akers of land, which affter
theire plowing up my moire they have thrown my land up in common.[293]
This is there kindness returned to me for lending them a hundred and
fiffty pounds fowre yeare gratis when none in the country would trust
her for five shillings. E Frek

---

[292] Thomas Barnes, the son of William and Anne Barnes of East Winch, married
Isabella, the daughter of Sir John Griffith and the widow of William Langley (Blomefield,
ix. 150). Their son, Henry Humphrey Barnes, was buried in East Winch on 21 February
1694/5, four years after the 1691 death of his father. Thomas Barnes' will stipulated that
if his son died without a lawful male heir, William Langley, a stepson, 'shall have all my
Mannors'; Barnes' wife was to live at East Winch Hall, enjoying during her natural life
the 'rents issues and profitts of all my Mannors Lands Tenements and hereditaments'
(PRO, PROB 11/405/128).

[293] Moire or moyre, a possible variation of mere and meare: marsh, bog, or swampy
ground; also a boundary.

20 Satterday, the 20, I received a fattall letter of the death of my deerst sister the Lady Norton from my cosin Mills in London.[294] **2.** Butt I humbly thank my God, affter my being allmost a week destracted for her, by the same hand I heard shee was recovered and sentt a most kind letter to me to come to her, which iff alive and able I purpose by Gods permision to doe in the spring. Eliz Freke

22 The bishop of London (Dr Compton) for himself and the clergy of London and Westminster to the number of a hundred and fiffty, i50 presented this adress to the queen, who subscribed itt himself and his brethren and then caryed itt to the courte to Kensington to her againss the Pretender:[295]

May itt please your majesty,

Our harts haveing all along accompanied the Church of England in our dutifull applycation to your majesty with the indignation shown [fol. 86v] att the presentt unpresented attemptt lately made to under mine nott only our constitution in the church and state butt our religion and govermentt allsoe, we were the less eager to lay hold on this occattion of approaching your throne because wee had offten and freely declared our selves on these heads from the pullpitt under the eye of your majesty and in the face of the whole world.

Butt the time is now come when we can noe longer be innocently sillentt since the acknowledgmentt of your majestyes tittle and heriditory authority is oppenly and boldly represented as in a plaine declaration in favour of the Pretender.

Wee looke upon the clergy as deeply involved in this malliciou callamy and therfore think our selves obliged to express our uttmos abhorance of any such disguised and tratiours intention; which our harts intirely devotted to your majesty are nott cullpable of harbering nor none butt the avowed or secred frinds of the Pretender would in order to facillitate there wicked and darke designes have endeavoured to fasten on us.

We have sworne and are steadfastly purposed to pay all dutty and alleageance to your majesty as to our rightfull and lawfull soveraigne whose tittle and crown by desentt has bin affirmed and recognised by all our leige people in full parliament.

[294] Elizabeth, the daughter of Cheney Culpeper (the older brother of Freke's mother born in 1640, had married Christopher Milles, who was buried on 22 January 1700/1 in Herne.

[295] The *London Gazette* (4734) and the *Norwich Gazette* (iv. 204) reprint the address presented on 23 August at Kensington and the queen's answer. Neither mentions the 150 clergy. Before Henry Compton (1632–1713) opposed the succession of James II, he had been bishop of London. William restored him to the ecclesiastical position, and Compton became in Anne's reign an increasingly zealous supporter of the established church.

And we know of noe other person who has any claime to our obedience, nor will we ever doe any thing either in or affter your majestyes reigne which may seem in the least favour of such pretentions.

On your majesty alone our eyes are fixed. All our vows and wishes are imployed for the length of peace and prosperity of your reigne and, when itt shall please God for our sins to withdraw soe invalluable a blesing, which all acknowledg the most illusturous house of Hannavour as the next heaire in the Protestantt line to have the only right of assending the throne and indisputable tittle to our allegiance and security from popery.

We thank God from the bottom of our hartts for the legall provision in this regard made to secure us from popery and arbitary power, which wee once through the devine assistance vigorously and sucessfully withstood when they were breaking in uppon our constetution. Nor shall wee faile to manyfest an equall zeale against them when ever and by whatt means soeever they shall mediate a retturne.

This we are firmly perswaded is the unanimous sense and resollution of the clergy nott only of these cittyes butt of the whole kingdome, as wee doubtt nott will appeer to your majesty when soever they shall have an oppertunitye of expressing itt in the next convocattion.

In the mean time wee shall nott cease to bow our knees to God and most ardenttly pray for a continuance to bless your armes and councell till they have subdued our restless enemies of our peace both att home and abroad, defeated the menaces of the proud and the devices of the craffty, and scatter'd all the people thatt delightt in warr.

23 This above address was presented by the lord arch bishop of London (Docter Compton) in person and subscribed by a (i50) hundred and fiffty of his immediatt clargy under his authority in London and Westminster the 23 day of Agust i7io.

To which her majesty gave this answer: I take very kindly the assurance of your dutty you give me in this address and the regard you express for the Protestant relegion. Eliz Freke

September 2d I transcribed this from the London Post Man September 2d, i7io: They write from Dublin thatt thatt citty haveing caused the effegye of King William which was latly most villanously defaced to be repaired and haveing putt a new trunchon into his hand in greatt solemnity, the 24 companies of the citty attending the same, the House of Commons came the i7 of September to the following resolution: nomyne contradycente, thatt the thanks of the House be given to the lord maire, shrifes, commons, and cittyzens of the citty of Dublin (who did errectt a statue in honour of King William the 3d of glorious memory) for their greatt zeale and care in repaireing of thatt noble monumentt of their gratitude to our late deliverer from popery,

and slavery, and the French powre and supporting the honour and
memory of thatt greatt prince in soe sollemne and publick a maner.[296]
E Frek

[fol. 87r]

i710 Munday morning, September the eleventh, my sister Austen
left me very ill att Bilney and wentt to London her selfe and i maide
Shee hired a whole coach to her self att Lin unknown to mee, EF.[297]

September 25 Monday, 25 of September, I were arrested in my
chamber by two rogues taken outt of Norwich jayle for the purpose by
Mr Carter, who cheated me of butt last year above ten pounds – by
name Beets and Hollond, who both seised me while I weer sitting by
my self in my chamber wrighting.[298] They both ransack my chamber,
and seized and carryed away whatt of my papers they thought fitt, and
broke my cane, and kept me frighted above three howrs whilst they
garded my door to serch my house and by itt to provok my passon,
which was my loss by Dawson of above a hundred pounds to Eliz Frek

November 3d Fryday nightt, November 3d, I were sitting in my
chamber all alone reading, when on a suden my head caught on fire
and in three minits time burntt all my head close to my haire.
And I being all alone could nott gett them off or any body to me thatt
itt was Gods greatt mercy I was nott burntt to death, and I doe humbly
thank him for itt.

December 2d Saterday night was the dreadfulest hurrycane of
wynd and weather for all thatt night allmost equall to the greatt wynd
November the 26, i703, as was likewise the fowrth day of this present
December.[299] These two winds have blown down my barns and
unthachtt allmost all my howses in this parish of Billney.

i710 The greatest providence in the world I were nott burntt to

---

[296] The entry for 2 September is also repeated on this date a year later (fol. 88v). An
asterisk and the notation 'see three leaves further to this marke' indicate that Freke
intended the more complete entry, which in this edition replaces the original. The
transcription is from the *Post-Man* (1909), which carried on 2 September 1710 the report
from Dublin of the 17 August 1710 resolution (*CJI*, iii. 792); Freke's transcription, other
than spelling variants, is accurate except for her error 'of September'. The vandalism to
the statue of King William in College Green occurred on 25 June 1710. The statue
erected in 1701 was the site each November of ceremonies commemorating the king's
birthday and his 1688 landing in England (J. T. Gilbert, *A History of the City of Dublin*, 3
vols. [Dublin, 1861], iii. 40–5).

[297] This and the next three entries have been shifted in this edition from fol. 94v, where
they originally followed the household inventory.

[298] See above, p 103 n. 186.

[299] The storm is not mentioned in the *Norwich Gazette*; Blomefield, however, notes the
'great tempest' of lightning, thunder, and hail that hit Norwich on 5 December 1710 (xi
432).

death, nott able to help my self or move outt of my chaire. For which mercy the greatt God make me ever thankfull. Eliza Freke

Decembr 2, 4, 5 December 2d, being Satterday nightt, was a most grievous storme of wind and raine as was the 4 and 5th of December litle inferryor to the greatt storme in November the 27, 1703. Thatt storme blow'd down allmost all my houses in the parish, and this has allmost perfitted itts ruiens.

1710/11 Jannuary the first, my unhappy birth day, I haveing all my tennants to dine with me to begin the New Yeare, I were like againe to bee burnt to death and to be knock'd att head by the fall of my chamber chimney then affire over the kitching. Butt by Gods providence and the help of my tennants and company, I were carryed away in my chaier, to which I have bin confined now a prisoner neer eighteen monthes with a rhumatisme and my tissick.

Febuary 22 I being very ill sentt for my cosin John Frek downe to me to settle my affaires and my will, as I did to my deerst sister the Lady Norton, and to remove five hundred pounds of mine which lay in the house by me of which I expected every day being robed by my servants and other rogues iff I should dye – which I dayly expected, I were soe ill.

24 Saterday my cosin John Frek went to Lin to gett me bills for itt.

27 He wentt to Elmen to Mr Warner to gett me bills, butt there he failed likewise as hee did about my law suite with Dawson.[300]

28 My deer sister Norton left Leigh and came to Bath for London to come downe to wretched mee two hundred miles, for which I hope God will reward her and for all her kindness to me and mine.

March 2 Fryday, March 2d, my cosin John Frek went to Norwich for me in my coach and carryed with him five hundred pound of mine to returne for London. Which hee did in two bills which was there paid him the 22 of March. Which compleated my three thousand pounds in his hand of myne now since my deer husbands death, being neer five years, June 2, 1706, the fattalles day of my unhappy life, tho my sons, Ralph Freks, birth day: to loose the best of husbands and blest with the undutifullest of sons to mee, I haveing nott heard from him in three years. Beesids hee has deprived for this five yeare of neer eight hundred pound a year my deer husband left me for my life and above twelve hundred pound in assetts as by accounts of Joseph Jervoise, accounts with my cosin John Freke whom I sent for Ireland to adminester for me, 1707. This is true, Eliz Frek. For which I humbly beg the greatt God to forgive him.

<hr/>

[300] Richard Warner, the son of James and Mary Warner of North Elmham, was a prominent attorney as well as a Norfolk justice of the peace. He died in 1757 at the age of eighty-nine (Carthew, iii. 125).

3 I paid my cosin John Frek for his jorney downe thirty guinyes.

5 The 5, fifth, hee returned from Norwich and wentt from Billney to London the seventh of March, being Wensday.

Tuesday, sixth of March, I sentt my maid Sarah to London to wait on my deer sister downe to my Billney, wher for three weekes she was dissapoynted of the stage coach and deneyd mine coming up to her And I a diseased criple with a rhumatisme and tisick confined to a chaire for this eighteen months past. Eliz Freke

[fol. 87v]

Satterday, March the 24, i7io, my deer sister the Lady Norton came downe to me from London to Billney; I fetched her in my coach from Seche.[301]

i7ii, March 25 Being the 25, shee was overturned in my coach goeing into the church yard affter shee had on my earnest reques come this long and kind jorney to mee.

Aprill ii From Venia Aprill ii they writt the emperor found himself indisposed, which proved to be the small pox; **i7** of which they being nott soe kindly as hoped for, he dyed of them the i7 instand aboutt i and i2 att night in convulltions to the greatt disorder of thatt and the disapoyntmentt of our English allyes.[302] The dauphin was taken ill at Mendan in the nightt between 9 and io a clock instantt, and the next day the distemper proved the small pox. **i2** The i2 they begun the forty howrs prayers for his recovery. **i4** And the i4 att six att night he lost his speech and dyed in convulltions att eleven a clock att night aged 49 years and 5 monthes and i4 days, born i66i the first o November; and hee was marryed in the yeare i680 to Mary Ann o Bavaria, sister to the ellector of thatt name, by whom he had three sons: the duke of Burgundy (now dauphin); 2d, the duke of Anjow; 3d the duke of Berry.[303]

i7ii, Aprill 24 They write from Dublin the i7 instantt thatt the Sunday before a greatt fire broke outt att the councell chamber which consumed the same as allsoe the treasury and most of the roles in the

---

[301] Setchey or Setch, by the River Nar about four miles south of King's Lynn.

[302] The *Daily Courant* (1969) reports that convulsions from smallpox seized the Holy Roman Emperor Joseph I (1678–1711) at four in the morning of 17 April (NS) and that he died at noon, not at night. With the emperor's death the Habsburg hope of controlling Spain diminished (Charles W. Ingrao, *In Quest and Crisis: Emperor Joseph I and the Habsburg Monarchy* [West Layfayette, Ind., 1979], 218).

[303] The *Daily Courant* (1961) reprints the 22 April (NS) news from The Hague describing the course of the dauphin's fatal illness; a similar version of the last days in the *Norwich Gazette* (v. 237) adds many of the biographical details Freke includes as well as a eulogy The son of Louis XIV and Maria Theresa, the infanta of Spain, Louis de France (1661 1711) was the father of Philip V, a central figure in the conflict over the Spanish succession

muster master generalls office and books, &c., in the survivour generalls office. All which with papers and books of severall other office were all burntt and consumed.[304]

May i Resolved thatt itt appeers in this presentt parliamet, i7ii, thatt of the mony granted for the publick service in the last parliamentt ther are still in arrears to Xmas i7io thirty five millions, three hundred and two thousand pounds, one hundred and seven pounds, eighteen shillings, and nine pence (35302i07–i8–9), of which noe accountt has binn given to the auditors.[305]

7 Monday morne my deer sister the Lady Norton came to my chamber and informed me thatt my servantt John Preston was a rogue burntt in the hand and thatt he had gott into my service under a falce cirtificate contrived with by my own maid Sarah Flowrs, who had lived with me above three years [and] was privy to itt and all this his theiffreys and rogeryes whilst with mee.

ii They both [took] all they could from me the eleventh of May and att midnight god into my house againe; and on Fryday I paid them both all off and turned them outt of doors, I nott knowing the many severall things they had stole from me, haveing hardly gon cross my chamber for allmost two years and then with a hard shifft to see my house allmost gutted by this rogue and whore, whose designe was on my life when my sister should leave me, they being provided with two case of pistols of my own and a long gun taken outt of my clossett for thatt purpose, as I were informed. Butt my God by my deer sister prevented itt.

i5 Tuesday, the i5, I gott warrants for apprehending of them, butt they crosed the watter, and I must be contented with my [fol. 88r] severall loses of all sorts and am most thankfull to God for my life. Eli. Frek

i7ii, May 23 Wensday, May the 23, being ill in my chamber and my deer sister Lady Norton by me, Spice the bayly came up to my chamber and arrested me att the suite of the rogue John Dawson, whome I putt into Norwich jaile a twelve month before for a debt of neer a hundred pounds he owed me of which I never had a peny affter my spending above a hundred pounds in law affter itt. He brok jaile (Mr Warner being my atturny) and impudently dar'd to come to my chamber and twice to arrest mee, E Frek. And the 24 of June the bayly sent me back my appeerrance againe – I paying his fees, which I did by Richard Taff.

---

[304] The report of the fire that destroyed the council chamber, including the surveyor general's office, located on Essex Street appears in both the *Post Boy* (2488) and the *Norwich Gazette* (v. 238).

[305] On 5 May the House of Commons considered specific arrears in the taxes of this amount reported on 24 April (*CJ*, xvi. 613, 629–36).

26 Aboutt the twenty six of May I had a letter outt of Ireland from my son datted the 12 of March 1710 and, I think, the first I have received from him this three years, which letter I transcribed and sent itt to London to my cosin John Frek to answer itt.

28 or some little time affter I had another letter from my cosin Arthur Barnard, which I likewise transcribed and sent itt to London for my cosin John Frek to peruse; and the next week I answered that as I thought fitt.[306] E Frek

28 or 29 I sentt Mr Warner, my atturny, a note under John Dawsons own hand datted June 22, 1706, wherin he acknowledges to owe me att the death of my deer husband fiffty pounds payable to me on demand. This note I sent Mr Warner by Mr Buck, minester of Billney. E Frek

June 14 I paid Mr Berners ten pounds for five thousand of reed, the worst was ever used by mortall, as I did likewise pay him 9 ginyes last year for three thousand allmost as bad; which is now the last ever St Maryes shall ever cheat me of.[307]

24 Midsomer Day, Sunday, the 24 of June, I humbly thank my good God I wentt in my own coach to my own church att Bilney, wher I received the blesed sacrament with twelve more pertakers with mee, amongst which my deer sister the Lady Norton. Wher I did in thankfullness to my God consecrate my new silver cupp and new bread plate and my new Common Prayer Book by Mr Buck, minester of the place, as I did last yeare a large sillver flagon I bought for this church consecratted by Mr Smith, vicker of Winch.[308] E Freke

27 The 27 of June, being Wensday, I did in my own coach endeavour to goe up to London to carry up my deer sister Norton, who had bin soe kind to me to doe penance heer with me att Billney for a quarter of a year, viz., from the 25 of March last past; which I shall never forgett.

29 Fryday, 29, I humbly thank God I gott safe to London with my

---

[306] Arthur Bernard (1666–1732), Francis' younger brother and the husband of Anne Power, had been an officer in the Bandon militia and the high sheriff of County Cork; later he would be elected to parliament and hold the position of Bandon's provost (Ffolliott, 35; Smith, ii. 214; Bennett, 484–6, 562–4).

[307] The 'remarkable species of reeds' found in the Freebridge marshlands was valued as 'a very durable and neat thatch for houses, and are said to last from thirty to forty years. Thatching is executed in this country in a style altogether superior to many other places' (John Chambers, *A General History of the County of Norfolk*, 2 vols. [Norwich, 1829], i. 371).

[308] The cup and cover along with the flagon remain in the safekeeping of the diocese. 'The cup, 7 1/4 ins. in height and 4 1/8 ins. in diameter, having only one mark, that of Jno. Jackson'. Both the cup and cover are inscribed 'Given by Eliz. Freke to the use of her Parish Church of West Bilney in Norfolk, where the corps of her deceased husband, Percy Freke, Esq., is deposited in a vault built by her under or near the Chancell, A.D. 1711' (Radcliffe, 'Church Plate in Norfolk', 265).

deer sister, with my fowre servants, and with my two coach horses and one horseman to rid by. For which great mercy God ever make me thankfull. Eliz Frek

[fol. 88v]

i7ii, Jully i5 In London I staid a fortnight and two dayes and rested my selfe and horses; and Sunday, the i5 of July, St Swithens Day, I left my deer sister Norton att her house and came affter diner from London in order to come downe to my own Billney with my fowre servants in my own coach. **i8** Wher with my two horses and one to rid by the coach, I doe most humbly thank my God I gott safe home in two days and a halfe to my own deerly beloved Billney the i8 of Jully.

Agust 7 I made an end of new reeding my little barne and the back house att the Maner Farme, for which I paide Gibs the reader for his work in itt ten pounds, fourteen shillings, and six pence; and I paid Mr Parker of Lin for rush rope for them, 3 grose and a halff, aboutt thirtty shillings; and for splints, eightt shillings; and for five thousand of reed for them, ten pound; and for carting the reed with twenty carts att six shillings a day cost me six pound; and the bridg mony and drink ther cost me fiffteen shillings; and a load of rye straw to rooff them cost me ten shillings.[309] Soe thatt the reeding of this barne cost mee with the maner back house thirtty pounds in a month time of redy mony, as wittnes Eliz. Freke. And nott a hundred of reed left mee <in the margin: 29–i7–6>.

[fol. 89r]

i7ii, September i2 Our greatt fleet new made by this queen for the South Sea Company (to fetch gould, of which this new lord of Oxford is made govenour) under the comand of Sir Hovenden Wallker, Major Generall Hill, and Benett, &c., came into the Spanish River Bay Septembr the i2, i7ii, in order to attack Quebeck.[310] **2i** Wher on

---

[309] Probably Nicholas Gibbs, the husband of Frances Thrower and the father of a son buried in West Bilney in 1707, though possibly either Luke or Thomas Gibbs, whose marriages are also recorded in the Swaffham parish register. A Thomas Parker of Chequer Ward is listed in the 1703 and 1704 land taxes of King's Lynn, but not identified by trade.

[310] Robert Harley (1661–1724), chancellor of the exchequer, was appointed lord treasurer and created earl of Oxford in May 1711, the month the House of Commons passed the bill to fund the national debt by offering creditors shares in the trading corporation known as the South Sea Company. Rear-admiral Hovenden Walker (d. 1728) was the naval commander of the expedition; after its failure he sailed to Jamaica to become its commander-in-chief, but he was later criticized for his leadership of the earlier Canadian expedition and struck from the list of admirals in 1715. He defended his conduct in *A Journal, or Full Account of the late Expedition to Canada*, published in 1720. John Hill (d. 1735)

the 2i day they gott up part of the river of Canada, which is i3o leagus long to Quebeck. **23** Which proveing very foggy all day and nightt, aboute forty leagus of Quebeck nine of our transportt ships struck up on the rocks and were all lost with att least 8oo men in them beesids ther store ship of provision; and with greatt diffillculty escaped our whole fleett of men of warr and convoyes, who were much damaged by the rocks, &c. This is a sad begining of getting gold by the conquest of new countryes, and for this sad accidentt the Queen Ann has given order to hinder the saileing of the fleett under Commodore Bennett by reason of the ill success of the expydition against Quebeck.[311]

Octtober 9 This day, being Octtober 9, came outt her majestyes proclamation for the sitting of the parliamentt the i3 of November nextt for the dispatch of mighty and importunatte affaiers.[312]

September 3d September the 3d, i7ii, I were warned in as the head of Billney to appeere before 9 or io comisioners for the drains of Sandringham Hey, which I utterly refused the doeing of for feare of a presidentt on the fens of Sechy River.[313] And I wrott to the bench this ensueing letter:

Sir,
    I received your warrants datted the 27 of Agust last wherein you are

[311] was appointed brigadier-general in command of the land forces. The name Bennett does not appear among the lists of officers included in *The Walker Expedition to Quebec, 1711*, ed. Gerald S. Graham, *The Publications of the Champlain Society*, 32 (1953).

[311] The account of the unsuccessful Quebec expedition follows closely that in the *Norwich Gazette*, v. 262, 11 October; Freke, however, confuses the date of the report from Canada (12 September) with the month the fleet entered the Gulf of Saint Lawrence and met disaster on the river (August). A John Bennett or Bennitt, commissioned as captain on 1 May 1695, was at this time in command of the seventy-gun *Lennox*, which in October was 'Designed on foreign service'. In November he was ordered to The Downs, where other ships were assembling 'to Cruize against the Dunkirke ships', but was then ordered to Portsmouth and later sailed to Saint Helena and the Cape (*Commissioned Sea Officers*, 30; PRO, ADM 8/11 and ADM 8/12).

[312] The *Norwich Gazette* (v. 262) notes and the *London Gazette* (4911) reprints the 9 October proclamation: 'the said Parliament shall on the said Thirteenth Day of November be Held and Sit for the Dispatch of divers Weighty and Important Affairs'. The commission from the queen for proroguing the legislative body was also read in parliament on 9 October (*CJ*, xvi. 693).

[313] The River Nar was known, among other names, as Sandringham Eau or Ea and Sechey. Proposals dealing with the flooding of lands and silting of rivers caused by drainage systems such as the Denver Sluice were pressing concerns especially in the Lynn area (Thomas Badeslade, *The History of the Ancient and Present State of the Navigation of the Port of King's-Lyn, and of Cambridge* [London, 1766]; H. C. Darby, *The Draining of the Fens*, 2nd edn. [Cambridge, 1956]). Concerned about the obstruction and flooding in the area from Sechey Bridge to Long Bridge, the general session of sewers proposed that the river 'might be Well and Sufficiently ditched Scowered & Cleansed by the Landowners on either Side' under penalty of five shillings a rod; commissioners and concerned owners were to meet before 20 September to resolve the issue (NRO, DB 9/10/fol. 9r).

pleased to dereictt me as the cheife inhabitantt of Billney to appeer att
the K[ing]s Head att Sechy iff I think fitt the 3d instantt.[314] Which tho
I am nott concerned in the effect of this warrantt, yett, gentlemen, I
think itt fitt to obey authoritye; and therfore I have sentt two of my
tenants to waite on you and receive your commands. Butt for this river
neer fowre miles from me, I humbly conceive I have noe concerne in
itt, itt haveing never bin done by mee this thirty seven years butt once,
trictt by Mr Person of Midleton injenuity aboutt seven years past
unknown to mee.[315] Nor had I ever ordered my attendance on itt before
either in Mr Freks time or my 27 years residence past. Therefore I
hope and intreatt the comisioners to concider me as I am, a woman
ignorantt and helpless and an unhappy widow poore and nessesitious;
thatt I may nott have any thing placed on me, I must be forced to
oppose you in my sons rightt. I am, gentlemen, with all due respectt,
your humble servantt,

Eliz. Freke

[fol. 89v]

17ii, September 4 I had a long letter from my deer son outt of
Ireland, which I answered him in September the 5, fiffth, being the
nextt post following. His was datted the tenth of Agust past.

6 Mr Barnes of St Marryes came to see me from the comisioners to
perswad me to nott oppose the comisioners,[316] butt I told him my fixt
resolution was to defend my sons right to my little abillity and nott be
catched by them in a fools trap, and thatt I had now neer a hundred
akers of land lye under water and durst nott turne itt for feare of a
presidentt of being brought into Sechy River or Sandringham Hea,
and thatt I would sooner spend a hundred pound to oppose them then
comply twenty shillings with them tho threatned 5000 l. against mee
att the sesions deep. Which when the time came I sent in my
appeerance, and itt was laid aside.

30 Henry Cross did penance for adulltry with Diana Davy in Billney
church, as did Diana Davy in June before, Midsomer.[317]

Octtobr i Monday, Octtober the first, Mr Buck wentt to Norwich

---

[314] Not listed in the Alehouse Recognizances of 1789.

[315] William Pearson or Peirson appears as a voter from Middleton in the 1715 *Poll for
the Knights of the Shire*, 143, and with his wife − Elizabeth Thurlow, whom he married in
East Walton on 8 June 1687 − in the Middleton parish records. He also served as a
commissioner of sewers.

[316] In the B text Mr Berners, not Barnes of St Marys, tries to sway her (below, p. 275).
Hatton Berners, was one of the commissioners of sewers at the meeting concerning the
dispute over drainage.

[317] Diana Davy gave birth that year to an illegitimate son, Francis, baptized in West
Bilney on 30 May 1711.

(my minester) to receive institution and induction of a liveing given him by Madam Brainswith.[318]

i I writt my third letter to Sir George Norton about lending of him twelve hundred pounds on his bond and judgmentt. Eliz Freke

i3 I finished my worke for a chamber, &c., being above six years aboutt itt, as is heer mentioned hard by. E Frek, i7ii

ii I entered Whittpitt Brack of my five akers, takeing the forfitter of her lease, she owing mee seven or 8 years rentt or more; and I can gett noe mony or account from Mrs Barns, now Mrs Edgworg, or her son Mr Langly for the severall years past.[319] And they haveing ploughed up my moyre with a designe to wrong me of itt, I, Elizabeth, did affter wrighting to Mr Langly the seventh instantt of Octtobr to stop my plough iff he thought fitt, I did the eleventh of Octtober i7ii putt in my own plough; and John Anderson, my then plough man, did then plough itt as farr as Tooly, one of Mr Langlyes tenantts.[320] And Luke Wingfield, one of my tennants thatt formerly rented itt, said was my due. **i6** And I left my plough there till the sixteenth of this month I ended itt, leaveing aboutt of whatt was allotteded my due for a moyre. Eliza Freke

[fol. 90r]

i7ii, Octtobr i5 By Gods permision I, being to goe in my own coach up for London nextt week to make up accounts with my cosin John Frek and place outt aboutt 3000 l. of mine in his hand — I have nothing to show for itt — and beleiveing I shall never returne againe home alive, doe think fitt and proper to make an inventory of some of the best things I leave in my house att Billney. Elizabeth Freke

And first in my uper closett over the hall:

i greatt haire trunk in which is

[318] Julian Branthwait was the widow of William Branthwait of Hethel; the Branthwaits controlled the Bacton living as lord and patron of Bromholm Priory. An inscription on the monument of her husband remembers her as the daughter of Thomas Berney of Swardeston; she died in 1727 at the age of eighty-eight (Blomefield, xi. 21, v. 112).

[319] In 1688 Madam Barnes received from Henry Richardson an eighty-three-year lease of the five acres known as Whitpit Brack at twelve shillings a year. A brack is a piece or tract of land, usually unenclosed and often uncultivated (*EDD*). Thomas Langley (1676–1762?), the second son of Isabella Barnes' marriage to William Langley, married Ann Edgworth, the daughter of his mother's third husband, Robert Edgworth, on 12 March 1709/10 in East Winch. At the death of his brother Roger Langley in 1716, Thomas succeeded to the baronetcy (Blomefield, ix. 150; John Bernard Burke and John Burke, *Extinct and Dormant Baronetcies of England, Ireland, and Scotland*, 2nd edn. (London, 1844), 298–9.

[320] John Tooley and Mary Bodley were married in Middleton on 26 June 1687; their son and daughter were baptized in East Winch; John Anderson's name appears in none of the local parish registers.

i little haire trunk with plats
i gold watch with its case and chaine
6 sillver servers, two of them new
i large silver chocolett pott and mill
i new sillver tea kettle and
i new frame and lamp to itt
i sillver snuff pan and snuffers[321]
2 large sillver candlesticks
2 sillver pintt cans
i2 large silver spoons
8 little double guilt spoons
6 litle sillver spoons, i outt
i large sillver poringer
i new sillver chamber pott
i new wrought tea box
i new milke pott and its cover
i little picture of my saivours sett with dimonds for my watch
i enameled hart sett with amathest
6 gold rings; i bag of gold fring
i gold seale, double coated
8 gold lockets on a ribond of frinds
5 gold lockets; two chains[322]
5 silver salts, three of them new
i little tortershell box with
i little pictur of my deer father, copy
i origanall of my deer unkle William Frek
i three pound peice in gold, given me by my deer father, Ralph Frek
i twenty shilling peice in sillver, given me by my mother in 1648
i weesell skin purs with silver medalion
    Given me by my deer sister Norton:
6 round stools, all of her worke
6 couchens to them, her work
2 long stools to them
i great easy chair, in her house I left in London
                    Eliz Frek

More in this greatt haire trunk is of my close, first, Eliz Freke

2 sticht whitt hollond petticoats, new
i under silk peticoatt, new

---

[321] Scissors-shaped implements for extinguishing candles and trimming their wicks kept
on snuff pans or trays.
[322] In manuscript: 'to change'.

i spoted bracade mantua lined with black, in London[323]
i spoted peticoatt to itt trimed with black, London
i new black cloth mantue, i7io, and
i black cloth peticoat to itt, i7io
i black vellvett mantua lin'd with cloth of gold
i black vellvett peticoate to itt bound with gold
i new bracade silke mantua lined (with changable), i7io[324]
i new petticoate to itt, i7io
6 yards of new bracade silk to this mantua
8 yards of new changable silk to line a mantua, i7io
io yards of new grasett for a coate, i7io[325]
i black and white satten mantua, i7io
i new peticoatt to itt trimed with black lace
i new callicoe mantua lined with purple silk
2 peticoats to itt; i whitt, i purple, i7io
i silk perdysway manta, new, London i7io[326]
i new perdysway peticoat to itt, London i7io
2 large peices of hangings of my own work for a drawing roome, i7ii
2 greatt easy chairs to itt, i7ii
i long couch or squab of the same, i7ii
4 other chaires of the same backs, i7ii
4 seats to them of the same w[ork], i7ii
4 stools of the same to itt, i7ii
2 peices for stools sticht in silke, i7ii
8 couchens stichtt in silk, i7ii
i sticht counterpoyne with silk, i7ii[327]
All these of my own work in six years.
i spotted wastcoatt of Mr Freks
i wrought wastcoat of his I worked, EF[328]
2 bags of slips to imbroder my work[329]
i paire of new black silk stays[330]
with my deer fathers picture framed
                                    Eliza. Freke

---

[323] A loose gown usually of silk or brocade fitted at the waist with a belt or sash, the mantua became increasingly acceptable formal attire (C. Willett and Phillis Cunnington, *Handbook of English Costume in the Seventeenth Century*, 2nd edn. [London, 1966], 176).

[324] Shot silk: a fabric woven or dyed to create a variegated effect.

[325] Grasett or grazet(t): a woollen material.

[326] Paduasoy: a smooth-textured, heavy-weight silk fabric.

[327] Counterpane: a coverlet for the bed, a quilt or bedspread.

[328] Worn by men under another garment such as a doublet, the waistcoat became by the end of the seventeenth century an outer garment, like a coat, buttoned at the waist and reaching to the knees.

[329] Hank or quantity of silk or yarn.

[330] Two pieces of stiff underbodice laced together.

[fol. 90v]

1711, Octtober 15. An account of whatt linnen I putt into my portmantle trunk in my clossett over the hall,[331] Eliz. Freke

2 paire of hollon sheets for my bed[332]
1 paire of fine hollon sheets for strangrs
12 hollon pillebers, used[333]
3 new diaper table clothes, never used[334]
16 new diaper napkins to them
1 long fine damask table cloth
1 shorte sideboard cloth to itt
11 fine damask napkins to them
1 long courser damask table cloth
1 shorter sidboard cloth to itt
14 damask napkins to itt
2 long damask towells to them
4 little laced table clothes
1 new tike squab to my worke[335]

My own clothes are

1 new black furboloe scarfe, 1710[336]
1 paire of new fine hollon sheets, never used butt washed upp, 1711
7 new shiffts, one of them nott made, 1711[337]
12 new cambrick hanchers, 1711[338]
8 yards of new cambrick in 2 p[ieces], 1711
4 new stripp cambrick arpons, 1710[339]
3 new night rails to them, 1710[340]
1 new single strip muslin arpon and
1 new night raile to itt, 1710

[331] Portmantle: northern dialect variant of portmanteau, a travelling-bag or case.

[332] Holland: white linen fabric, originally from Holland.

[333] Variant of pillow-bere: pillowcase.

[334] Table linen woven with a pattern.

[335] A cushion (squab) for a chair or sofa encased in a linen or cotton fabric (tike, an obsolete form of tick).

[336] A furbelow scarf was pleated, gathered, or otherwise trimmed with a flounce.

[337] An undergarment or smock known as a chemise in the eighteenth century.

[338] Napkin or small cloth of fine white linen fabric; also a kerchief worn on the head or shoulders.

[339] Striped apron. White or plain aprons were worn as outer garments about the house; without bibs and richly decorated with lace and embroidery, aprons also complemented dresses.

[340] Gown or loose wrap worn as nightdress.

5 paire of new gloves, i7io
3 new stript muslin arpons, i7io
3 new stript night rails to them, i7io
4 plaine muslin arpons, one unmade
4 plain muslin night rails to them, i7io
i new cambrick cravett, once used, i7io[341]
3 paire of hollon sleevs, new, i7io
2 paire of laced sleeves for me, i7io
i wrought cambrick head, laced, i7io[342]
2 new muslin heads, laced and dresed, never worn, i7io
i new plaine muslin head dres, i7io
2 paire of laced ruffells to them, never worne, i7io
2 laced sutes of head clothes and
2 quoifs, new, of my worke[343]
2 black and whitt silk hanchers, i7io
i new lute string hood, never worn, i7io[344]
i gause hood, new, never worne, i7io[345]
2 tippitts, one of them new velvett[346]
i new black silk arpon, never used, i7io
i new black crape hood, not used, i7io
i long crape scarfe to itt, worne

More in the portmantle trunk is putt in by me, Eliz Freke, Octtober i5, i7ii:

4 stomechers for stays
3 black silk scutions, of my sons[347]
3 new fans; 6 caps
4 new sticht caps; a sable for a cap
3 new men sticht caps; i5 sable tails
4 laced piners of my own work to be contrived[348]
i bag with severall collered and black new ribons; 3 parcell of whit
    thred

---

[341] Cravat: neck scarf or neckwear tied in bows and knots of various fashions.
[342] Head-cloth.
[343] Obsolete form of coif, a close-fitting cap covering the back as well as sides of the head, often tied under the chin and commonly made of linen and decorated with embroidery.
[344] Lustring or lutestring: glossy or lustrous silk fabric.
[345] Gauze: open weave as well as thin, transparent silk, linen, or cotton fabric.
[346] Tippet: cape or short coat covering the neck and shoulders.
[347] Scutcheon, eschutcheon or escutcheon: armorial bearing or coat of arms.
[348] Pinner: white cap with long flaps on each side, which were sometimes pinned at the breast; also a bib pinned on an apron.

io paire of specttles, never used, in a collered bagg and reading glass,
   i7ii
i bagg of Jamacoe spice, &c., i7ii
i little purse of spice
i little bagg of severall things, i7ii
3 parcells of lace of my own work
i canvase bagg with my 5 tallys for 3000 l. in the funds, E Frek[349]
i new sheett covers all
2 laced hanchers of muslin
i little pilleber with cruells left of my work[350] with one tin box of tea
              Eliz Frek

i7ii, Octtober the i6. A note of whatt I putt in the great black trunk by
the fire side, Eliz. Freke

i new plod quilt, never worne[351]
2 yards of new blue cloth for a livery
i linen damask cownterpoyn, new
i new head cloth to itt, never worn[352]
4 curtains to itt;[353] i chocolett mill
2 paire of vallence to itt[354]
i new Indian silk quiltt to my green damask bed, nott used
4 green damask curtains to it
2 paire of vallence to itt
3 plod window curtains to itt, green and whitt, for the best chamber
2 paire of vallence to them
3 plod scarlett window curtains to the dineing roome and
2 paire of valence to itt
i new tea table, given me by my sister Lady Norton; 7 q[uires] of
   paper
i new otter skin muff
4 setts of maps; 4 new tassels
i pilleber with cruels left of my work
          E Frek

[349] Exchequer receipts recorded on wooden rods notched to indicate the amounts, then split lengthwise and one half held by each party to the loan.

[350] Cruel, a variant of crewel, a form of embroidery done with worsted yarn.

[351] Dialect form of plaid.

[352] Cloth placed at the head of a bed.

[353] Curtains that hung from the canopy, enclosing the bed.

[354] Valence or valance, the drapery hung around either the edge of the bed canopy or the bedstead itself.

[fol. 91r]

i7ii, Octtober the i6. An accountt of whatt I putt in the greatt chest under the coffin in my closett, Eliz. Freke

5 whole peices of printed paper for hangings, yard wide
i cloke of my deer husbands, worne
i new grey coat and wascoatt for a livery
i grey cloth wastcoat to itt, both new
i black cloth coat and shamy briches to itt I made for a livery, little worn[355]
i blue cloth coat and wascoatt made for a livery, very little worne
i yellow cloth counterpoyne
i blue tartrain counterpoyne[356]
2 new large blanketts for the best chamber
2 other new blanketts, whipt[357]
2 large blanketts worne to the hall chest
    In the coffin over this chest is
2 boys to my damask bed;[358]
6 cushins, new; and 2 under blanketts.
                    Eliz Freke

Octtober the i6. In the lesser haire trunk in my closett is, E Frek,

2 paire of new course sheets
i4 new diaper napkins, never used
3 hollon wascoats, sticht, of mine
3 diaper table clothes, very little worn
i6 diaper napkins to them
i new larg course diaper cloth, unwhited
ii new napkins to itt of the same
i new umbrella, never used
i finer large diaper table cloth, much used
4 little courser diaper table clothes
2 towells; 4 hollon pillebers

i7ii, Octtober the i6. In the deep broad deale box is in my closett

i callicoe quiltt to the best chamber

---

[355] Variant of chamois, a soft, pliant leather; also an imitation cloth material.
[356] Tartan: patterned woollen cloth.
[357] Bound or edged with an overcast stitch or trimmed with embroidery or gathers.
[358] Ornamental figures of boys placed on the top of bed canopies (Tessa Murdoch, Victoria and Albert Museum).

i callicoe counterpoyne bound with scarlett
2 new grey hamer clothes laced with black to my coach[359]
2 other new hamer clothes bound with scarlett worsted, never used
i new patch work couchen, given mee
i little pilleber with some cloth coller cruells

Eliza Freke

i7ii. An accountt of whatt china and delph, &c., I putt into the deep box behind my closett doore, Octtobr i6

i greatt large jarr, given me by sister Austin
2 high deep open jarrs, by the same
2 greatt high bottles jars, by the same
i larg cover to the greatt jarr; all this given me by my deer sister Austen
4 small china jars for my cabenett
i fine wrought china suger dish with
i fine china cover to itt I bought
3 broad fine china dishes, given me by my deer sister Lady Norton, as was
i china japan tea table by the same[360]
5 fine china tea cups by the same
5 fine china plates to them
5 fine china chocolett cups by ye same
5 fine china plates to them and
i suger blat of the same; all this given me by my deer sister Lady Norton
6 little rattifye china cups[361]
2 china egge bolles, guilded
4 fine china tea cups
2 glass ink bottles; 2 glass salts
i china tea jarr for my cabinett
i china tea pott to itt
2 painted china cups
i2 white china cups for chocolett
6 white china cups for tea or coffy
3 fine china painted cups
6 china tea cups, dark brown
6 spotted china cups with handles to them

[359] Hammer cloth: the covering for the driver's seat.
[360] A japanned or lacquered tea table with a raised edge or gallery around the table top.
[361] Ratafia: liqueur or cordial.

    2 china tea potts with its covers
    i red Portingall tea pott and itts cover[362]
    5 red Portungall cups to itt
    4 little delph basons
    3 little delph basons more
    4 deep delph chocalett cups
                                Eliz Frek.

[fol. 91v]

i7ii. A further account of whatt I putt in the deep box behind the door
in my closett, Octtobr i6

    6 guiltt sconces, new, for candles, given me by my deer sister Lady
        Norton[363]
    i guild sconce to hold my tea cups[364]
    i lignum vite morter[365] and
    i lignum vity pestle to itt, cosin John Frek
    2 paire of lignum vite stands
    3 lignum vitte casters for suger, mustard, and peper[366]
    2 lignum vite cups with covers
    2 deep lignum vitte cups
    i lignum vyte cann
    2 lignum vitte little boxes, Eliz. Frek
    Of Tunbridge ware[367] is
        i paire of stands; i suger siffter
        2 powder boxes; 2 little basons
        2 little high cups; 3 little boxes
        i large punch cup; 2 little cups
        i little cup with a foott; i little ladle
    i milk strainer and i skiming dish
    i suger box and itt cover to itt
    i paire of new bellows in the drawer of my great haire trunke

[362] Portingall, an obsolete form of Portugal; unglazed ' "red china" teapots in imitation of Chinese Yixing ware' were earlier made (Robin Emmerson, *British Teapots & Tea Drinking, 1700–1850* [London, 1992], 57). R. J. C. Hildyard, assistant curator in the Victoria and Albert Museum Department of Ceramics & Glass, suggested a further association between 'red china' or *boccaro* and the Portuguese stoneware noted by William Bowyer Honey, *European Ceramic Art* (London, 1952), 79.

[363] Candlesticks as well as wall-mounted candleholders.

[364] Wall bracket or specifically, Tessa Murdoch has suggested, a giltwood shelf.

[365] Lignum vitae, a hard, dense wood from the West Indies and South America also used extensively as a cure for venereal disease.

[366] Castor: small container with a perforated top for sprinkling.

[367] Inlaid ware from Tunbridge of beech, sycamore, and lignum vitae.

4 pictture sconces with glass, Lady Getings[368]
7 little picters with glases over them,
with severall other printed pictuers and some blak cutt cloth, &c.
                        Eliz Freke

Over this china box is a flatt deale box, Octtobr 16, i7ii, is putt in

   i Indian writting box, inlaid, given me by my deer Lady Norton
   2 pictture sconces of my deer Lady Gettings with glass over them
   i picctture of my deer sister Choutt drawn by my deer Lady Gettings,
     with severall other printed papers

i7ii, Octtober the i6. An accountt of whatt books I putt into the deep
deale box by the fire side in my own closett, Eliz Freke

   i large old Bible, my mothers, folia
   i large book of Andrews sermons, folia[369]
   i large book of Bishop A Halls, folia[370]
   i book of Bishop Usher, folia[371]
   i book of Fellthams Resolves, folia[372]
   i book of Cassandria, a romance, folia[373]
   i book of A Cowlye, in folia[374]
   i book of Smith sermons, quarto[375]
   i other thick book of divynity, folia
   i book of Heaven Opened by Cooper, quarto[376]
   7 new books of my deer sister the Lady Nortons makeing and her
     deer daughter the Lady Gettings makeing, which I prise and vallue
     for ther authers[377]
   i book of mine of the New Testamentt
   i Psalme Book to itt with cutts
   i book of the life and death of the holly Jesus by Jerymy Tayler, in
     quarto[378]

---

[368] Pictures located behind the candles and protected from the flame by glass.

[369] Lancelot Andrewes, *XCVI Sermons* (1629), five editions by 1661.

[370] Joseph Hall, bishop of Norwich, a prolific author.

[371] James Ussher, archbishop of Armagh, many works.

[372] Owen Feltham, *Resolves* (1623), eleven editions by 1696.

[373] Gaultier de Coste La Calprenède, *Cassandra* (1652), many editions.

[374] Various folio editions of Abraham Cowley's poems.

[375] *The Sermons of Henry Smith* (1657), four quarto editions by 1676.

[376] William Cowper, *Heaven Opened* (1609), six editions by 1632.

[377] Frances Norton, *The Applause of Virtue. In Four Parts* and *Memento Mori* (1705); Grace Gethin, *Misery is Virtues Whet-stone. Reliquiae Gethinianae* (1703).

[378] Jeremy Taylor, *Antiquitates Christianae; Or, the History of the Life and Death of the Holy Jesus* (1649), nine editions by 1703.

i abstractt of P Helins geogriphy, quarto[379]

i new book of the wars of England and Ireland by the Lord Clarendon in short, quarto[380]

i history of King Charls the First from his birth to his death, old one[381]

3 new books of the life and reigne of King William the Third of blesed memory[382]

i new book of St Austins meditations[383]

i new book of Danyell Featly devotions[384]

i new book of the Xtian Patern of Christ[385]

i new book of Gerrads Meditations[386]

i new book of Quarles pomes, new printed[387]

i new book of the feast and fast of the church[388]

i new book of Reformed Devotions[389]

i new book of herrallldy, 1710[390]

i Practice of Pyeaty (2 Parbls of the Pillgrams)[391]

i Whole Duty of Man[392]

4 new books of state pomes[393]

[379] Peter Heylyn, *Microcosmus* (1621), enlarged as *Cosmographie* by 1652; seven editions by 1703.

[380] Edward Hyde, first earl of Clarendon, *The History of the Rebellion and Civil Wars … Faithfully Abridged* (1703).

[381] Possibly Peter Heylyn, *A Short View of the Life and Reign of King Charles* (1658); more recent are editions of Richard Perrinchief, *The Royal Martyr; Or, a History of the Life and Death of King Charles I* (1676).

[382] Works include J. S., *A Complete History of … Prince William III* (1702); *The Glorious Life and Heroick Actions of the Most Potent Prince William III* (1702); Abel Boyer, *The History of King William the Third* (1702); David Jones(?), *The Life of William III* (1702), three editions by 1705.

[383] Many editions of meditations attributed to Augustine.

[384] Daniel Featley, *Ancilla Pietatis* (1626), nine editions by 1675.

[385] Thomas à Kempis, *The Christians Pattern*, numerous editions and reprintings, including six between 1701–11.

[386] Recent publications of Johann Gerhard's 1627 meditations include *Gerards Meditations* (1695) and *Meditationes Sacrae* (1709).

[387] New editions of Francis Quarles' *Emblems* were published in 1701 and 1709; *Divine Poems*, in 1706.

[388] *Festa Anglo-Romana; Or, the Feasts of the English and Roman Church* (1678).

[389] Theophilus Dorrington, *Reform'd Devotions* (1686), seven editions by 1708.

[390] 1710 publications are Arthur Collins, *The Peerage of England* and George Crawfurd, *A Genealogical History of the Royal and Illustrious Family of the Stewarts*.

[391] Numerous editions of Lewis Bayly, *The Practise of Pietie* (1612) and many of Simon Patrick, *The Parable of the Pilgrim* (1665).

[392] The most reprinted work by this title is Richard Allestree, *The Whole Duty of Man* (1658).

[393] The series *Poems on Affairs of State* began appearing in 1689; a four-volume fifth edition was published in 1703 to 1707.

i book of cirgiary by Colebach[394]

3 New Attlanteses, writt by Mrs Manly[395]

i book of Bishop Andrews, unbound

i new book of Meditations of the Devout Soule, is my sister Austens, lent mee[396]

i Compleatt Herball by Peachy[397]

i new book of the life of the holy Jesus

2 books of Cullpepers phisick[398]

i Mirror of the Orracles of God[399]

i abstractt of Gerralds herball of my wrightine now in the great black trunke[400]

i thick history of the wars of England, Scotland, and Ireland[401]

i book of the popish plott and i book of the Westron Mirtroligye[402]

i6 small history books

2 new books of gardning; 2 old ones

i new book of the presentt actts of the parliament, i7ii[403]

i paper book of the same stile, i7ii[404]

i new book of the secrets of King Charls 2d[405]

i book of pryvatt devotions

i book of the Family Phisition[406]

i book of the Husband Mans Instructer[407]

[394] John Colbatch, *A Collection of Tracts Chirurgical* (1699) or *Novum Lumen Chirurgicum; Or, A New Light of Chirurgery* (1695).

[395] Mary de la Rivière Manley, whose New Atlantis works include *Secret Memoirs and Manners . . . from the New Atlantis* (1709), *Memoirs of Europe* (1710), and *Court Intrigues* (1711).

[396] Possibly Thomas Arundell, *The Holy Breathings of a Devout Soul* (1695); Charles Povey, *Meditations of a Divine Soule* (1703).

[397] John Pechey, *The Compleat Herbal* (1694).

[398] Among the many works, possibly editions of *The English Physician* (1652), *A Physicall Directory* (1649), or *Culpeper's School of Physick* (1659).

[399] Probably Nicholas Byfield, *The Marrow of the Oracles of God* (1619), thirteen editions by 1660.

[400] An abstract of John Gerard's *The Herball; Or, Generall Historie of Plantes* (1597), three editions by 1636, is in the vellum manuscript.

[401] James Heath's 984-page *A Brief Chronicle of the Late Intestine War* (1663) is the longest of the likely histories.

[402] John Tutchin, *The Western Martyrology; Or, Bloody Assizes*, five editions by 1705; the Popish Plot prompted numerous works.

[403] Possibly Samuel Blackerby, *The Justice of Peace His Companion; Or, A Summary of All the Acts of Parliament to June 12, 1711* (1711), William Pittis, *History of the Present Parliament and Convocation* (1711), or his *The History of the Proceedings of the Second Session of this Present Parliament* (1712).

[404] *A Succinct and Methodical History . . . of this Present Parliament* (1712).

[405] John Phillips, *The Secret History of the Reigns of K. Charles II and K. James II* (1690).

[406] Gideon Harvey, *The Family Physician, and the House Apothecary* (1676) or George Hartman, *The Family Physitian* (1696).

[407] *The Husbandman's Instructor, or, Countryman's Guide* (1690).

    1 book of tenant and landlord,[408] with severall other small books
                        Eliza. Freke

[fol. 92r]

i7ii, Octtober the i6. An accountt of whatt I putt in the thin flatt deale
box in my closett, EF

    1 large sillver flagon
    1 large silver cupp and
    1 silver bread plate or cover to itt
    1 new Common Prayer Book
    1 large embrodered table cloth
    1 large pullpett cloth and
    1 fine damask table cloth and
    1 embrodered pullpitt coushen

All which I, Eliz Frek, have seen consecrated and which I give att
my death to the chancell of Billney, where my deer husband lyes
and wher I hope to lye att rest; to be keptt allwaise att the Hall
and never to come under the authority of the bishop of Norwich
or the chancellor or the arch deacon, this church being my peculier,
a donative, and impropiation nither subjectt to licence, institution,
or inducttion, or authoryty from the bishopse butt the queen, me,
and my heirs. And when in the year i7io the bishop in my absence
turn'd outt Mr Buck for officiating ther in my church withoutt his
licens, I kept him outt seven months and refused the bishops
authority of placeing one heer, I keeping the key of the church
sentt to him. Iff they claimed any right in Billney, his best way was
to make a forcable entry by a new lock and key, for nither the
bishop or arch deacon or chancellour or their visittors should ever
come in ther butt by my authority.
                    Elizabeth Freke

i7ii, Octtober the i7. An account of whatt books is in the great chest in
my uper closett, Eliz Frek

    1 great book of the history of China
    1 of Homers Illiads, both Oglybys
    2 historys of Affryca, in follia

---

[408] Possibly George Meriton, *Land-lords Law*, five editions by i697; R. T., *The Tenants
Law*, four editions by i684.

i history of Ammeryca; these five books are all by Ogellby.[409]

3 history books of the reigne of King Charls the First writen by John Rushworth[410]

2 old history books of kings, &c., and greatt ones of England, Scottland, Ireland

i law book writen by Sir W Pellam[411]

i book of my Lord Wynttworth[412]

i law book by Sir Edward Cooke[413]

i book of Captaine John Smith first voyage to Virgina and conquest, folia[414]

i book of law by Sir Littleton for Ireland[415]

i history of the kings of England by Peetter Hellin, folia[416]

i history of Henry the 7th, folia[417]

i history of Richard the 3d, folia[418]

i history of her majesty of Denmark[419]

2 actts of parliamt[420]

Octtober i8, i7ii. Memorandum. I leave in my own closett when I goe to London:

ii4 quarts of strong cordiall waters and

36 pints of cordiall watters and

56 quarts of severall sorts of sirrups.

In all, iff right reconed by me, is i7 dosen. E Freke

Besids aboutt fowre dosen of cold stilld watters.[421] EF

[409] John Ogilby, *Atlas Chinensis* (1671); *Homer His Iliads* (1660); *Africa* (1670); *America* (1671).

[410] John Rushworth, eight volumes of *Historical Collections* (1659–1701).

[411] William Pelham (d. 1587), lord justice of Ireland; no law book has been identified.

[412] The 1641 trial and execution of Thomas Wentworth, earl of Strafford, occasioned several works by him; *An Impartial Account* ... (1679) also presents the impeachment proceedings.

[413] Works by Sir Edward Coke include the many parts of *Reports* as well as *Institutes*.

[414] Several folio editions of *The Generall History of Virginia* were published between 1624 and 1632.

[415] Numerous sixteenth- and seventeenth-century editions of Sir Thomas Littleton's *Tenures* appeared, all relevant to or 'for Ireland', though none is specifically about Irish law; nor are the few pieces written by Sir Edward Littleton.

[416] Peter Heylyn, *The First Table; Or, a Catalogue of the Kings* (1674).

[417] Francis Bacon, *The Historie of the Raigne of King Henry the Seventh* (1622), several folio editions.

[418] Two folio editions of George Buck, *The History of the Life and Reigne of Richard the Third* (1646).

[419] A *Life and Reign of the Late K. of Denmark*, Christian V, was published in 1700; none on 'her majesty' has been located.

[420] A number were published.

[421] Cold stills – pictured in John French, *The Art of Distillation* (London, 1667), 17 – heated liquids only to the point that they turned into drops.

i7ii. Memorandum. In the other little closett is within the cheese chamber aboutt 4 dosen of quartt bottles full and three hampers full of empty quarts and pints; besids is one deep tub full of empty bottles and a shallow tub full of more emty bottles. Eliza. Freke

[fol. 92v]

i7ii, Octtober the i8. An account of whatt I leave in the severall rooms of my house att West Billney now I goe for London, being designed for itt with Gods leave Octtober the 23, Eliz Freke

First in my own closett:

i greatt haire trunk, filld
i large portmantle trunk, fild
i great black trunk, filld
i broad deall box with the church plate, &c., I give to itt
with the imbroder table cloth, &c.
i broad deep box, fill'd
i deep box by the fire sid, with book
i old chest filld with books
i long chest with bottles
i long chest under the cofin, fil'd
i haire trunk with houshold linen
i deep box behind my closett door with china and delph, &c.
i box over itt fild, and in itt is
i inlaid wrighting box, &c.
i deale deep box with chocolett, &c.
i little scratore;[422] i coffin fill'd
6 other little boxs with severalls
5 cubbard with bottles, loctt
    severall bottles of cordiall water
ii4 quarts; of pintts of cordy water
36. And of the severall sorts of sirrups is
56 quarts and pints.
    In all, if right reconed, are aboutt
i7 dosen and aboutt
4 dosen of cold still'd watters.

---

[422] Scrutoire, escritoire: writing-table or desk, often portable; also, more generally, a bureaux.

i large fore glass to my coach
i fether bed

Eliz Frek

I leave in the parlor lockt:

4 pieces of green forrest tapstrey, very good, and the room hung
   round
i large fire gratt barrs
i picture of my deer fathers, given me by my deer sister Norton
i long cane squab, given me by my deer sister Austen
i2 cane chairs
i greatt ovall table
2 window curtain rods

Eliza Freke

i7ii, Octtober i8. I leave in the hall when I goe for London:

2 longe tables; i large fire gratt
i copper limbeck, holds a firkin[423]
i fire grate, under itt iron bars
i long bench fixtt the sid and head
i lock and key to the hall doore

I leave outt in the kiching under the care of Mary Ram:

2 tables, one long one and one little one
i long bench to the long table, fixt
i long dresser for pewter, fixt
5 rush chairs; i stooll; i crickett[424]
2 bacon racks; 2 haks for potts[425]
2 iron andiarns; i iron oven lid
i greatt fire shovle and i b[rass] candlest[ick]
i paire of tongus to itt
3 greatt brass kettles
i little brass kettle; i brass slice[426]
i brass stue kettle
i brass skillett; i new coper sauce pan
i brass chaffing dish; i iron gridiorn

[423] Alembic; firkin: a quarter of a barrel, usually eight or nine gallons.
[424] Cricket: wooden footstool or low stool.
[425] Hakes: pothooks.
[426] Spatula or other flat cooking utensil, sometimes perforated.

i brass ladle; i brass druging box[427]
i round brass dish for a pye or pud[428]
i new brass frying pan, i7ii
i new brass warming pan, i7ii
i new iron ratt trap, i7ii
4 pewter dishes, all good, and
i deep pewter dish, new, bought i7ii
i broad pye platte, pewter
i2 new pewter plats, bought i7ii
2 old pewter plates, good
i pewter salt sellor
i new tin pasty pan, bought i7ii
6 dishes and 6 new trenchers, i7ii

In the back house and milk house:

i coper furness of a battell sett[429]
i greatt chees press
i greatt mash tubb with its utinsells[430]
i squar stand to this mash tub
i large barrell tubb with 2 ears
i broad couling keeler with 2 ears[431]
3 cheese vates and there fallows[432]
i broad milk tray, devided; the other Luke Wingfield borrowed
4 pailes, 2 of them must be mended
2 broad milk bowls; i brown one
                    Elizabeth Frek

[fol. 93r]

i7ii, Octtober i8. A further note of whatt I leave Mary in the back house and dary, Eliz Frek

i sifting tub or trough for flowre
2 sives to itt; 3 hog trough
3 great milk pans; 3 shelves
i churne and itts dash; i iron peele

---

[427] Container for spices and for substances used in dyeing and in medicines.
[428] Pudding.
[429] Possibly a boiler or cauldron; the other apparatus and function are unidentified.
[430] Used to crush and mix malt for brewing, but also to prepare cattle and horse feed.
[431] A two-handled cooling vat for brewing; also a shallow household tub.
[432] Cheese moulds.

4 halfe barrells, brod hoopt, oke
3 new firkins, broad hoop, oke[433]
i fixt table in the pastry[434] and
2 shelves and i horse or ale stoole
i stand in the small beer seller and
i shelf and
i stand ore ale stoole in my own seller
2 shelves next the cole roome
                    Eliz Frek

7ii, Octtober i8. In the parler chamber:

4 peices of tapstry hanging immagry and 2 green under peices
2 tables, one ovall, i lerger one, i7ii
i tortershell cabinett, given me by my deer sister Norton
i chest of drawers to my scrutor[435]
2 varnished stands to my table
i greatt guilt looking glass
i large picture over the chimny
i large picture by the bed side
i great easy chaire
io other chairs, 5 of them ellbows
i cole grat, new, with its fender[436]
i pair of andiarns to itt and
i fire shovell tongs and poker to itt
i Indian silk bed head and tester to my green damask bed[437]
4 plod curtains on itt and
2 paire of plod vallence
i new feather bed and boulster[438]
i new boulster to itt; 2 pillows
i counterpoyne; in the drawers by
3 window curtains in the drawrs
2 paire of vallence to them
i tester sheett and
i head sheett, both belong to me
i fether bed and bolster in my closett I forgott with itts coverlidd
    and

[433] Small wooden cask or vessel used, for example, to hold butter or lard.
[434] Area where pastry is made; also a larder.
[435] Scrutoire, escritoire.
[436] Fender: low metal barrier in front of raised, open fire to contain falling coals.
[437] Tester: bed canopy.
[438] Bolster: long pillow or cushion placed at the head of the bed.

i greatt fore glass of my coach
i paire of bellows

Eliz. Frek

i7ii, Octtober the i8. In the hall chamber is

2 large peices of linen Indian immajary hangings
i sack cloth bedsteed with its toping[439]
i new feather bed to itt; 2 pillows
i new boulster to itt
i head and tester belonging to my plodd bed
4 haire water camlett curtains to itt[440]
i paire of vallience to itt
i large counterpoyne to itt in one of the drawrs in the parlor chamb*
i large wallnutt scruture[441]
i picture of my deer Lady Nortons
i longe table and i blankett covers all
i little ovall table, new, i7ii
4 Irish sticht chaires[442]
i fire grate fixt with bars
i red window curtaine

In the little chamber within the hall chamber is

i bed tester, corded
i new fether bed to itt and
i new boulster to itt
4 new curtains to itt, i7ii
i paire of vallence to itt

Eliz. Freke

i7ii, Octtober i8. In the dineing roome is

2 larg long peices of tapstry hangings the length of the room
i lesser peice of hangings, linen
i great wallnutt looking glass
2 tables, one ovall and one square one

[439] Bed frame or stand upon which the bed rests.

[440] Watered or water camlet: a fabric of various materials, originally silk and camel's hair, with wavy lines.

[441] Scrutoire, escritoire: bureaux.

[442] 'Irish stitch – white embroidery on a white background' (Rosemary Milward, *A Glossary of Household, Farming and Trade Terms from Probate Inventories*, Derbyshire Record Society Occasional Paper No. i, 1982, 27).

6 cane chaiers
i long pictture of my deer sister Norton
i long pictture of my deer neece Gettings, her only daughter, and
i monementt picture of hers – [443]
    these three given me by my deerst sister Norton, E Frek
i long picture of my wretched selfe
i blue window curtaine
i coffin for me and itts stand redy fixtt and leaded for me with the
    key of ye vault
Elizabeth Freke

[fol. 93v]

i7ii. I leav in the closett by the parler chamber Octtober the i8, E Frek:

i sett of paper hangins round itt
i greatt Brazile chest[444] in which is
i great long Turky work carpett
i new large baking pan and
i new falce bottom to itt, for fish
3 paire of new bras candlestiks
4 brass socketts to them and
4 brass save alls to them[445]
i paire of hurdles sodered with silver[446]
i bell and plate to itt for usquabath
2 long brass pipes to itt, all of them sodered with silver, for [   ]
i new greatt brass dish and
i new bakeing cover to itt and the pan
2 new little brass kettles
4 brass head and other parts of two paire of andiarns
i bell mettle skillett, the handle of itt brok outt by Amey[447]
i bell mettle morter and
i brazile pestle to itt
i little new brass morter and
i pestle to itt; i coper skimer
i tin dish cover; 2 pewter poringers
i tin cullender; 2 pewter stands
8 greatt pewter dishes

[443] Moniment or monument: the Westminster or Hollingbourne memorial.
[444] Brazil-wood: hard, reddish-brown wood valued in the seventeenth century for inlay.
[445] A save-all held the remains of the candle either in the candlestick or on the pronged
pricket of a candle pan, allowing the candle-end to burn.
[446] A hurdle is a strainer or sieve.
[447] Bell metal: a bronze alloy of copper and tin.

2 mazariens to them[448]
24 new French pewter plats
i large new butter plate
2 new choping knives; i hamer
i little copper limbeck top
i little coper bottom and tram to itt[449]
i pewter limbeck to the pott in the kiching chamber
i pewter cold still head
i blind marrabath head to the still in the hall of coper[450]
i old warming pan
i new bason; i new chambr pott
2 close stoole pans
i parcell of the paper of the hangings of the roome leftt
i table caire[451] and
2 iron frams for kettles, &c.

     Eliza. Frek

i7ii, Octtobr i8. In the other chest in the same closett is

i purple counterpoyn to the camlett bed in the hall chamber
i plod counterpoyn to the parler chamber
4 curtains and blue tartrin and
i paire of vallence to itt
4 stuff curtains to my own bed[452]
2 pair of vallience to itt
i blue tartrine quilt to my bed
3 blankets to my own bed

Octtober i8, i7ii. I leave in the east garrett chamber:

20 new deale bourds, i5 foot long
2 new horses to dry linen on
i new bottle rack; 3 firkins
i marble table in its case, black
i tin watter pott; i little firkin
i hamper with 2 new fore coach harnes, never used
i tray with white peas; 2 stools
9 sacks; i chest; 9 bushels of pease

[448] Mazarine: a deep metal dish or plate, often set on a larger dish.
[449] Tram: bench or frame supported by four legs or blocks.
[450] The head or capital condensed the vaporized distillate heated in the cucurbit.
[451] Care or cary: fabric used here apparently as a tablecloth.
[452] Stuff: a worsted fabric or a textile of any kind.

i longe table; i glass churne
2 horse harnes hallters; i lanthr[453]

7ii. In the west garratt I leave behind me Octtobr i8:

i new greatt powdering tub and covers[454]
2 little powdering tubs with covers
3 cheese racks; 2 doors, off
2 tables; 2 deal bed cases with corne[455]
i trundle bedstead; i alle stoole
i paire of mustard quarnes[456]
2 bushshells; 2 old chest
2 corne shovells; i new deale
i deale glass case; i old half bar[rel]
i2 little deep cheeses of last year
i good settle; 37 cheeses, this year

[fol. 94r]

7ii. A note of whatt I leave in my uper garrett Octobr i9

i new greatt kiching grate, with it
2 iron cheek; i iron purr[457] and
i iron fender and i greatt horse to warme beer belonging to itt[458]
2 irron andierns or racks to itt
2 other cob irons for a spitt[459]
i greatt jack in the chest, with its
i iron chaine, 2 wheels and lines belonging to itt.[460] The weights are
    in my own closed, being of lead, 4 stone fixt to an iron.
8 curtaine rods; i iron to smoth
i iron driping pan; 4 iron hoops
2 great bell mettle potts
i greatt old kettle; 2 iron hoop
i iron corne screene
i little brass pott

---

[453] Lanthorn(?) or lantern.
[454] Tub for salting or pickling meats.
[455] Bed case: bedstead.
[456] Obsolete form of quern, a hand-mill for grinding spices.
[457] Iron cheek: iron plate positioned on grate to decrease its size; purr: poker (*EDD*).
[458] Horse: 'beer tram' or iron stool placed in front of a fire (*EDD*).
[459] Spit racks or andirons with a series of notches or holders.
[460] Clock jack or mechanical device for turning a spit, driven by weights similar to those described in the next entry.

i new coper limbeck, never used
i new leaden bottom fitted to my cold still in the hall chimney
i sett of mallitia horse armor containeing i gantlett
i iron head peice and
i iron back peice and
i iron breast; the buff coatt Sarah and her rogue stole; the sword
  and pistols is in my own closett with the 2 belts and box.
i greatt iron swath rake
4 iron hows, 2 withoutt handles
i greatt iron brandlett to my stil[461]
2 iron saws; 9 sickles
2 iron cutting knives, i new, i7ii
2 mowing sives, one new, i7ii[462]
3 chimny hakes; i plough share
i greatt iron pin to my trass poles[463]
i sett of trace poles with ropes and wheeles to them
5 good traces; i whin knife[464]
3 good ridles and 2 old ridles[465]
i white horse signe
i new spining Dutch wheele and reels
2 sadles, one of the malita
i greatt chamber skreen, painted, with 5 leaves
i cowes hide, entire, and
i parcell of new tand leather

  Eliza Freke

i7ii. A further account of whatt I leave in the upper garrett Octtober
the i9, Eliz Freke

  i new sack cloth beadsteede with all pertaining to itt; the screwes are
    in my own closett.
  2 embrodering frames lyes with itt.
  i new fan; i new sowing baskett
  i new hamper with its cover
  i round hamper with its cover
  2 setts of coach harnes, viz., 4 paire
  4 whole mun barells, narrow hoopt[466]
  2 whole oken barells, braad hoopt

---

[461] Variant of brandreth: three- or occasionally four-legged grate for the hearth.
[462] Obsolete for sieve, but here Freke means scythe.
[463] Trace pole.
[464] For cutting furze, heather, or shrubs.
[465] Riddle: a sieve with wide mesh.
[466] Mum: malt liquor or beer brewed originally in Brunswick.

i great cheast; 2 black trunks, the things in them stole
i fine flax hichell; i old frying pan to rost cofy[467]
2 new entire setts of wood work for
4 fore coach horses, painted, and pins
2 iron anckors for a house
4 bridles and topings to my coach harness
i woden cradle
i old brass frying pan with its handle to roast coffy
Eliza. Freke

n the closett by the pasage is

i table and six shelves

n the kiching chambr is

i hung with printed paper
2 feather beds, new ones
2 old fether beds in the maids chamber
3 blankets; i bedstead there
i sack cloth bedstead in the chambr over the kiching, stand up intire
i long table; i cabinett of drawrs

fol. 94v]

May 27, 1712. A note of whatt cordiall waters I putt into the severall
cubards in my closett for my own use May 27, 1712, Eliza. Frek

n the greatt cupbord is of quartt bottles

i three quartt bottle of hott surfett watter, 1705[468]
5 quarts of pallsey watter, 1708, 1702
4 quarts of cordiall watter, double still'd, 1708[469]
2 quart of scurvigrass, double still'd, 1684[470]
6 quarts of duable still cordiall with cinaman, 1705

---

[467] Hitchel: obsolete and dialect form of hatchel, an implement used to comb flax;
ofy: coffee.
[468] Surfeit water: cordial of various herbs, roots, and spices 'against cholicks, gripings
n the stomach and bowels, flatulenties and vapours' (George Smith, *A Compleat Body of
Distilling* [London, 1725], 35–6, 126).
[469] 'All distill'd goods which are made proof, are call'd double goods' – one part of
liquor' added to two parts of distillate (Smith, *A Compleat Body of Distilling*, 94–5).
[470] Spoonwort, herb used to cure ulcers in the mouth and prevent scurvy (John Gerard,
The Herball [London, 1636], 401).

3 quarts of Angellicoe watter, first, i704[471]
9 quarts of lemon water and brandy, i705
5 quarts of rosemary water with licor
2 quart of tinture of lavender, i708
5 quarts of ague watter, first, i705
4 quarts of rosemary watter, i705
i quartt of hungary watter,[472] Lady Norton, i709
i quart of sirrup of saffron, Lady Norton, i7i0
   In all is 52 quarts. Eliza Freke

In the little cuppord over the greatt is of pint bottles – first cuppord has of pints:

2 pints of hungary watter for my wreched head, i709
io pints of aquamirabolus, i7i0[473]
i pintt of tinture of nuttmegs, i709
i pintt of snakweed tinture, i7ii
i quart of hungry water, Lady Norton, i7ii
i quart of spiritt of wine [and] rosemary, i709
   In all is i6 pint. Eliz Frek
i little viall of saffron watr

In the 2d little cupbord is even with this [   ]

[fol. 95r]

i7ii, Octtober 22 Tuesday, Octtober the 22, I sett outt in my own coach for London to place outt aboutt three thousand pounds I had then in my cosin John Freks hand and nothing to show for itt but justice, of which I have sufficienttly bilt on.

27 Fryday in my own coach I came to London and lodged in New North Streett in Red Lion Square for neer a month.[474]

November i7 Wher I were soe ill with my tissick thatt I were forced to goe to my deer sister the Lady Nortons house aboutte the end of November for more ayre, in Ormond Streett nextt doore to the

---

[471] Angelico or angelica water: cordial made from the herb angelica; its root was valued in treatments of lung afflictions and asthma (John Pechey, *The Compleat Herbal* [London, 1694], 5; Gerard, *The Herball*, 1,001).

[472] Distillate of rosemary flowers and wine.

[473] Aqua mirabolis: mixture of spices steeped in wine.

[474] '*North street*, on the N. side of *Red lion square*, near *High holburn*, extending toward *Ormond str*' (Hatton, i. 60).

church,[475] where I staied till the 7 of December i7ii all the whilst endeavouring to place outt my mony – Sir George Norton haveing for two month before wrott to me to come up to London and lend him thirteen hundred pounds. Butt affter he had given earnest for his coach, [he] was taken speechless with a parralitick, which forced my stay two months in London.

i8 I gave my cosin Mary Lackendane a lottry tickett cost me i2 l.–7 s.–o d. to try her [luck]; by which she gott nothing butt lost my mony.[476]

2i Transcribed outt of the gessett from Dublin att the prorogation of the presentt parliamt November io, i7ii: Resolved thatt whomsoever shall by speaking, wrighting, or printting arraine or condemne the princeples of the late happy revolution in i688 is an enimy to our most gratious queen, and to our constitution in church and state, and to the Hannavor succession and a frind to the Pretender (or Prince de St George as caled in France).[477]

i7ii, December 7 Fryday, December the 7, affter neer two months stay in London all the while allmost dead with my tisick, I did att last signe Sir George Nortons release of errors and lentt him in mony on his bond and judgmentt thirteen hundred pounds to be paid me againe the 2i of Aprill i7i2 with itts intrest for halfe a yeare, being i339 l.; which bond and judgmtt is in a trunk in my closett, as is the mortgage of Mr Steevens Westons mortgage deeds for twelve hundred pounds he borrowed of me to bee paid me in a yeare.[478] And I then passed accounts with my cosin John Frek, who owed me on itts ballance nine hundred and seventy pounds, for which I have his note. Eliz Frek

9 Sunday, the 9 of December, allmost dead, I undertook my jorney home againe to Billney; which tho by Gods mercy to mee I compased in five days with my neece Betty Austen, yett did itt allmost kill me.

i4 Fryday, the i4, in the night I gott home safe to my beloved Billney.

---

[475] St George the Martyr Church, Queen Square, Bloomsbury, built as a chapel by Alexander Tooley with private subscriptions in 1706 and consecrated in 1723 (Henry B. Wheatley, *London Past and Present*, 3 vols. [London, 1891], ii. 101).

[476] The government held two lotteries in 1711, a form of loan initiated in 1694 to meet the growing expenses of war. The first offered 150,000 tickets at £10 each and the other 20,000 £100 tickets. The drawing for The Adventure of £1,500,000 began on 6 October 1711; fortunate ticket holders won amounts of principal or debt obligations ranging from £20 to £12,000, depending on the tickets they held and the point in the drawing. All tickets paid six per cent interest for thirty-two years (C. L'Estrange Ewen, *Lotteries and Sweepstakes* [London, 1932], 134–8).

[477] *Post-Man* (2070), Thursday 15 November to Saturday 17 November.

[478] Release: renunciation of a claim or right of action (Jowitt, ii. 1,531, 1,532). Steven Weston mortgaged a property near Beaconsfield in Buckinghamshire worth £300 a year to obtain a loan of £1,200 at six per cent. The miscellaneous documents variously date the mortgage 1 or 7 December.

For which mercy the Lord make mee ever thankfull, tho tis now eleven months I have hardly gone crose my chamber. Eliz Frek

[fol. 95v]

January the first and my unhappy birth day I had all my tennants dined with me, and my neece Betty Austen entertained them.

i7ii/i2, January the 2d Goody Englebright brought me some mony latte att nightt, when my head being very bad I gave her an acquittance for itt in my own wronge a years rentt, viz., forty six pounds, and placed ten pound on her bond, nott knowing whatt I did till two or three days affter I found itt in my book thatt I had given her an accquitance in full for the year i7ii which should have bin for i7io.[479] And besids I allowed her in my own wrong two years taxes. All which I proved before Mr Buck, the minester, and Mr Smith and Mr William Fisk, and yett I lost my whole rentt and mony.[480]

January the i and i7ii/i2 New Years Day and my unhappy birth day I have by Gods permision, providence, and goodness to mee fully accomplished the seventieth yeare of my age. For which I doe most humbly thank him and begg whatt longer time he gives me of life may by me, Elizabeth Frek, [be] spentt in thankfullness and to my Gods glory and in his service, affter [I] have laine above five yeares in the tortter of a tissick and the severall distempers which dayly atend itt, nott able the least to help my selfe butt as lifted by two of my servants and noe frind neer me butt all cheats. And now I have begun this new year, I doe most humbly beg of my God frome the bended knees of my hartt a more moderate health then I have had this six yeare past my deer husband left me, being June the 2d, i706 (my sons birth day, i675).

i2 I lett my Hall Farme to John Whiting for 48 l. a yeare.[481]

i3 I read in the gassett thatt all three of the lyons in the Towre were dead in one day; they bled to death.[482] This is most strange to EF.

i8 of January the prince of Hanavor was by actt of parliamentt declared and made first peer of the kingdom of England call'd Greatt

[479] James Englebright rented Freke's Pentney farm; the Pentney register for this period is missing, and neither his nor his wife's name appears in the incomplete archdeacon's transcripts or West Bilney register.

[480] William Fisk appears on the 1704 Pentney land tax as an assessor as well as a resident of the Abbey.

[481] John and Catherine Whiting, whose two sons were buried in East Winch.

[482] Reports about the deaths of the Tower of London lions appeared in various gazettes, including the *Norwich Gazette*; none says the three lions bled to death, nor does Luttrell in his account (vi. 276).

Britton, hee being before duke of Cambrig. The actt was passed three times in one day, nott known before.[483]

26 My cosin Betty Austen gave earnest att Lin for her coach to London.

i9 The queen and parliamt [ordered] the bill to repeall the Generall Natturallixan Actt to bee engrossed.[484]

Febuary ii Monday morn and the ii of Febuary my cosin Betty Austen leftt mee and Billney and wentt to London, whither I bore her charges; and I there gave her by my cosin John Frek fiffty pounds to lay outt in plate to remember me by. My deer sister Austen sentt for her three times before I sentt her, tho she had another daughter with her and I alone.

i4 of Febuary, Thursday, I were taken with a violentt plurisy in my left side for which in the night I were by Mr Smith blouded, who made the orrifice soe wide thatt I bleed above threescors ounces before itt could be stoped. Which tho itt gave me some ease, yett for many months I lay very weake ever since with a most violentt cough, now eight monthes, expectting my last sumons and noe frind neer mee. E Frek

[fol. 96r]

i7ii/i2, Febuary 29 I received of Mr Thomas Langly fowre pound for 7 years of Whittpitt Brack and entered on itt by way of posesion and forfitted his lease of 83 years, which I this yeare lett to John Whitting with the Hall Farm.

March 2d The publick news tells mee thatt we have had buried within this yeare three dauphins and one daphiness in France (of the small pox) and thatt Sir William Windams house in Allbermall Street

---

[483] The *Norwich Gazette* (vi. 277) mentions 'the Bill for giving Precedency to the Elector of Hanover' was read three times within the hour and passed. On 18 January 1711/2 the House of Commons accepted without amendments the bill giving precedence to Princess Sophia, her son, and grandson in the succession to the English throne (*CJ*, xvii. 32; Luttrell, vi. 716). On 5 October 1706 at Newmarket Queen Anne signed a warrant creating Georg August, the future George II, a peer of the kingdom as duke of Cambridge, among other titles (*Post-Man* [1683], *Daily Courant* [1399]).

[484] The manuscript reads 'repealed' rather than 'engrossed'. The *Norwich Gazette* (vi. 277) carries the 22 January report from London, 'This Day the House of Commons read a Third time and past a Bill for Repealing the General Naturalization Act'. The 1709 act had granted naturalization to all Protestant immigrants. After failing early in 1711, the Tories succeeded in repealing the General Naturalization Act with a bill initiated in the House of Commons on 22 December 1711 and accepted by the queen on 9 February 1712 (*CJ*, xvii. 24, 34, 75).

was burntt downe to the ground by carlesnes of his servants, his loss computed att 30000 l.[485]

i4 I had a second letter from my daughter thatt she designed me a vissitt with her two eldest sons and to give a name [to] the child she went with, which iff a son I named Arthur, my husbands fathers name. E Frek

i7i2, March 25 Mr Buck, my minester, leftt the church of Gyton and Billney, hee being prefered by his wifes lady to a living att Bacton Madam Branswith gave him.[486]

i7 Thomas Pallmer, my tennantt, dyed of the small pox a hundred pound in my debt and fiffty more then he was worth.[487]

26 I paid Mrs Ferrer in full for her years news twenty shillings.[488] EF

Aprill i All Fools Day or the first of Aprill, being Tuesday, Mr Thomas Langly sentt to me to send two men to his and he would devide Whittpitt Brack with mee. My tennantt Whitting brought me this message, soe I did immediattly sentt John Whitting, my tennantt, and Roger Chapman, my servantt, and Henry Cross, my then tennantt, to devide itt with Mr Langly; butt hee never came butt sentt on Mr Wacy and another man who had known the land above thirty years before the moire was ploughed upp by Mr Langlys servants. In this devision I left outt of my partt land for a new moire. Eliz Freke, i7i2

3 Aprill The baylyes came and arrested my coachman, being Thursday, and carryed him to Norwich jayle withoutt soe much as permitting him to speak to me or give me an accountt of any of my things under his care, which was neer twenty pound loss to EF.

9 Thomas Pallmer, the son of the above Thomas Pallmer, dyed of

[485] The *Norwich Gazette* (vi. 281, 284) reports the deaths of the duchess of Burgundy on 12 February 1712 (NS) and her husband, the dauphin, on 18 February (NS) as well as the death of the third dauphin, the duke of Brittany, on 8 March (NS), all reportedly of the 'Pestilential' distemper, or measles. The duke of Brittany's brother Charles de France, duc de Berry, and Charles' son Charles, duc d'Alençon, also died not long after. The fourth dauphin, Louis, duc d'Anjou, lived to become Louis XV (François Bluche, *Louis XIV*, trans. Mark Greengrass [New York, 1990], 584–8). Sir William Wyndham had paid £7,000 for the house on Albemarle Street, a street near the northwest area of St James Street with 'excellent new Building, inhabited by Persons of Quality'. The occupants fled the March 1712 fire without clothing (Hatton, i. 1; Wheatley, *London Past and Present*, i. 14).

[486] Charles Buck was instituted vicar of Bacton on 5 October 1711 (NRO, DN/Sub 4/3), remaining its vicar until his death in March 1746. His wife, Mary, was buried there the previous year.

[487] The West Bilney register records no deaths for the years 1710 to 1716; the archdeacon's transcripts, however, indicates Thomas Palmer was buried on 17 March 1711/2. At his death he was the Wassell Farm tenant.

[488] Unidentified. The weekly *Norfolk Gazette* does not list its price; copies of London gazettes published three times a week still sold for as little as a penny.

the small pox; are both buryed in Billney church yarde.

Aboutt the sixth or seventh of Aprill I were sent to signe my son a commission; which I refused signeing my cosin John Freeks foolish bargains, assureing him by my letter I would never trust him with my grandchild thatt had wronged me soe basly in his trust to mee by my letter of atturney to him and giveing him since my widowhood above six hundred pounds in six years time. Tis true, Eliza. Freke. And I concluded my letter, from such friends, good Lord, deliver Eliz Freke.

20 I received a letter from my son outt of Ireland dated ye 30 of March as followes:

March 30, 1712

Deerst Madam,

Tho I am butt just outt of a severe fitt of the goutte and hardly able to hold my pen, yett haveing received a letter yesterday from my deer Lady Norton giveing me the ill accountt of your being outt of order in your health, I cannot butt express the very greatt concerne itt is to me, tho I trust in God you have before this recovered itt, which is the ferventt and dayly praiers of mee [fol. 96v] and my familly. I have this day wrott to my deer Lady Norton my thanks for Sir George and her kind invitation of mee and my family to Leigh; and I begg, deer madam, you will be pleased as soon as possible to lett me heer how you doe, for till then I shall be most uneasy and impattientt. My wife is now neer her time of lieing inn and presents her humble dutty to you, and I praise God my children are well and in the sumer shall pay you theire duty in England. And I am very sencible how much I am your debter in rentt besids every way elce in your goodness to me on all occasions. I shall trouble you this post with noe more butt thatt I am, deerst madam, your most obedientt son, Ralph Freke.

1712, Aprill 20 Sunday, the twentieth of Aprill and Easter Day, my daughter Freke was broughtt to bed of a daughter, which my deer Lady Norton and I named Grace, her only daughters name and my most deer and beloved neice. For which I have in my will given her five hundred pounds.[489] E Frek

21 Monday Mr Langly wrott to me to christne his daughter, which I refused them.

27 The Sunday affter they came to me both to desire itt of mee; butt I excused itt, my wantt of health and age nott permitt mee.[490]

---

[489] Freke entered the birth at Rathbarry in the parish register, noting that Frances Norton and 'my unhapy selfe the Grandmother' were godparents.

[490] Thomas and Ann Langley's daughter Susannah was baptized in East Winch on 28 April 1712.

The 22 from Parris is thatt the Chevilier de St George sister dyed att St Germons the i8 of Aprill of the small pox aged i9 years and eleven monthes. Borne in France the 28 of May i692, [she] is buryed the 30 in the monastry of the English Benedictans neer thatt of her father, the late King James the Second; and her harte was carryed to the nunnery of Chaillott.[491]

28 The old countes of Thannett dyed the 2i instantt of the small pox pox att above eighty years of age.[492]

i7i2, May ii Sunday morneing by the carllesness of my two maids Mary Ram and Mary Chapman, I lost all my clothes stole from me on Sunday morne by leaveing them outt all night, att least six weeks washing, for which I offered twenty pound to Mary Ram to recruitt them.[493]

i5 I had Diana Davy and Goode Kneeve whipt att the carts taile for cutting my wood and stealeing my hedges by a warrantt from the justices sitting, which I saw done outt of my window.[494] EF

24 of May Mary Chapman, Satterday night affter the loss of all my linnen, fell ill of the small pox. I removed her to the parish house.

June 3d Tuesday, the third of June, they apeered next to Thom Betts.

26 Wher I had two nurses to atend her and took as much care of her as of a neere relation, and I were bound for her and her husban Roger Chapman to Mr Younge thirty two shillings and her charge of the small pox and mony lentt her, above five pounds.[495] And affter neer all my care and charge, aboutt the 26 of June she run away affter spoyling me my bed, 4 blankets, 2 boulsters, 2 pillows, and coverlid, and sheets, and the i2 of July sent to me to come againe.

[491] The account of the death of Louisa Maria Stuart (1692–1712), the daughter of James II and his second wife, Mary Beatrice of Modena, and the sister of James Francis Edward Stuart, the Old Pretender, follows closely that from Paris on 23 April (NS) found in the *Evening Post* (421); the *Norwich Gazette* (vi. 290) also reports the death.

[492] Catherine, the wife of Thomas Tufton, sixth earl of Thanet, died on 20 April at the age of forty-seven; the London gazettes date her death either 20 or 21 April; the *Norwich Gazette* (vi. 290), 19 April. Her husband's brother Nicholas, third earl of Thanet, had been married to the second earl of Cork's daughter Elizabeth, whom Freke apparently confused with the sister-in-law. The third earl of Thanet's wife died in 1725 at the age of eighty-eight (*CP*, xii, pt. 1. 694–6).

[493] Mary and Robert Ramm's daughter Mary, baptized on 29 December 1692 at West Bilney, might have been the cook maid; the other maid was the wife of Roger Chapman, Freke's servant.

[494] Goody Kneeve may have been Dorothy, the wife of Richard Kneeve, two of whose children's burials are entered in the West Bilney register.

[495] A Robert Young was licensed in 1700 as a Norfolk surgeon from Wacton (Wallis, 676); no other Youngs appear in the neighbouring areas.

[fol. 97r]

1712, Jully 4 Thom Betts, the poor clark of this parrish, dyed of the small pox which hee took of Mary Chapmans nurse, whom he designed to marry as soon as recovered and said none could preventt itt butt God, tho he was above sixty years of age and took releife of the parish, to which hee leftt three children att his death to be provided for and keptt. EF

7 of Jully was Dunkirk surrendered by the king of France to the queen of Greatt Brittaine as a hostage or barryer for the expectted peace, and Major Generall Hill (Mrs Marshams brother) was by the queen made govonour of itt, and a casacion of armes proclaimed by England and France by sea and land till the two and twentieth of December 1712 whilst our allies with the Dutch and the emperrour fight itt outt with all their viggor.[496]

Agust 19 And the Post Man says wee have lost more conciderrable places in France this two monthes then we have gott in three years campaine besids the many thousand soules and millions of mony to the nation.[497]

24 of Agust The 24 of Agust a cessation of arms was agreed on to expire the 22 of December and proclaimed.[498]

I had a letter from my daughter datted outt of Ireland the 24 of Agust thatt her husband, her selfe, and childrin were coming over to mee. And in a most tempestious season they sett forth for this dreadful season of the yeare.

September 29 My deer son and daughter with their three children Percy, Ralfe, and Redman left Cork and took shipping for England in a man of warr, Captaine Paule, belonging to Bristow.[499]

Octtober 2d They were stormed all thatt day and night in a most

---

[496] The *London Gazette* (5029) reports the 7 July 1712 surrender of Dunkirk; the *Evening Post* (454) and the *Norwich Gazette* (vi. 301) carry the further news of Hill's appointment. Major-General John Hill, an officer in the ill-fated Quebec expedition, took possession of Dunkirk on 8 July as part of an agreement with the French preliminary to the Peace of Utrecht (G. M. Trevelyan, *England Under Queen Anne*, 3 vols. [London, 1930–4], iii. 217–22). Hill owed his military career in part to his older sister, Abigail Hill, Lady Masham (1670?–1734), the first cousin of Sarah Churchill, duchess of Marlborough, and a lady of the queen's bedchamber (Gregg, *Queen Anne*).

[497] No report has been located among the few issues for July and August that still exist.

[498] The *London Gazette* (5043) reports the queen's 18 August proclamation from Windsor suspending armed hostilities 'until the Eleventh of *December* next'.

[499] A rate 5 ship of 145 men and thirty-two guns named *Poole* was commanded by William Gray in the Lundy area, but Freke may mean a ship commanded by Captain Paul. Commissioned a captain in 1706, John Paul commanded the *Hastings* in September 1712, a rate 5 ship of 190 men and forty-two guns 'cruizing in the mouth of Bristoll Channell, & Convoys the Trade into the Sea bound to the Plantations' (*Commissioned Sea Officers*, 350; PRO, ADM 8/12).

dreadfull hurrycane of weather which continued till the 2d of October, Thursday nightt, when by my Gods greatt mercy to them and me (affter my being allmost frightned outt of my witts), they all landed safe att Bristoll. And Fryday morning, the **3d** of Octtober, Sir George Norton and my deer sister Norton sentt her coach for to fetch them to Leigh, where they rested themselves till the eleventh of Octtobr, Satterday.

ii And then they wentt all of them to the Bath, where they staid all aboutte five weeks; and then with my deerst sister Norton all wentt to her house to London in Ormond Street, where they rested themselves affter a most dreadfull jorney upp for aboutt three weeks more.

December 20 And came downe to Billney to wretched me and to my house Satterday, the twentyeth of December, my deer son and his lady and my three grandchildren, viz., Percy, Ralph, and Redman, with their master and three other man servants. Where I humbly thanke my greatt and good God they all came well and safe to mee and, I hope, to be a comfortt to miserable mee thatt have hardly gone outt of my chair and bed for above fowrteen months.

28 Saterday, the 28 of December, my youngest grandson fell sick after he had bin a weeke heer, which proved [fol. 97v] to be the small pox.

December 29 And they apeered on him Monday, the 29 of December, and hee had them in a most violentt maner by reason of the humour to his head thatt till the Twelfe Days was past, **January 7,** we dispaired of life for him, tho hee was the patients of children butt all over martered with the small pox to extremity. **29** Which confined him to his bed and to docters and nurses for a full month before hee rose, viz., 29.

Febuary 7 After which both my maids fell sick of the small pox, viz., aboutt the begining of Febuary fell downe Eliz Knopwood, who dyed of itt, and Martha Cope, who recovered itt.[500]

i4 And abouthe the i4 of Febuary fell downe of itt my servantt man who looked affter all my business and still lyes very ill of itt and lame March the 8, i7i2.

22 Mr Smith, vicker of Winch, came heer and preached att Billney church, when I engaged him to give the sacramentt heer a Midlentt Sunday, being the eightt of March, and to serve the church till next Michellmas i7i3. E Freke

23 I wrott a complaining letter to the chancellour of Norwich thatt since he chalenged my church in his courte by the bishops order to know why itt had bin kept aboute ten monthes vacantt withoutt the

---

[500] The burial is not recorded in the incomplete West Bilney and Pentney archdeacon's transcripts.

service of God in itt, of which I would complaine to [the] arch bishop of Canterbury.

25 The 25 of Febuary dyed the king of Prusia, much lamented, of a longe, lingering sickness, 56 year of his age.[501]

28 Satterday, the 28 of Febuary, Mr Henry Pine, son to the Lord Chiefe Justice Pine and heire to him, had some words with Esquire Theophilus Bidulph (son and heir of Sir Michell Bidulph) about Docter Sacheverall. Wheron was a challeng wherin and neer the corner of St James Parke Mr Pine was stabed in his right breast six inches deep and dyed on the spott; and Mr Bidollph was wounded aboutt fowre inches in the belly, of which he lay still weak (iff nott dead) March 4th.[502] Mr Lord Chiefe Justice Pine of Ireland was this Mr Henry Pines father (and Mr Freks neer relation) and left him an estate of above two thousand pound a yeare in England and Ireland when he dyed, which was in Aprill 2i, Aprill the one and twentieth, i7io, and lyes buryed in Sary att his fine house there, i7io, leaving only this son Mr Henry Pyne, who has three daughters.[503]

i7i2/[i3] of March i5 Being Midlentt Sunday, Mr Smith of Winch preached att Billney and affterwards gave the sacramentt there; where I doe most humbly thank God I weare a most miserable unworthy pertaker of itt with my few neighbours, my son goeing outt of the church, tho I had nott seen him in allmost seven years before. And twas with the greatest of diffyculty and the help of fowre servants I compassed [fol. 98r] to my church and misery I sate ther (and nott lessened to see my son sett frowning on me ther for an howr for I

---

[501] Frederick I (1657–1713), elector of Brandenburg and first king of Prussia, was allied with England against France. News of his death on 25 February (NS) appears in a number of London gazettes; the *Flying-Post* (3343) has a biography of the deceased king.

[502] None of the gazettes that report the duel fought on 28 February near Chelsea mentions the nature of the quarrel. The *Post Boy* (2779) states that Pyne was mortally wounded 'on the Right Side of his Body, and died on the Spot, and the other dangerously wounded in the Belly 5 Inches'. The *Evening Post* (558) further reports that a coroner's inquest 'brought in Theophilus Bidolph Esq; and the two Seconds, guilty of wilful Murder'; on 6 March Biddulph was 'committed to Newgate'. The *British-Mercury* (407), 22 April, notes Biddulph was 'only found guilty of Man-slaughter'. The son of Michael Biddulph's first marriage to Henrietta Maria Witley, Theophilus (1685?–1743) assumed the family baronetcy upon the death of his father in 1718; he died without a male heir in 1743 (*CB*, iii. 300). Henry Pyne, the son of Richard Pyne and Catherine Wandesford, was born at Waterpark in 1688, educated at Trinity College, Dublin, and represented Dungarvan in parliament from 1709 until his death. He left his wife, Margaret, the daughter of Sir Richard Edgcombe and Anne Montague, and three daughters, Anne, Catherine, and Elizabeth (Morris, 'The Pynes of Co. Cork', 708–10; PRO, PROB 11/542/179).

[503] Richard Pyne died at Ashley Park, one-half mile south of Walton-upon-Thames in Surrey. The parish records indicate the burial of 'Sir Richard Poyne, Lord Chief Justice of Ireland', on 22 December 1709. The link with Freke, other than via the marriage to the Norton family, is unknown.

know nott whatt) (except itt were his feare of my coming alive home againe). This his cruell usuage of me gave me a greatt trouble, tho I were att the sacramentt, where I had nott bin nor in any church in two years before by my miserable tissicke. And affter diner when before Mr Smith, I asked him iff hee had nott latly received mercyes enough from God: first from his deliverance by the severall tempest by sea last Michellmas Day when soe many ships were lost and himselfe, his wife, and three sons were all preserved by Gods providence; and since thatt, his youngest son, John Redman, lay sick heer with me (and att my charge) allmost a month given over of the small pox; besids severall other mercyes received. His answer to me was I talked to him as iff he were butt eighteen years of age, when att this very time hee owes mee above three thousand pounds in redy mony I can lay him up for.

19 And since Sunday, which is now fowre days, my son hass gone by my chamber doore and never called on me to see how I did butt twice (and I soe very ill). My greatt and good God forgive hime and supportt unhappy mee, his wretched mother, Elizabeth Freke. The like was his eldest son Percy Freke dereicted to doe, who for above a week pased my chamber neer twenty times a day [and] never once call'd in to see mee, his grandmother. Tis butt as my deer husband before me has bin treated by them both and there eldest son in the yeare 1705 in London. E Freke

23 Monday, 23 of March, Docter Sacheveralls three yeare were expired of silenced for preaching; **29** and the Sunday after, being Palme Sunday, he preached the first time affter the expiration of his three years sentence before a numorous auditory att St Saivours Southwork. His text was Luke 23, verse 34 (Father forgive them for they know nott whatt they doe). And another sermon he preached outt of the 26 of Jeremiah, the 14, 15, 16 verses – Sachever, I am in your hand; doe with me as itt seemeth you good. But know, &c.[504]

29 Palme Sunday her Majesty putt on the order of the St George on one side of her and the order of the St Andrew of Scotland on the other side of her, she being the first soveraigne thatt has ever done both nations the honour of wearing these two orders together.[505]

---

[504] News of the sermon by Henry Sacheverell (1674–1724) on Palm Sunday, 29 March, and the celebration at the expiration of the parliamentary prohibition against his preaching appears in the *Evening Post* (565, 568) and the *Post Boy* (2788, 2791). His Gunpowder Plot sermon of 5 November 1709, thought to be critical of the government and the hereditary right of succession, had led to his impeachment, conviction, and three-year prohibition from preaching. 30,000 copies of his Palm Sunday sermon on Luke 23 were said to have been printed as *The Christian Triumph*; the sermon on Jeremiah is not mentioned in the gazettes and was not published (Geoffrey Holmes, *The Trial of Doctor Sacheverell* [London, 1973]).

[505] The queen's Palm Sunday appearance was not a newsworthy event in the London gazettes; no copies of the *Norwich Gazette* have survived after the 26 July–2 August 1712 issue (vi. 304).

1713, Aprill 5 Sunday and Easter Day, the 5 of Aprill, I wrott to my cosen John Freke to buy for me a pattentt of a barronett for me, Elizabeth Freke, to presentt my son and daughter with, hee being by my Gods blesing on my industrious endeavours now entitled to affter my death full two thousand pounds a yeare in England and Ireland, and his two eldest sons provided for by me, Eliz Frek, who when I maryed Mr Freke in the yeare 1671 had but two hundred pound a year. I am by my Gods, by my husband, [fol. 98v] and my weak endeavours blest to see my selfe and my son, Ralph Frek, the head of my grandfathers familly and of my deer fathers, Ralph Frek of Hanington, Esqr, tho I had nott nor my husband, Percy Freke, Esqr, one foott of his or theire estates butt whatt I bought since I were marryed, my deer fathers being settled (for wantt of heirs) on his youngest brothers son of above fiffteen hundred pound a yeare long before I were marryed, who now enjoys itt. Yett were I [blest] by my deere fathers bounty and goodness to mee: I had allways his helpe whilst he lived of above twenty thousand pounds att severall times for a help to me. And this was Gods mercy to Eliz Frek. All which two thousand pound a year I have seen settled on my eldest grandson, Percy Frek, hee being the 28 of Aprill thirteen yeares of age, 1713. And besids this I doe by my Gods blessing settle on my second grandson, Ralph Freke, of my own industry, now aboutt ten years of age, two hundred and three pounds a yeare in the exchecker for 99, ninety nine, years and two thowsand pound on a mortgage on Sir George Nortons estate (my brothers) and the intrest to run on att six percentt till my grandson comes to one and twenty years of age. Thus am I blest with my Gods dayly mercyes to me nott only in the blesings of chilldren butt thatt I am able to see a subsistance settled on them before I dye. For which the great God make me for ever thankfull to him whose gift itt is and bless my son (and forgive him all his undutifullness to mee) thatt none of his, my sons, children may be to him as hee has to mee, his unhappy mother, Eliza Freke. 1713

Aprill 26 Sunday, the 26 of Aprill, I left my house att West Billney and went for London with my son and his wife and his three sons and his fowre men and my coachman and maid, wentt up for London affter they had bin all with me above fowr monthes heer with ther disorderly servantts. **29** And I came to my deerst sister Lady Nortons house Wensday, the 29 of Aprill. And the day I left my house my daughter came rudely into my chamber and told me I owed her husband fiffty pounds and twenty pounds, when hee now owes me above five, 5000, thousand pound, and they had of me heer above three hundred pound of Mr Rolfe and my selfe, and by the tenants discharges. In which time ther youngest son lay two month dyeing of the small pox, who infectted fowre of my servants, of which one of them dyed. I will nott say more then from such another time, good Lord, deliver mee and make thankfull to God. Eliz. Frek

[fol. 99r]

1713, May 14 My son and daughter being both desirous of more quality, I did aboutt the midle of May purchas by my cosin John Frek the pattentt of a barronett from the queen, for which I paid and for the ingroseing of itt and the quiettest est above five hundred pounds and gave my cosin John Frek for his trouble forty guinyes.[506] And this my deer sister Norton gieving my son and daughters rude family the freedome of her house, I staid in London nine weeks and on my own charge kept there disorder familly. And I paid for coach hire five pounds, 16 shillings, tho I had a coach of my own in London, and for meatt and drink for him and his family to ther own apoyntmentt, and gave my daughtter fiffty pounds for her own spending. And I paid Mr Cross eight ginyes for drawing his picture and severall other things. And yett all deserved noe thanks, tho for nine weeks I kept open house for all comers and goeres to them both and all their acquaintance.

June 24 Wensday and Midsomer Day, the 24 of June, being very ill by a voylentt fitt of the colick, I atempted my goeing outt of [London] in hopes of a little quiett (haveing had none in six months before) and being quitt tired outt. And my son apprehending my death neer came in the coach downe with mee, tho I begg'd the contrary of him.

28 And by Gods great mercy to mee I came home in my own coach in five days, being Sunday late att nightt, the 28 of June, very ill. Heer my deer son (now Sir Ralph Freke) staid with me till the six of Septembr, being Sunday morning.

Jully 16 In which time his groome and his honestest servantt of the fowre stole a maire he vauled att twenty guinyes, and aboutt twenty pound in gold and sillver he run away with, and left him severall bills to pay in Linn. Hee had trusted the mony with him to cary and pay itt.

Jully 7 My son, Sir Ralph Frek, proclaimed the peace and had itt with prayers in the church and with cakes, wyne, and a barrell of ale,

---

[506] Ralph Freke was created a baronet on 4 June 1713 (*CB*, v. 15). James I instituted the rank of baronet in 1611 to honour men of 'qualitie, state of living, and good reputation' who were 'at the least descended of a grandfather by the fathers side that bare Armes, And have also a certaine yeerely revenue in Lands'. After the restoration of Charles II the patent fee of £1,200 and the £1,095 for maintaining thirty foot soldiers for three years could be lessened through a royal warrant to the exchequer, which then issued a discharge of debt or *quietus* (Francis W. Pixley, *A History of the Baronetage* [London, 1900], 97–8; 101, 140).

and a greatt burne fire in the common of aboutt two or 3 load of wood besids, &c.[507]

Septembr 6 Sunday, the sixth of Septembr, my son (and his bosome frind Gin) leftt me and begun his jorney for London by way of Northamton, wher Gin had perswaded him he might buy a sett of good coach horses as he did a little before att Norwich, both which jorneys were lost. However, the morning hee left me [fol. 99v] my son broughtt me another bill of above a hundred pounds and ten pound in his debtt, which 100 l. I paid my son as by accountt outt of whatt I left to bury mee. E Frek

September 11 Fryday nightt I humbly thank my God my son with his boy and my coachman and his six or 7 pampered horses gott safe and well to London in order to goe for Ireland, wher I doe most humbly beg of God to send him and all his children safe affter hee and his familly have a twelve month come Michellmas Day nextt, which now wants butt one day, left thatt kingdome and his children lost there time of schooling. Three or 4 days before my son left me I asked him to leave me his seccond son and I would putt him to schoole and provide for him; butt he flattly deneyd me, as did my daughter for her youngest son thatt lay sick of the small pox butt seven years of age. Tis the last trouble I shall beg of my children. My good son left me the whole estatt in my hand for a twelve month past and butt two farms on itt lett, nor any stock on itt, and the warrener run away with neer two hundred pounds from mee. God forgive him all his barbarityes to me and grantt his children may nott pay my score to him as hee has dealt by his father and mother. Eliz Freke

14 I was arrested by Thomas Garrett for nine pound for my apeerance. He told me hee would carry me to jayle to my warrener Last (which has lain vacantt now a twelve month, as has done the Maner Farme and Croses). This John Last cheated mee of a hundred and fiffty and a years rentt in my waren of a hundred pound a yeare; and affter I had by two writs putt him in the Castle of Norwich, he dared me three or fowre times in my chamber, and this by the favour of Mr Rolfe, my atturney.[508]

---

[507] The queen received the Peace of Utrecht ratification ending the War of the Spanish Succession and on 4 May, the eleventh anniversary of the war's beginning, signed an authorization proclaiming the peace; 7 July was appointed as a day of public thanksgiving for the 'Blessing of Peace' (*London Gazette* [5118, 5136]).

[508] The tenant was perhaps the John Last who married Elizabeth Hall in Swaffham on 12 January 1701/2. Freke's attorney was probably Edmund Rolfe (1649–1726), who followed his father Francis Rolfe as town clerk of King's Lynn and was twice mayor besides fulfilling various judicial assignments. His son Jonas (1677–1725), however, was also an attorney and could conceivably have been employed. A Rolfe had also managed the Bilney estate for Freke's brother-in-law before she bought it (R. T. and A. Gunther, *Rolfe Family Records* [London, 1914], 50).

Agust i5 Aboutt the midle of Agust I had another sumons from the chancellour of Norwich to apeere att the bishops courte and answer why I did nott place a minester in my church heer att Billney, which now by my selfe and the bishop of Norwich has bin kept vacantt for a yeare and a halfe this Michellmas, with greatt threats to mee. Which I decline to doe for feare of being tricked by him and brought into his courts and soe loose my peculer by his lycence. E Freke

i9 However, aboutt the i9 of Septembr I wrott this following letter to Doctter Thomas Tanner, chancellour of Norwich.

[fol. 100r]

A letter I wrott to Doctter Thomas Taner, chancellour of Norwich, affter his thundering arest of mee, EF:

i9 of September i7i3

Reverend Sir,

My son, Sir Ralph Freke, being amongst some gentlemen last week was informed thatt you designed troubling me aboutt my church being vacantt, nottwithstanding in severall of your former letters to mee you asured mee affter six monthes vacancy itt was lapps to the bishop and thatt his lordship would fill my vacansy himselfe, which my pryde of such a patron to this place and church made me very easy in. Now a full year in his lordships charge, who has taken noe care for itt or for xings, sacraments, or buryalls this sickly time or soe much as the proclamattion for the peace, which my deer son saw as grandly performed both within the church and att nightt as iff you had bin there presentt on my charge. Together with xings and buryls and a sacramentt last Midlelent Sunday, viz., the i5 of March, have I trespased on his lordships priviledg, tho I have butt two familyes in the parish above this twelve month.

Sir, I must needs say noe tongue can express the trouble itt has bin to me to [have] 9 or ten of my sons familly added to mine and have no place to serve God in or church in the parrish to resortt to. You, sir, displaced Mr Buck thatt I placed inn, tho coalatted by the lord bishop of Norwich vicker of Gyton, and for noe reason mentioned butt wantt of maners. This, sir, is in my own justifycation. And now, sir, I am further inform'd, which I cannott beleive, thatt you threaten me with an excomunycation; you need noe such trouble, for iff his lordship or your selfe hang butt a cobweb cross the church doore, I promise you thatt on the faith of a Christtian I will never offer a voyalence to itt my life.

Sir, I am nott now ashamed to have itt seen inside or outside; butt iff any injury be offered to my reputation, I shall immediatly withdraw my extravagencys outt of itt and leave itt as naked as I found itt and never laying outt more on itt.

Sir, I were a few days since warned, tho I have nott seen itt, to fill the church with a minester; which I am endeavouring to doe, tho my acquaintance in this country is very little. Therfore I am promised att Wishbich and Lin one to enter itt att Michellmas and serve itt once a fortnight with his care for all parish dutyes. And then, I hope, his good lordship and your selfe will be pleased since he is accepted by our good and gratious queene, my patroness, and confirmed by actt of parliamentt. I confess I little thought of coming to this affter all my troubles, [fol. 100v] butt I will rest my self sattisfyed thatt church is best thatt has most of quiett in itt. And had I bin able to have crosed my chamber, which I have hardly done this three years past, to have waited on his lordship and your selfe, I should nott have doubted to have convinced him and you of my integerity in the hardshipp I have received in your courts by proctters, &c. This longe scrole, sir, begs your pardon and leave to subscrib my selfe

Your humble servantt,
Eliza Freke

Subscribed: To Doctter Thomas Tanner, chancellour of Norwich, &c.

1713, Octtober 5 Before I had placed in my curatt in this church, the arch deacon of Norwich, Doctter John Jeffryes, sentt his thunderbolts by his proctters of excommination to mee iff I did nott immediatly pay him his fowre years affter he had cheated me of twenty five years by my ignorance and his proctturs threats of me.[509] And att the same time I saw Pentny twenty seven years in arrears to him he durst nott demand.

Octtobr 12 Tho I am thus tormented by thatt dam'd court to make me loose my peculer in this church, perhaps the finest in England, I wrott this insueing letter to the arch deacon Jeffryes:

Reverend Sir,

Brockett, your procttor,[510] broughtt me last Monday your threattning bull, as grand as iff from the pope and as mercyfull as iff from the Turke, demanding fowre years arrears of tith due to you of seven

---

[509] John Jeffery (1647–1720) received a Cambridge doctorate in divinity two years after his 1694 installation as archdeacon of Norwich, a position he held until his death (Venn, ii. 465; *Fasti Ecclesiae Anglicanae*, 45).

[510] Brockett does not appear among the proctors listed in Carter, *The Norwich Subscription Books*, 70. Among the Brockets at the inns of court, a John Brockett of the Middle Temple was called to the bar on 3 June 1698 (*Middle Temple Register*, i. 223). See also miscellaneous documents, below, p. 323 n. 58.

shillings a yeare, which oughtt to have bin for twenty seven years as is now due this Michellmas att Pentny butt thatt I have by your self and rogues of procttors by my ignorance and there threats forcst from me and for quiettness sake to suffer a depryvation of my rightt to be wrested from mee by you. Butt now, sir, since I have soe lately paid you all your demands, I ought to be sattisfyed how they come to be due to you; for the law allowes itt mee (and in another man itt would be sacralidg, tho nott in you). Nor need I informe you, sir, thatt the rubrick in the church now allowed by our good queen and confirmed by actt of parliamentt is thatt all things relatteing to the church are to stand fixtt as settled in the second yeare of King Edward the Sixth time by him settled (which allows you no tithes), [fol. 101r] from which and by whome I am entittled to my right and claime of my peculer in this place and shall when occation offers prove itt under ten crowned heads. And the revertions made since King Edward the Sixth (1547) gave this place to as Fullguston has noe mention made of the church.[511] Nor is there either in morgage or sale any mention made of the church (as recorded or enroled) – and I am the twelfe person has bin posest of itt since thatt time – in either my mortgage and purchas deeds when all the little messages, riviletts, and drains are specified in them. I confess my deer father offten told me amongst all his good works (which were numorus) thatt affter he had bought this estatt hee had laid outt above 200 l. to cover the church and chancell, just falling, for a conveniency for whatt child he should give itt to. And I have bin as carefull to support itt.

And now you and your courte is endevouring to molest me in my just rightt; which rather then submitt to, I am resolv'd to pull itt downe and build upp my houses with itts stones since I can keep noe minister to itt for your courte. And iff I doe pull itt downe as I sett it up, you can doe me noe hurte for itt nor your selfe neither. And, sir, is itt nott a shame to your carractor to send your procttters aboutt with such threatts for seven shillings a year, when your own contience and my selfe can tell you thatt you have wrongfully forced from me by threats, &c., five and twenty years pay, as apeers on record, by my fears and ignorance. Which iff you please to serch as I have done and an abstractt of itt by me from King Edward the Sixth guift, I am sure, sir, you will abominatt the sacralidg of itt and I hope be soe sinceble of the injury done me by your selfe and Mr Chancellour as to returne itt me againe. And now I have given you my sentiments, I oughtt to be sattisfyed by

---

[511] Richard de Fulmodeston or Fulmerston, a 'great buyer of Church lands and property' (Rye, i. 236), obtained the West Bilney holding at the dissolution of the priories in the reign of Edward VI; from him the manor was conveyed to Thomas Mildmay (Blomefield, viii. 354).

my lord bishop and your selfe for the injury done me by you. Nor shall I refuse waiteing on you both in the queens court and the arch bishops you paying of my charges.

Sir, I am ashamed to trouble you under such a stile as this does presentt itt selfe to you, butt force has noe law. I shall only begg your pardon and leave to subscrib my selfe

Your humble servantt,
E Frek

Sir, I have with my own hand paid you 28 years in my own wrong of ignorance.

Subscribed: For the Reverend Doctter John Jeffryes, arch deacon of Norwich, att his house there. Post paid 3d.

[fol. 101v]

1713, Octtober 9 Octtober the ninth, being Sunday, my son, Sir Ralph Frek, and his wife and his three sons (Percy, Ralph, and Redman) left London in order to goe for Ireland after a twelve month stay heer in England; when in May I presented him and his wife with the pattentt of a barronett, which I have well paid for since. However, itt fixes this estatte of West Billney from being sold by them and I hope may bee of advantage to the marry of my severall grandchildren, which my God has blest him (and me) with. And for this and all my kindness to them I have nott had a letter from my son above this halfe yeare.

1713, Novembr the 3d I thank God my son and his familly landed saffe in Dublin from Chester. Att the parliament there where they weare all in greatt heats against the Lord Chancelour Phips favouring the Pretendor, &c., affter aboutt 6 weeks sitting they were by the queen prorogued to the tenth of nextt Agust and the citty left to 3 lord justices care.[512]

1713, November the 4 The 3d or 4 of November dyed Narscyssas Marsh, lord prymmate of Ireland, in the seventy second yeare of his age. He was bred up under my deer father att Oxford and by him prefered to the being lord prymate of all Ireland. His carractor in the publick news is he was nott only a father to the fatherless and a husband to the widdow butt a receivour for the poore, for all his greatt incoms were laid outt in charytable and pious uses for them. Wittness

[512] The *Daily Courant* (3798) has an 18 December report from Dublin about a parliamentary attempt to remove Constantine Phipps (1656–1723) from his position as lord chancellor of Ireland (*CJI*, iii. 993). Phipps was accused of supporting the Pretender; but parliament was prorogued until 10 August 1714, then dissolved until 12 November 1715. In the interim and a new monarch Phipps was removed from his position and returned to England (J. Roderick O' Flanagan, *The Lives of the Lord Chancellors and Keepers of the Great Seal of Ireland*, 2 vols. [London, 1870], i. 536–54).

one thing of many where att Drogheda he has buyltt a noble fabrick and endowed itt for ever for twenty clergymens widdows, each to have an apartmentt and twenty pound a yeare perr anum. **2i** Taken outt of the gassett the 2i of November by me.[513] Eliza Freke

i7i3, November i5 or i6 Monday, the i6 of November, my kiching doore being oppen, came up into my chamber two ruffins, viz., Thom Garett and Goodbody of Saffum, and brought me a peice of paper to insertt my name;[514] in which I absolutly refused to doe, offering iff I owed any thing to any one I had mony to pay itt. And therfore I would nott subscribe my name, which these two rogues swore twenty times they would make me doe alive or dead. My two maids being in my chamber they turned downe stairs as fast as they came round up to me, [so that] I might have noe wittness of there words and acttions to me, shutting the doore affter them to frighten me. Thus these two rogues stood pulling and pinching of me for above two howrs the clock in my chamber, and spitting on me, and threw the table I have rested my self on for three year past with all there force [fol. 102r] against me, and towre me by my arms and shoulders. And when I said they would kill me, they said they cared nott; and Goodbody said they came for thatt intentt, all the while calling me the worst names thatt there mouthes could utter. Att last they concluded to throw me down the staires and by thatt way to stopp my breath; when both these rogues, Thom Garrett and Goodbody, tore me by my arms by all their strength outt of my chaire and pull'd me to the stair head to throw me downe. Which they had scartainly done had nott Goode Whiting and Sconce with my two maids stood just before me to break my fall, crying they were goeing to murder me, and beged me to subscribe itt.[515] Which (lifes preservation and above three howrs contest) I sett my hand to there paper. From whence last week these rogues sent me word iff I had noe bill to show thatt they had made me one should att the nextt

[513] Narcissus Marsh (1638-1713), archbishop of Armagh and primate of all Ireland, died on 2 November. Born in Hannington, he entered Magdalen Hall, Oxford in 1655, won a fellowship at Exeter College, and later received both his masters and doctorate in divinity. His diary does not acknowledge any role Ralph Freke might have had in either his education or later career. He was appointed lord primate of Ireland on 18 February 1702/3, long after Ralph Freke's death ('Archbishop Marsh's Diary', *The British Magazine*, 28 [1845], 17-26, 115-32). Among the gazettes that announce the news of his death, Freke's characterization of Marsh follows very closely one found in the *Post Boy* (2888).

[514] Robert Goodbody, the husband of Elizabeth Turner and father of several children baptized and buried in Swaffham, was himself buried in the church of St Peter and St Paul on 7 January 1715/6.

[515] John Whiting had married Ann Fowler on 12 July 1713 in Swaffham, a year after his wife Catherine had been buried in East Winch on 23 April 1712. Goody Sconce was probably Elizabeth, the wife of John Sconce, who is listed in the land tax records of 1704 as well as in the Pentney archdeacon's transcripts; she could also be the Sconces' daughter-in-law Margaret, the wife of Strett Sconce.

assises reach me body and goods; which being now butt a fortnightt to itt, I were faine, haveing noe frind in a hundred mile of me, to submitt to there unreasonable demands of neer twenty pound paid besids charges and to my atturney. Besids aboute fowr month have I now laine on the wrack of misery they have putt me to in my shoulder and arme, nott able to sitt or lye downe. This is the misserable condition I live in. God give me patience. E Freke

1713, Decembr 13 From Dublin they wright thatt on Thursday last Mr Jacob Twisleton was taken into custody by a serjantt att armes.[516] Hee was our state trumpeter butt about six years agoe went for France, where hee turned Roman Catholick. Hee came into England with the duke de Amon, the French ambasador, and brought over severall medalls of the Pretender.[517] Hee is charged with deserting the queens service and goeing into an enimyes country and returning withoutt pardon or pass.

14 Letters from Dublin advise thatt they are prepareing bills to attaint the Pretender with a conciderable reward for any thatt shall apprehend him. On Monday before was ordered thatt leave bee given for heads of a bill thatt the subjects may have the benifitt of councell in case of ffellony or treason and a list of the names of all Irish papist thatt are licenest to carry armes and by whome. Taken outt of the London gassett.[518]

December 31 And thatt ther are 18 pettitions by the Wigs against pretended undue elections; 8 or 9 tryed, and they turne outt all church members.[519]

Aboutt the 27 or the Sunday affter Xmas Day I had a sermon and a sacramentt in Billney church preached and given by Mr Smith, the vicker of Winch, and another last Aprill, for both which I paid him forty shillings and sentt him my stray mare and gave his son ten shillings and his daughter an arpon cost me in London neer twenty shillings more.

[516] Jacob Twisleton was apprehended and on 12 December ordered delivered to the lord chief justice of queen's bench. Twisleton had been in France serving the Pretender and had returned without authorization (*CJI*, iii. 966–7, 977). Freke's entry follows closely the account of Twisleton's life in the *Post Boy* (2904).

[517] Louis, duc d'Aumont (1666–1723), was the French ambassador extraordinaire to England from 1712 to 1713 (*Dictionnaire de Biographie Française* [Paris, 1934–], iv. 635–6).

[518] The news from Dublin in the *Daily Courant* (3798) and the *British-Mercury* (443) includes the 10 December parliamentary resolve to appoint a committee 'to bring in heads of a bill to attaint the *Pretender*' and all who have supported his treason (*CJI*, iii. 967). The *Daily Courant* (3794) and the *Post Boy* (2905) carry reports from Dublin that the Irish parliament ordered a committee on 7 December 1713 'to bring in heads of a bill, that the subject may have the benefit of counsel in cases of felony and treason'; they also mention the 8 December vote to bring before the House of Commons 'a list of the names of all *Irish* Papists, that are licensed to carry arms' (*CJI*, iii. 962, 964).

[519] Follows verbatim the 12 December news from Dublin in the *Post Boy* (2905).

i7i3/i4, January first Fryday, New Years Day and my unhappy birth day thatt I entred my seventy third yeare, I had as usuall all my tennants and neighbours dined with mee. Where tho I have nott bin hardly cross my chamber this three years, yett I made them all wellcome; and twill be my last time I shall see them all together. And I doe most humbly beg of God iff hee spare my life longer itt may bee to serve hime. Eliza. Freke

[fol. 102v]

i7i3/i4, January the i6 The sixteenth of January I had a letter from my Lady Freke from Dublin outt of Ireland which informs mee of hers and the chilldrens good health and thatt Sir Ralfe, my son, lyes there very ill of the goute in Dublin. Itt was very wellcom to mee to heere any way hee was alive, itt being confidently reported in this country hee was one of the six gentlemen cast away att Rings End in the herbor of Dublin.[520] Soe thatt I can truly say thatt from the 9 of Octtober lastt to the eightt of Febuary I have never gone to bed or rise outt of itt with dry eyes and thatt I have paid those tears due to his death in his liffe to him. For which I humbly begg of God to forgive me, Eliza Freke.

i7i3/i4, Febuary ii Thursday, Febuary the eleventh, Mr Harvy was heer from Gyton to informe me thatt the nextt Sunday hee was ordered by Thomas Taner, chancellour of Norwich, to excominycatte mee for nott releasing the rightt of my church into there scandelous courte,[521] where itt has never bin yett, itt being my owne peculer in which I have on my own charge keptt a minester above this forty years withoutt ever haveing him questioned in all the foregeoing bishops times; [yet Mr Buck] was turned outt by this chancelour for wantt of good maners, tho coalated by this bishop to Gyton.

i4 Vallintines Day, the fowrteenth of Febuary, being Sunday, this Mr Harvy excominycated me outt of my church, for none of my neighbours elce would doe itt. Before which I took outt my plate and whatt elce I had given itt and left the church tite and whole and nott soe much as a quary in the windows broke or the least breach in the church yard, and soe with an inventory of whatt I left in the church delivered itt to the care of the chancelour of Norwich, Thomas Tanner. And now I hope I am rid of all the spirittual black coats. Butt the key

[520] Ringsend, a 'small town', now within the city of Dublin, located on the east side of the River Dodder (Lewis, *A Topographical Dictionary of Ireland*, ii. 516).

[521] Benjamin Harvey was instituted vicar of Gayton on 8 October 1711, replacing Charles Buck. Harvey, who would later become rector of Stody, received his BA from Corpus Christi in 1707 (NRO, DN/Sub 4/3; Venn, ii. 322).

of the church I keep to my selfe and ordered the chancelour to make another to the south doore.

1713/14, Febuary 14 Sunday, the 14 of Febuary, dyed King Phillips queen of Spaine, daughter of the prince of Wolfenbattle, sister to the empress, and grandchild to the king of France. Shee had a long sicknes and expired the above day. All our courts are in mourning for her, even the zar of Muscovy. Outt of the gassett.[522]

[fol. 103r]

1713/14, Febuary the 15 Monday, the fiffteenth of Febuary, aboute two a clock in the affternoone was heer the dreadfull'st storme and hurrycane of wind for severall howers was ever heard, which did an infinitt deale of damage to many people in this country and mee in perticuler, itt haveing hardly left a house or barne standing in the parish.[523] And three blown downe to the ground att Knopwoods, and his dary and dwelling house lyes quitt naked, as does the head house of the Wassell House Farme. And all the back house stable and outt housing lyes quitt naked. And the Hall, my own house, is quitt unkeptt, and Holtens house and barne I had just mended up made as bad as ever. And the Maner Farme the barne allmost all downe and the stable and house ruinated, and Greens stable barn,[524] &c., quit to the ground and all the roof of his house blown off. And most trajocall to behold is this parish now, and soe is my lodg of the warren; butt which is most my concerne is the church, which now being outt of my care will, I feare, soon fall to decay, itt being much harrased with this wind.

13 When the chancellour sentt me word he would excominicate me, I putt up those things I gave the church for my own disposall wher I lye.

As first one large sillver flagon, cost me above fiffteen pound; one large sillver cupp to itt and itts bread plate or cover; and one new Common Prayer Book in Turky leather imbost and gilded; and one new vellum book for xings and buriall; a register; and one imbrodered table cloth, pullpitt cloth, and couchen of my own worke; with one fine damask table cloth, &c. Eliz Freke

The things I leftt in the church are as followeth: one south door into the chancell from my house; one old communion table railed in by me; two long seats; one chest in which is putt in by me one greatt

[522] The *London Gazette* (5207), *Daily Courant* (3844), and *British-Mercury* (451) report the death of Philip V's wife, Marie Louise (1688–1714), on 14 February 1714 (NS). None of these gives her genealogy or says that the courts are in mourning.

[523] Blomefield notes the brief but 'violent wind' that on this date 'did great damage by sea and land' (iii. 435), as does Paul Richards, *King's Lynn* (Chichester, 1990), 36.

[524] Probably that of Charles Greene, who rented land on the common.

Bible; one Common Prayer Book, allmost new; one old book (of, I think, Erasmus); one little sillver cupp and little bread plate; one pewter flagon; one old table cloth; one hollon table cloth; 3 silk couchens to my seatt in the church; 2, two, folding doors outt of my chancell into the church – wherin is the pullpitt, and under itt the clarks seate; and over the chancell doors is the armes of England in a large scution with the Lords Prayer, Beliefe, and Ten Commandements. And more is my seatt and eighteen more; three bells, new roped; and one funtt for xings; and a carraige for dead people with itts black cover; and one long lader; with two dores, one north, the other south. The north one I have the key of, and I wrott the chancellour word he might make one to the south doore. This inventory I sentt him to answer itt againe to Sir Ralph Freke and Elizabeth Frek.

II. REMEMBRANCES, 1671–1713

[fol. 3v]

Some few remembrances of my misfortunes which have atended me since I were maryed (in my unhappy life), which was i4 of November i67i

i67i, November i4 Thursday, the i4 of November and Childermas or Cross Day and dreadfully rainey, I was in London pryvatly married to Mr Percy Freke by Docter Johnson, my Lord Russells chaplin, in Coven Garden Church in London.[1] My husband was the only son liveing of Captaine Aurthur Frek and grandson to Mr William Freke, the only brother of Sir Thomas Frek of Dorshetshire, who was my grandfather, and his son Mr Ralph Freke [was] my own deer father. And my deer mother was Sir Thomas Cullpepers daughter of Hollingburne in Kentt. Her name was Cicelia Cullpeper, who dyed in or about i649 and left me, the eldest of five daughters, aboutt six or seven years of age and lyes buryed in the chancell att Hollingburne – where lyes six more brothers and sisters of myne which dyed young and my deer sister, the wife of Sir George Choutt, who lived his widow i2 years and dyed of the small pox, as did her only daughter, and are both inter'd in the chancell in Hollingburne.[2] And affter aboutt 6 or seven years being engaged to my deer cosin Mr Percy Frek and all my three surviveing sisters maryed, viz., Cicelia maryed to Sir Georg Choutt in Kentt, Frances marryed to Sir George Norton att Abbots Leigh neer Bristoll, and Judith, my youngest sister, marryed Collonell Robertt Austen of Tenterden in Kentt, I, the eldest, Elizabetth, as above, was maryed i4 of November i67i to Mr Percy Frek withoutt my deer fathers consentt or knowledg in a most dreadfull raynie day (a presager of all my sorrows and misfortunes to mee).

i672, Jully 26 Being Thursday, the 26 of Jully i672, I wear againe remaryed by my deer father, who then gave me himselfe to Mr Frek by Docter Uttram att St Margaretts Church in Westminster in London in a dreadfull windy day as my other was rainey (by a license keptt in

---

[1] Cross Day, or the Exaltation of the Holy Cross, is celebrated on i4 September, not i4 November, and is not traditionally associated with Childermas or Innocents Day. See above, p. 37 n i.

[2] The Hollingbourne parish register indicates Cicely died on 6 January i650/i; her monument, which adds that she was forty-one years of age at her death, names the five surviving daughters. The burial of the youngest, Philippa, is not recorded in the register, nor are many of the earlier deaths of the other siblings. See Introduction, p. 5 and n. 8.

Mr Freks pocked 4 or 5 years).[3] Both which days of my marriage have bin true prognostications of whatt I have undergone since for full forty years past, being now 1712, Elizabeth Freke. And I look'd on them as dredfull emblems to mee.

1672, Agust 26 Mr Freke, coming over St James Park aboutt 12 a clock att nightt, challenged my lord of Roscomon either to fightt him presently or pay him downe a thousand pound my lord owed him;[4] butt the King Charls, being in the park, prevented the presentt quarell. And the next morning by three a clock ten men of the lifegard seised him in his bed and carryed him away to Whitt Hall immediatly before Secetaory Coventry,[5] I nott knowing whatt it was for more then the loss of my 1000 l., and the begining of my troubles and my disobedience in marrying as I did withoutt my deer fathers knowledg.

1673, Febuary 14 In or aboutt Febuary 14 my deer father, Mr Ralph Frek, was pleased to bestow on me for a portion a mortgage on Sir Robertt Brooks estate of 500 l. a year neer the Green Man in Epping Forrest, 5 miles from London, thatt I might have a subsistance for my life.[6] Which Mr Frek unknown to me sould to Sir Josias Child, a bruer in London, for (5664 l.) five thousand six hundred sixty fowre pounds or thereaboutts.[7]

Jully 7 Which nither my deer father or my self or any of my 5 trustees knew any thing of till about Jully the 7. This was nott kind done, for by itt I were turned outt of doors and nott a place to put my unfortunatte head in and my mony in a bankers hand, viz., Allderman Forths, who all three brothers soon affter brook for a hundred thousand pounds.[8] But I thank God the little wee had there we gott safe outt two days before they broke, butt my deer father lost by them twelve hundred pounds. This was Gods greatt providence to Eliz Frek.

[fol. 4r]

1673, September 15 Aboutt the middle of September Mr Frek endeavouring to place the remaineing part of my fortune on an estatt in Hamptshier of one Mr Coopers and trusting to one Mr Worldlyge

---

[3] William Owtram; 26 June 1673 in the register: above, p. 37 n. 2.

[4] Wentworth Dillon, fourth earl of Roscommon: above, p. 38 n. 3.

[5] Henry Coventry: above, p. 38 n. 4.

[6] See above, p. 38 n. 5.

[7] Josiah Child: above, p. 38 n. 6.

[8] John Forth, a London alderman from Cripplegate (1668–76), and his brother Dannet, an alderman from Cheapside (1669–76), were master brewers with commissions to farm Irish revenues. They were also among the original stockholders in the Royal African Company (Alfred B. Beaven, *The Aldermen of the City of London*, 2 vols. [London, 1908–13], i. 134; ii. 190, 102; J. R. Woodhead, *The Rulers of London, 1660–1689* [London, 1965], 71–2).

ιs his agentt in itt, wee were cheatted by them both, [so] thatt on his composition my husband was forced to loose att least fiffteen hundred pounds as the least loss besids a 3 or fowers [years] law suite, their cheatt being above 25 hundred loss to me and the estatte.[9]

Thus was three of my unhappy years spentt in a maryed <deleted: several words> lyfs comfortts in London, wher I twice misscarryed, and] where I lost two thousand five hundred pounds outt of my six thousand seven hundred sixty fowre pounds. And I never had of itt, to my remembrance, five pound of itt and very little of my husbands company, which was no small griefe to mee, I being governed in this my marriag wholly by my affecttions withoutt the consentt or knowledg of any of my friends. And now beeing apprehensive all my fortune vould bee thus spentt, I resolved to goe for Ireland and try my fortune there while something was left; which I did attemptt. Eliz Freke

1674, Jully 14 Aboutt Jully 1674 my husband and my family wentt downe to Hanington to my deer fathers, Mr Ralfe Freks, to take our eaves of him in my way for Ireland, and wher I staid aboutt a forttnightt. And from thence I wentt to Abbotts Lygh to Sir George Nortons, his lady being my own sister, who was then redy to lye inn.

Agust 2d Agust the second I came there. **4** And my deer sister was broughtt to bed Sunday morning, the fourth of Agustt, of a most lovely fine child, butt itt was a daughter. **12** Which on my deer sisters desire I staid and christned itt with my Lady Balldin, the grandmother, the 12 of Agust by the name of Grace.[10] And heer I staid att my deer sisters till the two and twentieth day of Agust lyeing wind-bound for a shipp and a wind.

22 Aboutt the 22 of Agust I wentt to the Bath with Mr Frek, where I lay for a ship and wind for aboutt a month. In which time my deer father, heering I were nott gone for Ireland and were with child, sentt his coach and horses to fetch me from the Bath to him to Hanington.

Octtober the 7 Where Mr Freke and I wentt with my little familly the 7 of Octtober; who very kindly received mee with my deer auntt Frek and did soe treatt me till I were able to goe for Ireland, which was aboutt ten monthes.[11]

March 7 Sunday morne, March seventh, 1674/5, God took to himself my deer sister Sir George Chouts lady of the small pox, as did her husband aboutt twelve years before of the same distemper, who continued his widdow from two and twenty years of her age to her death. And she left behind her one son and one daughter, viz., Sir George Choute, a barrenett and a fine gentleman now liveing in 1712

[9] Richard Cooper's manor of Ditcham and Sunworth: above, p. 39 n. 7.
[10] Ellen Baldwin; Grace was baptized on 10 August (above, p. 39 n. 8).
[11] Frances Freke: above, p. 40 n. 9.

and a single man, and her daughter named Cicelya, her mothers name and mine.[12]

i675, March 26 Aboutt the 26 of March my deer sister, being imbalmed in London wher shee dyed, was carryed downe to Hol longburne in Kentt to be there intter'd. Where shee was in the chancel in my deer mothers grave, which was above 20, twenty, years past when I were butt seven years of age and the eldest of five daughter alive, and nott mist by us, haveing soe indullgentt a father and good an aunt in my mothers sister to breed us up.[13] Eliza. Freke

Aprill 5 God took to himselfe my deer neece Cicelia Choutt of the small pox neer a month affter the death of my deer sister, who lye buryed by her deer mother in Holingburn chancell in Kentt.[14] They both dyed in London to my griefe.

June 2d Wensday, June 2d, my deer son, Ralph Frek, was borne att my deer fathers att Hanington aboutt three in the affternoone (the very same day and hower my deer husband dyed and left mee an unhapy widow in i706[15]), and I haveing fowre midwifes with me for him, of which one was a man midwife. He was borne soe weak as to bee baptised immediattly by my deer father and Sir Georg Norton for his godfathers and my auntt Frek for his godmother and Lady Thinn. I were 4 or 5 days in labour of him; and all my fowre midwifes affirmed him severall howers dead in mee to my husband and my Lady Thinn and to my deer Lady Norton, all with mee in my extremity severall dayes with my aunt Freke. Att last being allmost spentt and without any further hopes, [fol. 4v] itt was agreed by them all my son should be taken in peices from mee on ther conciderration I cold nott live an howr longer. Butt whilst the man was putting on his butchers habbit to come aboutt me, my greatt God thatt never failed mee (or deneyed me my reasonable request) raised me up a good woman midwife of my Lady Thins acquaintence, one Mrs Mills, who came in att this juncture of time and for three howrs in her shifftt work'd till by Gods providence and mercy to mee I was saffly delivered.[17] And tho of a dead child hurtt with severall great holes in his head, my God raised him up by life to mee soe farr as the same night to babtise him of my deer fathers name (Ralph Freke).

3 The nextt day I putt him into the hand of a good surgion, who came every day from Highworth to dress him (I being soe weak as not

[12] George Choute: above, p. 40 n. 10.

[13] Cicely was buried on 12 March (above, p. 40 n. 11). Frances: above, p. 40 n. 9.

[14] Hollingbourne monument: above, p. 41 n. 12.

[15] '1712' in the manuscript.

[16] Mary or Frances Thynne: above, p. 41 n. 14.

[17] The midwife Mrs Mills is not listed in the Wiltshire Articles of Subscription, nor can she be identified with the Anne Milles in the Highworth parish register.

able to stirr); who dayly attended him for six weeks and att last by my Gods greatt goodness and mercy to me recovered him.[18] For which, great God, make me ever thankfull for spareing my child and raiseing up his poor servantt. Eliz Frek

Jully 7 My son was taken with a through thrush in his mouth and his head with which he was againe given over for dead and carried from me to be burryed.[19] Butt from this misfortune my God raised him up againe, I hope, to bee his servantt and a comfortt to his poor afflicted mother for my deer sister Choutt, whome my God tooke from me about two months before and was to have binn with me in this my extremity. Soe my joy was turn'd to mourning by the loss of my deer sister and her daughter, tho I had my deer sister the Lady Norton soe good to be with mee.

September 15 Aboutt the midle of September I sett outt againe from Bristoll Faire for Ireland, the first time of my goeing over thither;[20] and I left my only son (with my deer father care over him) att Highworth att nurse, hee being then aboutt ten weeks old. In Ireland att my Lord Inchequeens house I staid aboutt eight monthes.[21]

December 14 When my deer father sentt for me over to England, my son being cripled by the carlessness of his nurse [who] aboutt 14 of December brok his legg shortt in the hackle bone and keptt itt pryvatte for a quarter of a yeare.[22] My deer father and sister Norton took him away from nurse and Hiworth and placed him by my father att nurse Deveralls, wher he lay aboutt a quarter of a year in [her] lapp nott able to move or stirr.[23]

January 8 Mr Frek and I in Ireland all the whilest knew nothing of itt till aboutt January 8. Dispaireing of his life, my deer father sentt for me in hast againe. Where when I came over aboutt the begining of Aprill, by Gods blessing I againe recovered him from his cruches with my poor, weak endeavours; and now, I thank my God, is straitt and goes well, and noe signe of these misfortunes, butt is the father of three fine boyes alive now in Ireland, 1712, which God of his infinit mercy spare to Eliz Freke.[24]

1676, Aprill 14 My deer father sentt for me againe outt of Ireland to my son, he haveing bin given over by the doctters and surjanes.

---

[18] His name does not appear in the Wiltshire Articles of Subscription.

[19] Thrush: above, p. 41 n. 16.

[20] Bristol Fair is not listed on contemporary maps; the Bristol archivist, J. S. Williams, does not 'know of any name existing in the past'.

[21] Rostellan, the estate of William O'Brien, second earl of Inchiquin: above, p. 42 n. 19.

[22] Hackle-bone: hip bone.

[23] Anne or Jane Deverell: above, p. 42 n. 18.

[24] Percy, age twelve; Ralph, age nine; and John Redman/Redmond, age six.

And aboutt the end of Aprill or the begining of May, I landed att
Bristoll, wher I sentt to my deer sister the Lady Norton then att Leigh
to come to mee.

May 7 Which shee did with a sad accountt of my son being a quite
cripple. And thatt my father and shee every day expectted his death
hee would nott invite me to Hanington to see him.

June i5 Aboutt the midle of June my deer father came up to London
to mee to sattissfie me aboutt my son, whose life he said he dispaired
of; and hee advised mee to be contented since all was done for him
thatt could be done; and then hee invitted me to Hanington from
London to see my son.

Jully 7 or 8 When to the best of my remembrance, aboutt the
begining of Jully my deer father sold to my deer husband the estate o
West Billney in Norfolk, my brother Austen nott liking of itt for my
sisters portion.[25] Hee paid my brother for itt downe in redy mony fowr
thousand pounds and to my deer father more, aboutt seven hundred
sixtty six pound.

September 29 For which he made over Billny for itts securyty and
aboutt the end of September following settled itt on mee and my son
being then little more then a twelve monthes old and in a faire way o
recovery. Which bond of Mr Freks to my deer father of 766–i4–id
when I came outt of Ireland he was pleased to give me up to pay for
my jorney and as a helpe to my loses of 2500 l. by Cooper. E Freke

[fol. 5r]

i676, December i4 Aboutt the midle of December Mr Frek
purchased of my deer father Leeds Castle in Kentt for two thousand
pound due then to my father on itt. My husband paid my father downe
on the bargaine five hundred pound; and hee was to stand outt the
law with the Lord Cullpeper in my deer fathers name, which in two
years cost my husband neer a thousand pounds in law; and gave my
deer father eight hundred bond charged on my West Billney, which
my husband was to pay my deer father when we recovered itt by our
decree in chancery then depending.

23 Butt affter all our charge in law and possesion given us for 5750
l. and the tennents atturned to my deer husband, [by] the base King
James the Second and villinaus Lord Cullpeper, my cosin jermine, wee
were withoutt our knowledg turned outt of all our posesion and by
them; and Chancellour Finch nott alowed or permitted a heering for
itt affter itt had cost my husband soe much in law and the shriefe and

---

[25] The miscellaneous documents (below, p. 320) note that Austen sold the property
back to his father-in-law on 30 June 1675.

iis twenty fowre baylyes a hundred pound for giveing us the posession.[26]

24 Aded to this, Mr Frek returned from Leeds Castle in Kentt illmost dead with his jorney to London the Xmas Eve in frost and now. Eliz Freke

i676/7, Febuary i2 While King Jams, Lord Cullpeper, and Lord Chancellour [Finch] jugled together with threats to reverse our decree given my husband by actt of parlamtt, which was done by them in Candlemas tearme following, Febuary i2, i676/7. Soe affter our attendance about three month more in London to obtaine a heering from his unjust courtt, wee were deneyed itt, tho Mr Frek butt to be cast by law or begin his suit againe.[27] This is true. Eliz Freke

i677, May 2 Aboutt the second of May I lay in of annother son in South Hamptton Square in London which by hard labour and severall rights was dead borne and lyes buryed att the upper end of St Gilles chancell in Londdon with one of my Lord Hallifaxes in the same grave.[28] Eliza. Freke

Jully 20 I wentt downe with Mr Freke againe to my deer fathers, Mr Ralph Freks, to Hanington to goe for Ireland, England being then full of plots and troubles, where I staid aboutt a month and wentt for Bistoll to gett a shipp for our passage. Butt King Charls and King James had commanded an imbargoe on all ships and passengers nott to cross the seas withoutt their permitt, which was deneyed us.[29]

Agust 25 Wee wentt pryvattly off att Pill[30] in a boatt to a shipp the 25 of Agust, and my second time of goeing for Ireland, on a Satterday, when I left my son att Hanington with my deer father under the care of his dry nurse, Goode Deverall. But wee were by tempestious wynds all like to bee lost thatt day. **26** Att last compased Illford Combe, where I stayed Sunday, Monday, and Tuesday.[31]

28 And a Wensday by two of the clock in the morn the wind changed, when I wentt with Mr Frek to sea againe and came thatt night within a watch of reaching Watterford. **29** Butt on a suden arrose the most hidious tempest of wind and raigne which brought us back againe nextt day att nightt to Lundy, where we with 4 ships more lay dispaireing of life with our mast downe and our cabin shutt upp and

---

[26] Atturned: see attornment (above, p. 44 n. 23); Thomas, second Lord Culpeper and Heneage Finch: above, p. 44 nn. 22 and 25.

[27] According to Stephen Ellison, Deputy Clerk of the Records, no parliamentary records of the decree exist; nor has the lord chancellor's reversal been documented.

[28] The child of George Savile, first marquess of Halifax (1633–1695), and his second wife, Gertrude Pierrepont, whom he married in 1672. Lord Halifax would become lord privy seal and speaker of the House of Lords as well as the author of *The Character of a Trimmer* (*HC*, iii. 396–8).

[29] Charles II, France, and Holland: above, p. 45 n. 28.

[30] Cockerne Pill on the River Avon: above, p. 46 n. 29.

[31] Ilfracombe: above, p. 46 n. 29.

our anchors lost, roleing on an anker till nextt day att night.[32] **30** Wher tho night, dispaireing of life wee attempted the barr of Barstable, ir which wee expected our last. Butt by Gods infinite mercy to us wee safe landed att Barstable aboutt sun setting to the amasementt of al thatt saw us. Wher with Captaine Jeffryes we staid aboutt a weeke.[33]

September 5, 6 Wee wentt to sea againe; and by Gods mercy to me wee all landed safe in Cork harbour, tho persued by several Algeriens, September 6, i677.[34] For which mercy the greatt God make me ever thankfull and grantt I may never forgett his goodness to me whilst I am, Elizabeth Freke.

i678, May io I wentt againe for England with Mr Frek by the desire of my deer father, Ralph Freke, Esqr. Wher affter a short stay Mr Frek went for London and unknown to my deer father or mee sould outt his right in Leeds Castle to Alexander Cullpeper for (250о l.) two thousand five hundred pound, tho he had promised my father to settle itt on mee and for which my deer father gave me up my bond my husband owed him of 800 l., eight hundred pounds, as he did another nott long before of 760 l. due to him on our estate in Wes Billney.[35] Which were then both very wellcome to us [fol. 5v] and done by my Gods dereicttion, who allways provids for. Eliza Freke

i679, Aprill 3d Dureing this our stay in England Mr Freks mother dyed Aprill 3d in Ireland. On which news we went up againe for London to endeavour for a pasage over for Ireland; wher Mr Freek fell sick of an ague and feaver to death doore thatt I were forcst affter six weeks stay to hasten downe to my deer fathers againe to Hanington **June 2d**, wher he lay sick of a quinsey and plurisy aboute six weeks more.

July 23 Affter which, tho he was very ill, wee wentt to Bristoll to my deer sister Nortons.

i680, Agust i8 Where by Gods mercy to me and my deer sister kind care of him, he with my son, Ralph Frek, endeavoured our jorney for Ireland and took shipping aboutt the i8 of Agust i680. **2i** Where by Gods greatt mercy to mee my husband, my son, and my selfe were safe landed att the Cove in the Greatt Island neer Cork the 2i – my son then being just five years of age the second of June before and his

---

[32] Lundy Island: above, p. 46 n. 30.

[33] Barnstaple: above, p. 46 n. 31; since the Frekes left without official permission, the officer would probably not have been John Jefferys, a captain in the royal navy not listed among the fleet during July to November 1677 (*Commissioned Sea Officers*, 243; PRO, ADM 8/1).

[34] Reports from Falmouth and Deal stress the danger the Algerian men of war posed. The *Mary* of Cork and the *Elizabeth* from Falmouth were stopped in August 1677; the *Constance* from Weymouth was boarded in October (*CSPD*, 1677–8, 324–5, 395).

[35] Alexander Culpeper represented Lord Culpeper (above, p. 46 n. 32).

rst coming over for Ireland and my 3d time.[36] For which mercy the
reat God make me ever humbly thankfull. Eliz Freke

Septtember i6 I came with my husband and son to Rath Barry,
here my husbands sister Barnard had cleered my house of every thing
ood I left in itt, even to seven years letters past between us before I
aarryed and my cirttificate of my privatt marraige the first time.[37]
esids shee took away from me all my plate and linnen of my own
efore I marryed her brother to the value of above two hundred
ounds, engraven with my own coate of armes in a lozenge. And tho
ay husband was his mothers executor, yett all was by his kind sister
arnard conveyed away from him and mee thatt I had nott the valuy
f five shillings of hers or my own leftt mee, or one scrip of my linnen,
r a spoone to eate with, tho I had neer two dosen. Only she sentt my
usband a bill of eighty pound for burying his mother.

November Butt with much adoe and high words I gott a little of
ay plate againe. This was the good usuage I had in her familly and
aying the death of my husbands mother to my doore (for carring away
er son) att neer fowrescore years of age.

i68i However, in Ireland I staid with my son allmost 22 monthes;
a which time Mr Freke contracted with the earle of Barrymoor for his
state of Rathbarry, for which we were to pay, as to the best of my
emembrance, fowrteen hundred pounds besids our lease of sixty three
ears due on itt.[38] This being concluded on, Mr Frek made me writ to
ay deer father to creditt me with a thousand pound on Billney security
nd to settle itt presenttly on my son; which accordingly I did. And my
eer father immedyatly returned itt to mee on my husband and my
ond rather then charge my Billney with itt, as he was pleased to say.
his mony my husband presently drew over, and with some more we
ad finished his purchas of Rathbary, and has now, I thanke him,
ettled itt on my son on his marraige with Sir John Meads daughter
n the yeare one thousand six hundred ninety nine).

November 22 And aboutt November the 22 we paid of all to thatt
amily and made all the hast we could for England, my deer father
aveing sentt for me and my son to come over to him and receive his
ast blessing.

i682, Aprill 30 Soe thatt in Aprill I left Rathbarry and wentt to
Kingsaile with my son to attend for a shipp for England; wher I
ttended a fortnight and had the oppertunity of a man of warr in
hich I putt my selfe and son, I haveing noe friend to take any care
or me.

---

[36] Great Island: above, p. 47 n. 34.
[37] Mary Bernard: above, p. 47 n. 35.
[38] Richard, second earl of Barrymore: above, p. 48 n. 36.

May 10 And wee went outt to sea, to the best of my remembrance
Sunday morne, the tenth of May. **17** Where by Gods infinite mercy
affter strikeing three times on the sands wee landed safely att the Pi
att Brisstow with my son and fowre servants.

22 Att Bristoll I staid till I could send to my deer father to fetch me
who aboutt the 22 of May sentt his servants, coach, and horses to fetc
me to him to Hanington. Eliza. Freke

[fol. 6r]

1682, May 24 The 24 of May I with my sone came to my dee
fathers to Hanington safe and all my mony spentt in my travills. So
soon as I came to my deer fathers, affter he had bid me wellcome, he
made me promise him thatt I would nott leave him while hee lived
which I redily and gladly did. And then he bid me take noe care for
should wantt for nothing his life; who made his words good and treate
me and my son with the greatest kindness imaginable. A grea
allterration itt was [from] whatt I found in Ireland from my husban
and his friends.

1682, July 7 And on my looking a little mallancolly on some pas
reflections, my deer father fancyed I wanted mony. And my deer fathe
withoutt saying one word to me broughtt me downe presently in tw
baggs under his coatt two hundred pounds, which 200 l. hee charge
me to keep and nott to lett my husband know of itt, to buy mee needl
and pins. As this was very kind in my deer father, soe the very nex
post I wrott my husband word of itt to Ireland, hopeing itt might be
meanes for my continuance with him; butt Mr Freke presently foun
outt a use for itt.

Agust 15 Butt I had the contience to keep itt for my own use (I no
haveing seen two and twenty shillings the two and twenty monthes
were in Ireland). Which with more my deer father had given me a
severall times and itts intrest made up eightt hundred pounds, whic
Mr Freke took from mee and soe left me a beger againe.

1682/3, Febuary 18 Aboutt the midle of Febuary my husban
came to my deer fathers to Hanington unknown to me to fetch me fc
Ireland back with him and my son; which by the ill usuage I the:
received, I positively refused goeing with him ever more (alledging m
promise I made to my deer father to stay with him his life). Whic
when thatt would nott doe, I insisted on the ill usuage I received i
Ireland from him and his friends. Besids, his parting with me last a
Kingsaile stuck deep in my stomock, tho to this day (1712) I never le
my deer father or any friend I had know of the least difference betwee
us or any unkind usuage received from my husband or his familly i
Ireland for fear of grieveing of my deer father, butt with grief of ha

enough [prepared] to take my last leave of him and goe over againe with Mr Frek for Ireland.

i683, Jully 24 When att my parting with him, my deer father gave me his blesing and with it the bond of my husbands and mine for a thousand pounds I borrowed of him for the purchass of Rathbarry.

25 Thus I haveing staid aboutt thirteen monthes with my deer father, with a heavy hartt – being the last time I ever saw him – I leftt him and Hanington Thursday, the 25 of July, and my son att schoole with Mr Turner att Summerford, aboutt seven milles from him.[39]

26 I came to Bristoll and took shipping att Pill incognito; **29** and by Gods greatt goodness and mercy to me, tho such turbelentt times wee both came safe to Corke the Satterday following, being both of us garded before the maire there for plotters in England stole over to be searched by the presentt maire; who being one Mr Covett, well known to my family, was over and above civill to us and treated us like a gentleman and bound for our loyallty and commanded all our things on shipp board to be presently delivered to us and the citty of Cork to give us the respectt due to our quallity, to the amasementt of all beholders.[40]

i683/4, January the first Aboutt the first of January, my unhappy birth day, my deer father sentt me over to Ireland a hundred pound for a New Years gift, and dereicted me thatt Mr Frek medled nott with itt, butt bid mee to make hast over to him hee might see me againe before he dyed with my husband, wher I should meett my two sisters, the Lady Norton and my sister Austen.

Febuary 24 Butt itt being just affter the dreadfull hard winter, I could nott gett a shipp, tho hee said whatt ever itt cost me hee would pay the charge of our jorney and give me his last blessing.

i684, March 26 In order to itt Mr Freke lett Rathbary to Mr Hull for one and forty years and putt off all his stock to John Hull for the renting of itt the May affter.[41] Unknown to me Rathbary and the land aboutt itt were contracted for by John Hull for two hundred and fiffty pounds a year, and fiffty pound a yeare for Mr Hungerfords farme, and a thousand pounds for our liveing stock of horses, about thirty; cow beast, aboutt three hundred; and sheep, 2500; and lambs, 700.[42]

[39] Somerford Keynes, Gloucestershire; Isaac Turner(?): above, p. 49 n. 38.

[40] Aftermath of the Rye House Plot; Richard Covett: above, p. 50 n. 39.

[41] See above, p. 51 n. 43.

[42] Before his death in 1681 Thomas Hungerford held considerable land in the Rosscarbery area; his heir Richard, who married a daughter of Emanuel Moore, gained further property on Inchedowney Island near Clonakilty; John, another son, came into the holdings at Cahirmore (*A Census of Ireland, Circa 1659*, ed. Séamus Pender [Dublin, 1939], 209; *Clerical and Parochial Records of Cork, Cloyne, and Ross*, ed. W. Maziere Brady, 3 vols. [Dublin, 1863–4], i. xl–xli; Ffolliott, 39, 41).

[fol. 6v]

i684, March 26 Mr Frek, resolveing I should goe and live with my deer father to sattisfye him in his soe earnest desire whilst he lived, contracted with John Hull for the letting of Rathbarry to him for a lease of one and forty years att the yearly rentt of three hundred pounds a yeare including Mr Hungerfords farme of Croneges in itt and took of him twenty ginnaes earnest. And hee was to buy all our liveing stock, viz., aboutt thirty working horses besids coach horses and sadle horses, and aboute three hundred cow beast for the paile and plough oxen besids young stocke, and aboutt two thousand five hundred sheep and aboutt seven hundred lambes – all goeing away to my greatt joy and sattisfaction thatt I myght goe to my deer father, Ralph Frek, Esqr to Hanington. Elizabeth Frek

Aprill 24 Butt oh, the sadest of fates thatt ever attended poor mortall was mine, for on the 24 of Aprill my God took to himself by death my deer father to my greatt griefe and unspeakeable sorrow before I could gett a shipp to see him to receive his last blesing, which of all things in this world I desired. In the eighty ninth yeare of his age hee joyfully gave up his soule into the hands of his God, and his body to bee privattly intered in the chancell att Hanington just affter the hard wintter, and leftt me, his unhappy child, ever to lamentt him.[43] Eliza. Freke

i684, May i John Hull, Mr Freks tennantt, came to Rathbarry by six a clock in the morning when my house was full of company and demanded the possesion of my house, tho hee had promised me 3 weeks time to remove my goods. Butt nothing would prevaile butt I must be immediattly thrown outt of doors, which I was thatt day with all my goods in my house. Butt this inhumanity the country heering o: sentt in all theire carts and horses and removed them to Dunowen aboutt a mile distantt, when I lost allmost halfe of them in their removeall.[44] Butt my greatt God revenged my cause on this bruitt Hull for in the yeare i688 King James the 2d came for Ireland and by the Irish seised all thatt ever he had in the world and gave away Rathbarry to Owen Maccarty, the loss of which with all his goods and his own estate broke his hartt, he haveing nothing leftt for his wife and family to subsist on.[45] Hee lyes buryed there with one of his children in the open partt of the church of Rathbarry amongst the common Irish to his etternall infamy. Elizabeth Freke

Jully 7 Being Monday and the 7 of July, Mr Freke and I took

---

[43] Hannington monument and register: above, p. 51 n. 41.

[44] East or northeast of the castle towards Ardfield or Clonakilty: above, p. 51 n. 44.

[45] Owen MacCarty or Macartie: above, p. 52 n. 45.

hiping att Kingsale in a man of warr with Captain Clemontt and
came round to England by longe sea. Thatt nightt wee were grievously
tormed and like to be lost on the Goodwin Sands neer Dover.[46] **12**
Butt by my Gods greatt mercy to us wee safe landed att Billingsgatte
he Satterday following. For which greatt mercy greatt God ever make
hankfull. Eliz. Freke

Agust 4 Mr Frek wentt into Norfolk to West Billney, leaveing me
in a lodging in London in Brownlow Streett with my cosin Clayton,
wher I lay aboutt ten weeks and never had my husbands company ten
imes.[47]

17 Hee returned outt of Norfolk to London the seventeenth, wher
ee staid with me in London aboute a month.

September 17 And then Mr Freke wentt againe for Ireland with
he Lord Inchequieen, unknown to mee till the nightt before he wentt.[48]
And he leftt me with my son and a man and a maide att lodgings att
Mrs Murryes in Brownlow Streett to shifftt for my selfe and familly,
my husband then declareing before his nephew Barnard and the three
Googins this estatte of Billney would nott find him in bread and
cheese.[49] Boughtt by my deer father for five hundred twenty six pound
a yeare of the Lord Richerson and now lett me, Elizabeth Freke, for
476 l.) fowre hundred seventy six pound a yeare besids forty six pound
a yeare att Pentney, in all itt [is] lett for five hundred and twenty
pounds a year by wretched me, Elizabeth Freke, 1712.

Septtember 28 Being thus left by my deer husband and nott a
place now to putt my unhappy head in either in England or Ireland
and butt fiffteen pound in the world to shifft for my selfe and familly –
being my self and my son, a man and a maid servantt, – all which I
aid outt butt 4 pound in a suite of second mourning for my son to
were for my deer father, I resolved to try my fortune amongst my own
riends.

Octtobr 15 And heering my sister Austin was very ill affter her
being brought to bed of a dead childe, I wentt downe to Tenterdine to
my deer sister Austin, I makeing [fol. 7r] a vertue of nessecity.[50] Where
with my sister Austen and my brother I staide with all the kindness
hey could express to me till the 15 of June followinge.

November 8 And all this while I heard nott a word from Mr Freke
whether he were alive or dead, butt with my Lord Inchequine; when
aboutt the 8 of November following I had a letter he was with my lord
afe returned to Bristoll, wher he should stay a week to mend up their

[46] Long sea and John Clements(?): above, p. 52 n. 46; Goodwin Sands: above, p. 52 n. 47.
[47] Brownlow Street: above, p. 52 n. 48.
[48] William O'Brien, second earl of Inchiquin: above, p. 42 n. 19.
[49] Francis or Arthur Bernard and the Gookins: above, p. 52 n. 49.
[50] Heronden estate at Tenterden: above, p. 53 n. 50.

ship, which was fiered by green hay and all the pasengers like to be smother'd. Heer in Kentt I staid with my deer sister and my good brother till I feared a trespass on them.

June i5 When on my earnest entreaty my sister broughtt me up in her own coach to London with my son and my two servants, I now resolveing to try for a subsistance in Norfolke affter five monthes stay with my deer sister Austen. And being very poore, I presented her in London with six sillver plates cost me thirty six poundes. Eliza Freke

i685, Febuary 6 Febuary the sixth King Charles the 2d dyed, nott withoutt suspisioned of being poysoned by his French whore, made a little before dutches of Portsmouth and her son duke of Richmond,[51] and by the conivance of King James and his queen, his own brother.

June i5 I came from my sister Austins att Tenterden, wher I had staid as before. And the times being then very troublesome and I noe place to putt my head in for my selfe and son and three servants by reason of the duke of Monmouth landing in Dorsettsheire all roads being stopt by King James, I sentt downe my son againe to Kentt and with my sister Austen, and Richard Clark to Norfolk, and staid my selfe and my maid with my deer sister the Lady Norton till the rebellion was over.[52]

Jully io The duke of Monmouth was broughtt to London under a greatt gaurd by King James from the west of England, being Fryday and putt in the Towre. And Wendsday, the **i5** of Jully, hee was most barbarously beheaded on Towre Hill, chopping his head, shoulders and neck in five severall places.[53]

3i Then the 3i of Jully I sentt for my son home to me outt of Kentt to goe with me to Linn and shellter my selfe there. When as soon a he came and I had given earnest for fowre places in the stage coach he fell sick of the small pox, soe thatt I were faine againe to returne to my deer sister the Lady Norton to Brownloe Streett.

Agust i4 I staid with her there and att Epsome for my son to drinke those watters till the i4 of Agust, a fortnight, till they came outt to my greatt torture and distracttion, Mr Frek being then in Irland and my mony bein all gone, I think, butt one three pound peice of gold (given me by my deer father) which my sister would nott lett me have a doctter with.[54] And tho I dispaired of his life, yett then my greatt good God looked on me and spared mee his life by the kindness and care of my deer sister the Lady Norton, with whome I have bin now fiffteen weeks with all the kindness and frindship immaginable. E Frek

---

[51] Louise de Kéroualle and Charles Lennox: above, p. 53 n. 51.

[52] James Scott, first duke of Monmouth: above, p. 54 n. 52; Richard Clark, her servant

[53] See above, p. 54 n. 54.

[54] Epsom: above, p. 54 n. 56.

Septtember 29 Thus left, still I attempted againe to seek my fortune for my bread to Billney; wher att last, I humbly thank God, I gott to Linn in the stage coach my self and my son, Ralph Freke, two men and a maid the 29 of September; wher being a stranger I could hardly gett a lodging, where I lay privatly till the eight of Febuary following.

December 24 Mr Freke came over from Dublin in Ireland by post, I haveing [hardly] heard of him or from him in three quarters of a yeare by reason of the imbargoe of King James. Heer while Mr Frek was in this kingdome, he was dayly importuneing of mee to sell my Billney to Sir Standish Harts Tongue for the like in Ireland;[55] butt my God gave me the resolution and courage to keep whatt I had rather then by parting with itt be keptt by my frinds.

Febuary the 8 I came to my thacht house in West Billney with Mr Frek from Linn to take possesion of thatt estate, and the first time of my coming theither to the estatte my deer father settled on me and my son in 1675, and where I have staid, I humbly thank my God, allmost twenty eight years, viz., till 1712. When I came I had nott a bed to lye on, a stoole to sitt on, a dish to eate outt of, or any thing nessesary for a poor mortoll in this world; butt were dayly threatned I should nott nest my selfe ther, for they would starve me outt, seing I would nott partt with my estatt.

i3 Affter six weeks stay in Norfolke and fowre days stay in Billney, he took coach heer and wentt for London in order to goe for Ireland againe and left wretched me heer to seek my fortune amongst a pack of bruite beast who endevered my rhuien [fol. 7v] as by their threats to me dayly, and my deer father dead, Mr Freke gone to sea, and my self quitt a stranger in this country. Leftt with nither mony or bed or the least of goods or credid, I gott into the Wassell Farme house and sett my selfe up to farmeing (whilst my deer husband wentt for Ireland).

Aprill 4 Which was where att sea hee was twice like to bee cast away; butt by Gods greatt mercy to mee thatt never fail'd me, hee was att last saffly landed in Ireland the fowrth of Aprill 1686. For which mercy God make me ever thankfull, E Freke. Where he staid from me till the 14 of June 1687. Elizabeth Freke

1687, April 9 Goode Mammons house nextt to mine was aboutt ten a clock att nightt burntt downe to the ground with overheatting her oven for Goode Saywells christning, and the poore widdow woman burntt to death in itt by the trechery of Goode Cheny perswading her to fetch outt a dish on Saterday nightt.[56] And tho I were up my selfe

---

[55] Standish Hartstonge: above, p. 55 n. 57.
[56] Mary Mammont and Mary Sowell: above, p. 56 n. 58. Edward Cheney's daughter Elizabeth was buried in West Bilney on 19 May 1687; the register does not include his wife's name.

calling, yett nott one of the parish would come to mine or the poor womans releife in this her distress. E Frek

May 26 My deer sister Austen came to see me in my thach, poor house (with my deerst neece and god-daughter Mrs Grace Norton) in her own coach from London to fetch me up amongst my friends and to give me her husbands creditt in my husbands absence. Butt I thank God I had learned the way of shifting better then borrowing and ever esteemed itt more honorable to unhapy me, Eliz Freke.

June 6 My deer sister Austen and my deer neice left me att Billney, and they both wentt back in their own coach to London.

i4 And then aboutt the i4 of June came over Mr Freke from Ireland very unexpectted by mee affter he had left mee sixteen monthes and three days.

September i9 Mr Freke wentt againe for Ireland affter he had staid with me aboutt three monthes and five days, when he took from me neer six hundred pounds. Which with more of mine in London added to itt, hee bought my coppy hold estate in Pentney of forty six pounds a yeare and putt in his own life in itt for wreched me to renew.

i688, March 27 March 27 Mr Freke came againe to West Billney affter he had staid from mee and his only child neer i9 monthes, he being prosecuted by Captaine Buttler, which had Mr Freks company given him by King James, butt affter halfe a years persecution in the wars was by the favour of my Lord Cappell dismist and sentt for England and came to me to Billney the 29 of March.[57] Eliz Frek

Aprill 5 Richard Clark, my servantt and friend, dyed with me att Billney of a creek in his neck. Hee lived with me neer 8 years heere and in Ireland, and a good and faithfull servant hee was and a greatt help to me in Mr Freks absence.[58]

29 My cosin Percy Crosby, my husbands sisters eldest son, dyed att West Billney and lyes burryed in Billney chancell neer the south doore by my vaultt I made for Mr Frek. They both dyed in the compass of a month affter Mr Freke came outt of Ireland. Hee was one of King James marters and was buryed about the i9 of May following.[59]

---

[57] Edward Butler(?): above, p. 56 n. 59. Henry Capel, Baron Capell of Tewkesbury (1638–1696), would later be a lord justice of Ireland, becoming in 1695 lord deputy. Although his earlier influence on the Irish affairs involving Freke is unknown, he had family links with Ireland: his brother Arthur, first earl of Essex, and his brother-in-law Henry Hyde, second earl of Clarendon, had served as lord lieutenant of Ireland (*HC*, ii. 6–11).

[58] Clark was buried in Bilney on 5 April 1688.

[59] The entry should be for the year 1690, when he was buried on 20 May (above, p. 58 and n. 65). The antecedent of 'they' is ambiguous. The death of Percy Freke's sister Agnes Crosby has not been dated; her son Percy, however, died a month after Percy Freke's brother-in-law Francis Bernard, who lost his life defending Castle Mahon on 15 April 1690 (Bennett, 289; Ffolliott, 35, 36).

1688, November 15 The good prince of Orang, King William the Third, came over outt of Hollond to be our deliverer from popery and slavery. God sentt him when wee were just past all hopes to be our hellper and releived us when we were past all hopes. He landed neer Exeter, in the west of Dorsettshier, with aboutt 12 saile of ships of his own and aboutt 12 thousand men in them. Against whom King James went with neer 60000 to oppose him, butt wantt of courage carryed him back to London, when hee with his queen and pretended prince of Walles run for France.[60]

1689, Febuary 13 King William and Queen Mary, the daughter of King James the Second, were proclaimed king and queen of England and were both crowned the eleventh of Aprill following, 1689.[61]

Octtobr 25 I wentt to London to see my friends and deer sisters affter I had staid in my thacht house fowre years by my selfe dureing the heatt of the warrs of King James. In London I staid with them aboutt seven weeks; and then I returned home againe to Billney December the 18 most thankfull to God for my poor thacht house, where I did enjoy eight years of quiett and comfortt – more then all my life ever afforded mee.

1690, March 4 Mr Freke left mee att Billney and wentt againe for Ireland, I nott knowing of itt two days before, to endeavour the getting of his estate there given to Maccarty by King James of 800 l. a yeare and himselfe was outtlawed by him [fol. 8r] for an absentee and all his estatte and goods given away to Owen Macarty and his greatt house att Rathbary burntt downe by the Irish, which held outt for a garrison for Kinge Charls the First nine monthes under his father, Captaine Arthur Freke, with three hundred Protestants in itt.[62] Eliz Freke

June 4 King William came over for Ireland to the conquest of itt, where King James the 2d was, to take the posesion of itt for the English Protestants; on which King James soon wentt off. He landed June the 13 and foughtt the battle of the Boyne Jully the first, where hee was shott through his had and into his shoulder as hee passed the Boyne with the English army, and posest himself of Dublin July the third, and returned againe for England to the greatt joy of all good Protestants in Jully.[63]

1691, Jully 1 My servantt Henry Crutland shott off his hand with killing of a pigion. He lay under the hand of a surgion fowre monthes in a most sad condition; and then by his importunity and the parishes

---

[60] William landed in Devon on 5 November (above, p. 57 n. 61); James did not join his wife and son in France until two weeks after they had fled (above, p. 57 n. 63).

[61] See above, p. 57 and n. 64.

[62] The defenders left Rathbarry Castle in October 1642; see Introduction, p. 7 and n. 19 and above, p. 58 n. 66.

[63] Had: hat; see her history of the Irish war, above, pp. 145–7.

I took itt to cure, which I humbly thank my God I did – I effecttually did itt. He was the patients creture ever I saw. He held his own hatt before his face whilst his fingers and wrist was sawed off and never cryded, oh, or shed one teare.[64]

2i I had my last tryall with Captaine Spillman of Norbrow against Doching, who carryed to Norwich councell against me and himselfe rid by my door with sixteen wittneses against me; and Mr Frek in Ireland and I had only my son and good servantt Richard Clark. And yett God gave itt on my side against him in the publick courtte.[65] Eliz. Freke

1692, March 30 Mr Frek, haveing now left me to shift for my selfe above two yeares, never lett me have any quiett butt commanded me to leave Billney and goe over to Ireland to him there. Wher affter half a years conciderration I forcst my selfe to undertake thatt jorney for [Ireland] with a heavy hartt; and in order to itt, March the 30 I wentt with my son and servants to London in my deer sister Nortons coach and leftt my house and goods with James Wallbutt, my then servantt butt affter my cheating tennantt.[66]

Aprill 2d I came to my deer sister Austins, who lived then in St James Streett in London, my brother being then one of the lords of the admireallty; wher by reason of the French invation I staid till aboutt Jully for a shipp.[67]

May 24 I putt my son, Ralph Freke, being within one week of seventeen yeares of age (viz., the second of June following), to Mr Du Veales, a French Hugonett, to learne French and all other quallifications of a gentleman; and I paid for his dyett and chamber fowre and forty pounds a yeare.[68]

Jully 25 And when I had seen my son settled and in my two deer sisters care, I wentt to the Bath Jully 25; and wher I rested my selfe neer a month for shipping, my hartt allwaise failling me in thatt jorney. From the Bath I wentt to Bristoll to be more neer the shipping.

Agust 14 And aboutt the midle of Agustt I took me a lodging on Bristoll Green neer the cathedrall church, where I stayed for feare (and for shipping) till the 2d of Octtober.

Occtobr 2 When on the 2d of Octtober I mustered all my courage and took shipping when I wentt to sea with Captain Poole.[69] **5** And by Gods infinite mercy to mee I came to the Cove in Corke Thursday,

---

[64] Henry Cruckland was buried in Bilney on 9 November 1693.

[65] Mundeford Spelman and John Dochin: above, p. 59 n. 71. Richard Clark was dead by the time of the trial, which W locates in King's Lynn.

[66] James Wallbut: above, p. 59 n. 72.

[67] See above, p. 60 n. 73.

[68] Du Veil and De Veille: above, p. 60 n. 74.

[69] William or Benjamin Poole(?): above, p. 60 n. 75.

the 5 of Octtober, where thatt morning the French privatteers had taken two ships outt of thatt harbour and kild the captain and stript all the passengers in itt and sett them naked on the shore aboutt two howrs before I landed.

26 Aboutt Octtobr the 26 I came into Corke late att nightt, wher in a boatt wee were all like to be lost on the key. Nor could I gett a lodging in the citty. Att last Mr Edwards took me in, beleiveing I belonged to Mr Frek (tho I concealed my name).[70] Where next day I fell sick with the hardness of my jorney and coldness of the water and were given over by the docttors there, and Mr Frek gone butt the night before to parliamtt of Dublin.[71]

November i2 Butt still my God spared my life to know more misery, for on or aboutt the midle of November I came with my servants a horse back to Rathbarry, from whence I had bin absentt eightt years. Where when I came, I found my house quit burntt downe: only two little rooms, and neither chaire or stoole fitt for a Xtian to sett on, or a bed to lye on, or meatt or drink to sattisfye nature, and noe stock butt two sheep and 2 lambs and 4 little garrans horses worth aboutt ten shillings a peice.

December 2i In this deplorable condition I staid till neer Christmas the Irish parliamentt adjorned, when Mr Frek came home affter I had bin thus shifting aboutt from place to place to hid my wretched head for above three years and a quarter. However, in this misserable place and condition I staide allmost frightned outt of my witts for above three years and a halfe and sick all the time with the colick and vapours, and [fol. 8v] thatt I were given over for death, and hardly ever wentt downe the staires all the time I were in Ireland, viz., 4 year and a halfe. And tho I have undergone more then mortoll tongue can speak, I never knew whatt vapours were till this prospectt given me in Ireland, the misfortune of which I expectt to cary with me to my grave. And tho seventeen year pastt, I still labour under all the misfortunes of itt. And thatt with an humble thankfullness too I have seen the fall of most of my enimise and am able to subsistt withoutt the help of my friends. Eliza Freke

i693, March 29 Att the assises att Corke Mr Freke had a letter to goe for England in hast for my son to goe over for Ireland. When on Easter Munday, Aprill the i7, hee left me att Rathbarry and wentt to Kingsaile for a shipp.

May i5 And hee landed in England aboutt the midle of May. From thenc hee wentt to London, where he staid (and att Billney) aboutt a month with my son and broughtt away from Billney all my plate, linen,

---

[70] Dr and not Mr in W, but unidentified (above, p. 6i n. 76).
[71] Percy Freke represented Clonakilty (above, p. 6i n. 77).

and other goods I had bin eight years a getting together of whatt was valluable, and all unknown to mee, in hopes by itt to make me reside in Ireland. This is the hard fate of Elizabeth Freke.

i693, Agust i6 However, aboutt the midle of Agust my greatt and good God brought both my husband and son saffe home to me to Rathbarry unlooked for and unexpected. For which mercy the Lord make me ever humbly thankfull.

November 2d When on November the second a greatt Dutch shipp was cast away and lost with all the pasengers in her on Rathbarry strand by overshoutting his course for the Old Head of Kingsaile.[72] They were dashed to peices amongst our rocks and all there goods and persons lost butt fowrr men Mr Frek took up and buryed in Rathbary church. This was a sadd sightt to mee that howerly expected my deer husband and onlly son, who came to me home safe to mee. For which mercy the greatt and good God make thankfull Eliz. Frek.

i694, November 3d Mr Frek was made shrife doe all I could to the contrary November i694. Hee kept his first assises in the city of Cork, where I were with him, and had two and twenty handsome proper men in new liveryes to attend him besids those thatt run by his horses side. The two judges were Lord Chiefe Justice Pyne and Sir Richard Cox where thatt assises were condemned twenty eight persons to be hanged and burned – and one young English man, an only son whose life I begged, itt nott being for murder and his father an estated man in Devonshier.[73]

i695, March 2d Mr Frek wentt to Dublin to give up his shriefs accounts, wher was by the Lord Drahaday a match proposed to him for his eldest daughter with my son and 3000 l. with her (the Lady Ailce Moore).[74] A fine lady she was, but I cared nott to be a servantt to any one in my old age <deleted: a line and a half>.

May 28 Mr Frek returned from Dublin from giveing up his accounts of shrivalldry to Rathbarry full of the proposition of this greatt match with this fine lady, which my son was quite smitten with and angry enough with me I would nott be there.

Agust 22 Mr Freke wentt againe to Dublin to the parliamentt, where he staid about three months, and had againe this match earnestly againe proposed for his son outt of hand and the mony of her portion to be paid me downe. Butt I could nott think her <deleted: quality> proper for my son, clog'd with seven or 8 brothers and sisters.

Octtober 22 Mr Freke sentt for my son from Rathbarry to Dublin

[72] Old Head, Kinsale: above, p. 62 n. 78.

[73] Freke was high sheriff of Cork; the other chief justice was Richard Pyne (above, p. 62 n. 79).

[74] Ealce, not Ailce, in W: Alice, the daughter of Henry Moore, third earl of Drogheda (above, p 62 n. 80).

to see this young lady aboutt fifteen years of age, where he was very kindly received and entertained by the Lord Draheda and his lady together with the young lady.

December 20 Wher my son and Mr Frek staide in Dublin till aboutt the 20 of December, when my husband and sone came from Dublin full fraight with letters from Lady Poorscort and there frinds presently to finish the match or my sonn would goe for France.[75] But I cared nott to bee frightnened outt of my mony nor my son too <deleted: several words>.

Aprill 14 Mr Freke and my son wentt againe for Dublin to finish this greatt match or break itt quitt off. Which affter aboutt three weeks stay and atendance there was brok quite off, my son being tied to live wholly in thatt parte of the country at above a hundred miles from me, which I thoughtt very hard (and my husband and I to be their pay master) to trust my only son when [fol. 9r] they had ten children might have as well trusted me with one att least to have lived in twenty milles of mee. Butt they found my sons inclinations soe farr fixed towards this lady thatt they resolved to bring me to any tearms. And soe farr they did prevaille on Mr Frek thatt he offered my Lord Drohade and his laddy downe on the naile six thousand pound to by the young lady a joynter any where in the county of Corke of six hundred pounds a year. Besids which I then promised to settle West Billney on them in the county of Norfolk because to oblige my only son and them. But itt nott being then excepted, Mr Frek was offered itt on better tearmes; when I refused itt, tho my son was bitterly angry with me.[76]

May 28 And on aboutt the 28 of May home came Mr Frek and my son from Dublin. In which jorny my son fell very sick of a high feaver thatt Mr Frek was faine to putt in att Watter Park, the house of Sir Richard Pynes, nott being able to reach further, being given over by all the doctters for death. Butt my greatt God had still mercy on me and restored him to me againe (by the good Lady Pines care), I hope to be his humble servantt and a comfortt to his unhappy mother.[77] EF

June 2 My son, Ralph Freke, was of age of one and twenty years when I gave him for a New Years guift two hundred pound, which my deer father sentt me for my birth day for a New Years guiftt aboutt two monthes before he dyed, and five pounds for a purse to putt itt in. Eliz Frek

5 I left Rathbarry in order to goe for England affter I had staied

---

[75] Elizabeth Powerscourt: above, p. 63 n. 81.

[76] Alice Moore married Sir Gustavus Hume (above, p. 63 n. 82).

[77] Catherine Pyne, mistress of Waterpark: above, p. 63 n. 83.

there aboutt fowre years and a halfe a miserable life, and most of my time ther sick of the distempers then reigning affter King James warrs (questionable whether the plague). From thence I wentt to Corke to try for shiping.

25 Where and aboutt the country I staid till the 25, i696, of June; when my impationce of being gone, I ventered my selfe on shipp board a very cracy ship of Captaine Townsend with 2 men and 2 maids and my husbands sisters son Thomas Crosby, who was vexation enough to Eliz Frek.[78]

Jully i I landed affter a weeks saile att Plymouth, where I mett Collonel Robertt Frek, my neer kinsman, then govenour of thatt towne, who was extreamely kind and civill to me, and offered twenty pounds for a coach to carry me to Portsmouth and to goe along with me rather then I should goe to sea againe, and had borrowed for me Madam Founds. Butt my small acquaintance there, tho earnstly prest, I denyed itt.[79]

6 Sunday, the 6 of Jully, I went to sea againe, where we lay beating up and downe till Thursday in a tempest and mist – I lay nott knowing wher we were. **io** Which forced us to an anker for two days more; soe thatt being in a tirrible storme and the ship and boatt both very crazy, I durst nott venture againe to sea butt anckered on the Goodwin Sands.

i2 I sentt for the queens pillate boatt and putt my selfe and family in att a ginny a person; and tho with greatt hassard, by Gods greatt mercy to me wee landed saffe on the beech att Deale. Where being ill, before I could be taken outt a greatt wave carryed me off againe to sea thatt every body thought me lost. When on a suden another greatt wave forced my boatt to the beech againe, where aboundance of people looking att mee by there strength and graples hall'd her to an anchor. Thus my greatt and good God preserved me round the world in a leaky shipp and boatt.

i3 We landed saffe att Deale when a ship of 300 tun was lostt and all itts crue with itt.[80] From thence I hired the Canterbury coach for London and two horses for my servants.

i4 Where att Maudlin in Kentt I were besett with 5 highwaymen, one of which told me I would never reach Cittingburne and bid my boy behind the coach drink hartily for itt was his last he should ever drink.[81] And soe we both run for itt and, I doe most humbly thank my God, just gott to the townds end before them to Cittingborn.

i6 From Cittingburne I hired this coach to Rochester, and soe to

[78] Isaac Townshend(?): above, p. 64 n. 85.
[79] Robert Freke: above, p. 64 n. 86; Petronell or Anne Fownes: above, p. 64 n. 87.
[80] Goodwin Sands shipwreck: above, p. 65 n. 88.
[81] Maudlin and Sittingbourne: above, p. 65 n. 89.

Graves End, where I come on the i7 and landed latte att nightt. **i7**
Where coming outt of the boatt, a roghy watterman stole every ragg
of my clothes from me, one suite of which I would nott have taken
thirty pound for them, being sure I shall never have such another. In
this pickle with att midnight I gott a coach and came to my deer sister
the Lady Nortons.

July i8 And the next day my deer sister Austen fetched me in her
house in Sohoe Square, wher I staid aboutt a week in both places and
then wentt to lodgings of my owne neer Sohoe Square neer my deer
sisters.[82]

2i I gott my usquabath on shore, which cost me six pound the
costome of itt; and itt was soe mingled as itt was quitt spoyled by the
seamen.[83] [fol. 9v] This was my severall disapoyntmentts when I came
for England and noe place to putt my unfortunate head in.

i696, Agust 22 And to add to my troubles, in or aboutt the 22 of
Agust itt pleased God to take to himselfe my brother Austen a Satterday,
about two a clock in the affternoone, and left my deer sister in a greatt
deale of trouble. Tho he left her a good joyntter, yett he left her two
daughters, women grown, and her youngest son, Thomas Austen, with
never a peny provision for them and a considerable debtt for her eldest
son to pay.[84] He was just entered the sixth of Agust before the fiffty
sixth yeare of his age, the goutt breaking in his legg or foott aboutt
three weeks before.

23 Hee was buried in Bexly the next day att night, latte att nightt,
in the famyly vault.

Septtember 5 I came againe to West Billney to bare walles to my
thacht house, where every thing of mine thatt was good was taken
away from me, even to my very bed to lye on, tho I left 8 good fether
beds when I wentt for Ireland and a good stock and all things nesesary.
And I found nothing butt five farmes in my hand and the tennants of
them run away with aboutt 500 l. of my arrears of rentt.

December 2i I leftt Billney and wentt to Lin Regis to Mr Benetts
to finish my leases and accounts and to endeavour for some new
tennants affter James Wallbutt, who had the looking affter this my
estatte, had fallen the rents of whatt I left itt neer fifty pounds a yeare
and lost me above 500 pounds in mony.[85]

3i I wentt up againe to London and came to my deer Lady Nortons
in Covent Garden, where I staide with her aboutt three days.

January i And January the first I wentt to my own lodgings in Red

---

[82] Soho: above, p. 65 n. 91. 'August' in the manuscript.
[83] Usquebaugh, an aqua vitae: above, p. 66 n. 92.
[84] Robert, Judith, Elizabeth, and Thomas Austen: above, p. 66 n. 93.
[85] An unidentified Lynn attorney: above, p. 67 n. 95.

Lyon Streett very sick, over against my deer sister Austins, very ill and in the doctters hands; where I staid neer five monthes.[86]

Febuary 16 In which time, viz., Shrove Tuesday, Febuary 16, my deer neece and god-daughter, and my deer sister Nortons only child, was privatly marryed to Sir Richard Gettings, who soon brok her hartt and an unspeakable grief to my deer sister, her deer mother, and to me, whom I loved as my own lyfe and would have spared mine to have saved hers.[87] Eliza Freke

1697, Aprill 17 I came downe againe to my Billney with my deer sister Austen to see and endeavour to gett me a place to putt my unhapy head in by my renting of the Hall in Billney. Butt in this I was likewise disapoynted too by my Lady Richerson, who chose to lett itt to a little Shepherd befor me, tho I offered her the security of my sister Austen, and Sir George Chouts bond and my nephey Austen vallued att above ten thousand pounds.[88]

May 18 I heard of my sons being like againe of a violentt feaver in Ireland, which soe tiryfied and frightned me thatt I had noe rest in mee. And affter eleven week stay heer in Billney att my thacht house, the Wassell Farme, I lefft Billney and with my deer sister Austen came for London, the great God having recovered my son. For which I am ever thankfull to him. Eliza. Freke

1697, June 29 I left Billney and came to London June the 29 in order to goe to Tunbridg to drink the watters for my better health, and I carryed my deer sister Austen along with me affter I had staied with her in Red Lyon Streett till Jully the 20.

Jully 20 Aboutt three week I continued with her very ill, when wee both wentt together to Tunbrige, where I staid very ill till the 24 of Agust.[89]

Agust 24 When I returned againe and brought her back to her own house in London Barthollmew Day, to her house in Red Lyon Streett, affter five weeks stay att Tunbrig.

September 15 Where I staid with her very ill, rather worse then better for the watters, with the fright of my sons sickness till September the 15 I fell downe quitt sick att my sister Austins of a mallignantt feaver called by the name of the plague feavour, of which rained much in London. And aboundance dyed of itt, and my deer neece the Lady Gettings; and those thatt lived were martered by itt.[90] Of which I keptt my bed two month in the hands of docters and appothycaryes, every

---

[86] Red Lion Street: above, p. 67 n. 96.

[87] Grace and Richard Gethin: above, p. 67 n. 97.

[88] George Choute and Robert Austen: above, p. 68 n. 99; the Shepherds: above, p. 68 n. 100.

[89] Tunbridge Wells: above, p. 68 n. 101.

[90] Malignant fever: above, p. 69 n. 102.

day expecting my last. Which att last fell from my groyne to my ankle of my left legg, wher itt broke when noe surjoin would medle with itt, twas all soe [fol. 10r] black and mortifyed. Thus I lay for neer three monthes more, all concluding nothing butt my death, and Mr Frek and my son both in Ireland. And att the same time my own maid lay ill of the same, which settled in her back before itt broke. She kept her bed with itt neer six month before itt brok in the same doctters and apothycarys hands I were. Thus we lay and my deer neece for above half a yeare, and affter all my God raised me up againe a miserable specttle (and took my deer neece to himselfe) to receive more of his mercys to unhappy me, Elizabeth Freke.

1697, Octtobr 11 God took to himselfe my deerst neece the Lady Gettings, my deer sister Nortons onlly child, of this feaver, who gave up her pyous soule to God Tuesday, the eleventh day of Octtober. Who as she was used all her life to afflictions bore them to her last and most sainttlike gave up her soule to God. And her end was a presidentt for the best of bishops and all the world to immitate, to the griefe of her deer mother, my deer sister, who has inter'd her in my own deer mothers grave att Hollingburne, wher lye seven of my sisters and brothers and is a very fine monementt errected for her, as is likewise in Westminster Abby.[91]

Febuary 16 I left my deer sister Austins house just recovered of my feaver tho hardly able to goe or stand and **19** came a Satterday, the 19 of Febuary, to my own Billney againe to take in Mr Freks name possesion of my house I had bin kept outt of for 28 years by the Lady Ann Richerson, who was burntt to death in her clossett aboutt the Christmas before and concealed itt from me.[92]

21 Which I took posesion of Munday, the 21. And with itt God gave me a house and place in England to putt my poor unfortunate head in; which is more then I have had or could purchas, tho marryed above six and twenty years, to rest my wearied carcass in butt tost from place to place and to the trouble of both my deer sisters. And this is, as I remember, the seventh time since I have bin an unfortunatt wife thatt I have come to an empty house with nothing in itt butt bare walles just redy to fall on my head, as was the church and chancell with the rest of the houses in the parrish in the posesion of the Lady Richerson. Elizabeth Freke

1698, Aprill 8 My husband and son, affter leaveing of me to seek my fortune above three years by shiffting for my selfe all alone, both,

---

[91] Cicely was the seventh sibling buried in Hollingbourne; Grace's monuments are in the chancel of All Saints Church and the South Choir Aisle of Westminster (above, p. 69 n. 103).

[92] Anne Richardson died in Honingham on 31 January 1697/8.

I humbly thank God, landed saffe att Minhead in Devonshieir aboutt two howres before a most dreadfull storme happened.[93]

i3 They came both to London saffe the i3 of Aprill and downe to West Billney the 23 day to mee, which was a greatt mercy in God to mee and unlooked for. Which providentiall mercy God grant may nott be forgoten by me, Eliz Frek.

May 30 Mr Frek and my son wentt to London aboutt a great match for him severall times proposed to him, and Mr Freke had severall good offers for him; butt none would he see or heer of, I suppose haveing before made his choise where he marryed of Sir John Meads daughter.

Jully i6 They both returned from London to Billney withoutt sattisfying Mr Frek in the seing of any one fortune, tho beg'd by his father to see severall proposed.

23 My deer sister Norton sentt me towards furnishing my bare walles the fine tortershell cabynett in my best chamber with severall peices of fine china for itt, which are secured in my closett.

25 My deer sister Austen sentt me downe towards my house furniture a long cane squab,[94] now stands in the parlour, and five greatt jarrs for my best chamber, now in my closett carefully laid up by Eliz Frek.

29 I bought my green damask bed and all my tapstry hangings for the two chambers and the parlor and the dineing roome with my two great glasses and new coach lined with a damask and scarlett silke coffoy for my selfe and severall other nessesarys all outt of my own mony, which cost me above three hundred pounds.[95]

Agust io Mr Freke and my son left me heer att Billney all alone againe with two maids and a man and a hundred pound a yeare in my hand and nott one peny to stock itt, he haveing taken the rest of my thousand pound to buy the estatt att Pentney of forty six pounds a yeare of coppy hold in his own name and life putt in itt. Elizabeth Frek

[fol. iov]

i698, Agust i5 The i5 of Agust my husband and son came both safe to West Chester from Billney and took shipping the nextt day, butt were tost up and downe by stormes and tempest till the five and twentyeth of September, and were putt into five severall harbours.

Octtobr i Att last in an open boatt withoutt any thing of shellter or

---

[93] Minehead: a Bristol Channel port in Somerset, not Devon.
[94] A couch.
[95] Damask: silk or linen fabric with a figured or patterned weave; glass: mirror; coffoy: caffoy, caffa, an imported fabric or silk cloth comparable to damask.

subsistance, every howre expectting the fate of a mercyless sea, my greatt and good God of his infinite mercy landed them both saffe in Dublin affter haveing bin neer seven weeks cast up and downe the sea to my unspeakable tormentt and torture. For which mercy of God to mee I doe humbly beg I may never forgett to be thankfull. Elizabeth Freke

November 3d Affter this through frightt I could nott stay any longer att West Billney nor have any rest day or night in my mind butt left my house and servants and **6** came up to London to try my frinds kindness to me in there company for whatt time they could spare me.

30 When on the thirtyeth of Novembr my deer sister Austen came downe with mee, which was a greatt kindness and comfortt to me in this my deplorable condition; wher shee staid with mee confined to my chamber in bare walls till the fourth of Aprill following. For which I am ever thankfull to her. Eliza Freke

1699, March 5 My son, Ralph Frek, was marryed in Ireland to Sir John Meads daughter Mrs Eliza Mead.[96] Hee had with her three hundred pounds a yeare land in Ireland; or iff Mr Frek liked to sell the land, he would give with his daughter fowre thousand pounds in mony. This match my only son never asked my consentt in or my blesing. For which I have and doe forgive and begg of God to doe the like in forgiveing of him too and wish him better fortune then I, who marryed withoutt my deer fathers knowledg or consentt. For perhaps I mightt have opposed this match, I heering my son wish (to cross mee) thatt he mightt never prosper iff hee marryed there to thatt lady fiffteen years of age. God forgive him, and [I] doe. Eliza. Freke

Aprill 4 My deer sister Austen lefft me affter shee had done pennance with mee aboutte fowre month. Itt was a greatt kindness to me then, indeed. And then she returned home againe to her house in Plumtree Streett in Holborn in London.[97]

June 13 I wentt with Prebend Bradrup and his wife to London affter they had staied a week with me heer att West Billney.[98] I hired a coach to our selves thatt wee mightt travill att ease up to London, where I stayed aboutt a fortnightt.

Jully 1 I returned from London home to West Billney, when I new slatted and made the whole chancell of Billney tightt and glased itt and whited itt together with the church, lefft just redy to fall by the Lady Richerson. And I made the brick and stone pillers in the church yard to support itt, and I boughtt the materialls for itt att Pentney of Mr Carter.[99]

---

[96] John and Elizabeth Meade: above, p. 72 n. 110.

[97] Plumbtree Street: above, p. 72 n. 111.

[98] Richard and Ann Broadrepp: above, p. 70 n. 106.

[99] Anthony Carter, who was buried on 26 September 1713 in Pentney, where he and his wife Ellen had buried at least two children.

Aprill 23 And aboutt the Easter before I gave to this chancell of mine in West Billney a handsome table cloth for the communion table embrodered of my own and my deer mothers worke and a pullpitt cloth and couchen all embrodered on purple cloth. Elizabeth Freke

1700, Aprill 30 The thirtyeth of Aprill one thousand seven hundred my son Freks eldest son was borne and christned by the name of Percy Freke, my deer husbands name. Hee was borne two days before the last quarters change of the moone att Castle Mahon in Ireland.[100] And I humbly begg of God to give him his grace, and to blesse him and make him his servantt, and to bless him with a long life and health, and thatt he may be a greatter comfortt to his parents then my son Frek has bin to mee, his mother, thatt was borne butt to two hundred pound a yeare and by Gods blesing on my industry has affter my death above two thousand pound a yeare. And I have provided for his two eldest sons. Eliza. Freke

June 19 I went to London to see my two deer sisters, and I staid att my deer sister the Lady Nortons in Brownloe Streett. I staid till the one and thirtieth of Jully.

Jully 31 I came home from London with my neece Judith Austen to keep me company and Mrs Willis to waite on mee. Where att Billney wee all staide till December the second, when I wentt up to London againe with my neece Judith Austen and Mrs Willis, I haveing lett partt of my house outt to Henry Fish the Michellmas before.[101]

[fol. 11r]

1700, Decembr 5th I came to London to my deer Austins in Plumbtree Streett, where the very next day I fell downe rightt sike and soe stuft up with my tisick I could nott fetch my breath or goe cross my chamber butt lay under the hands of doctters and surgions till the midle of Febuary following.[102]

1701, May 10 I came home againe to Billney with my two maids and a boy.

And aboutt the end of May I had a letter from Bristoll from Mr Freke on his landing there aboutt the 20 of May butt very like to dye of a dropsey and scurvy – distempers hee purchased in Ireland into the bargaine of his estate there, hee haveing now this time in Irland from mee allmost three years wanting one quarter. E Frek

June 17 Tuesday, I heering Mr Frek was like to dye att the Bath,

---

[100] Freke also says Percy was born on 28 April (above, p. 73 n. 112); Castle Mahon was the Bernard residence (above, p. 64 n. 84).

[101] Judith Austen's older daughter; Freke's maid: above, p. 73, n. 113.

[102] Phthisic, a chronic cough, asthma, or lung disease.

ho nott well able, leftt my house and servants att Billney and came to
Bath[103] the 2i of June, above two hundred miles in fowre days. Wher
ho I found him very ill, yett I humbly thank God he was well enough
o chide me, tho I had nott seen him in neer three years before this.
Tho itt was nott kind, yett nott come unexpectted by me. E Frek

Jully 9 I left the Bath and with Mr Freke came to London the i2
of Jully. **25** And I came home by my selfe to Billney the 25 of Jully.
And I left Mrs Evans my servantt and his man to come home with
him the 30 of Jully, where and in England Mr Freke staid till Agust
he i8, i702.

i70i, Jully i8 My son Frek had his second son borne, which was
babtised by the name of John, the grandfathers name of the mothers
side; who in the yeare i705 hee was shott to death in the head in
London in Norfolk Streett on Sunday aboutt two of the clock by the
carlessness of my sons servante Peryman.[104]

Septtember 30 My own son, Ralph Frek, leftt Ireland, given over,
as I was informed, by six phissitions there, to try for the Bath. And by
Gods greatt mercy to him and mee hee landed safe at Minhead, a
seaportt in Devonshiere, just before a most grievous storme. And hee
came to the Bath aboutt the 6 of Octtober and drunk the waters ther
and bathed for aboutt 5 weeks, by which he found greatt good.[105] For
which mercy the greatt and good God ever make thankfull his humble
servant. Eliz Freke

i70i, November 8 I thank God my son was soe well recovered as
to come to London with my deer sister the Lady Norton, where they
both staied aboutt a fortnight. **22** And then both my son and my deer
sister came downe to Billney the 22 of November and staid both with
me till the i9 of January following.

January i9 My sister Norton and my son left Billney, Mr Frek sick
in his bed of an ague and the goute; **2i** and my selfe was taken with a
violent ague for aboutt a fortnight too. Thus when we most wanted
our friends, wee had none. Butt my greatt and good God never yett
failed me, his child and servant. Eliz. Freke

29 Aboutt this time my sister and my son leftt London and wentt to
Bristoll for a shipp for Ireland. Where att Sir George Nortons my son

---

[103] 'London' in the manuscript.

[104] 'A very pleasant regular and spacious' street on the river side of the Strand between
Arundel and Surrey Streets (Hatton, i. 59) 'esteemed the best both for Buildings, and
Pleasantness of a Prospect into the *Thames*' (Strype, ii. bk. 4, 118), Norfolk Street no
longer exists. John was born in Rathbarry (above, p. 74 n. 116). Richard Perryman:
above, p. 82 n. 131.

[105] By the beginning of the eighteenth century the spas of Bath were increasingly
popular (above, p. 110 n. 202).

lay wind-bound till the eightt of March, Sunday, remarkable for the death of our good king, William the Third.

March 8 This our good Protestant king and dellyverer dyed Sunday aboutt ten a clock and on Innocentt Day (as did his good and pious Queene Mary of the small pox), both a loss irrepairable to this nation. And hee was kild by a fall from his horse which broke his coller bone, which being by his surjones ill handled soon ended his days to the sorrow and grife of all good Protestants.[106]

13 Fryday, I humbly thank my God my son landed saffe in Ireland on his own estate att Balltimoor and came next day to Rathbary and **15**, a Sunday, to Kingsaile to Sir John Meads, wher his wife was, being the 15 of March.[107] For this greatt mercy, good Lord, make me thankfull. Elizabeth Freke

25 Thom White, my tennantt, stole away from me in the nightt with above threescore pound, and carryed away all his goods, and left his wife and three children to the parish.[108] This was the very next house to me, and by his pretended religion to the church, &c., I could nott have suspected of him.

[fol. 11v]

1702, June 9 Mr Freke and I wentt up to London to my deer sister Austins, where my husband took up of my mony of East Indy stock a thousand and fowre pounds to buy Irish debenturs to buy more Irish land with.[109] I was very unwilling to partt with itt, being my own saveings of 24 years at Billney, all alone by my selfe; butt I was bound and must obey. Att my sister Austins I staid a full month allmost dead with my tisick and could nott fetch my breath or stirr cross my chamber, tho I were blouded above twenty ounces and laid outt for dead.

Jully 9 Then by advice I wentt into the country to Abbots Leigh to my deer sister the Lady Norton to accompany Mr Freke to his shipp, where wee both staid till the 18 of Agust. On which day, being Tuesday, hee took shiping att the Pill and carryed with him above a thousand pounds of mine, itts foundation laid by my deer father, Mr Ralph Frek, and part of the industry of my affter life.

Agust 20 On the 20 of Agust, I thank God, Mr Frek landed safe att Watterford in Ireland. From thence he wentt to Cork, and soe to Rathbarry, where he found, I thank God, all his young familly well.

September 9 On Wensday, the 9 of September, I left Abbots Leigh,

---

[106] William did not die on Innocents Day (above, p. 75 n. 117).
[107] Ballintubber, near Kinsale.
[108] He rented the White House (above, p. 75 n. 119).
[109] Stock transactions: above, p. 71 n. 109; government debentures: above, p. 75 n. 120.

where I had bin kindly treated by Sir George Norton and my deer
sister for two monthes. These two good friends and my neece Betty
Austen, whom I brought downe with mee, I left att the Bath.[110]

i2 And I came to London from Bath the i2 of September.

i9 And the i9 I came home to my West Billney very ill with my
jorney of fourteen weeks runing up and downe and kept my chamber
till the end of November. In all which time I never heard from either
my husband or son, only by my cosin John Freke thatt Mr Frek [was]
goeing for Dublin **25** and thatt I must immediattly returne him fowre
hundred pounds to finish his Irish purchas with the Lord Sidney;[111]
which I did on my creditt to my cosin John Freke. Thus is above i4,
fourteen, hundred pounds of my two thousand gone this yeare in
debenters for Ireland.

Octtober i5 Aboutt the i5 of Octtober I received a letter from my
cosin John Frek thatt my son Ralfe Frek [asked him] to begg of me
fowre hundred pound to entitle him to his deer fathers trad of
purchasing of land which lay neer his house. All which I imediattly
did. Soe thatt is gone this yeare (i702) eighteen hundred pound of my
mony outt of the Indy trads, for all which I never had soe much as a
letter of thanks from either husband or son. This is too true. E Frek

3i I seised the stock of Goody Fish whatt was nott conveid away in
my absence for fowrscore pounds. Whereof I gott little of money, yett
I gott a greatt deale of trouble and three farms in my hand, kept neer
a year before I could lett them.[112]

November 2i The 2i of November I had a letter outt of Ireland
from Mr Freke thatt hee had now finished his purchass of my Lord
Sidneys land, which he said cost him three thousand pounds. Of which
he tooke from me fowrten hundred pound in debentures att aboutt
seventy pound, and fowre hundred [given] my son did allmost break
my trad to sett up theirs in Ireland.

December 2 I had another letter from Ireland, from Dublin, from
Mr Frek, and the first I have had in three months from him, in which
he sentt me a fine to levy [and] release my rightt of Rathbary of three
hundred pounds a year to settle itt on my son.

22 Which tho I had severall times deney'd him in, yett being willing
to secure itt to my son and his heirs, I now did itt beefore Sir John
Turner and his brother Allderman Turner of Lynn on the 22 of
December, when I sentt my son fowre hundred pound to purchas
Dirryloan with.[113] For which I never had soe much as his thanks for

---

[110] Elizabeth, the younger daughter of Robert and Judith Austen.
[111] The estates of Justin MacCarthy forfeited to Henry, Viscount Sidney (above, p. 77
n. 123).
[112] Margaret Fish: above, p. 76 n. 122.
[113] John and Charles Turner: above, p. 77 n. 126; Derrylone: above, p. 77 n. 125.

itt. This tis to have butt one child, and him none of the best to me
neither. Butt God forgive him and give patience to me, his unhapp
mother, Eliz Frek.

1703, May 8 My deerst sister the Lady Norton came downe to me
to Billney outt of her pitty and charity to doe penance with me, whe
had kept my bed and chamber for seven months beffore. Whose ver
sight soe revived me thatt I were in a little time most sencible of thi
her indullgentt kindness to mee.

[fol. 12r]

1703, May 7 I had a letter from Mr Frek outt of Ireland to desire
me on all accounts to meett him att the Bath; and iff I would, he would
live comfortably with mee and never more leave.

June 1 Which tho I fattally knew the strength of his promises, yet
thatt nothing might lye att my doore, though I had kept my bed and
chamber seven month very ill, my deer Lady Norton being with me
made a hard shift and wentt up to London with her June the first
Affter she had done penance heer with me three weeks, she took the
trouble of carring me with her to the Bath. This kind visett God grant
I may never forgett and reward her for itt.

3 of June I came to London, where I stopt to make up my account
with my cosin John Frek. Where outt of my two thousand pound and
itts intrest I found Mr Frek had taken up of itt all butt five hundred
pounds; and outt of this 500 pound hee took up of my cosin John Frek
a hundred and thirteen pounds and nine shillings, which money I were
faine to pay for Mr Frek to him. And then being little more then three
hundred and sixty pound, I sould itt quite outt of the Bank of England
itt then bearing a greatt price, I thought I could nott doe better, the
bank runing high.[114] Thus ended my fiffteen hundred pound given me
by my deer father with my 18, eighteene, years improvementt and
intrest of itt brought to 360. Eliza Freke

Jully 1 I left London and wentt to the Bath, there to meett Mr
Freke; wher I staide of till the thirteenth of Jully.

13 From thence I went to Leigh with my deer lady and sister Norton
wher I staid with her till September, butt noe Mr Freke came over.

September 15 Soe like a foole I returned home; as I came to my
own house att Billney affter runing about for above fowre monthes and
to the greatt diseasment of my selfe and vexation of me, to see all
had thus borrowed away by my husband and son and carried for
Ireland unknown to mee. Eliza Frek

---

[114] The *Post-Man* (1134) states that bank stock on Tuesday, 1 June, was 131. The stock
which opened the year at 126½, ranged from 129¼ to 132¾ during the month of June

November 26 or 27 was the great hurrycane of wind for a whole night and day, being Fryday, thatt was ever known in England since Olliver Cramell dyed.[115] Which wind did blow downe allmost all my houses and putt me to above five hundred pound charge in presentt stopping of gaps. And the Wassell Farme I lived in, both house and barne, quite blown downe besids severall others.[116]

Decembr 16 Aboutt December the 16 Mr Frek came over from Ireland by Chester full of the goutte; and from thence, ill as he was, he came to London the 23 of December and by my cosin John Frek sentt for me up to London to him. Where in lodgings and att my sister Austins hee kept his bed neer six weeks before I were able to goe to him.

Febuary 10 However, I came up to him aboutt the tenth of Febuary, when hee was in his second lodgings. Wher when I came, he refused to see me for moveing thatt little remaine of my mony outt of the Bank of England. Butt heering I were on my returne home againe, hee wrott to me to my sister Austins iff I would come to him to his lodgings all should be made up between us and thatt hee would goe downe with me to Billney and live there with me for thatt he found frinds were butt indifferendt cementers between man and wife. In obedience to this his promise I wentt thatt night in a chaire to my deer husbands lodgings in St Martains Lane, where I received his check for takeing my mony outt of the bank.[117] On which I promised him to make itt fiffteen hundred pound and lay itt out for his third grandson bearing my deer fathers name.

March 3d Which I did on the 3d of March, I haveing itt my life and the dispos of itt att my death; both which were granted me.

16 And soe we came both comfortably home together, leaveing London and my two sisters the sixteenth day of March. **18** And by Gods blesing to us wee both reached home to Billney Saterday night, the 18 of March, affter he had left me and this place for neer two years, one year of which I never heard of him or from him whether dead or alive. This has bin the hard and uncomfortable fate of Eliza Freke.

---

[115] Oliver Cromwell (1599–1658), lord protector of England, died on 3 September 1658; the storm, which occurred on 30 August, was later dated by some to coincide with his death (Evelyn, iii. 219–20 and 220 n. 2).

[116] The storm on the night of 26 November 1703, 'the like not known in the memory of man' (Luttrell, v. 363–4), lasted about four hours and did extensive damage in London and especially the coastal areas of southern England (*London Gazette* [3971], *Daily Courant* [405], and *Post-Man* [1213]). Daniel Defoe's account, *The Storm* (London, 1704), says that seven ships with a value of £3,000 and twenty men were lost at King's Lynn, another ship was missing, and the damage to buildings in the town was £1,000 (174–5). Paul Richards assesses the loss at six ships and thirty sailors in *King's Lynn*, 76.

[117] 'A very great Through-fare both for Foot and Horse, and is well inhabited, having good built Houses, especially the Western Side' (Strype, ii. bk. 6, 68).

1704, March 25 The 25 of March I received a letter from my daughter outt of Ireland how ill my son was of a dropsy and how much his legs pitted. **27** On which I writt to them both to hasten over to me for cure in his own native country, where, I bless God, he was finely recovered, I hope to be a comfortt to mee, his unhappy mother Elizabeth Frek.

[fol. 12v]

1704, Jully 25 Tuesday the 25 and St James Day I went up into my uper classett to fetch down six pound to pay Scerry the mason for new tilling part of the Hall blowne downe by the late hurrycane of wind.[118] Which I coming the second paire of staires, my head was soe taken thatt I fell downe greatt part of them against the stone wall of the window, [which] ston'd me soe thatt I were took up dead. Till Mr Frek, heering that noise of my fall and noe complaintt, made a shift to gett outt of the bed, who had nott bin outt of itt in six weeks before knocked and caled company to help me upp, and laid mee on a bed allmostt incencible – my head and face soe battered with the wall, and my back almost brok against the stairs, and both my knees brok. Thus I lay some weeks, and about ten of my uper teeth knoctt outt, of which was fowre of my eye teeth, all fell outt by the roots. And the artt of three blouders could nott make me bled one dropp. About two howrs before I had this dreadfull fall, I were forewarned of itt by my dream and told itt Mr Frek, who chectt my superstition. My dream was, viz. I thought I were up on a long lader in the garden a looking over the house where Skerry had bin att work. Wher affter I had staid a quarter of an houre, I called to my maid and told her my lader was falling therfore come quickly. Me thought I saw her run, butt before she came to me the lader and I were fallen downe; and thatt I was by a greatt many people taken up dead and ladd on my best chamber bed; and tho I survived this fall, I should live miserably till I dyed. I have found butt too true; for tho I have escaped this greatt fall with my life, yett never have I had one days comfortt or ease since, though now within two monthes of seven yeare since. Eliza. Freke

May 18 or 19 Mr Frek was taken very ill of a sore throatt of which thatt yeare aboundance dyed, which turned him into a violent feaver; when I watched with him 8 nights together every night expectting his last. The violent paine of which turned him into the goute, where itt brok in one of his feett, with which he was for aboutt three monthes

---

[118] Probably Michael Skerry, who married Lydia Betts in Narford on 16 October 1699. The Pentney register bills record the baptisms of four of their children and the burials of two.

onfined to his bed and chaire. And itt being the goutt broke ther, noe
octer or surgion would medle with itt. But my God gave me the
ourage and aded his blessing to my care and skill thatt by Gods greatt
aercy to him and me he is now whole and restored to his health
gaine and this day, being the sixth of Agust, is able with me to goe to
hurch and render my God thanks for his infinite mercy to him and
vretched mee.[119] Eliza. Freke

1704, Jully 26 My son, Mr Ralph Frek, and his wife and his two
ldest sons, Percy and John Frek, took shipp att the Cove in Cork in
ae Shoram frygate, a man of warr.[120]

Agust 3d They sett saile a Wensday in the evening and landed att
finhead the third of Agust in the evening and from thence took a
aarchantt and came to Pill, where my deer sister the Lady Norton
:tched them in her coach to Leigh to Sir George Nortons and
resented my daughter Freke with a dymond necklace valluable att a
undred pounds. Att Sir George Nortons they rested themselves aboutt
x week, viz., till the i5 of Septembere.

Agust 30 Then aboutt Wensday, Agust the thirtieth, Mr Frek sitting
a a new chaire by my greatt barne doore to see a load of barly goe
ato the barne – I was butt just gone from him, I think, for a couchin
or him; and the horsses very gentle, withoutt any provocation the cartt
a the twinkling of an eye run itt selfe full against that chaire Mr Freke
vas setting in and broke itt all to bitts, to the amasementt of all thatt
aw itt. And in this distress God liffted my deer husband up for shellter
ehind the barne doore, thatt had nott rise in a twelve month before
vithoutt att least one to help him. For which mercy the Lord make
ae for ever thankfull to him. Eliza Freke

September 6 Wensday and the 6 of Septembr, about twelve a
lock att noone one of my best houses in the parrish, Jams Wallbutt
ould ale in, full of company was burntt downe to the ground in the
ompass of three hours time. And nott one bitt of itt saved. The loss
f which was to me neer three hundred pound besids the wantt I have
f itt for tennants. EF

fol. 13r]

1704, September i8 Monday, the i8 of September, my deer sister
ae Lady Norton with my son and daughter and my two deer
randchildren Percy and John Frek wentt to the Bath with their three
ervants, where they all staied till the 26 of Octtober.

Octtober 28 And Satterday, the 28, they all came safe to London

---

[119] Freke retains the dating and tense of the passage from W adapted here.
[120] HMS *Shoreham*: above, p. 79 n. 128.

to the fattall lodgings my deer grandchild was kild in in Norfolk Street
Which beefore they wentt to London, I beged them to leave itt wit
mee; I would take care of itt. And I did att the same time forewarn
these my children of thatt lodging. Butt nothing comes by chance.

November i6 My son and daughter and my two grandchildre
and thyer three servants sett outt of London in a hired coach
themselves towards West Billney, **i8** and came down to Mr Freke an
mee Satterday, the i8, affter they had bin in England neer fowr
monthes, [my son] loaded with his dropsicall humour and soe bigg an
fatt I hardly knew him.

January i The first of January, being my birth day, I beged M
Freke to give my son Freke a New Years guiftt, which he most kindl
did of fiffty pounds. And I gave him ten pounds in crown peices, an
I paid above thirty pounds for cord for his toyles to catch deer with i
his park of Dirryloane.[121]

2 Mr Freke and I being in my chamber alone, I were saying befor
my own maide that my deer husband had given my son fiffty poun
for a New Years guiftt, which I was glad of. On which my daughte
that allwais stood harkning att her chamber doore, flew into Mr Frek
chamber and told him to his face hee might be ashamed to speak
such a tryffle before my servantt, tho itt was more then all the frind
she had ever gave liveing and dyeing butt her bare portion, and furthe
said to me thatt she would kick my maid downe stairs and iff I di
nott presently turne her outt of doors shee would be gone her self
Thus were I hectored in my own house and forcst immediatly to turn
her outt of doors thatt had lived soe many years with me and soe fi
for the attendance of my deer husband. This is true. Eliz Frek

i705, May 7 Monday, the 7 of May, I hired a whole coach att Lin
and sentt up all my young familly to London, and I gott Mr Frek t
goe with them thatt they mightt be att noe charge with coming to m
and to sett them downe where ever they desired except in Norfo
Streett wher they lay last. Butt to cross me, noe place would serv
them butt thatt. I likewise desired of them to leave with me both the
children; I would take care of them. Butt iff nott, I begg'd of them th
youngest, being something like my son. Butt I weer denyed in all.

io May the tenth I sentt my daughter up a hundred pounds, unknow
to Mr Frek, to ease there expences in London, and then I beg'd he
since she had deneyd them to me my grandchildren might b
immediattly carryed outt of London for feare I should loose them.

27 And this I begged by my letters to them the 27 of May, for I ha
noe quiett in mee. To all which I were nott allowed by them the civilit
of an answer, tho I had kept them and there familly above si

---

[121] Near Clonakilty: above, p. 77 n. 125.

onths, being eight of them and three pampered horses, att house and
provided] neer two hundred pounds in mony and five fine milch asses
d a little horse to little Percy. And while they were heer, I paid above
n pounds in apotharys bills for them besids doctters. For all which I
ver had soe much as thanks from my undutifull son or his wife. Eliza
reke

June io My deerst grandchild Jack Frek, which I had soe often
gg'd, on Sunday aboutt two a clock (in my blind eyes the loveliest
ild ever I saw and like my son) was by Mr Mullsons his landlords
n (and the place I had soe warned them against) shott to death in
e eye with my own sons pistolls by his cook Perrymans fault of
rlesly laying of them.[122] [fol. 13v] For which I beged my son and his
ife hee mightt be turned away, alleaging here was like to have the
me accidentt thatt day hee left my house, being the seventh of May,
her he discharged these very pistols charged with a brace of bulletts.
e lett them off, and neer twenty in the room come to take there leave
' my son, when two persons very hardly escaped itt and left its mark
' remembrans in the stone wall of the chimney. Yett for all this, all
e intrest I had could nott remove this French beast from my son.
his was a faire warning before I lost my deerst grandchild. Butt hee
ust pay for all theire undutifullness and cruellty to me the most
ttall'st thing thatt ever hapned to me, for this same shott kild my deer
usband.

i3 Wensday, the i3 of June, my deerst grandchild dyed. Aboutt 5 a
ock in the morning he gave up his soule to God for there undutifullness
mee, for elce my God would nott have taken from me roott and
anch as hee did butt to show his judgments to them. Butt God
rgive them both theire barbarity to the best of fathers and the
dullgents of mothers. Eliz Frek

i8 June the i8 my deerst grandchild was brought downe to Billney
bee intered in my vault there I made for Mr Frek and my selfe
der the chancell there. I then paid the herse man for bringing of
m six pound. And then I buryed him very handsomly with a greatt
peearance of my neighbours, my child being thatt day hee was inter'd
st three years and eleven month of age, bein borne the i8 of Jully,
d now lyes att the upper end of the vault with his grandfather Percy
rek, Esqr.

2i Thursday, the 2i of June, affter my deer grandchild was murdered,
y son and his wife wentt to devirtt themselves att the Bath. Shee staid
London six weeks; in all which time tho butt a few doors off, shee,
y cruell daughter, had nott the civility to goe once to see Mr Frek,
id up with the goute by the death [of] his deer grandchild, nor would

[122] Mullson or Molson: above, p. 82 n. 130.

soe much as lett her eldest son, Percy Frek, goe to ask his blesing th
day they went outt of London, tho Mr Frek lay very ill and never mor
smiled or enjoyed himselfe affter the murder of this his belove
grandchild. God forgive them.

Jully 7 Satterday, the seventh of Jully, my deerst cosen and husban
came home to me to Billney soe alltered as to frighten mee. Hee wa
soe swelled and with griefe for my child and his childrens cruell usag
to him for two monthes together in London, the extream malloncal
of which hee never recovered to his dyeing day, which was the secor
of June (my sons birth day), little more then eleven monthes,
compleatt all my miseryes together. God forgive them.

Septtember 19 My son Frek, his son, and his wife took shippin
and his family with his father and mother in law, Sir John Mead, too
shipping att Pill from Sir George Nortons on Sunday morning in
man of warr, Sir Charls Rich master, **24** and by Gods blessing arrive
safe att Kingsaile a Fryday nightt, the 24.[123] Nor has my son bin so
civill to me to lett me heer one word from him since the murder of h
child, tho I buryed itt and heer kept his familly above halfe a yea
and gave them two hundred pounds and my daughter a suite of clot
cost me above thirty pounds; and I paid, unknown to Mr Frek, a
theire extravagentt bills run in heer. Yett all has nott deserved thank
For which, good God, lay nott these his crueltyes and undutiffullne
to mee to his charge butt forgive him as I, Elizabeth Frek, his unhapp
mother, doe.

December 25 Mr Freke goeing to church with me to the sacramer
complained of a shortness of his breatth which soe increased on hi
thatt by New Year Day turned to soe violent an astma I thought I
would have died with itt. Every howre [he] was like to be choacke
and I affrighted outt of all my sences. [fol. 14r] And every howre
expected when he should be choaked.

1705/6 By New Years Day [it] increased soe on him I every da
expected his death – and my house full of invited company, all invite
his tennants for the New Years. I did immediattly send to Doctt
Barker of Lin and to Dr Thomas Shortt of Berry and to Mr Goodw
the surgion, butt all to little or noe purpose.[124] Thus my deer husban
lay for two month languishing in the hand of fowr doctters and surgio
and never closed his eyes or wentt into a bed to lye downe. Then
was concluded amongst them he must goe to Saffum.

Febuary 21 Wher on Thursday, the 21 of Febuary, he went in h
own coach against my reason or consentt; which jorney, tho butt
miles, stir'd the dropsicall humour soe with a violentt purge he too

---

[123] Charles Rich: above, p. 83 n. 133.
[124] Robert Barker, Thomas Short, and John Goodwyn: above, p. 84 n. 134.

om Docter Barker as forced his dropsey into his legg.

25 Wher itt broke Munday, the 25 of Febuary, when I sentt for 4 octters againe to him, viz., Dr Shortt of Berry, Doctter Barker of Lin, Doctter Duckett, and Doctter Cosins with Shelldrick.[125] Butt all to noe urpose, for by ther computation itt run in his right legg, as I were iformed, neer eight gallons, forced downe by a vyollentt purge given im (from these doctters). Which now being surgions worke, they left ı the hand of Doctter Cosins of Saffum to compleatt this barbarity, ıd all withoutt my concentt or approbation forced my stay there to ːe my deer husband murdered by five doctters, two surgins, and three oothycaryes.

30 Febuary 30 I sentt againe to Berry to Docter Thomas Shortt for Il ther consultations together. Mr Frek for all this two months never ay or nightt wentt into a bed, I setting up all the while by him, when ıey all gave me my doome: imposible to save his life to the equanoction.

1705/6, March 14 I were by these doctters to remove my deer osin and husband more in the ayre of Saffum; which I did to Mr Life tt twenty shillings a week one roome, who was soe cruell to me.[126] ʼho I kept them all in meat, drink, and fireing, yett he would nott ford me a bed to rest on for my selfe or deer husband.

18 Soe thatt the 18 of March, Monday, I were overperswaded by Mr ıbbott, minester of the parrish, to goe to his house and there take a round roome att twenty shillings a week; and they were to board mee ıd my husband, son, and cosin Crosby att ten a peice the week and ve shillings a week a peice my five servants.[127] Butt this was the arbarous place of all to me, where from Christmas to this time my ːer cosin never lay downe in his bed, as I, Eliza Frek, can testifye ıatt sett up with him as one of the fowre watchers. I never wentt into ıy bed six nights in the time of his sicknes.

24 Sunday, the 24 of March, my deer husband sentt Mr Towrs to ıe to goe presently and make hime a vaultt under Billney chancell ıatt wee mightt rest there with my grandchild John Freke (shott to ːeath in London) together.[128]

25 Lady Day I sentt for carpenters, massons, and workmen, all I ould gett to goe aboutt thatt dreadfull worke, and brought with me ʻom Billney his own bed he used to lye on there greatly to his attisfaction. And by this time with my setting up with him neer three ıonthes, I had two greatt holles broke in my left legg, an aditionall ıisery to whatt I dayly laboured under I dayly reckned would kill mee.

[125] Henry Cozens: above, p. 85 n. 138; Tobias Sheldrake: above, p. 85 n. 136.
[126] Family of Nathaniel Life: above, p. 85 n. 139.
[127] Thomas Ibbot: above, p. 85 n. 140.
[128] Henry Towers: above, p. 86 n. 141.

1706, March 26 My deer husband wentt into this his own bed an hardly rose outt of itt for six weeks longer with the ullceration of h legg.

[fol. 14v]

1706, Aprill 28 The 28 of Aprill Sunday nightt latte my son Fre and his nephew Crosby came outt of Ireland to see Mr Freke, who la in a deplorable condition, hee haveing left his house of Rafebarry th third of Aprill before. Where soon affter my son received a letter of h wifes being safe delivered of a son named John Redman Freke (tho m deer husband desired his name might be Arthur, his own fathers name butt itt was deneyd him and nott to bee purchased by me, his unhapp mother).[129]

May i Affter sitting att the table att Mr Ibbotts thinking Mr Fre had bin in a sleepe, Mr England, his curratt, came into the room were sitting with Mr Life, both of them drunke, and like two bea called mee crassy woman.[130] And Life said hee [had] two pisstolls i his pockett redy charged would soon rid me outt of the way. Butt I di nott mind itt; my troubles were soe grievous on me for him.

2 of May Mr Freke cal'd his servants and the people of the hous to know whatt the matter was his wife was soe abused and thatt befor his son and my cosin Crosby, whom he made sett up all night wit him, and locked me outt of his chamber hee might send a challeng b him to them by sun riseing to fightt them both. And after he wou have the law against them.

3 Unknowne to wretched mee till nextt day they came both on the knees to mee and offered me whatt sattisfacttion I required of then Soe tender was my deer husband of my honour, tho too true, for m grife had made me very little better then crassed with seeing him ly fowre monthes in thatt misery and my own legg broke in two holes fu of pains.

9 of May 1706, Mr Frek, being very desirous to have his vaultt red and I being in great torture of my own legg, sentt me to Billney to tr to rest my selfe for a few days; when I left him, I thought, in a fin condition and under the care of fowre docters and Doctter Cosins, h surgion, with my own son and cosin and fowre servants to watch wit him. And I sent allmost every day to see him.

23 Butt by thatt time I had staid att Bilney ten days, he sentt awa

---

[129] John Redman or Redmond was born on 14 April (above, p. 86 n. 142).

[130] Thomas England received a Cambridge MA in 1705, the year before he w ordained a priest and signed the Articles of Subscription (Venn, ii. 104; NRO, DN/Su 4/2).

r me, for to my sorrow his legg was gangreened all over thatt now I
uite dispared of his life by Docter Cosins managementt. Whom I told
ee had murdered my deer husband in my little absence by his
rdygreass oyntmentt, tho I paid him five pounds a week for neer six
onthes together.[131] This is true. Eliz Freke

1706, June 2d Sunday, the 2d of June, God took to himselfe my
eerst cosin and husband aboutt three a clock in the affternoone, my
eer sons birth day and the very howre he was borne in, in a fitt of
e astma. They being all att church, noe mortall was with him butt
y wretched selfe; [dying] in my armes, which quite distracted me,
e] bid me nott stirr from him. Butt my amased condition was such
 my crying outt soon fill'd the house outt of the church to be a
ittness of my unhappy and deplorable fatte.

3 I carryed my deer huband in a herse from Saffum to Billney, to
hich place he had a greatt appeerance of the country and outt of
affum; wher I rested him in his vault, being wraped in lead. And I
aveing all the bells in the severall parishes tolleing till I came to his
wn church att Billney, wher in a double leaded coffin I rested him till
e 7 of June in the vaultt suitteable to his quality and desertt and my
usband. All which cost me with his vault makeing and doctters and
rgions and apothycaryes, &c., and buryall above eleven hundred and
ffty pounds, as by his bills to show. Eliz Freke

3d of June, Monday, my cosin John Frek came from London. I sentt
r him to bury my deer husband, I nott being [able] to support my
lfe in itt. Which I did.

ol. 15r]

1706, June 7 Fryday, the seventh of June, I did inter my deer
usband in the vault under Billney chancell with a vast appeerance of,
think, all our part of the country and all the gentry by me invitted,
ith 8 gentlemen to carry him and eight more to carry up the pall. All
ad rings, gloves, scarfs, and hattbands; with wine, cakes, and ale,
hatt ever they would drinke. He had an appeerance, as I were told,
f above seven hundred people att his funarall. And I, his unhappy
ife, spar'd noe charge in all his sickness, death, and buryall, which
st me above (ii50 pounds) eleven hundred and fiffty pounds, as by
y bills above to show. And with my husband I did inter my deer
randchild Mr John Frek, kild by some accidentt with my sons pockett

---

[131] Verdigris, formed from the exposure of copper to acetic acid or moist air, became
e basis of 'fretting' or caustic tinctures and ointments used 'with much discretion' to
eat ulcers and postules (Thomas Blount, *Glossographia* [London, 1670], 678; Nicholas
ulpeper, *Pharmacopoeia Londinensis* [London, 1683], 105).

pistolls the tenth of June before in London, 1705. Affter which Mr Fre
never enjoy'd himself, butt hee sentt him downe to me in a herse t
bury him. Which I did the 18 of June with the appeerance of all m
neighbours and tennants. Eliz Frek

24 Midsomer Day, the 24 of June, I were sent for up to Londo
ther to prove my deer husbands will, who made me his executor an
gave me all he had both in Ireland for my life, viz., (850 l.) eigh
hundred and fiffty pounds a yeare in Ireland and twelve hundre
pound arrears, which my son took from me; and in England this estat
of West Billney, which was my owne, for I brought itt to him, and th
of Pentney, both now lett in 1712 for above five hundred pound a year
and two hundred pounds a yeare in the exchecker for ninty nine year
Soe with my son and familly I wentt wher I staid and putt my sel
and family in mourning, and I gave my son a hundred pound to bu
him mourning for his father – himself and his man, and I gave m
cosin Crosby a whole suite of mourning and ten guinyes to buy him
horse.

Jully 4 I did with my cosin John Freke in Doctters Commons prov
my deer husbands will, who left me, as above, 850 l. a year in Irelan
and 1200 l. in mony there, and 500 l. a yeare heer at Billney an
Pentney, and above 200 l. a yeare in the exchecker besids his persona
estatte there and heere.[132]

22 July the 22, being Monday, I leftt London and came in my ow
coach to my Billney with my deer sister Austen, who in pitty cam
downe with mee; where, I thank God, we both came well home th
24. Twas an unexpected kindness from her to me, her unhapy siste
Eliz Freke.

And now give me leave to recon up the misfortunes I have undergon
for this year past, 1705 and six.

1704, Jully 25 Saint James Day, 25 of Jully,[133] I goeing into my upe
closett for five pounds for the masons, coming downe from my close
with the mony in my hand, my head turned and I fell downe severa
staires and cryed outt I had broke my back. Butt recovering my sel
in a little time, I stood on my feett againe, when by an unknown han
(or I know nott how) I were thrown downe the rest of the greatt staie
against the stone wall of the window. Which Mr Freke being sicke
the goutt, of which he had keptt his bed six weeks, came hastily an
well outt to take me up; butt finding me dead was so affrighted h
durst nott move me butt call'd up all the people in the house to tak

---

[132] Doctors' Commons on Knightrider Street was the site of the prerogative court
Canterbury where Freke would have gone to prove the will.

[133] This and the next two entries are misdated in the manuscript 1705.

ne up, which fowre of my servants made a shiftt to doe and in aboutt
wo howrs broughtt me to my self. And in this condition I lay severall
veek and were bloded sixteen times butt could nott bleed. And with
his fall struck outt ten of my teeth.

Agust 2i Then aboutt the one and twentieth of Agust Mr Freke
ventt to my great barne to see a load of barly come in. Hee had a
new, strong chaire carried outt for him to sett in. And the horses were
is gentle as could [fol. 15v] be. When on a suden, sitting in my chamber
itt work, I heering a greatt outt cry went to be satisfyed of the occation
of itt [and] found the cart horses had turned the taile of the cartt
igainst the chaire Mr Frek was setting in and in the twinkling of an
eye or a moment broke itt all to little peices. Butt my God did help
ny husband off redily from the chaire behind the barne doore or hee
had bin broke to peices with itt, thatt had nott rise from such a low
chaire by himselfe in above two years before. This was a perticuler
providence to me affter my grievous fall downe staires; which fall of
mine I were forewarned of in my dreame thatt morning and told Mr
Frek of itt nott above an howre before I fell, who begg'd me nott to
goe up stairs thatt day. Butt to avoide superstition I wentt. And besids
the loss of all my teeth, I shall carry the marks of in my head to my
grave by itts continuall disorder there. Butt my God has hitherto
preserved me from all.

i704, September 6 Aboutt the sixt of September I had one of my
pest houses in the parishe burnt downe, Jams Walbutt sold ale inn;
which, tho full of company and severall of my servants in itt, none
knew itt was on fire till redy to fall. Which I could nott build such
another house for three hundred pounds.

i705, June io My deer little grandchild John Frek was shott to
death on Sunday aboutt two a clock with my sons pockett pistolls by
his man Perymans careless leaveing them redy charged. **i3** Mr Mullsons
son shott him into his head by one of his eyes; with which he dyed the
3 of June and was sent downe for me to bury the i8 of June. **i8** Which
I did in my vault with his grandfather, being thatt day three years and
eleven monthes old. This was my fatte, who a month before my son
and daughter deneyed me this childs company I offten beged to be a
comfortt to me and my deer husband.

i706, Sunday 2 Sunday, June 2d, God took from me my deerly
beloved husband affter I had bin his wife thirty six years and contracted
o him seven years before. He dyed my sons birth day and aboutt the
same howre he was borne and in the sixty third yeare of his age, which
att last was taken from mee with an astma and dropsey affter seven
monthes labouring under itt.

Agust 6 I wentt into my uper closett for two bottles of wyne and
fell downe the great staires with the two quart bottles in my hand,

when my deer sister Austen runing up against me broke my fall or
must have bin immediatly kild. This was Gods providence to me, Eliza
Freke.

30 As was Agust the 30. I being in my uper closett Sunday morne
two of my servants told me Mr Adams was come to call me to church
When I makeing hast downe stairs, I fell downe the great staires to the
bricks to the parlor doore and were by fowre men taken up dead. And
every body concluded all my bones were brok to peices with my heade
and face, and noe surgion could I gett. Butt my good God thatt never
failed me recovered mee of this withoutt the help of mortall man when
my house full of company howrely expected my death. This was
another peice of providence to Eliz Freke. For which God ever make
me thankfull for all these and many more signall mercyes to mee
Elizabeth Frek, and grant I may never forgett them.

1706, November 14 The 14 of November and my weding day
renewed my coppy hold estate att Pentney by Charles Turner, which
Mr Frek gave up to the lord of the maner, Mr Noes, to the use of hi
will. I call'd a court of copy hold tennants on purpose for itt, and
paid Mr Charles Turner fourteen pound for his renewall of itt besid
his fees and engrosing of itt.[134]

[fol. 16r]

1706, November 23 I had a letter from my cosin John Frek that
my son was in Dorsettshier with my cosin Robertt Frek att Upway
affter I had bin allmost frightned outt of all my sences for fear of hi
being lost att sea by the late tempestious stormes, for neer fowre
monthes in perpetuall feares, he goeing outt of London in greatt hast
the 19 of Jully before to goe home to his famyly from Bristoll Faire.

25 And I never heard he was alive till November 25 I wrott a letter
to him since he did nott goe home to come to me and nott thus to
expose himself. My sons answer to me was he would acknowledg the
kindness withoutt charging the debt of obligation on mee.

December 23 I wrott a letter againe to my son as I thought my
dutty to admonish him of his errors. I had only as usuall a rude answer
for itt. A coppy of [the] letter I wrott is in my whit vellum book of
remembrances, 1706.[135] Thus my son and Thom Crosby with three of
Mr Freks best horses I gave him run up and downe the country from
the death of Mr Frek till the eight of March following to my unspeakable
griefe, a day most remarkable for the death of our good king William

---

[134] Charles Nowyes, lord of Ashwood Manor, and copyhold: above, p. 89 n. 147.
[135] W, fols. 67r–v: above, pp. 89–90.

he Third. And then, itt being Sunday, hee took shiping in a man of
varr, and by Gods greatt mercy to mee and him he came safe over to
iis familly in Ireland affter hee had thus run aboutt exposeing himsellfe
and me above eleven monthes heer in England to the griefe of me, his
afflicted mother, Eliz Frek.

1706/7, January ii Sir John, my daughter in laws father, dyed of
an appoplexy, and my son then in England runing aboutt the country.
Hee was a greatt loss to me and my familly in Ireland.[136]

Febuary 24 I carryed my deer sister Austen home and her maid
n my coach to London, wher I wentt to settle my business in order
or my voyage for Ireland, ther to prove my deer husbands will and to
ake posesion of his bounty to mee. Butt there I were soe afflicted with
my asttma thatt I were faine to gett home againe as fast as I could.

1707, Aprill i5 I came outt of London, being Easter Tuesday, nott
ible to stirr or goe further with my grievous tissick butt settled my
exchecker funds; and I then made my will by Mr Richard Turner.[137]

6 And the next day came outt of London, wher by Cambrig I had a
grievous fall in my new coach, my coachman being drunk. To the
amasementt of all thatt help'd me up wee were nott kild, being then
ixty six years of age; which was seconded by another lifting me outt
of my coach.

i9 However, att last by Gods mercy to mee I came alive and safe
home to my Billney the ninteenth of Aprill. For which mercy God
nake me for ever thankfull. Eliz Freke

And I were faine to send my cosin John Frek with my letter of
atturny for Ireland to prove my deer husbands will and ther to settle
my affairs, and gave him in part for his jorny before I left London a
hundred pounds and two hundred pounds more when he returned, tho
he ruiened me in my estate there by falling all my rents and gave away
welve hundred pounds from me and brought me over nothing butt
himselfe.

i707, Aprill 2i My cosin John Frek sett outt of London for Ireland
by way of Chester, before which I paid him Mr Frekes lagacy of a
hundred pounds and gave him another in part paymentt for his jorney.
Butt God forgive all falce frinds. For this yeare was a dreadfull yeare
o me as ever poor mortall ever underwentt, being i707. My distractions
or Mr Freke rendered me a mark for all the rogues and knaves of this
country; and those frinds I most trusted most deceived me, besids my
own sons undutifullness to me, which affter the loss of Mr Frek was
enough to have brok [fol. 16v] the hart of any mortall butt my wretched
elf. Butt now outt of all I am by my greatt and good God delivered,

---

[136] John Meade: above, p. 91 n. 150.
[137] Possibly Richard Pyne's trustee.

tho itt has confined me to my chamber by sickness and tisick with a[n] astma for six years past and sencible of noe comfort.

i707, May ii I had a letter from my son outt of Ireland and th[e] second I have had since I buiered his son John Frek, which was kil[d] in London, datted from Rathbarry, which was two years wanting on[e] month.

io And May io I had a letter of my cosin John Freks landing i[n] Dublin affter he had bin fowr days att sea in the packett boatt an[d] seen eleven ships taken from Hollyhead by privatteers, of which I than[k] God hee escaped [and] went safe to Rathbarry.[138]

i707, Agust 2d My cosin John Frek left Dublin, whither my so[n] wentt with him, and came back in the packett boatt to Chester; **i9** an[d] from thence to London Tuesday, the i9 of Agust. From whence he[e] brought me the dismall account of my affairs in Ireland and my great loses there by Mr Jervoyce[139] and nott mended by his jorney thithe[r] which cost me to him three hundred pound thatt ten weeke hee wa[s] there besids his fall of my rents 200 l., two hundred pounds, a yea[r] and giveing away my arrears of above twelve hundred pounds mor[e] Lett me be a warning to trust friends with letters of aturny.

3i Being Sunday, I fell downe the greatt staires by the parlor door and were taken up dead. A surgion was sentt for to bleed me, wh[o] pricked me in both my armes and feett sixteen times withoutt on[e] spoonfull of bloud. All said I must dye, butt outt of this misfortune m[y] God raised me againe. EF

September 29–30 Munday, September the 30, I discharged M[r] Adams from my church for his debauchery affter I had dispenced wit[h] his notorious life thirty six years for his wife and childrens sake. No[w] forced to remove him.[140]

Octtobr i3 Monday, Octtobr i3, I wentt up to London againe to be[e] sattisfyed how my kinsman John Frek had managed my Irish affaires.

i6 And the i6 I came to London, whither with my long jorney and th[e] inhuman accountt my kinsman gave me added with itt his managem[ent] thatt the next day I were taken with such a violent asttma and tisick tha[t] for seventeen weeks I could nott goe outt of my chaire butt lifted to m[y] bed fowrteen weeks of this time. All which time none thatt saw me though[t] itt imposible for my life. This my foolish jorny to London and my i7 week[s] sickness ther cost mee above three hundred pounds, to which aded t[o] the three hundred I gave my cosin John Frek for his jorney and m[y] sons usuage of me in Ireland has rendered mee an example for th[e] trust of frinds and children. Both which my God forgive and grant

---

[138] Holyhead: above, p. 92 n. 151.

[139] Joseph Jervois: above, p. 92 n. 152.

[140] William Adams: above, p. 93 n. 153.

may only reley on him who helps the helpless and releives the oppresed thatt trust in him as does his humble servant. Eliz Freke

1707, September 29 And affter all these usages to mee in my sick and weak condition, my cosin John Freke never lett me have any rest till I had made a lease to my son of me 850 pound a yeare in Ireland lett by my deer husband in 1703 and reduced by this my truste with my letter of aturney in the yeare 1707 to the rentt of 664 pound a yeare in order to lease itt to my son for the yearly rentt of 350 pounds a yeare, which he did Michellmas 1707. From which time to this day, being Agust the 22, I never had one peny of rentt butt one half years, tho now itt is 1712. Soe thatt there is now due to me from my son above three thousand pound besids my personall estatte. Is this kind or faire in my cosin John Freke, whom I made choice of to be a trustee for mee; or is itt faire in him by the powre of my letter of atturny to him to take away my estate from me in Ireland given me by my deer husband of 850 l. and my personall estate of above twelve hundred pounds and give itt [fol. 17r] to my son, who had 800 l. a yeare settled on him to live on? From such friends and friendship, good Lord, deliver mee and forgive my son his undutifullness to mee, his poor unhappy mother, and grant his children may nott pay my debtt by their undutifullness to him is the dayly prayer of Eliz Freke.

Febuary 14 Vallentines Day, Febuary 14, I came home againe to my Bilney in hopes there to rest my poore, weryed carrkes affter I had squandered away neer seven hundred pounds in litle more then a quarter of a yeare besids doctters, meatt, drink, or close in 18 weeks time. Butt this is my least of suffrings, for affter I came home I mett with an infinite sortt of loses and troubles from all my tennants and the country. Heer fowre times were I arrested in the hundred court, unknown to me, by Harry Towers and his rogry crue, whom I had bin soe kind to as to lett him cheatt me of above 200 l. besids my guifts to him and lentt him more outt of my pockett thirty pounds. Yett in the hundred court for thirty shillings hee made itt cost me neer a hundred pound. Then came in nextt the atturney Charls Turner of Linn, who arested mee with an execution body and goods for eightt pound from the shriefs courte when I had neer 800 l. in my house and I did nott know I owed a farthing to either. And this Charls Turner cheated me of above two hundred pounds butt few monthes before.

Jully 20 Then thirdly came in the rogue Thom Garrett, who before ten justices of peace att Saffum swore against me att the sesions of a royett, asault, and battry and for stealling of nine, 9, akers of grass and hay. The grand jury brought itt in ignoramus, and the gentry of the country ashamed of my usuage.[141] Butt my help was and is in my God.

---

[141] Swaffham sessions; ignoramus: above, p. 96 n. 162.

And the shame to my selfe I could very hardly beare. Then came in the rogue Dawson, who cheated me of above a 100 l., hundred pound, with my severall other tennants, all which picked holes in my leases to cheatt me of my rentt.[142] For which I had a tryall att the assises att Norwich against Towre and Thom Garrett for my rentt and cutting downe neer a hundred liveing trees – oke, ash, and elme – and convey[ing] them away the time above I were sicke in London.

Jully 22 Where I carryed with mee to Norwich eight wittnesses, my tennants, [and] kept them there a week drinking, when all the time I were nott allowed to know when my heering was by the rogue Self, my aturney to whom I then gave five ginyes. When in the compas of a quarter of a houre, Sir John Trever gave the suite against me on the oath of Charls Turner and Henry Towrs withoutt ever axamining one of my witnesses, they both swearing I never sued any body butt I cast them and made them begers.[143] This is true and the best of my usage since my widowhood; and tho I have soe offten and weekly complained to my kinsman John Freke, yett withoutt releive or help from him or any of my other frinds.

November 25 Att last to compleate all my misfortunes Charls Turner of Linn, an atturny, earlly in the morning the 25 of November sentt the shrifes two baylyes to carry me to Norwich Castle for eight pound on my body and good when I had eight hundred pound by me in my house besids plate. Butt to God I made my complaint, who signally lett me see his justice and goodness to mee in the fall of my enimise. For Charls Turner, soon affter he came from the asises, his eye dropt outt of his head on his book and his wife dyed from him; and nott long affter God took him away to accountt for his perjury.[144] And for Henry Towrs, [fol. 17v] soon affter he came home, viz., aboutt a five or six weeks, hee, Henry Towers, was taken ill of a feavour of which in aboutt three days he dyed. Which tho early in the morning, he was forcst to be carryed outt in the garden presently and be next morn privatly laid in the ground for feare of anoyance.[145]

November 26 And Garrett and Dawson have spentt ther substance in cheating of me [and] are now little wortth, thatt rented above a hundred pounds a yeare of mee.[146]

Besids by my ignorance, cosin John Freks nott letting me know I

---

[142] John Dawson, the Manor Farm tenant: above, p. 100 n. 176.

[143] Thomas Selfe: above, p. 96 n. 165. Sir John Trevor was master of the rolls (above, p. 144 n. 258); W, however, refers to Lord Chief Justice Trevors, who is Thomas Trevor (above, p. 97 n. 166)

[144] Charles Turner's wife Mary died on 28 December 1708; he died on 11 December 1711 (Carthew, iii. 129).

[145] Henry Towers was buried at North Runcton on 27 May 1709.

[146] The manuscript date in the margin includes the year 1707, an apparent misdating.

oughtt to lease my land in my own name, his leases expireing with
him, I lost by these severall tennants:

First by Thom Garrett above a	ioo pound
By the rogue John Dawson I lost above a hundred and fiffty	i5o pound
I lost by John Fish in mony and farms aboutt	57 pound
And by Dick Cross aboutt in mony and farme	6o pounds
And by Towres and Charls Turner I were cheated above	200 pounds
Besids my charge of law in Norwich courte and the county courte and in running up and downe to defend my selfe in six severall suits and with my removeing them cost me	250 pond
In all	88o l.

In all which troubles and abusses placed on me nott one friend or
relation of my ever apeered to my comfortt or asisstance; noe, nott my
cosin John Frek, whom I had made choise of to be my truste. And I
thoughtt I had obliged him, giveing this severall sums of mony as:

First in i706 I desired Mr Frek to give him a hundred pounds in his will to assistt me, which I paid him Jully i706 when I wentt to London to prove my deer husband will in Docters Commons.	ioo l. EF
Then March 7, i707, when he wentt for Ireland to give away my estatte there and to reduce itt from 850 l. a year to 664 pounds a yeare, I gave him in gold more for this foolish jorney for me there to file his will a	ioo l. EF
Novembr i8 I presented my cosin John Frek more in mony, for I hoped his kindness and friendship to me before I knew whatt was done for me in Ireland. I then presented him with more in redy mony	200 l. EF
i708, Jully 2i I more gave my cosin John Frek for a gratuity to asist me the intrest of a thousand pound for a year halfe, which was att least	78 l. EF
More I gave to his neece Betty Gilles[147] on his accountt	50 l. EF
Which he said he accepted as to himself, with three years intrest on itt.	
More I gave my cosin John Frek when hee came down to me, i7io, for a week stay and returneing mee 500 l. from Norwich in March 6	32 l. EF

[147] Elizabeth Gyles: above, p. 95 n. 159.

More December i7ii when I made up my accounts
with him, the intrest of a thousand pound for 9
monthes   25 l. EF
All this in six years, which comes to the sume of   595 l.
                                                                                E Freke

Besids the severall thousand pounds I am a looser by him and was
never five pounds to my knowledg the better for his assistance since
the death of my deer husband. For all his ill usuage of mee God forgive
him, and from such friends and frindship, good Lord, deliver. Eliz
Freke

September 29, 30 Being Monday, I discharged Mr Adams from
his further attendance on my church att Billney and paid him downe
ten pounds affter I had borne with all his debaucharyes of all kinds six
and thirty yeares for his wife and childrens sake and placed in Mr Buck
in his roome.[148] E Frek

And for all these my civilitys to my cosin John Frek, he wrott me
two rough letters March io, i708[/9], which I keep in memory of him,
which did nott want there answer from me, Eliz. Frek, to be treated
by him soe barbarouslly and soe civily by strangers. Oh, thatt my God
would give me a better health thatt I might nott trouble my frinds. Eliz
Frek

[fol. 18r]

i709, Aprill 25 Mr North wrot to me Garrett had affter neer a ioo
l. charge to mee refer'd his difference to him and desired me Mr
Hatten Berners might be my refferee and nott Mr Hoste. I presently
writt to Mr Berners to oblige me in this refference the 27 instant att
Midletowne taverne.[149] **27** Where accordingly both came, butt nothing
was done in itt, only forty shillings for me to pay for wyne and our
dinner.

May i3 I sentt to John Dawson for some mony, who owed me
above a ioo l. for rent for the Maner Farme; who allwaise promised
butt never paid me any, takeing the advantage of my leases want of
renewall.

i4 On which the i4 I destrained him, who had drove off all his stock
from my land; and on his promise of paying me, I released my
distress.[150] Which as soon as done the next day, being Sunday, hee rid
into the Hall a horse back by three a clock in the morning and bid me

---

[148] Charles Buck: above, p. 103 n. 187.
[149] Mr Barnish is the referee in W (above, p. 99 and n. 175); James Hoste: above,
p. 100 n. 178; the Crown: above, p. 99 n. 175.
[150] Distrain/distress: above, p. 104 n. 188.

enter for the doors were all open. And every thing was caryed away: locks, keys, gates, &c., to the vallue of a i5o pound lost to mee; briges, fences, and drains, above fiffty pounds more loss to mee. E Frek

i708/9, January 29 John Fish, my tenantt, dyed, who rented Billney Closes; before which his son Thom Fish run away all his stock from my grounds, who owed me by his bills as proved before Messrs Berners and Good neer a hundred pound to be due to me besids my loses of twenty pound alowed Luke Wingfield to take them for the first yeare and all the gates and fences gone, which cost me neer twenty pound more, and the fall of the rent 4 l. a year.[151] Yett Robertt Good, his executor, had the contience to wrong me of fiffty seven pounds. Thus am I used.

i709, May 25 All my six coach horses Mr Frek left me being kild and dead by my servants, I bought mee a paire of coach horses of Mr Berny[152] cost me 35, thirty five, pound, a gellding and a mare, by Mr Buck to goe to London with in order to goe my selfe for Ireland – my self to endeavour to settle my business there before my death and to retreive my cosin John Freks imprudent bargaine he made for me with my son by my letter of atturney intrusted him with.

June 2i Tuesday, the 2i of June, I left my house and begun my jorney for London, and Mr Buck, my chaplin, rid up with me by the coach side. I was very ill, and I took him with me to make up my accounts with my kinsman before I wentt for Ireland.

24 Midsomer Day I came into London to my lodgings in Red Lyon Streett; **30** wher Thursday, June the thirtyeth, my great coach mare was stole from me by one George Marllo, who was taken on his back att Barnard. He shoulder shot him and cutt off his taile and his eares.[153]

Jully 2 Soe thatt I was faine my selfe to hire a coach and horses to goe in persuite of him. In this my cosin John Freke would nott assist me. Ther Mr Berners, my next neighbour, offten offered me to goe and release her and to be bound for my prosecution of itt.[154] Which I did, and affter paying all there charges I could nott have her till I were bound over by Justice Hadly to prosecute the man for felony att St Allbons sesions.[155] Thus were I tormented runing aboutt for five days together before I could gett my mare.

i3 Then the i3, Wensday, I went with my cosin Herlackendone[156] in

[151] See above, p. 99 n. 173.

[152] John Berney: above, p. 108 n. 196.

[153] High Barnet or Chipping Barnet: above, p. 108 n. 197; shoulder-shot: archaic term for a shoulder strained or dislocated.

[154] W does not describe Berners as a nearby neighbour; Hatton Berners' will lists no property in the immediate area (PRO, PROB 11/537/269).

[155] George Hadley: above, p. 109 n. 199.

[156] Katherine Harlackenden: above, p. 93 n. 155.

my own coach to St Albons sessions to prosecute this poor roge Morly and to hang him, or I must loose my mare – above twenty miles from London. This was grievous to me, butt goe I must or forfett my bonds to the queen and my horse to the lord of the maner, which cost me neer twenty pounds butt a month before. When I came on the sessions bench, I declared I would sooner loose both [horses] in my coach att there doore then hang this poor man, which angered the justices and the bench very much. And the lord of the maner was redy there to demand him iff I would nott except [fol. 18v] the queens bounty of forty pound to convictt this miserable criminall, who stood in iron fetters before me bowing [and] pirced my hartt.[157] Thus in the greatt tavarne in St Allbons I spentt three days more.[158] Att last I were to be bound to the Old Bayly sessions in London; which I utterly refused my further prosecution butt offered to pay all ther full demands, which cost me above ten pounds more then the maire was then worth.

1709, Jully i5 To conclude, St Swithins Day, Jully i5, I left St Allbons and came in my own coach to London griveous ill and tired, allmost outt of my life.

25 Where I staide till the 25 of Jully, when thatt day I sett outt in my own coach with my deer sister Austen for the Bath in order for Ireland. Wher, I thank God, I came safe in fowre dayes, butt very ill with my tissick, to try for help of the doctters there.

Agust i2 Butt finding noe good in them nor their watters, after a fortnight stay there I went on my jorney to Sir George Nortons to see my deer sister there. Where I staid for a man of warr and my Lord Chiefe Justice Pine till September i2, in all which time noe ship to be gott.[159]

September i2 Soe thatt winter drawing neer and the watters very high, the ways bad, and my selfe very ill, I were forced to returne home againe.

i9 And [with] the help of two of my sisters horses, by the Oxford Road I compased to London to my sister Nortons house in five days time in Ormond Streett in London, where I staid one week very ill of my tisick.[160]

---

[157] The earlier remembrances note she was bound 'in a bond of forty pound to the queen to prosecute'. The sum, however, could be related to the 'parliamentary reward' of forty pounds given private citizens by 1692 and 1706 statutes for the prosecution and conviction of those accused of various crimes, including theft (Leon Radzinowicz, *A History of English Criminal Law and Its Administration*, 3 vols. [London, 1948–57], ii. 57–9; Elizabeth Wells, Bodleian Law Library).

[158] Among the inns located on Holywell Hill, the Bull Inn was described by a late seventeenth-century visitor to St Albans as 'the greatest that I have seen in England' (*History of Hertfordshire*, ed. Page, ii. 474).

[159] George Norton's brother-in-law Richard Pyne: above, p. 110 n. 204.

[160] From Bristol to Malmsbury, through Purton and Highworth to Faringdon, and via

26 And the Fryday affter, I humbly thank God, I sett outt for Billney, where I came safe in five days, **29** – time enough to enter my house and fitt my self with servants. Soe thatt in the compas of fourteen weeks I have gone with these my two horses above five hundred miles and spentt att least three hundred pounds). For which mercy and severall other deliverancyes both by watter and land lett me never forgett to be thankfull to my great and good God whilst I live, Eliza. Freke. And I brought home with me a large sillver flagon for my comunion table cost mee above twelve pounds to give to my church here att West Billney affter I had used a pewter pott for 28 years.[161]

Octtober 20 I discharged Mr Buck, my minester there, the bishop haveing suspended him for preaching withoutt his licence, which I refused to except or take to lessen my wrightt to thatt donative, itt being my peculer and nott his.[162] And I wrott a letter to this presentt bishop of my discharging Mr Buck and thatt I would except none under his licence except he would pay them, my church haveing neither tith or gleab belonging to itt butt my bounty and charrity and which I had maintained thirty six years withoutt the Norwich courte, in whose jurisdicttion I would nott come or subjectt my church to withoutt he would please to endow itt.[163]

1709, November 29 I had a very civill letter from the bishop thatt rather then my church should be vacantt I should fill itt to my pleasure to have devine service in itt, hee being unwilling to contend with me. Butt, however, his chancellour, Docter Tanner, Gahezy like tormented me with his proctters and baylyes.[164]

December 19 Soe thatt I wrott againe to the bishop to London thatt I would fill the vacency of West Billney iff my right was allowed by his courts in Norwich. Butt hee haveing placed his displasure on my church doore and in my absence whilst I were att Bristoll goeing for Ireland, my church never haveing had an inquest on itt before for above this forty years by the severall bishops and the minester when I came to itt (Mr Peirce) lived in a little twenty shilling house of mine by selling ale, I beg'd leave of his lordship to defend my rightt or to

---

Oxford or Abingdon to London; rather than through Marshfield to Chippenham, Marlborough, and Reading (John Ogilby, *The Traveller's Guide* [London, 1699], 14–15, 20–4). Ormond Street: above, p. 109 n. 201.

[161] Silver flagon: above, p. 110 n. 205.

[162] Donative and peculiar: above, p. 113 n. 209; p. 115 n. 216.

[163] Letter, W, fols. 74v–5r: above, pp. 111–12; glebe: above, p. 115 n. 216.

[164] Thomas Tanner: above, p. 117 n. 222. Gehazi, the servant of Elisha who pushes the Shunammite mother away from his master (2 Kings 4:27), is cursed with leprosy when in his greed he deceives Naaman, compromising the trust of Elisha for money and garments (5:20–27). Proctors were trained in Roman and canon law (above, p. 123 n. 228).

endow itt and dispose of itt as he thought fitt.[165] And whatt ever hee gave I would add as much to itt. Eliza. Freke

[fol. 19r]

i7io, January first New Years Day and my unhappy birth day sentt to Mr Smith of East Winch to come and give the sacramentt at West Billney, itt being Sunday, thatt I mightt see my silver flagon consecrated. Where he did come, tho Mr Edgworth forbitt him. Fo which I gave him twenty shillings, and his two clarks five shillings, and his son and daughter ten shillings.[166]

4 And I clothed Thomas Betts three children and gave poor Mary Frek five pounds, and to Ann Freke I sentt twenty shillings, and to the parish for Walbuts children I gave them forty shillings for Jame Wallbutts chilldren; which coms to ten pound, nine shillings.[167] E Freke

30 of January I sentt John Dawson with two baylyes to Norwich jayle, cost me above five pound, for above a hundred pounds he owed mee, E Frek, for rentt affter I had tryed all faire menes with him til he said he had me in his pocked and iff he had a thousand pound nott one peny should I have, &c.

i709/io, February 2d My honoured good cosin Hamillton dyed of an appoplexy. Shee was taken speechless the Sunday before and on Tuesday nightt dyed of itt. She was my own aunts eldest daughter and my mothers own sister. Shee lyes buryed att Hollingburne in the chancell by her father, my Lord Cullpeper, and dyed in the seventy second yeare of her age, leaveing a greatt posterity behind her of grandchildren, whom by her prudence all seventeen shared in her bounty of kindness to them.[168]

March 2d Thursday and the second of March my deer sister Austen came downe to me. I fetched her from New Markett in my own coach who found me alive, I thank God, butt very ill, haveing hardly moved outt of my chaire since last November. And soe I still continue under the hand of a mercyfull God for above this six years past or ever since my unhappy widdowhood. E Frek

i7io, March 25 I entered Mr Smith, vicker of Winch, into my church my curratt, butt hee being a very weak man was nott able to hold itt (or elce afraid to anger the bishop).

---

[165] Arthur Peirse/Pierce: above, p. 119 n. 225.

[166] Robert Edgworth: above, p. 128 n. 232. Joyce, who was baptized on 23 December 1698, and Thomas, who was baptized on 18 May 1695.

[167] Betts and Wallbut children: above, p. 117 n. 219, p. 59 n. 72; the sisters Mary and Ann Freke are unidentified (above, p. 116 n. 220).

[168] Elizabeth, the daughter of Cicely Freke's sister Judith and her husband, James Hamilton (above, p. 128 n. 233).

Aprill 25 Affter a shortt tryall [he] gave itt me up againe Aprill the 25, 1710, soe I paid him for his two sermons twenty shillings and gave his two children a crown a peice. And by the perswation of my deer sister Austen and to oblige the bishop, I were perswaded to except Mr Buck againe, vicker of Gyton, a Kentt man, who entered my curratte dureing my will and pleasure and while he behaved himselfe well to the church and me with a trust on my generosity for his time or subsistance whilst in itt.

27 On these tearmes he entered my church the 27 Aprill.

30 Where the 30 of Aprill, bein Sunday, he was sentt for away to bury his own mother in Kentt. Where in London and in Kentt he staide till the 8 of Jully, soe thatt I had from him butt five sermons this quarter of a yeare or 4 months.

Agust 9 Mrs Barns husband (Mr Edgwarth) was arrested for fiffty pounds hee bought his wife with by nine baylyes att Winch Hall affter his greatt brags of her greatt fortune of i2000 l. Wher affter the breaking of 9 or io locks, [they] found him run up in his own chamber chimney with two pistolls charged in his hand.

io Betimes in the morning Mr Edgworth stole outt of this country rather then stand such another shock next day and leftt his daughter married to Mr Thom Langly and the estate of Winch under a mortgage of sale to Mr Cotten while Mrs Barns and Mr Edgworth made the best of their way for Ireland.[169] Affter all there great brags of two thousand pound a yeare, [they] wentt over in a cole barke and left there children to make the best of whatt they could gett for ther subsistance, which he told me this winter was nott thirty pounds a yeare and never a farthing portion with his wife. This is true. Eliz Frek

22 I received a letter of the death of my deer sister Norton; **24** and from London by the same hand I heard of her recovery and did send to mee to come to her.

23 The bishop of London (Compton) with a hundred and fiffty of his clergy under him subscribed an adress to the queen against the Pretender or prince of Walles and presented itt himselfe, which is printed in this sessions of parliamentt.[170]

---

[169] Langley marriage: above, p. 164 n. 319. Robert Perryman transferred the 7 March 1708/9 bond secured by the East Winch property to Charles Cotton in trust for John Cotton of Cutler's Hall, London (NRO, 12336 30C4).

[170] Besides the gazettes (above, p. 154 n. 295), the address appears in John Swynfen, *The Objections of the Non-subscribing London Clergy, against the Address from the Bishop of London* (London, 1710), sigs. A2r–v, and Abel Boyer, *The History Of the Reign of Queen Anne … Year the Ninth* (London, 1711), 180–2.

[fol. 19v]

i7io, Septtember ii The eleventh of September my deere sister Austin leftt Billney and me very ill in itt and went for London, where she sentt to her two daughters to meett her, unknown to mee. She hired a coach to her selfe and maide att Lin, tho I offered her mine. Soe when I saw goe she would, I gave her twenty pound to pay for itt I mightt receive noe further pitty or obligation on thatt accountte. Nor would itt have troubled mee soe much had shee gone to a house of her owne to have left me soe; butt itt was to goe and boarde att Wye Colidg, wher in little more then a yeare shee and her daughters both were to seek a new habitation.[171] Which I could nott butt resentt most unkindly from her affter I had pinched my self back and belly these severall years in these severall sums to serve her and hers by these guifts to her following, to the uttmost of my memory. Eliz Freke

		l.–s.–d.
i When I wentt first for Ireland, i675, I presented my deer sister with the Imperiall Bible cost me outt of my pockett besids the binding to Mr Oglyby[172]		50–0–0
2ly When I wentt my second jorney for Ireland, being aboutt i677, I then gave my deer sister all I were possest of my own in this world, which was aboutt, to the best of my memory, 400 l. Which against my will she putt outt to Mr Lee;[173] which for severall years was in danger of itts being lost, butt I saw my brother receive itt when he was in the admyrallty office.		400–0–0
3ly In or aboutt the year i682 when I had scraped some more mony together and were then goeing for Ireland, I gave my deer sister all I had againe in the world; and I did returne itt her by my cosin John Freke with all thatt my deer father then gave me while with him, which my cosin John Frek of Bristoll[174] said he paid my deer sister and was		250–0–0

[171] Wye, ten miles southwest of Canterbury, was the site of a school established in 1447 by the archbishop of Canterbury John Kempe 'for the celebrating of divine service, and for the education of youth in this parish'. In the early eighteenth century Lady Joanna Thornhill founded a grammar school for the parish poor (Hasted, vii. 355; Philipot, *Villare Cantianum*, 374).

[172] *The Holy Bible*, illustrated by John Ogilby and printed by John Field, 2 vols. (Cambridge, i66o).

[173] Four Lees are in *A Collection of the Names of the Merchants Living in and about the City of London* (London, 1677), sig. E8v, none by profession and only by address; nor do any appear in the lists of goldsmiths 'that keep Runing Cashes'.

[174] Possibly a mistake for Freke's Middle Temple relative, though the Freke genealogy

4ly Then I staid fowre yeare and a halfe in Ireland, all which time my sister and my nephew Austen received my rents of West Billney.[175] When Mr Blith of Linn and James Wallbutt charged my nephew with his receitt of two hundred and fiffty pounds, nott one peny had I of this butt one bill Mr Worrell gott me of aboutt twenty pound, which money [he] owned the receitt of in a letter of thanks to mee.[176]   200—0—0

5ly Then in or aboutt the yeare 1696 when I came last outt of Ireland, when aboutt the 22 of Agust my brother Austin dyed and left his two daughters and youngest son nott one peny butt near 3000 l. debtt to pay, I gave this my sisters two daughters all I were mistress of in the world, viz., 100 l. a peice.   200—0—0

6ly Then aboutt the yeare 1697 I gave my deer sister to bind outt her youngest son, Thom Austen,[177] to a marchantt in Cork   100—0—0
And I paid itt to Mr Freke for his master more for him   030—0—0

7ly In or about the yeare 1700 when my deer sister lived in her little house in Plumtree Streett, when she putt all her joynter into my nephews hand for portions for her two daughters, I did then furnish her best chamber intirely and gave her in mony besids to her better subsistance   200—0—0
Then all I had saved att my Billney.

8ly Then more I sentt her up to London in a box of suger cakes to buy her something to remember me, Eliz Freke, by when shee lived in Plumetree Streett   030—0—0

9ly Then in or aboute the yeare 1707 the very first mony I saved in my widowhood of my exchecker funds I gave my deer sister Austen more when I came outt of London   100—0—0

---

indicates a John Freke was born in Bristol on 15 July 1647, the son of Thomas and Elizabeth Freke and the husband of Sarah Wickham, whom he married in 1672.

[175] Robert Austen.

[176] William Blyth, listed in the 1690 Lynn poll tax as a beer brewer residing with his wife in Chequer Ward (NRO, KL/C47/12–15), is taxed for property in Kettlewell and Paradice Wards as well as Jewes Lane in the 1693 land tax (KL/C47/8). A Francis and Elizabeth Worrell baptized several children in Swaffham, where she died in 1711.

[177] Austen left her younger son only five pounds 'haveing approved himselfe the whole

And more att the same time, Mr Langly bond of
London of   050–0–0
Sume is   i6io–0–0
                                                             Eliza Freke

[fol. 20r]

And att the same time, i707, I gave my deer sister my coach, which
cost me att second hand fiffty five pounds when I went into mourning
lined with a silk cafoy and butt one jorney used, viz., to London.

	l.–ss.–d.
ioly And more in the year i707 I gave my two neeces, her daughters,	20–0–0
iily More then I sentt my neece Austen by my sister a silver bason cost mee	25–0–0
And a sute of night close cost me for her to lye inn into Mrs Giels[178]	7–0–0
i2ly Then in September i710 I gave my deer sister to pay for her coach to London	20–0–0
i3ly More I gave my neece Betty Austen, i7ii, when I brought her down hither for two month. I paid for her jorney back and gave her besids for her to by her some plate to remember me by – tho my sister [sent] for her fowre times in thatt two months, tho I were soe very ill. I gave her	50–0–0
Sume of both is	i732–0–0

                                                            Eliz Freke
This I pincht my selfe every way for, and yett my sister would nott
bear my malloncally one winter. My God forgive her and raise her
and hers upp better friends then I have bin to her and them is the
dayly prayer of Eliza Freke.

i710, June 2d Whitson Tuesday and the 2d of June, aboutt noon
sitting in my sisters chamber, I were on a suden taken allmost blind
with vapours in both my eyes thatt I could nott see the meatt on the
table. Which have contynued with me in a greatt degree ever since,
being now above three years and the first of vapours ever I weer
sencible of in my life.

Course of his Life, the worst the most undutifull and unnatrall in all his words and
actions to mee' (PRO, PROB 11/560/201).

[178] 'My neece Austen' is described in W as Judith Austen's daughter-in-law (above,
p. 95); she was Jane Austen, the wife of Robert and daughter of William Strode (CB, iii,
78–9). Presumably the occasion is the birth of their son Robert, baptized in Tenterden
on 11 April 1708. Mrs Giels was Judith Austen's cousin Elizabeth Gyles or one of her
daughters, Elizabeth and Anne, to whom Austen bequeathed belongings.

September 9 Mrs Barns, now Mrs Edgworth, sentt to mee to give her leave to vissett mee affter a twelve month unhandsome usage of mee in plowing up my moire of my five akeres and deneying me any acquitances of itt, nor paid mee any rentt in almost a dosen years to the forfitture of the land.[179]

ii Shee sentt againe to me of the same errantt, which I deneyed her both times all correspondency with her and her family, tho great offers of frindship made me.

18 She sentt to me againe thatt she had business with mee from Ireland to impartt to mee. All which I deney'd her in.

20 Mrs Edgworth supprised me with her vissitt to West Billney.

2i I writt againe to the chancelour of Norwich, Doctter Thomas Tanir, thatt I did except Mr Buck as curate to my church butt dureing my pleasure and independantt of any sallary from me for his maintenance; and thatt I would be plagued with noe more drunken priest as I had bin with Mr Adams for six and thirty years past for my deer fathers sake, who placed him in Billney and Pentney, and I had soe long bourne with his notorious life for his wife and childrens sake; and thatt since the bishop of Norwich (Doctter Trimnell) gave me soe little thanks for whatt I had done for a church in his dioces (tho my peculer), I did intend to make thatt advantage of itt the queen had given mee by turning itt into a convicttle, soe I sentt the bishop word; and thatt I were in treaty with three desenters of Wisbich aboutt itt,[180] butt my contience would nott permitt my doeing of itt wher I hope to rest my self in with my deer husband, Percy Freke, Esqr, and my deer grandchild kild in London, Mr John Freke, aged 3 years, eleven months.

i7io, September 25 Monday, 25 of September, I were sitting by my selfe in my chamber awrighting with my doore shutt on me when two greatt rogues of baylyes came up into my chamber, one taken outt of Norwich jayle for thatt purpose, the other pretending to be a gentlemans servantt. They both came up to my chamber and arested me [fol. 20v] for an apperance to John Dawsons suite, whom I had putt into the jayle of Norwich for a hundred pound debt due to me, Eliz Freke. These two rogues serched all my papers in my chamber and boxes. Beets kept my chamber doore whilst the other serched my papers, and I all alone the while my servants afrighted went outt of my house. They took whatt papers they thought fitt, amongst which one with my name on itt. Butt I calling outt of my window my servants up, I found there designe was to robb mee by there endevouring to

---

[179] Moire or moyre, possibly mere or meare: marsh, bog, or swampy ground; also a boundary.

[180] Conventicle: an assembly or meeting place especially of Protestant Nonconformists gathered for worship. The Cambridgeshire village of Wisbech was not noted as a centre of dissent.

take my gold watch on the table by me. And as soon as they gott my name on a peice of paper I were awrighting, I know nott whatt they did with itt. Butt presently John Dawson, my prisoner, was released outt of Norwich jaile, tho I had paid Mr Warner my atturney ten pounds before hand for my tryall of him att Norwich assises.[181] Thus am I cheated of all hands, for by their rogery and my inabillity of stiring I lost my debt of above a hundred pound and all my charges from this to Warner and his baylyes; thus am I used by all the rogues of this country since my unhappy widowhood enough to distractt any poor mortall did nott my God supportt mee. Since which nor one friend or relation has ever appeered to my assistance in any or all my troubles, butt my dependance is wholy on God.

26 Mrs Barns, now Edgworth, came againe to me att six a clock in the morn, wher she staid till noon. I told her my business did not admitt of a longer visett.

November 3d Fryday nightt I were sitting alone in my chamber reading some partt of my will when on a suden I catchtt all a fire and burntt downe to my haire and all my head cloths cleer off, and I nott able to help my self or take them off. Soe thatt itt was only Gods mercy and providence I were preserved from being burntt to death. For [this] mercy God make me ever thankfull. Eliz Freke

December 2d Satterday nightt, being December 2d, was a most dreadfull storme allmost equall to the greatt storme thatt was the 26 of November i703 – which storme cost mee in my houses and barns above two hundred pounds. Which tempest continued two or three days to the torture and terror of Eliz Frek as well as charge.[182]

i7io/ii, January first New Years Day and my unhapy birth day I haveing all my tennants with me to begin the New Yeare, I were like againe to be burntt to death and kild by the fall of my kiching chimney into my chamber; butt by the mercy of my God and the help of my severall tennants, I were carryed away in my chaire, to which I had bin confined neer fiffteen monthes with my tissick and rhumatisme. Butt from this sad misfortune my greatt and good God did still preserve his poor servantt. Eliz Freke

Febuary 22 Being Thursday, my cosin John Frek came downe to me to Billney, whom I sentt for from London, fowre of my servants conspireing to murder me, viz., my coachman burnt in the hand, and my own maide thatt had lived neer fowre years with me, my cook maid, and Henry Ettrige, her rogue; all which had robed me one way and another of above a hundred pounds, and my own maid knew I had five more in my trunke in a sillver chamber pott.

---

[181] Richard Warner: above, p. 157 n. 300.
[182] Great tempest: above, p. 156 n. 299.

24 Satterday, 24 of Febuary, my cosin wentt to Linn to returne this mony to London for me by bills.

27 Tuesday, 27, my cosin in my coach wentt on my desire to Ellman to Mr Warners aboutt my suitt against John Dawson.

March 2 Fryday my cosin John Frek in my coach carryed with him this my five hundred pounds to Norwich for me to returne to London to compleatt my 3000 l. in his hand of mine.

5th Then Monday, the 5 of March, my cosin returned from Norwich and brought with him bills for the returne of my 500 pounds and staid with me one day, for which and his jorney I gave him thirty guinyes.

7 Wensday, the 7 of March, I sentt my maid Sarah [fol. 21r] up to London to waite on my deer sister the Lady Norton downe to me to Billney, from whence I would have brought her in my own coach butt could nott prevaile with her to exceptt itt. And happy itt was for me shee did nott, for next day affter shee came, being Sunday, I would force her to goe to church in itt; my rogue of a coachman John Preston overturned my coach on my sister side by the church yard gate on purpose to murder her. Which the violence of the fall broke the pole and my coach to peices, cost me above twenty shillings the mending. And itt was the greatest mercy in the world my deerst sister was nott killd, tho shee and Mr Buck, my minester, were both very much hurtt.

24 Satterday, the 24 of March, my deer sister the Lady Norton and her maid with my divell of a servantt came downe to mee on my earnest desire to her affter shee had attended for the stage coach three weeks and allwayes disapoynted by this divell Sarah, thatt had lived neer fowre yeare with me a theiveing life [and] was now with the rogue her husband disstrustfull of my deer sisters discovery of itt in them to me.

25 Soe on the 25, Sunday, they had combined to murder her this way and to kill my horses with itt, which had bin scertainly done had nott the church yard bin full of people to see my deer sister. While I satt a cripple, neer eighteen monthes a cripple, and could nott stirr butt by my fowr servants cheatted me of all the moveables in my house and all my mallitia armer, buff coate, &c., which allone will cost mee neer twenty pounds to recruitt itt. E Frek

i7ii, Aprill i7 The Emperer Joseph, this emperers elder brother, dyed of the small pox att Viena the fifth day of there appeering between eleven and i2 att nightt.[183] And the dauphin was taken ill with them att Parriss Aprill the seventeenth, which likewise proved the small pox and came outt aboutt twelve att nightt the fourteenth day.[184] Att night he

---

[183] The Holy Roman Emperor Charles VI's older brother Joseph I died on 17 April (NS); see above, p. 158 n. 302.

[184] Louis de France: above, p. 158 n. 303.

lost his speech, and att eleven hee fell into convulltion fitts and departed this life (as did the emperrour, in fitts). The dauphin was aged nine and forty years, 5 monthes, and i4 dayes, being borne att Fountaine Blue the first of November i66i, and was marryed to Mary Ann of Bavaria, i680. He leftt three sons behind him, viz., the duke of Burgundy, the present dauphin; and the duke of Anjow, called kinge of Spaine; and the duke of Berry.

24 They write from Dublin in Ireland of the i7 of Aprill that the Sunday before thatt a greatt fire broke outt in the councell chamber which consumed the same as allsoe the treasury, and most of the roles in the master generalls office and books in the surveir generalls office with severall other offices were burntt.[185]

May i Resollved thatt itt appeers to this presentt parliamt thatt of the mony granted for the publick service in the last parliamt there are in arrears 35302i07, viz., three millions, five hundred and thirty two thousand, one hundred and seven pounds, of which noe accountt has bin given or laid before the auditers.[186]

7 Munday betimes in the morning my deer sister the Lady Norton came into my chamber and told me she had nott slept thatt nightt for feare of mee; and then shee informed me my coachman was burntt in the hand, John Preston, and the rogery between him and my maid Sarah Flowre nightt and day, and of the theviryes committed in my house to a greate vallue.

ii Fryday, the eleventh of May, I charged her and him with itt, and paid them both the full of there wages and bills, and discharged them both. I saw them goe outt, and att midnightt they were all lett in againe to compleatt their theiveryes. Butt my deer lady, haveing locked the staire head doore by her chamber, disapoynted there further rogerys thatt nightt. This maid Sarah had the command of all my mony and goods in my house, and they both designed as soon as my sister left me to have murdered mee and had fitted for thimselfe two long laders to reach the highest window in my house. All which [fol. 21v] they had made a tryall of the robing of my closett, then warme they said. This all done by a falce cirtificate brought me by my own maid, his whore.

i7ii, May i6 I gott warrants for them, butt they were both fled from Lin affter they had cheated me of above a hundred pounds and above seven dosen of bottles of cordiall watter and wyne in half a yeare besids a great trunk of linen and all the rogues tricks were to bee shown a Christian. For which they endeavoured to murder my deer sister in my coach for makeing this discovery of them. Butt still my good God

---

[185] Essex Street fire: above, p. 159 n. 304.
[186] Tax arrears: above, p. 159 n. 305, which correctly cites the figures.

prevents and preserves mee and them thatt trust in him as I, his poor
humble servant, doe. Eliz. Freke

May 20 I had a letter from my son outt of Ireland datted March
the i2, i7io[/ii], and I think the first I have had from him this three
years. Which letter I transcribed and sentt itt to my cosin John Frek to
answer itt.

23 Wensday, the 23 of May, Spice the bayly came up into my
chamber and arested me att the suite of the rogue John Dawson and
William Johnson and Thom Selfe, a cheating atturney of Linn, three
[of] the greatest rogues a jayle can afford.[187] Butt Spice, affter he had
arrested me, sentt me word iff I would pay his fees his prosecution
should cease and he would send mee my warrantt; which for quiett
sake I did.

And I being to goe to London next day, **26** of May, I had another
letter outt of Ireland from my cosin Arthur Barnard, which I likewise
transcribed and sentt to my cosin John Freke to answer.[188]

28 I sentt a note of fiffty pound under Dawsons hand he owed mee
by Mr Buck, the minester of the parrish, datted the 22 of June i706,
wherein he accknowledges to owe me then fiffty pounds. Which note
I sentt to Mr Warner, the attorny, to gett for me and paid all his bills
and gave him ten pounds to try itt and for seventy seven pounds more;
all which hee keeps together with Mr Freks will and will returne none
of them to me, tho I have offten sent for them.

i7ii, June i4 June i4 I paid Mr Berners ten pounds for five thousand
of the worst reed I ever used in my life and sentt twenty carts for itt
as farr as Laire Brigg, as I did the i9 of Octtober last nine ginyes for
fowre thousand, and fetched itt att fiffty shillings a thousand.[189] Which
was very bad reed; butt since itt is the last mony I will be cheated of
att St Marryes, I must own itt a good bargain and witt cheap boughtt
by Eliz Freke.

24 I humbly thank my God I did on Sunday, being Midsomer Day,
goe to my church att Billney and his house in my own coach, where I
had nott bin in neer a twelve month before, and there with my deer
sister the Lady Norton receive the blesed sacramentt with twelve of my
neighbours parrish by Mr Buck, my then minester. Where I conceratted
a large sillver cupp and plate cover for the bread; and then I did in
thankfullness to God presentt itt att the communion table with a new

---

[187] William Johnson had baptized a daughter Sarah in Pentney on 10 November 1700
and may be related to Thomas Johnson (above, p. 101).

[188] Arthur Bernard: above, p. 160 n. 306.

[189] Apparently a Berners of Wiggenhall St Mary. Brig is an older form of bridge (*EDD*);
P. Mason of the Norfolk Family History Society has no doubt about 'Laire being a
Norfolk corruption of Nar'. One possible crossing might be Sechey Bridge. St German's
Bridge near the Berners was over the River Great Ouse.

Common Prayer Booke covered with blue rushy leather cost me 23 shilling, as was a large sillver flagon I brought downe the Michellmas before.[190] Eliz Frek

27 Being Wensday, I did in my own coach endeavour to goe up to London to carry up my deer sister the Lady Norton, who had bin soe good and kind to me as to doe pennance with me att Billney a quarter of a yeare, two months of which time I stirr'd nott from my bed. Which kindness and the saveing of my life from fowre ruffin servants in my house I can never forgett. Butt twas God dereicted itt for me.

29 Fryday, the 29 of June, I humbly thank God I came safe with my sister Norton to London with her and my fowre servants, where I staid and rested my selfe aboutt a fortnightt.

[fol. 22r]

i7ii, Jully i5 I returned back to my Billney againe tired in my own coach with my two horses and fowre servants and a horseman by. And by Gods greatt mercy to me I came home Wensday, the i8 of Jully, and I left my deer sister att her own house in London. Affter which itt raigned for a fortnight withoutt ceasing, which uncovered all the slats of my own house, being Sunday. I expectted itts fall.

Agust 7 I made an end of new reeding my barne and Taffs back house, both blown downe; and I paid Gibs the reed layer for itt ten pound, fowrteen shillings, and six pence, and for 5000 of reed and itts carraige sixteen pound, and for rush rope and rye straw for the roofe thirty shillings.[191] Soe thatt this my little barne cost me in thaching and reed, rush rope, and straw, with itt carraige above thirty pounds besids the back house of the maner house.

30 Fryday, the 30 of Agust, I arrested Mr Langlyes cartt loaded with corne on Whittpitt Brack for a dosen years rentt, to pay seven, affter I had tryed all faire means with him and his mother, Mrs Barnes, and ploughing up my moire, concelling my aquittance with a designe to cheatt me of my land as they had done of my other things.[192] Which I released on his promise of coming to an accountt with me att nextt Michellmas.

September 2 or 3 I were warned in as the head of Billney to appeer att the K[ing]s Head in Sech before nine or ten comisioners for the drains of Sandringham Hey;[193] which presidency I utterly refused and wrott this ensueing letter to them:

[190] Silver cup and cover: above, p. 160 n. 308. A miscellaneous document notes that the chalice and Book of Common Prayer 'cost me allmost eightt pounds' (B, fol. 33v).

[191] Nicholas Gibbs(?): above, p. 161 n. 309; Richard Taff: above, p. 105 n. 192.

[192] Whitpit Brack lease: above, p. 163 n. 319.

[193] General session of sewers: above, p. 162 n. 313 and p. 163 n. 314.

Sirs,

I received your warrant datted the 27 of Agust last in which you are pleased to dereictt itt to me as the cheif inhabitantt of Billney to appeer before you att the K[ing]s Head att Sechy iff I think fitt the 3d instantt. Which tho I am nott concerned in the [effect] of this warrantt, yett, gentlemen, I think fitt to obey authority; and therfore I have sentt two of my tennants to waite on you and receive your commands. Butt for his river neer fowre miles from me, I humbly conceive I am noe way concerned in itt, itt haveing never bin done by me for this thirty seven rears past butt once, unknown to me, Mr William Person trickt Mr Frek into itt – he being very ill [and] would nott goe from his word – aboutt the year 1703, a stranger to these matters, in a pretended visitt ust as he came outt of Ireland.[194] Nor were I ever ordered my attendance on itt before dureing Mr Freks time or my residence of 29 yeare heer on the spott. Therfore I hope and intreatt you gentlemen comisioners to concider me as I am, a woman ignorantt and helpless and an unhapy widow poore and nessesitous; thatt I may nott have a hing placed on me, I must be forced to oppose in my sons rightt. I am, gentlemen, with all due respectt, your humble servant,

Eliza Freke

September 6 Thursday, the sixth of September, Mr Berners came over to see me with the result of the river and to perswad my complyance, but I utterly refused itt; and I told him I had above a hundred akers now lye under Wormngy watter I durst nott cleer or nedle with for fear of presidents and being brought an abbetter to the Sechy River and thatt I would sooner spend a hundred pounds to oppose them then contributte twenty shillings towards itt.[195] Eliz Freke

1711, September 4 I had another long letter from my son outt of Ireland dated the tenth of Agust before, which I answered to him the 5 of September and dereicted itt to Dublin.

30 Dyany Davy and Henry Cross did both pennance in Billney church for adulltrye.[196]

Octtobr 1 Monday Mr Buck, my minester, wentt to Norwich to receive institution and induction for a living given him by Madam Branswith, his wifes mistress.[197]

---

[194] William Pearson/Peirson: above, p. 163 n. 315.

[195] Barnes of St Marys in W (above, p. 163), but Hatton Berners was a commissioner of sewers (above, p. 163 n. 316). The area in question was at the western side of the estate, near what was then called the Wormegay Fen. See also below, p. 314 n. 46.

[196] Diana Thomson and Thomas Davy were married in Bilney on 29 January 1701/2; Henry Cross married Frances Johnson in Pentney on 20 August 1704.

[197] Julian Branthwait: above, p. 164 n. 318; institution and induction: above, p. 114 n. 210.

1 And the first of Octtober I writt my third letter to Sir George
Norton to lend him 1300 l., thirteen hundred pounds, for a yeare, which
I did the 20 of November. Eliz Freke

23 Tuesday, the 23 of Octtober, I wentt to London and left only
Mary Ram, my cook maid, in itt.[198]

25 And Thursday, the 25, I came safe and tired to London with a
paire of horses. The 26 I writt to both my deer sisters where my lodging
were.

[fol. 22v]

1711, November 2d I discharged my coachman John Anderson
November 2d for runing up and downe a nights with my coach and
horses, which hee had in fowre or five places soe galled thatt I could
nott use them once in above two monthes and cost me above ten
pounds before I could stirr outt in my coach againe. The 4 of November
I putt away Bety Hempsell for runing away with thirty shillings from
me.

7 I gave my cosin Mary Lackendane a lottery tickett cost me 12–7–
6, twelve pounds, seven shillings, and six pence.[199] I paid my cosin John
Frek for itt. Affter I had taken this grievous jorney to London, the 7 of
November I received a dismall letter from my deer sister and Mr Jones
Sir Georges stuard, thatt in six minits he was taken speechless; and my
deer sister wrott to me to come downe to her.

13 Tuesday, being very ill, I removed my lodgings from Mrs Loyd
in New North Streett, wher I were allmost dead, and with great
diffyculty gott to my deer sisters house in St Georges, next door to the
chapple; wher I staid aboutt a fortnight.[200]

14 Wensday, the 14 of November, my weding day, I writt to my cosin
John Freke to take my mony outt of the East Indy Company and to
place itt in the Bank of England for me in hundred pound ticketts
might command itt, being 3100 l.

15 My cosin John Frek came very early in the morning very angry
with me and brought with him, as he said, the three thousand pound
ticketts, which hee said was as secure in his hand. I told him my
reputation was all I had to live on, and I had nothing to show for this
my mony butt his memorandum, and thatt hee had refused me his
bond which I vallued nott att six pence. Twould be beyound all
discretion for me to have three thousand two hundred pound in his

[198] Mary Ramm: above, p. 194 n. 493.

[199] Harlackenden and lotteries: above, p. 189 n. 476.

[200] North Street: above, p. 188 n. 474; on Ormond Street near St George the Martyr
(above, p. 189 n. 475).

ιand thatt had nott a foott of land for the security of, Eliza Frek. Thus ιngry, away he went outt of my dineing roome, which I took no notice οf. Butt I disposed of partt of itt, viz., i300 to Sir George Norton on ιis bond and twelve hundred pounds on mortgage to Mr Weston, ιnd left now in my cosin Freks hand io56 pound of mine on his ιemorandums.[201] Eliza. Freke, September, i7i2

i7ii, November 9 Transcribed from The Hague corrantt (Tournay): Οn the first instantt the marble stattue of the king of France which ιtood over the Port Royall of our cittydal was taken downe and putt οn bourd a vessell to be sentt to England, the same being a presentt to ιe duke of Marlbrow.[202]

i5 Transcribed outt of the gassett from Dublin att the progation of ιis presentt parliamentt November io, i7ii, these words to September ₂d, i7i2: A motion was then made and the question putt and resolved ιhatt whomsoever shall by speaking, writting, or printing arraine or ₂ondemne the princeples of the late happy revolution in i688 is an ₂nnimy to our most gratious queene, and to our constitution in church ιnd state, and to the Hannavour succession and a friend to the Ρretender. Taken outt of the Post Man by me, EF, November i5, i7ii.[203]

i7 I was in London November i7. Itt being Queen Elizabeths birth ιay, ther was like to be an insurection with the mob there by there ₂urning of the pope, the divell, and the Pretender (called prince of ιWalles) all together, butt by provydence was stopt by the queens timely ending of her gardes removed those occations.[204]

December 7 Fryday, the 7 of December, I signed Sir George Νortons release of errors and took his bond for (i300) thirteen hundred ₂ound and judgmentt to bee paid mee againe in a yeare.[205] And I did ιhe same to Mr Steven Weston, lentt him twelve hundred pound on ιis mortgage. Both which are now in a trunke in my closett att Billney ἱor saffty, Eliz Freke, i7i2. And have now in my cosin John Frek hand οf myne a thousand fiffty six pound cleere besids from December last ιhe intrest of itt. Eliz Frek

9 Sunday, Decembr the 9, I left London very ill and with my cosin Βetty Austin and my three servants sett outt for Billney, which with

---

[201] Steven Weston: above, p. 188 n. 478.

[202] The news from the Belgian city of Tournay or Tournai is quoted in the *Evening Post* 353); John Churchill, first duke of Marlborough: above, p. 147 n. 272.

[203] The i November 1711 resolution (*CJl*, iii. 931) appeared in the 15–17 November ιssue of the *Post-Man* (2070).

[204] The procession of effigies included 'a Pope, the Pretender, and the Devil between ιhem'. A detachment of foot guards sent to Drury Lane at two in the morning seized ιhe figures (*Norwich Gazette* [v. 268]; *Protestant Post-Boy* [34]). Elizabeth I was born on 7 Ϩeptember 1533; her accession was on 17 November 1558.

[205] Release: renunciation of a claim or right of action (Jowitt, ii. 1,531, 1,532).

being five days and nights on the road did allmost kill mee, tho in my own coach.

[fol. 23r]

i7ii, December i4 Fryday night late, December i4, I gott home againe, I most humbly thank my God, after five days being on the road to my beloved home of Billny, affter my being neer two month confined to my chaire in London. Nor did I in all thatt time stirr outt butt once to gett some mony to pay fourteen pounds for my horses keeping and care. Thus am I used by every body.

i5 of December, Satterday, I had a second letter from my deer sister Austen to send away her daughter to her againe (which was a comfort to me in my sad condityon) att the furthest by Candlemas; which I promised to doe. Tho haveing another with her and affter my kind giveing her above fiffteen hundred pound, shee might have spared this awhile to me, Eliz Frek; for I had deserved itt and more of her thatt have bin to her like a mother from her childhood. Butt my God forgive her and be my supportt. Eliz Frek

24 Munday, Xmas Eve, I had a very kind letter from my deer sister Norton.

i7ii/i2, January first New Years Day, or the i of January, my unhappy birth day, I had according to old custom all my tennants dine with mee with neer twenty dishes of meatt and whatt ale and brandy they please to drink, with cards butt noe musicke.

2d James Englebright of Pentney came latte att night and broughtt me some mony, and I being very ill gave them an acquitance in my own wrong for i7ii which should have bin for Michellmas i7io.[206] Which they took advantage of me of itt, tho I sentt my servantt Roger Chapman to them the next day for itt. By which I lost a full years rentt, and I allowed him besids two years taxes for one of sixteen pounds besides their bills. This is most barbarous usage of me; butt I must beare itt Gods time, I nott being able to help my selfe.

January i This New Years Day and my unhappy birth day, i7ii and i7i2, I have by my Gods permission and greatt goodness to me by his mercyfull providence fully accomplished this day the seventyeth or threescore and ten year of my age. For which I doe most humbly thank him, and I doe begg of my God whatt time he gives me more of life may be by me spentt and dedicated to his glory in thankfullness for all his greatt mercyes to mee, Eliza. Freke. And tho I have laine above this three monthes in torter and misery night and day with my tisick and cough, yett I had 26 of my tennants dined with me thatt day.

---

[206] In the other version his wife brings the money; see above, p. 190 and n. 479.

2nd I thank God; and by his permision as I have begun a New eare, I doe most humbly begg of him on the bended knees and from my hartt he will be pleased to bestow on me, iff my God think fitt, a more moderatte health then I have had this six years past since my deer husband left mee, being June 2d, i706, haveing hardly bin downe airs since six times.

3d Thursday, the 3d of January, I past my acounts with Henry Cross efore my neece Austen and Daniell Wallis of Lin, when there apeered due to me on the ballance last Lady Day i7i2 eighty three pounds, ffteen shillings and all taxes and charges allowed him to thatt day by me.²⁰⁷ Eliza Freke

i2 I lett my lands of my Hall Farme to John Whitting with the little ouse in which John Sad lived in for forty eight pounds a yeare besids my reserves.²⁰⁸

i3 I read in the publick newes thatt all the three lyons in the Towre f London were dead and thatt they bled to death. This is strange tho ue.²⁰⁹

i9 Satterday I had a third letter from my sister Austen to send her daughter away; she wanted her, tho shee had her eldest then with her nd neer forty years of age. And this is the sister thatt has had all the ndustry of my life.

2i I writt her word I would doe itt by Candlemas iff posible, as she efore dereicted.

i8 of January the prince of Hanavar was by actt of parliamentt made me first peer of this kingdom of England call'd Great Britton, hee being efore duke of Cambrigg; which pased the House three times in a day y the House of Lords and Commons, a thing never knowne beffore me same day.²¹⁰

ol. 23v]

i7ii/i2, January i8 January i8 was Mr Robertt Wallpoole expell'd me house for five hundred pounds brybery by the House of Commons nd comitted prisoner to the Tower dureing the sesions of parliamentt y the queen and parliamtt.²¹¹

---

²⁰⁷ Henry Cross rented the White House in 1708; Daniel Wallis, a vintner, was made freeman of Lynn in 1709–10 (*Freemen of Lynn*, 217).
²⁰⁸ John Whiting: above, p. 190 n. 481.
²⁰⁹ Tower of London lions: above, p. 190 n. 482.
²¹⁰ Georg August: above, p. 191 n. 483.
²¹¹ The *Norwich Gazette* (vi. 277) states that on Thursday, 17 January, the House of ommons voted Robert Walpole 'to the Tower, and Expelled him for being Guilty of a igh Breach of Trust and Notorious Corruption'. Walpole was charged with using his osition as secretary at war to gain a 'Sum of Five hundred Guineas' and a 'Note for ve hundred Pounds more' from forage contracts supplying troops in Scotland (*CJ*, xvii.

The nineteenth the parliamt ordered the bill to repeale the Generra Naturallyxan to be engrosed.[212]

26 My neece Austen gave earnest for her coach to goe home to m sister.

24 I entered my farme att Pentney by putting my padlock on th doore of Englebrights affter hee had cheated mee of neer sixty poun besids two years texes of sixteen pound by misdateing my acquittanc a yeare in my own wronge.

February ii My neece Betty Austin left me and Bilney and cam safe to London in three dayes. I gave her five pounds to bear he charges and fiffty pounds in London to buy her some plate, and neve more will I be troubled with friends paid by my kinsman John Freke

i4 Thursday I were taken with a violentt plurisy in my left side.

i5 Fryday, i5, I sentt to Mr Smith to bloud me for itt att night i my bed; where before I could have any ease, I lost above threescor ounces of bloud att the age of above seventy years and have labouere ever since under soe violentt a cough and weakness as to bee unculpabl of any business or comfortt. And with the violence of my cough fc fowre monthes wantt of rest and soe much bleeding, I am allmo tottally deprived of my eye sightt, an insuportable griefe to me. An noe friend neer me, tho I have this fowre monthes every day expectte my last summons, which with most humble patience I doe attend ti my God shall release his miserable servant out of all my miseryes c raise me as he shall see good and best for Eliza Freke.

i7ii/i2, March 2d The publick newes tells me thatt we have lo: by death three daulphin in France of the small pox, &c., and on dauphyness. And March 2d Sir William Windoms house in Allbermal Streett, being Sunday, was burntt to the ground by the carelessness c two servants, who to scap the fire leapt outt of the window in a garre [and] were bruised to death.[213]

Febuary 29 I received of Mr Langly fowre pound for neer twelv years rentt due to mee outt of Whittpitt Brack and gave him a acquitance to last Michellmas. And from thatt day I entered the lan in my own right and lett itt to John Whitting this yeare by way c posesion, he haveing ploughed up my moire.

March i4 I had a second letter from my daughter outt of Irelan thatt shee did intend to bring over her two eldest sons this sumer t see mee and to give a name to the child she now goes with and t

30). The imprisoned Walpole was reelected from King's Lynn; the House of Commor however, declared the election void (*CJ*, xvii. 128–30). Walpole remained in the Tow until 8 July 1712 and would not return to parliament until the next year (J. H. Plum *Sir Robert Walpole: The Making of a Statesman*, 2 vols. [London, 1956], i. 178–84).

[212] General Naturalization Act: above, p. 191 n. 484.

[213] Royal deaths: above, p. 192 n. 485. William Wyndham: above, p. 192 n. 485.

igne my sons comision. I answered itt: for the first she was wellcome
o me, and for her children the care was too greatt to entrust me with;
ff she would stay to take care of them, they are wellcome. And for the
hild shee now goes with, iff she approve itt, I named itt Arthur, my
usbands fathers name. And for my sons commision, I were too old to
ake jorneys to London. Nor would I be troubled with them downe to
ne nor sett my hand to confirme my cosin John Frek follyes with Kelly
y giveing away my right which he maintained.

1712, March 25 Mr Buck, my minester, left my church att West
Billney and wentt to his new liveing Mrs Branswith gave him, soe thatt
am now destitute of a minester to my church; for which I hope God
ill provide me one.[214]

26 I paid Mrs Farrer for my years news ending Lady Day.[215] E Freke
16 Sunday morning my tennantt Thomas Pallmer dyed of the small
ox. He then owed me three half years rentt of seventy five pounds,
vhich I am in greatt hasard of loosing or I must undoe the poor
viddow who lost her husband and her two eldest sons of this fattall
distemper.[216] A quiett man he was, and he leftt three children behind
im.

fol. 24r]

1712, March 30 A coppy of a letter I received from my son outt of
reland 30 of March:

Deer Madam,
Tho I am butt just now outt of a severe fitt of the goute and hardly
ble to hold my pen, yett haveing received a letter yesterday from my
deer Lady Norton giveing me the ill accountt of your being much outt
of order in your health, I cannott butt express the greatt concerne itt
s to me, tho I trust in God you have before this recovered itt, which
s the ferventt and dayly prayer of me and my family. I have this day
writt my deer Lady Norton my thanks for favouring mee with her
etter and Sir George and her kind invitation both shee and Sir George
give me and my family to Leigh; and I begg, deer madam, you will be
pleased to lett me heer as soon as possible how you are, for till then I
shall be most uneasy and impatientt. My wife is now very neer her
ime of lyeing in and presents her humble dutty to you. I praise God
ill my children are well and in the sumer, God willing, shall pay you
here dutty in England. And I am very sencible how much I am your

---

[214] Charles Buck became vicar of Bacton on 5 October 1711 (above, p. 192 n. 486).
[215] See above, p. 192 n. 488.
[216] Thomas Palmer was buried on 17 March 1711/2; his widow was Mary Palmer.

debter for rentt besids every way elce in your goodness to me on all occasions. I shall trouble you this post with noe more butt thatt I ever am, deerst madam, your most obedientt son. Whilst,

Ralph Freke

1712, Aprill 1 Mr Langly, being Tuesday, sentt to mee thatt iff sentt two men to Whittpitt Brack hee would send two more to them and devide Whittpitt Brack. Which I did my servantt Roger Chapman my tennent John Whiting, and my tenant Henry Cross to see it devided by Mr Langly, who sentt Mr Wassy and another man who had known this land for thirtty yeare beffore. And in this devition left land for a new moire to be made againe and then lett itt outt to John Whiting. E Frek

3d Thursday, 3d of Aprill, three rogues of baylies came to arrest M Langly and mising of him violently forced away my coachman and carryed him to Norwich jaile withoutt letting him see me or give me an accountt of any thing of mine in his care, soe thatt by him I am a greatt looser, haveing trusted him above neer five pounds before hand and his wife as much more with the small pox besids the loss of all my own linen and my household linen. E Freke

4 I sentt Mr Langly of Winch word whatt these rogues of baylye said att my house (thatt tho they had miss'd him now they would soon have him alive or dead) and invited him to shellter himselfe in my house.

6 And I writt a letter in his behalf the sixth and sentt itt open to him to his mother (on his desire). EF

9 Wensday, the 9 of Aprill, Thomas Pallmer, Junier, dyed of the small pox, as did his father aboutt three week before, viz., the 17 of March; by whom I feare I shall loose neer a hundred pounds and have my farme in my hands.

1712, April 2 And aboutt the second of Aprill I had another letter outt of Ireland from my cosin John Frek in London to come up and signe my sons commission, thatt have hardly bin cross my chamber this twelve monthes withoutt the asistance of two to help mee, with my astma and very shortt breath with a fixtt plurisy in my left sid. And in shortt, I refused coming up or permitting the commisioners to come downe to mee, E Frek.

7 or 8 I answered this my cosin John Freks letter and thatt I did thankfully except his release of my trust, assureing him I would never trust him with my grandchildren thatt had wronged me and my deer husband of soe many thousand pounds as he had done by my letter of aturny to him, tho he had bin gratifyed by me in six years six hundred pounds att least. And from such friends and frindship as to wronge me of three thousand pounds together, good Lord, deliver mee. Eliza Freke.

i5 Tuesday late att night Mr Langly came to my house (hee and his lady haveing had a greatt difference the Sunday before, being the i3 instantt, for which his wife and frinds feared some mischiefe might have befallen him). About eleven a clock att night I sent to Mr Smith, vicker of Winch, [fol. 24v] I had him in safty and would keep him my prisoner till he released him.

i7i2, Aprill i6 Who came for him the nextt evening, which he did late att nightt, being Wensday, i6 instantt.

i8 And the i8 I wrott a letter of advice to her to be more moderatt with her husband, pattion being seldom the wifes advantage and might force him to bee desperatte. In recompence of this my civillity to them (they selling all the fruitt of ther garden to Goode Penington):²¹⁷ I sentt my maid for aboutt a dosen pound for sirrup for sick people; they both deney'd me a handfull, tho I sentt mony for them.

i7i2, Aprill 20 Easter Day and the twentyeth of Aprill, being Sunday, my daughter was brought to bed of a daughter, which my deer sister the Lady Norton and I named Grace, my sisters daughters name and my beloved neece and god-daughter.²¹⁸

2i Mr Langly wrote to me to christne his second child, which I refused by my inabillity of being able to stirr besids my resolution fixt against itt att my age to undertake whatt I could nott performe.²¹⁹

Easter Day and the 20 instantt I invited my new tennantt, his wife, and his two children to diner. And the first time I ever saw her, she was full of care aboutt her lyeing in; butt I bid her leave those things to God, for I saw death in her face. Thatt night she rid home to Winch and dyed the nextt day, being Easter Monday.²²⁰

27 I wrott to my Lord Richerson aboutt the purchas of High House and Westicar Abby, Mr Jallops estatt by mee; who promised me his service and favoure when come to be sold, who was now outt of England and knew noe time of his re[turn].²²¹

26 Satterday in Easter Week an execution came on Mrs Barns estatt, the impropryations of the church and tithes of Winch, for eight hundred

---

²¹⁷ Probably Mary Penniton of East Walton. Francis Penniton and Mary Carman were married on 19 May 1684 in East Walton, where several of their children were baptized and at least one buried.

²¹⁸ See above, p. 193 n. 489.

²¹⁹ Susannah Langley: above, p. 193 n. 490.

²²⁰ Catherine Whiting was buried in East Winch on 23 April 1712.

²²¹ William Richardson: above, p. 114 n. 212. High House Manor, along with Westacre Abby, came into the Yallop family through the marriage of Charles Yallop and Helen/Ellen Barkham. He was the son of Sir Robert Yallop and Dorothy, the daughter of Charles Spelman (Blomefield, ix. 162–3; Clarke and Campling, eds., *Visitation of Norfolk*, 5 [1934], 250).

pound debtt due to Doctter Thomas Shortt of Berry for phisick for her in arrears.

22 From Parriss the gassett mentions thatt the sister to the Chevilier de St Georg, King Jams son call'd the Prettender, dyed att St Germons aged 19 years and eleven months old of the small pox. Borne in France the 28 of May 1692, [she] was buryed the thirtyeth in the monastry of the English Benedictons neer thatt of her father, the late King James the Second; and her hartte was carryed to the nunery of Chaillott.[222]

28 The publick news says there are three severall transportt ships arived with aboutt two hundred men prisoners from France which reportt thatt all the prisons in France are now cleere and the prisoners released.[223]

28 The countiss of Thanett dyed of the small pox very aged, above eighty; and Petter God, a member of this presentt parlimentt for Lewis in Susses, did hang himselfe last Thursday, the 17 of Aprill 1712.[224]

1712, May ii By the carelesness of my two maids Mary Chapman and Mary Ram, I lost all my own linen and all my houshold linnen left outt a Satterday nightt to whitten, unknown to me; [it] was stole all by sun rise on Sunday morning – I haveing butt aboutt three days before turned outt of my house Diana Davy and Goode Kneeve for stealing of my fences and cutting of my wood, which I proved against them att the justice sitting which was the 15 of May.[225]

15 With aboundance of ill language the 15 they broughtt a warrantt from Justice Pell against mee; on which att the justice sitting I wrott to the bench my complaintt against Goode Kneeve and Diana Davy, who ordered them both a good whiping and whatt further I pleased.[226] Which I saw done to them both outt of my window att the carts taile **27** of May, Satterday, till the bloud spun for example sake. And iff further complaintt to be sentt to Bridwell.

24 of May, Satterday, my own maid Mary Chapman complained of

---

[222] Louisa Maria Stuart: above, p. 194 n. 491.

[223] The *British-Mercury* (326) carried on 22 April the news from Falmouth 'that the three Transports which exchang'd Prisoners from France, report, that all the English that were Prisoners there, are now cleared'.

[224] Freke apparently misidentifies Catherine, wife of the sixth earl of Thanet (above, p. 194 n. 492). The *Norwich Gazette* (vi. 289) states that on 14 April 'Peter Gott, Esq; Member of Parliament for Lewes, in West Sussex, was found dead in his Bed, having taken a Dose of Liquid Laudanum, and as a finishing Stroak tyed the Tail of his Shirt about his Neck'. Gott represented Sussex from 1708 to 1710 and Lewes, in West Sussex, from 1710 to 1712 (Geoffrey Holmes, *British Politics in the Age of Anne* [New York, 1967], 222, 492 n. 12).

[225] Mary Ramm and Goody Kneeve: above, p. 194 nn. 493 and 494.

[226] John Pell's name appears among the officials who signed the 1704 Pentney land tax as well as among those officiating at the 1708 Swaffham general quarter sessions (NRO, C/S2/6). He was apparently not educated at university or at the Middle Temple, Gray's Inn, or Lincoln's Inn.

er head and back, which I then told her would prove to bee the small
ox. Three days she lay very ill, and on Tusday, the third of June, [fol.
5r] they appeered. Wensday I removed her outt of my own house into
little house in the parrish and took her a nurse att a crowne a
eek for neer three weeks besids meatt and drink, doctters, cordialls,
pothycaryes; wher she lay past all recovery neer a forttnight as Mr
mith and all thatt heard of her condition said itt was imposible for
er recovery. Besids I am sure forty shillings would nott pay for her
ordialls shee had outt of my closett besids another nurse for above a
eek to tend her, Goode Man.[227]

26 Blind she was the second day, and soe she lay till aboutt the 26.

30 And affter neer a monthes care and charge of Mary Chappman
nd the loss of all my clothes and above five pounds in mony I trusted
em with as iff my neer relation, up shee gott and run away Thursday,
e 30 of June or there after. She had spoyled me a fether bed, two
oulsters, 2 blancketts, two pillows, and a coverlid, and a paire of sheets.
nd I paid Mr Hogan her apothicarys bill and two and thirty shillings
r close for her and her husband, which I were on my word bound
r, and part paid her coming downe.[228] Away she run to Norwich jaile
) her husband and never soe much as said God buy. And all this I
id in pitty to her as a stranger and her faithfull promise of paymentt.

Jully 4 Thom Betts dyed, the clark of this parish for above thirty
ears, of the small pox caughtt of this my servantt; which leftt three
hildren behind him to the parrish charge, two of them sick of the
mall pox when he dyed.

7 of Jully was Dunkirk delivered up to the queen of England, call'd
3reatt Brittaine, by the king of France for a barrier of the peace, and
Major Generall Hill (Mrs Marshams brother) was then made govenor
f Dunkirke by the queen and a cesation of arms proclaimed between
rance and England for two monthes whilst the states and the Dutch
nd the emperor and all there and our allies kept on the warr with all
here vigor against France and Spaine.[229]

Agust 19 And the news Post Man sayes [England] lost all to the
rench king in Agust and Jully of those places in France, &c., which
he English have bin in three compaines a getting with the loss of soe
nany thousands of soules and the expence of soe many millions of
nony to this nation.[230]

24 of Agust a suspention of armes was agreed to for fowre monthes,

[227] Mary, the wife of James Mann, whose daughter Sarah was baptized in Pentney on
4 June 1718.
[228] Persivall Hoogan, apothecary, was made a freeman of King's Lynn in 1708–9
(*Freemen of Lynn*, 216).
[229] John Hill and Abigail Hill, Lady Masham: above, p. 195 n. 496.
[230] No report has been located among the few July and August issues that exist.

which is to expire the two and twenty of December nextt, betwee
England and France and was there published with the usuall cer
monyes.[231]

September 29 Munday, 29 of September, my deer son and h
lady and my three grandchildren Percy, Ralph, and Redman left Cork
in Irland and tooke shipping for in Captaine Paule, a man of war
where they were all fowre dayss att sea till Thursday nightt in a mo
dreadfull storme and hurrycane of weather till I were allmost frightne
outt of my sences.[232]

Occtobr 2d Butt att last my good God landed them all safe a
Bristoll Thursday night, the 2d of Octtobr. And Fryday, the 3d o
Octtobr, Sir George and my deer sister, his lady, sentt her coach an
fetched them to Leigh, where they all staid till Satterday, the eleven
of Octtobr.

ii Then they all wentt in my ladys coach to the Bath, wher they a
staide till the 2d of December by reason the high waters were unpassabl

November 27 Then aboutt the end of Novembr they all came t
London with my deer sister the Lady Norton, where they were severa
times like to be lost by the high watters.

December 2d Att last by Gods greatt mercy to me and them (thre
coaches being thatt week lost with part of there pasengers), they cam
all safe to London aboutt the 2d of December to my deer sister Norton
house in Ormond Streett, next doore to St Georges Chaple, wher the
staid till aboutt the 18 of December.

18 Thursday, the 18, they came from London and came downe t
wretched and miserable me the 20, St Thomas Eve, Satterday. I humbl
thank my God they came all safe and well to me to West Billney afte
my frights for them three monthes. E Freke

[fol. 25v]

1712, December 28–31 Satterday, the 28 of Decembr, my younges
grandson, Redman, affter he had bin att Billney aboutt a wee
complained hee was not well, which to him proved the small po
Which a Monday, the last of Decembr, came outt full on him and o
which he lay dangerously ill for the whole month of January to th
dispaire of his life allmost as by the judgmentt of his docter and h
two nurses.

January 15 My maid Martha Coop and Elizabeth Knopwood fe
both sick of the small pox, of which my cook maid dyed of itt star
madd in aboutt ten days time by the docters gieving her a vomitt whe

---

[231] Queen's proclamation: above, p. 195 n. 498.
[232] Probably Captain John Paul rather than the ship *Poole* (above, p. 195 n. 499).

hey were coming outt.[233] And shee was the first of i4 I had under my
)erscription. Butt my own maid Martha recovered itt by Gods blesing
)n my endeavours, as did my deer child.

Febuary i4 Satterday my man Isack fell sick of the small pox,
,vhom I putt outt of my house, being very ill my selfe and quitt tired
,vith doctters and nurses for above neer two monthes.

22 Mr Smith, vicker of Winch, being Sunday preached heer, when
[desired him to adminester the sacrament att Billney church on
Midlentt Sunday, being the i5 of March, and contracted with him to
;erve the church till nextt Michellmas i7i3. E Freke

23 Monday I wrot to the chancellour of Norwich, Doctter Taner, a
:omplaining letter of the bishops neglectt of this parrish in turning outt
Mr Buck, whom I placed into Billney, and to leave the parrish and
:hurch now eleven monthes unserved and destitute of a minester as itt
has now bin.

25 The kinge of Prussia dyed the 25 of Febuary between twelve and
)ne of the clock in the 56 yeare of his age much lamented.[234]

28 Satterday, the 28 of Febuary, Mr Henry, only son and heire to
the Lord Chiefe Justice Pine of Ireland, haveing had some words with
Mr Theoffphylus Bidolph (son and heire of Sir Michell Bidolph) (aboutt,
as tis said, Dr Sacheverall), foughtt neer the corner of St James Parke;
wher Mr Pine was stab'd in his right breast six inches deep and dyed
on the spott, and Mr Bidolph was wounded in the belly, of which he
lyes very weak iff nott dead March 4, i7i2[/3].[235] This Mr Henry Pyne
was the only son of the late Lord Chiefe Justice Pine (and neer kinsman
to Mr Frek), who dyed att his own house in Surry about the one and
twentieth of Aprill i7io and leftt behind him this his only son heire to
neer three thousand pound a yeare in England and in Ireland.[236] (Butt
God is just as well as mercyfull). Mr Henry Pyne has left three daughters
in Ireland all heireses.[237] And this Lord Chiefe Justice Pine when he
was a young man unfortunately kild a substantiall cittyzen in Cheapside
for takeing place of him as he was leading att nightt the Lady Brodrick.[238]
Butt itt is remarkable how Gods justice [works]: affter forty years and
a greatt estate aquired of above two thousand pound a yeare, his only

[233] Mary Ramm is earlier identified as her cook-maid; W states Knopwood died (above,
p. 196 and n. 500).
[234] Frederick I: above, p. 197 n. 501.
[235] See above, p. 197 n. 502 and Henry Sacheverell, p. 198 n. 504.
[236] Richard Pyne died in December 1709 (above, p. 197 n. 503).
[237] Anne, Catherine, and Elizabeth, none specifically named in his will (above, p. 197
n. 502).
[238] Lady Brodrick was probably Alice, the wife of Sir John Brodrick and mother of
Alan Brodrick, Lord Midleton (c. 1656–1728), who succeeded Richard Pyne as chief
justice of king's bench (*CP*, viii. 701–2). A Richard Pyne was convicted and then pardoned
of manslaughter in 1671 (Morris, 'The Pynes of Co. Cork', 704).

son should bee sudenly taken off by the same unhappy fatte and M
Bidolph lives.

March i5 Being Midlentt Sunday I had a sacramentt att Billne
church adminestered by Mr Smith, vicker of East Winch, and by m
Gods greatt mercy to mee I weare one of the comunicants with m
daugher in law. Butt my son went outt of the church where I had not
bin in allmost two years before nor my son with me above this seve
yeare. My greatt and good God forgive him this and all his othe
mistaks to Elizabeth Freke.

[fol. 26r]

i7i3, Aprill 26 Sunday, the 26 of Aprill, I leftt Billney and cam
for London with my son and my daughter and her three sons an
theire fowr servants.

29 In my own coach I came to my deer Lady Nortons house o
Wensday nightt, the 29 of Aprill, with my two coach horses and fiv
persons in my coach besids lumber and beyound my expecttation well
concidering I had hardly moved from my chaire in seventeen monthe
before. This was a greatt mercy to mee, and for which my God eve
make me humbly thankfull, his servant. Eliz Frek

May 5 Tuesday, the 5 of May, was the peace proclaimed by th
order of the queene and persuantt to the actt of parliamtt, butt such
peace I never heard of in my life. The greatt God send us a good en
of soe odd a begining, itt appeering to wiser heads then mine to be
seprate one.[239]

---

[239] On 5 May 1713 a proclamation of peace between England and France wa
announced with 'great Solemnity', the gazettes observe, and greeted with 'great Rejoicing
(*Flying-Post* [3371], *Evening Post* [583]).

III. MISCELLANEOUS DOCUMENTS

A. Account of Expenses Related to Percy Freke's Fatal Illness

B, fol. 37v, i side]

7i2 An accountt of whatt I laid outt on the sickness, death, and buriall
of my deer husband, Percy Frek, Esqr; taken outt of the severall bills
in my uper closett and paid by me, Elizabeth Frek, his unhappy wife,
within the year of i707[1]

Butt now comes the dismalls and fattasst day of my life, for on the
second of June, Sunday, aboutt three a clock (the very day and howre
my son was borne, hee being then thirty two years of age), my deer
husband, Percy Frek, Esqr, to compleatt all the miseryes of my life,
affter seven monthes torture of a dropsey and an astma, in which time
   think I never wentt seven nights ,into a bed butt I were one of the
three thatt watched with him nightt and day for fear of him. Eliz Frek

	l.–s.–d.
i705, Decembr 25 Christmas Day goeing to the church att West Billney to the sacramentt with me, hee complained of a shortnes in his breath.	
27 For which I sent to Linn to Mr Goodwin to bleed him twice att io s. a time and paid him for it	i–o–o
January 3d He still growing worse and worse, January 3d I sentt immediattly to Berry to Doctter Thomas Shortt a horse and man and kept him with me three dayes, every howre expectting his last breath. For which I paid him fowre ginnyes	4–6–0
And io the man and horse.	0–io–0
i4 I sentt to Doctter Barker of Lin and to Mr Goodwin the surgion and paid	2–3–0
20 I sentt againe to Doctter Barker of Linn for two days stay with me and paid	2–3–0
23 I paid Mr Goodwin the surgion for three dosen of lemons and oranges	0–i2–0

[1] An earlier version, apparently completed by the end of i709, appears in W, fols. 35v–39r. The later account from the B text is included in this edition because it is the final version and because the tone of the revision expresses the deepening discontent of Freke's last years. Variations in the entries of expenses have not been noted; the notations supplementing the foliation are Freke's.

I paid James Wallbutt and Betty Fox for three
weeks atendance on him nightt and day and watching
with him   2–0–0

Febuary 4, 1705[/6] I sentt againe a horse and
man to Berry to Doctter Thomas Shortt, and I paid
him for his fowr days   4–0–0

And the man and horse more   0–10–0

I sentt to Doctter Barker to joyne with Dr Shortt
and paid him   2–3–0

Febuary 8 I sentt then to Doctter Jeffryes to
Norwich a horse and man for two dayes and paid
them for their jorney and the doctter   2–10–0
Who bid me hast away or he would soon dye; which
I did.

9 And I sentt againe to Lin to Mr Goodwin and
Doctter Barker and paid them   2–0–0

And by these three doctters advice I bought my
deer husband of white Lisbon wine a little vesell cost
mee att Linn   3–0–0

And 3 dosen of lemons and oranges which cost me
more   0–12–0

12 I paid Mrs Langly for two quarts of old hock,
viz., sowr w[hite] wyne,   0–10–0

13 Being Sunday, I paid Mr Towres for drawing
Mr Freks will   1–1–6

As I did Mr Godard before of Lin for two or three
days[2]   1–1–6

15 I sentt againe to Doctter Barker withoutt any
hopes and paid him   1–1–6

18 I paid James Wallbutt and Mrs Sad[3] for two
week attendance on him   0–16–0

20 I haveing noe quiett in my mind, I sentt againe
to Burry to Doctter Thomas Short a horse and man
and paid the doctter 4 ginys   4–6–0

And man   0–10–0

21 I sent to Mr Sheldrick of Saffum and Doctter
Barker of Linn and paid them, every momementt
expectting my deer husbands death,   2–1–6

---

[2] Several Goddards are listed in the Lynn land and poll taxes.
[3] Ann, the wife of John Sadd, one of Freke's tenants. She was buried in West Bilney
on 3 January 1706/7.

22 When itt was agreed and consented to by my
~~~er husbantt thatt I should send againe presently
~ Doctter Thomas Shortt of Bery a man and a horse
~d to Doctter Barker and Shelldrick of Sawfum;
~hich I did. When itt was unanimously agreed thatt
~y deer husband should goe the nextt day to Saffum
~ be there murdered, as he was. For which I payd
~em all for this fattall consulltation   7‒7‒6
    Beffor which I sentt againe to Norwich to Doctter
~effryes] a horse and man, who sent me word he had
~ry little hopes. And I paid them   i‒i3‒6
23 Thursday, Febuary 23 or theraboutt, in the
~ening against my sence or consentt he was removed
~ Saffum, there to dye by artt, in my coach with
~o servants and a maid servant; wher thatt night he
~me. These docters with the advice of Doctter
~ucked gave him soe strong a purge before I gott
~ him forced all the humours into his right legg,
~hich Monday 25 broke to my amasmt.   i‒i‒6
                                                          49‒5‒6
                                                          Eliz Frek

~3, fol. 38r, 2d side]

Febuary 25 Which Monday, the 25, this jorney
~nd his strong phicksick, itt broke in his right legg
~nd soe frightned mee, the runing of itt, thatt I
~resently sentt away againe a horse and man to Bery
~ Docter Thomas Shortt, Doctter Barker of Linn,
~octter Duckett, and Cosens; and I paid them ther
~verall fees as before to Shortt and the man   4‒6‒0
    And the man and hors two days i2 s. and to Doctter
~arker of Lin 2 days   2‒i2‒0
    And to Doctter Duckett and Cosines more was   2‒3‒0
~ll these to consult my deer husbands condition to dye
~y artt.
March i I haveing noe quiett in me sentt away
~gaine to Bury to Doctter Short and to Doctter
~arker of Lin and to Doctter Duckett of [   ]; paid
~em   3‒4‒6
    And to Cosins and Shelldrick I paid them more   2‒3‒0
6 For a dosen and half more of whitt Lisbon wine   2‒0‒0
    And for 3 dosen of lemons and oranges, i2 shillings,
~nd severall other things taken up by them   i‒6‒0

io I paid Peeter, Mr Frek man, i–io–o and two
more watchers for a fortnight[4]   2–18–

i5 I paid Mr Minican for a chaldron of cole i–i5–
o and bring itt to Saffum[5]   2–7–

i6 Heer at Saffum I paid for one little roome att
Mr Minakins with a pallett for Mr Frek only and
the dyett of him and his man for three weeks 8–8–
8, and gave her two elder chilldrin 5 shillings.   8–i3–

 And I paid James Minacan his brother for a weeks
attendance   o–12–

i7 Then he was advised to goe more into the
country ayre to Mr Lifes, a mile from Saffum; where
Thursday, the i7, Mr Frek, my selfe, and three of my
servants wentt, where wee were barbarously used
and staid there butt fowre dayes on a ground flowre.
I paide him by Mr Henry Towre, who knew how to
be generous with my pockett,   3–io–

 And gave to his servants which deserved nothing
of mee   o–5–

And all this time from New Years Day my deer husband
never went into a bed or shutt his eyes to sleep, I
watching with him always.

i8 of March, Monday, I came to Mr Ibbotts, the
minester of Saffum, where for a little ground room
I paid him for three week withoutt bed or any thing;
and the worst place of all, yett I paid him for lodg   3–io–

i9 Heer att Mr Ibott I sentt for my deer husbands
own bed and chair to Billney hee used to sitt in,
who was very much pleased with itt. And the i9 of
March wentt into a bed. When I contracted with
Mrs Ibbott to board Mr Frek, my self, and three
servants, hoping more for my own ease: Mr Frek and
I att ten shillings a week and my three servantts att
five shillings a week a peice and one shilling a peice
for all strangers. Soe I paid two porters for removeing
our things from Minakins to Lifes and from Lifes to
Mr Ibots, the minester of Saffum, and worst place of
all   o–i5–

---

[4] Peter Good.

[5] The remembrances characterize James Minican as one of 'Mr Freks two men'; th
surname does not appear in the Swaffham parish register. Chaldron: thirty-two bush
of coal.

22 I sentt againe for the doctters of Bery, Doctter
rker, Doctter Dockett, Cosins the surgion, and
elldrick to consult together once more. I paid   5–10–0
23 Heer I paid againe for three weeks watchers
d attending him   2–10–0
     More I paid James Large[6] for keeping my coach
d three horses a month att stable, every howre
pectting my fate,   5–7–6
     And more hee brought me in for strangers horses
d tenants   0–14–0
24 I paid Mrs Ibott before hand for our boards
d lodging   5–0–0
     And I gave her daughter and maid more   0–10–0
     I sentt againe for a chaldron of coales to Linn   1–15–0
     And I paid Sheringham[7] for caring of them from
n to Saffum   0–12–0
1706, March 25 The 25 of March my deer
sband sentt Towers to me to goe home immediatly
make him a vault of the north side of Billney
ancell and large enough for me to lye by him and
s little grandsonn murdered in London.
26 And sentt againe to Doctter Dockett and paid
m more   2–3–0
                      Errors excepted sume is   68–10–2
                                                                  Eliza Freke

, fol. 38v, 3 side]

1706, March 26, Doctter Cosins, Mr Freks
rgion, sentt to Mr Frek and mee to pay him in
artt for his months attendance by Mr Towrs and
r the dresing of his legg, to be paid him in London;
r which he demanded twenty pounds, which I
nediatly paid him by my cosin John Freke and by
y deer husbands order.   20–0–0
     More I paid att Mr Bottoms for shop goods I knew
othing of taken up by their order   1–12–0

---

[6] Among the Larges in the Swaffham register, a James Large married Ann Moare on
May 1685, and James and Alice Large baptized children in 1697 and 1706.
[7] Possibly Robert Sherringham, who was buried in Pentney on 25 October 1721; an
nne and Robert Sheringham baptized a son in Narford in 1708.

And more I paid Cullum the knacker for six
jorneys to Raymond and elcewhere for a milch
ass[8]   o–18–

25 or 26 I sent Mr Towers aboutt makeing Mr
Freks vaultt under the north side of Billney chancell,
and Mr Freke was nott easy except I wentt my selfe
and dereicted itt – and 5 men to goe aboute itt as
fast as they could. And I gave them 5 shillings earnest
and was to give them 5 pound whene the wall was
begun. Which I did.   5–5–

29 I wentt to boarde with Mrs Ibbott and paid
her before hand more,   io–o–
the other 5 pound being for a little room to dress my
meat in for three weeks and the maid to lye in.

30 And now I paid of all my small bills more att
Saffum   i–5–
And for a new wicker chaire he could never use
or sitt in   o–io–
And for a new greatt easy chaire I sentt for from
London   5–o–
And the carrige of itt to Saffum to Mr Large more   o–io–
Neither of which could my deer husband sitt in; they
both were too strait for him. The last is in the best
chamber.

1706, Aprill 6 Sunday night late, the sixt of Aprill,
my deer son came from Ireland to see his deer
father, with Thom Crosby. Where in the town I were
faine to gett a room for him and Mr Crosby and his
man att Thomas Cullams, the neerst house to Mr
Frek,[9] and to board them at Mr Ibotts att ten shillings
a week a peice.

8 of Aprill I paid Mr Penington[10] more for a
challdron of coals   i–i5–
And to Sherringham for the carraige of them from
Lin to Saffum   o–12–
And for carting of half a hundred of fagots from
Billney   o–7–

---

[8] Several Culhams appear in the Swaffham parish register. The earlier ledger h
Raynum: either South or West Raynham.

[9] Thomas Culham and his wife Elizabeth Thorpe, whom he married on 13 Octob
1689, had buried in Swaffham two of their four children baptized there.

[10] Probably Francis Penniton, who lived with his wife Mary in East Walton. See abov
p. 283 n. 217.

i4 I paid for wine and brackfasting for my son
nd Crosby and Towrs and their servants to Mr
arge for eight dayes   3–i8–o

And I paid more for drink and lodging for my
wre servants   2–i2–o

i5 I paid more a shop book for two new wascots
r Mr Frek, stockins, shooes, and 4 caps for my
er husband   i–i4–io

And for a paire of new cruches for him, the
icks   o–io–o

2i of Aprill I paid Mrs Ibbott more for our months
oard, viz., my deer husband and my self and my
n and Thom Crosby and our 4 or five constantt
rvants,   io–o–o

22 I paid James Large for a month keeping my
ree coach horses in oates and hay and stabling
d coach house   5–7–o

And more for by horses came to vissett my deer
osin   o–i4–o

23 I paid Mr Large more for wyne my son, Towrs,
d Crosby had   i–i5–o

25 More I paid for two watchers a month and
mes Minickin a week   i–i8–o

And I gave more to Petter and my sons man for
ere watch   o–io–o

27 I sentt againe to Doctter Duckett, who came
aine to him to noe purpose, and I gave him by
y deer cosins order   2–3–o

Errors excepted sume is   78–i5–io

Eliza Freke

, fol. 39r, 4 sid]

i706, May 5 I paid more to Mr Large severall
lls taken up by my son and Thom Crosby, Mr
owers, and Thom Chaffin, and all theire gess to
y son and there followers for wyne and alle, &c.,
ken up by his order. Which bill the wretch Towrs
ought me to pay from Large of Saffum, being   4–io–o

i5 The i5 of May more I paid for them and ther
rvants in shop bills unknown to me   2–o–o

2i And I paid more for two watchers a month for
y deer cosin and husband   i–8–o

22 More I paid Mr Large of Swaffum for keeping
my coach and three horses att oatts and hay for a
month, coach house and stable   5–7–

And more for by horses of strangers and
tennantts, &c.   0–10–

1706, June 2d Sunday, the second of June, aboutt
three a clock in the affternoon my deer husband
departed this life, and noe mortall with mee butt my
wretched self till I scrimed them outt of the church,
and left miserable me for ever to lamentt him. Hee
dyed the same day and howre my son, Ralph Frek,
was borne affter he had laine allmost seven month
under the hand of fowre doctters and 2 surgions and   13–15–
three appothycaryes who all had the honour of   78–15–i
murdering of him. And my self, Eliza Frek, and   68–10–
three other watchers – two men and a woman –   49–5–
every night with him before his death. EF   210–6–

1706, June 3d I caryed my deer husband away
with me to Billney in a hearse I had from Lin with a
vast appeerance of company – gentry, tennants, and
neighbours – which did all attend him to his vault
att Billney affter ther brackfast att Saffum att Mr
Larges. For which I paid Mr Large that day for itt   5–10–

And carryed with me in wyne and ale for there
suppers   2–14–

And I paid to three parishes for three pasing
bells as I wentt through them thatt day for tolleing
them   1–0–

And I gave the maid of the house and the poore
att the door   1–0–

And to the pasing bell more att Saffum I paid
more   0–10–

June 3 On Monday night my cosin John Frek
came downe to me; I sentt for him to inter my deer
husband in his vaultt, where I placed him sheetted
in lead in a double coffin till I could provide for his
buriall. My cosin Frek found me allmost distracted
and this my house full of company.

7 Fryday, June the seventh, I inter'd my deer
husband, and I had all the gentry in the country of
my neighbours with all my other neighbours and
tennants, a vast appearance. Which day and soon
affter I paid these following bills, taken upp most of
them by my cosin John Frek, the day he was buryed:

I paid for a falce coffin for him, bays, hapses and
henges, and bays   3–12–0
    I paid for wyne thatt day taken up att Lin by my
cosin John Frek   7–10–0
    I paid for macaroons and biskits for this fattall day   4–15–0
    I paid Mr Bagg of Lin for two barrels of old beer
for that day[11]   4–10–0
    And the carraige of itt more was   0–5–0
    I paid Mr Priest of Lin for the crap suitt and sheet
he was laid in[12]   3–10–0
    I paid Mr Priest for scarves and had bands for the
parlor   10–0–0
    I paid for three dosen and a halfe of scutchens   9–5–0
    I paid for two Saffum men for the coffin and lead
for the coffin my deer husband now lyes in, being
double leaded,   10–15–0
    Given to the poor of the three severall parishes
and there bell tollers more when I came through them   2–10–0
    I gave Mr Adams, the minester, mourning and a
had, and making itt cost me, Eliz Frek,   8–10–0
          Errors excepted itt comes to   89–ii–0
                        Eliz Frek

[B, fol. 39v, 5 side]

1706, June 7 Paide Mr Wallgrave of Lin for
twenty gold rings for the bearers and minesters and
gentry for thatt dismall day[13]   15–10–0
    Paid Mr Scarlett of Saffum for gloves for this my
fattall day[14]   15–13–0
    More he cheated me of them, two gunyes   2–3–0
    Paid James Minakin more for 13 weeks attending
my most deere husband (Percy Freke, Esqr)   5–10–0

[11] John Bagge, a merchant who was made a freeman of Lynn in 1694–5 and later
served as an alderman and mayor, was the 'founder of a family of Lynn merchants and
lawyers'. The Bagge family had a brewery in King Street (*Freemen of Lynn*, 205, 218, 225;
Rye, i. 19; H. L. Bradfer-Lawrence, 'The Merchants of Lynn', in *A Supplement to
Blomefield's Norfolk*, ed. Clement Ingleby [London, 1929], 175).
[12] Timothy Preist is identified as a milliner among the freemen of Lynn and in the
1690 Lynn poll tax; the 1704 land tax indicates he had property in the New Conduit,
Sedgeford Lane, and Chequer Wards (*Freemen of Lynn*, 186; NRO, KL/C47/12–15 and
KL/C47/35–44).
[13] Charles Waldegrave, a goldsmith who was made a freeman of King's Lynn in 1709–
10, resided in the Sedgeford Ward (*Freemen of Lynn*, 217; NRO, KL/C47/46).
[14] Thomas Scarlet, who married Elizabeth Caps in Swaffham on 8 February 1707/8.

Paid Mr Sparrow more for black bays for his fallce
coffin[15]   i–12–0

Paid Thomas Cullam his bill for my sons lodging,
and his man and attendance, and drinking mony
brought me by Hary Towrs   8–17–0

Paide Petters jorney to London to fetch my cosin
John Frek   i–12–0

More I paid Mr Wallgrave for a vellvett pall and
ten black clokes for this my fattall day of entering my
husband   4–15–0

June 14 More I paid Mr Larg for wine taken up
by my son and the wretch Henry Towers unknown
to me till he brought itts bill   2–18–0

17 More, paid Mr Towrs his cheating bill for my
vault brick and for work men for itt and there work
of itt   84–5–0

22 I likewise paid him more for the carriag of the
brick and frame   ii–5–0

I paid Docett the carver for a white marble
scutchen for the vault bespok by my son and Mr Towrs
and paid for by me, Eliz Frek,   2–13–0

I paid Mr Clark for his herse from Linn to Saffum[16]   i–15–0

More I paid Mr Robison for paintting and leading
of this vault[17]   6–16–8

23 More I paid by Mr Adams to Mr Browne for
arch and boards for this vault[18]
The others, Mr Towrs told me, were stole before   io–o–o
used whilst Mr Towrs was a week drinking with
Thom Crosby att my charge att Saffum att Mr
Large.

More I paid Mr Hall the lime burner for
eightt challdron of lime and the carraige of itt to Billney
church yard for his vault   17–15–0

[15] Robert Sparrow resided in the Sedgeford Lane Ward; made a freeman as a woollen
draper in 1662–3, he was also mayor in 1687–8 and 1696–7 (NRO, KL/C47/35–44;
Freemen of Lynn, 172, 198, 206).

[16] Peter Sykes has suggested that William Clark, the innkeeper of the Globe Inn, may
have rented horses for hearses.

[17] The W version has 'Robenson the plumer'. John Robinson, a plumber, was made
freeman of King's Lynn in 1685–6 (*Freemen of Lynn*, 197).

[18] Perhaps Oliver Browne, a carpenter whose name appears in the list of those made
Lynn freemen in 1680–1 and in the 1704 land tax for the Kettlewell Ward (*Freemen of
Lynn*, 191; NRO, KL/C47/35–44).

24 Midsomer Day, being the 24 of June, wentt to
ondon to prove my deer husbands will with my
wn coach and fowr horses and my son and Thom
rosby and 4 servants and Towrs to Brand, when I
ave my son to beare my charges up to London   io–o–o

My expences there and bills paid by me there are
, follows:

29 I gave my son Freke to buy him and his man
ourning   ioo–o–o

I then paid Mr Freks lagacy to my cosin John
reke of   ioo–o–o

I then gave Mr Freks kinsman Thom Crosby
ourning and made itt up all compleat; hatt, stockens,
oos cost mee   i3–i7–o

And then I gave him, Thomas Crosby, to buy him
horse ten giny.   io–i5–o

Jully 4 I more gave my son my two best coach
ares and my deer husbands own rideing horse. I
ere offered for them   55–o–o

And I sentt my daughter, his wife, a new suite of
lk closhes trimed with silver lace. I paid my cosin
hn Freke for it   30–o–o

I then paid my cosin John Frek Mr Chambers bill
r fowre gold locketts and ten gould flowered rings for
y sisters and frinds in London he gave for me, EF,   i4–i2–6

i4 And I then gave Mr Towers for cheating of me
bove two hundred pound deep a silver headed cane
st me   2–io–o

And more I gave him a silver tankard, new, cost
e   8–5–o

And to him, his son, and wife 3 gold rings and a
ckett cost   4–io–o

Errors excepted   532–8–6

Eliz. Frek

3, fol. 4or, 6 sid]

i7o6, Jully i4 More I gave Mr Towrs for his
retended service to me whilst I were a month in
ondon (in a purse) 6 l., which was onlly hee took
e in one Whitrig, the greatest rogue in Norfolk,
to my Hall House. Which when I came from
ondon cost me above 20 l. to gett off.   6–o–o

And for goeing 3 miles to the Lord Richersons for
me, I gave him more   i–i–

i6 More I paid my Cosin John Frek bill for Mr
Ashhurst for cloth for mourning for Sir Georg
Norton and my two sisters and himselfe   25–5–

I paid Mr Ashhurst more for nineteen yards of
cloth bays for my self a weed by my cosin John Frek   5–17–

I payd more to my cosin Gyels for a mourning
black crap suite[19]   6–5–

I paid more to Mr Sparrow of Lin for bays Towrs
had taken up and, as he said, forgott to place itt to my
accounte, E Frek   i–ii–

i8 or therabouts more I paid my cosin John Frek
the probatt of my deer husbands will (Percy Frek,
Esq)   4–6–

More I paid for mourning for my self and two
servants   io–i2–

2i I boughtt me a new mourning coach cost me
to Mr Shepherd   45–0–

And fowre new harneses to itt cost me ten pounds   io–o–

I staid in London a month att my sister Austins,
wher my nesesary expences of my selfe and three
sarvants and 4 horses cost mee   30–0–

25 I returned home to Billney in my own coach
with my deer sister Austen in a most distracted
condition, Elizabeth Freke. Where att Billney I paid
more these bills following, which I feard being brok:

Agust i4 I paid more to Doctter Cosins of Saffum
for his paines in the murdering of my deerst cosin
and husband forty gynyes.   43–0–

And I payd more to Mr Sheldrick, his apothycary,
for pump watter[20] and his attendance on him these two
bills brought me by Henry Towrs   26–i6–

2i More I paide the queens tax for honour or his
quallity mony[21]   5–6–

I paid more Mr Hall the lime burner for the vault
and for the raiseing of the chancell and painting the
rails of itt   5–7–

---

[19] Elizabeth Gyles, sister of Freke's attorney John Freke.

[20] Medicinal water from the pump rooms of spas.

[21] A tax first imposed in 1695 'according to the rank and condition in life of person
upon births, marriages, and burials' (Dowell, *A History of Taxation and Taxes in England*,
46).

29 I paide more to Mr Priest of Lin for gloves of
kid and cordevan taken up by Henry Towres – I
knew nothing of them – by John Frekes order   3‒10‒0

1706, Septtember 3d I paid more for boards
taken up by Henry Towre, who said they with the
arch for the vault were most of them stole outt of
he church yard, wher he ordered the placeing of
hem, while he sate drinking att Saffum on my
account, unknown to me,   8‒0‒0

I paid Mr Audly the apothicary for goods taken
up att his shopp before I wentt to Saffum, unknown to
me, Eliz Frek,[22]   3‒2‒6

15 As I did likewise for things taken up of him in
Mr Freks sick[ness]   3‒10‒0

And I likewise paid the Bery appotycary for things
of Doctter Short   0‒11‒6

I likewise paid Mr Godard, the Lin apothicary,[23]
or severall things taken up by my daughter Frek when
shee was att Billney, 1705,   6‒10‒0

Octtober 14 I likewise paid my deer sister Austen
her bill for severall small things taken taken up by
Mr Freks order   8‒15‒0

And I likewise then paid my sister Austen for the
herse thatt brought downe my deer little grandchild
shott to death in London, Mr John Freke, who now lyes
with my deer husband in the vauld,   6‒10‒0

November 12 When I were allmost broke with
paying of all these severall bills, Mr Towrs brought
me another long bill from Mr Large of Saffum for
wyne, &c., which he said my son and hee knew to
be due   15‒0‒0

14 Mr Towrs brought me severall other bills for
drinke and for lodging and shop goods taken up
unknown to me, Eliz Frek,   12‒0‒0

Errors excepted sume is   293‒16‒6

Eliza Freke

[22] The King's Lynn poll tax of 1690 and 1703 land tax identify John Audley as an
apothecary residing in the New Conduit Ward (NRO, KL/C47/12‒15 and KL/C47/26‒
34, 45).
[23] Unidentified by profession in the tax lists and unlisted in Wallis.

[B, fol. 40v, 7 side]

November the 14 I new took my lease att
Pentney Mr Freke gave up to the use of his will before
three bond tennants, viz., Mr Adams, John Fish, and
Mr Throll, Febuary 21, 1705; and I paid Mr Charls
Stuartt of Pentney courte for its renewall and for the
new takeing of my copy hold estate there[24]   14–10–0

    And his clarks fee for engrossing of itt, Mr Ling,[25]   1–10–0

    21 I likewise paid the severall quitt rents att
Norwich by Mr Charls Turner, viz., procu[rations]
and sinydoll and keks[26] and the kings,   13–18–0

    And I gave himself half a guiny for a pair of gloves   0–11–0

December 2 I likewise paid Mr Turners cooper
for wyne taken up by the order of Mr Frek when
my son and daughter were heer   7–10–0

    14 or thereaboutt I likewise paid Mr Finch for
nails (1 box), two years nails taken up of him for the
tennants, and things of iron work by the tenants his
bill of   13–10–0

    I likewise paid John Willson the smith his bill whilst
I were att Saffum there fowr months and did nothing   5–8–0

    Decembr 21 I likewise paid Mr Thimblethorbs
bill for which he threatened to arrest me in the queens
exchecker of   6–14–0

    And I likewise paid the arch deacon of Norwich
his seven years bill for quit rents of   4–6–0
for which Clark threatned mee to putt me in the
spirittuall courte. Which now I stand outt for in ther
defiance. Eliz Freke

    And I likewise paid Mr Demee his bill of quitt
rents,[27] who said he would putt me presently into the
exchecker iff I did nott send itt to Norwich to him. I
then paid him   5–8–0

---

[24] Throll is neither in the parish records nor among the tenants on any of Freke's lists.
A number of Stewards appear in the archdeacon's transcripts of Pentney, none named
Charles. Nor has he been linked with the Charles Stuart who studied law at Middle
Temple or who held the advowson in Hillington, Norfolk (*Middle Temple Register*, i. 243;
Blomefield, viii. 468).

[25] Possibly James Ling, who married Mary Pinchback in Swaffham on 1 April 1680; a
Henry Ling and a John Lyng are also listed in the 1689–90 King's Lynn poll taxes
(NRO, KL/C47/10 and KL/C47/12–15).

[26] Meaning unclear.

[27] Most likely James Demee, the owner of Surrey House in Norwich, who died on 1
September 1718 at the age of fifty-nine (Blomefield, iv. 158–9).

Thus were I threatned and torne to peices for mony
when first I were a widow allmost to my distraction,
soe thatt from December 1705 to December the one and
twenty 1706 I have paid in bills   73‒5‒9
besids my liveing, and travilling, and servants wages,
and the minester twenty pounds a yeare, work men,
and the plague of law and ther atturneys.

I say I have payde in the seven foregoeing sids in the sickness,
death, and buriall of my deer husband, Percy Frek, Esqr, as appeers
in the severall bills filed by me in my closett and by me taken outt
December 18 and paid by wretched me, Elizabeth Frek, the sume
of ii85‒18‒0, as by ther severall sids may be seen to bee eleven
hundred eighty five pounds, eightteen shillings. Which mony ought
to have bin all paid by my son, Mr Ralph Freke, and nott to have
had me, Elizabeth Frek, threatned with a jayle as I were by these
Norfolk rogues; as did Charls Turner of Lin send his two baylyes
to my closett (where I were sitting the 25 of November 1707) with
the shriefs execution on my body and goods for eight pound of
which I knew nott thatt I owed him one farthing. Nor did hee give
me warning butt to carry me away to Norwich Castle jayle when
att the same time I had in my closett eight hundred pound by me,
Eliza. Frek. Affter my haveing paid ii85‒18‒0. This is the usuage I
have had in Norfolk; therfore, son, take heed and beware of my
fate. Eliza Freke

The sums on the severall sids are as followeth:

i: 49‒5‒6
2:    68‒10‒2
3:    78‒15‒0
4:    89‒11‒0
5:   532‒8‒6
6: 293‒16‒6
7:    73‒5‒9

Errors excepted sume is   ii85‒ii‒0
Elizabeth Freke, 1712, Septembr 29

B, fol. 41r]

1712, September 14 Besids these severall sumes paid by me, Eliz
Frek, and forcst from me the yeare my deer husband dyed and left me,
being the second of June 1706 …[28]

---

[28] Omitted is a more detailed variation of the legal and financial troubles with tenants
Freke recalls in her second remembrance (above, pp. 257‒8).

[B, folio 42r]

i7i2 Thus have I lived neer seven years in my widowhood in continuall trouble and to see the fall of most of my enimies withou the assistance, help, or comfortt of one friend. Tho my cosin Joh Frek, who pretends to be executor with me to my deer husbands wi tho in my distreess I offten complained to him, hee never did me five shilling curtisy since I were an unhapy widow, though I had oblige him above five hundred pound deep; only on my letter of atturney i the yeare i7o7 to him dereicted [he] gave away my estate in Ireland o 85o pounds a year my deer husband left me for three hundred an fiffty pounds a yeare. And my arrears then due in i7o6 att the death o my husband he told me was above i2oo pound. I never received of i one peny, tho I paid him 3oo pound for his jorney. This is true, a wittness my hand, thatt from such friends and friendship, good Lor deliver mee. Elizabeth Frek, dated September i4, i7i2

B. West Bilney Manor and Tenants

[B, fol. 28r]

A true accountt of the rents of West Billney bought by my deer fathe of my Lord Thomas Richerson and given to my sister Austen are a followeth, i672:

The severall akers are, iff right reckned by me, Eliza Freke,	2698 aker
Of which in the common is 4oo akers and in the warren is	io62 aker
And the tennants enclosed akers are, besids whatt I have bought,	i648–22 r–2oo
In all is bought by my deer father, Ralph Freke, Esqr,	2698 aker
And the rentt of West Billney then was lett tennanted for	557 a year
Outt of which to be deducted to the minester	2o–o–o a yeare
And to the Lord Oswellston quitt rentt more	2–io–o a yeare
And for other small quitt rents is more	2–i8–o a year
All which is	25–8–
Which taken outt of the above 557 l. remaines cleer due	532–i2–

An accountt how the rents of West Billney were fallen the fowre years my brother Austen had itt under the managemt of Mr Rolf of Lin Regis when I bought itt, Eliza. Freke, i676. Tennants names are as olloweth – D signifyes the Lady Richerson dowre:

Dowre-	i is Thomas Turner, the Hall	98–0–0
	2 William Bish, Paws Farm	6i–0–0
	3 Robert Ram, the warren	64–0–0
	4 Richard Coe rents	38–0–0
	5 John Plattfoott rentt was	30–0–0
	6 is John Chapman	26–0–0
	7 is John Fish, passture	i7–0–0
Dowr-	8 Parsnage Farme is	28–0–0
	9 Thomas Unkles is	i2–0–0
	io John Plattfoott, medow	4–0–0
	ii Will Thorpe	4–0–0
	i2 John Benson	4–0–0
	i3 John Greene is	4–0–0
	i4 is Henry Dawdry	4–i5–0
	i5 Thomas Day is	2–i2–0
D-	i6 Thomas Shepherd is	2–0–0
D-	i7 Wiliam Walles	i–i5–0
D-	i8 John Downing is	2–0–0
	i9 John Green, now Barkam	i–i6–0
	20 Ralph Ram, Barne Meadow	3–5–0
	2i Ralph Ram, Long Close	3–0–0
D-	22 Ralph Ram, Spar Fen, i3 Akers	3–0–0
	23 Rentt hens is	i–0–0
	In all is, iff rightt reckned by mee, Eliza Frek, coms to	4i4–3–0

[W, fol. 4iv]

An accountt how Billney stands now lett by me, Eliz. Frek, with itts akers and rentts from Michellmas last, i708

The Hall Farme now in the hand of Richard Taff is now lett for by me, Eliz Frek, for containing i76 akers:

		l.–s.–d.
ii akers	in one ploughed peice just before the house att ten shillings the aker is	75–io–0
5 akers	One peice of hay ground just below itt at io shillings	5–io–0
		2–io–0

		l.-s.-d.
9 aker	One ploughed peice just below the medow with 2 akers of bordrs	5–0–0
6 akers	of ploughed land att the head of the orchard lett att	3–0–0
9 akers	of hay pasture just nextt to itt lett att	5–0–0
2i akers	of plough land and one of pasture in the same field	io–io–0
6 akers	of pasture or hay land just before the 20 akers	3–0–0
i5 akers	of plagh land just by Betts house lett att under rentt	
3 aaker	of pasture just by itt lett for both	9–io–0
4 akers	of courser pasture on the other sid of Betts house lett att	2–0–0
i aker	of plough ground and house in which Sad lives lett att	2–io–0
i5 aker	of pasture and plough ground, formerly Jams Wallbutt	7–io–0
2 akers	of pasture just before Betts house lett att with the house	3–0–0
i6 akers	of cow pasture called Dyes Close now lett att	8–0–0
24 akers	of fen ground adjoyning to the parsnage lett att	i2–0–0
5 akers	of carr ground[29] in Dyes Close lett att	i–5–0
	The little house lett for by Dyes Close	2–0–0
i8i akrs	Errors excepted, this coms to just	79–i5–0

i708, September 29. The Wassell Farme, wher I lived in King Jams time 8 years, now lett for by me, Eliz Freke, for   50–0–0
to Thomas Pamer, I reserving three roomes and the seller outt of itt with the little house thatt goes to Pentny by the lane, E Frek, i708

Akers belonging to the Wassell:

		l.–s.–d.
2i akers	in the common field by the warren is of ploughed land lett att ten shillings an akere comes to	io–io–0
3 akers	of ploughed in the Clamp just by lett att i3 s.–4 d. the aker	2–0–0
7 akers	of plough land and pasture in Alltus, att i3–4 an aker	4–ii–0
4 akers	of pasture just before the little house, i3– 4 an aker	2–i2–0

---

[29] Carr: boggy land or meadow formed from drained bog.

5 akers	of plough land just before the head house, i3–4 an aker	3–5–0
1 aker	of plough and pasture called Clamp Aker, i3–0	0–i3–0
30 akers	of pasture for cows with Ollivers peice for hay att 6–8 per aker	io–0–0
io akers	of passture or hay ground call'd Kings Medow, io–0 per aker	5–0–0
30 akers	formerly belonging to the Hall Farme in three severall ten aker peices att ten shillings an aker, io–0,	i5–0–0
iii akers	Errors excepted comes to	50–io–0

Luke Wingfield now rents of me in Billney by the yeare the sum of   62–io–0

lett by me, Eliz Freke, Michellmas i708:

ioo akers	The Parsnage Farme, containe a hundred akers more or less, is now lett to him for the yearly rentt of	25–0–0
27 akers	now lett to Luke Wingfield for the yearly rentt of	9–io–0
50 akers	Billney Closes, the uper partt, now lett att	20–0–0
70 akers	The lower part of Billney Closes of seventy akers with	
30 akers	lieing nextt to Wallton Common, both lett for	8–0–0
277 akers	Errors excepted, which comes to	62–io–0

Which whole three farms lett att 4–6 pence the aker, one with annother come to 62–6–6, the land worth half as much more. Besids I give this years rentt into the bargain. Eliz Frek

[W, fol. 42r]

i708, Michellmas, September 29. Henry Crosse farme, or the White House Farme, lett by me to Henry Cross for the yearly rentt of forty six pound, ten shillings a yeare for the terme of seven years, with itt akers and price,   46–io–0
Eliz Freke
Imprimus   l.–s.–d.

2i	In the field by Saffum rode is 21 akers att io shillings an aker is	io–io–0

3	Three akers more in Saffum field, 3, belonging to Dawson, io shillings an aker	i–10–0
5	The Horse Close lett att five, 5, shillings the aker	i–5–0
5	akers call'd the Hoppground, 5 shillings the aker	i–5–0
23	akers of pasture for cowes, 23, called Juells, io	ii–10–0
3	akers of pasture by the Hall, 3, called Billneys, io	i–10–0
i	aker of plough land in the common field, i, by the warren, i8	0–i8–0
7	akers of wheat land by the common field, 7; by Pentny road, i3	4–ii–0
i3	akers withoutt the warren, i3, att five shillings	3–i5–0
i8	akers of plough'd ground by the house, i8, att io shillings the aker	9–0–0
io	akers call'd Funells Medow, io, att io shillings	4–10–0
3	akers of ploughed land by the house, 3, att io shillings	i–10–0
	In all, iff right reckned by me, E Freke, is io7.	
	Errors excepted, the rentt coms to	46–i2–0
		Eliz Freke

[W, fol. 43r]

A true accountt how West Billney is now lett by me, Elizabeth Frek, last September i708, when 5 tennants in my absence run away with my rents and arrears to aboutt my loss of in the compass of a year and half time, as will apper, in my unhapy widowhood and inability of goeing outt of my chamber,[30] Eliz. Frek

	688–0–0
John Benifield, the warren, lett att	55–0–0
John Benifield his pasture farme	39–0–0
Common Hous, now Wick lives in, lett at	5–0–0
Richard Taff for the Hall Farme	45–0–0
To him for Dyes Close and the fen	20–0–0
To him for Wallbutts grounds, hous burnt	7–0–0
To him for Sads house and Betts pittle[31]	3–10–0
Luke Wingfield of East Walton, Priers Close	9–10–0
And the Parsnage Farme att	25–0–0
And Billney Closes att	28–0–0

---

[30] B, fol. 28r, has a variation of this account.
[31] Pittle: variant of pightle, a small enclosure or field.

William Knopwood, Hoss Paws Farme	60‒0‒0
Thomass Pallmer, the Wassell Farme	50‒0‒0
Henry Cros, the White House Farme	46‒10‒0
The Maner Farme in my hand	48‒10‒0
Henry Lindo,[32] the Comon Farm	12‒10‒0
John Bonion of East Wallton	4‒0‒0
Daniell Coats, the Comon Farme	8‒10‒0
Sconces house and the Parish House	4‒0‒0
Maddam Barnes	0‒12‒0
Rentt hens	0‒16‒0
Errors excepted	472‒8‒0

More, I lett Mr James Englebright att Pentney a
arme I bought of my own mony of copy hold estat 46‒0‒0
   Both which estates coms to, iff noe mistak in the
eckon of them, May 28, 1709, 518‒8‒0
   Eliz Freke

Outt of this is the minester I pay now,
Mr Buck, 20‒0‒0
And the kings rentt 2‒10‒0
And quitt rents aboutt 1‒10‒0
   24‒0‒0

And for this 20 year last past I have paid the parliamtt tax of neer a
hundred pounds a year besid my loses this two years past of above five
hundred pounds since a widow. E Frek

[B, fol. 28v]

An accountt how West Billney stands now lett by me this Michellmas
712, Elizabeth Frek, in my unhapy widowhood, with the severall
tennants names thatt rentt itt att present
Imprymus
. The Hall Farme now in the hand of John Whitting
lett for 48‒0‒0
2 Richard Tofts, the Maner Farme lett to him for 48‒10‒0
   And to him Dyes Close and the two fens lett to him
   for 20‒0‒0
   And to him more the Alle House Farme burnt down 7‒0‒0
3 Is the warren to John Benifield for 55 l. and his
pasture 39 94‒0‒0
4 Is the Wassell Farme lett to Thomas Pallmer for 50‒0‒0
6 [sic] Is Henry Cross Whitt House lett for 46‒10‒0

[32] He lived in East Walton, where he was later a church warden of St Mary the Virgin.

7 Is William Knopwood Paws or Bishops Farme lett to
him   60–0–c
8 Is Daniell Coats in the common lett to him for   8–io–c
9 Is Charles Greene in the common   5–io–c
io Is Luke Wingfield of East Wallton, Pryers Close   9–io–c
   To him more is Billney Closes lett at   28–0–c
   And more to him is the Parsnage Farme lett att   25–0–c
ii Is Henry Lindo of East Wallton, to 2 Whin Closes
and 7 akers   i2–io–c
i2 Is John Bonion, two peices lett him for   3–io–c
i3 Madam Barnes, Whittpitt Brake, 5 akers, 5 perch   0–io–c
i4 Is Robertt Wattsons house and pittle   2–io–c
i5 Sads house and Sconces house, and both is   3–0–c
Rentt hens att Xmas is i6 shillings   0–i6–c
And Parish House in hand
             Errors excepted, sume is   472–i2–c
i6 Is in Pentney one farme in the hands of James
Englebright lett for   46–0–c
         Soe thatt both make up the sume of   5i8–i2–c
                                Eliz Freke

[W, fol. 42v]

i7i3/i4, March 4 An accountt of whatt lands belong to the Maner
Farme of West Billney, taken outt by mee, Eliz Freke, and lett to
   30 akers of mowing fen ground, high land, lett att
   50 akers of fen ground lett att
   io akers of high mowing ground lett att
   3 akers of fine mowing ground lett at, in Pincens Hill,
   4 akers in the pound peice of fine hay
   3 akers in the home stall of fine hay
   4 akers of fine pasture belonging to the Alle House Farme
   2 akers more of mowing ground fine hay, to the Ale House
   8 akers of plough ground belonging to the Ale House
   i aker more of plough ground call'd Dadrys Ale House
   8 akers of plough ground on Pinsons Hill and
   3 akers of plough ground att Hamenstad
   3½ akers more of plough ground before this house
   3 akers more by the warren field plough land
   3½ akers more in the waren field plough land by Knop

C. Ownership of West Bilney

[W, fol. 112r]

In i547 of King Edward the 6th and the 3d year of his reigne[33] I find in a maniscrip amongst my wrightings of Billney the third yeare of King Edward the Sixth reigne, i547, thatt this king grants the maner of West Billney in the county of Norfolk and all messagges, tennaments, lands, meddows, pastures, feedings, commons, wasts, warrens, and herrydettrementts, &c.,[34] late parcell of the possesion of the pryory of Pentney, to Richard Fulcauston.

Febuary io and the 3d of Elizabeth[35] Fullcauston grants this said maner to Mildmay and to his heires by deed inrolled with a fine betweene the said partyes with all itts perquisits to him and his heires, as is above mentioned.

Febuary the 22 and the i5 of Queen Elizabeth[36] Mildmay bargains and sells by deed inrolled this above estate of the maner of West Billney to Francis Windham and his heires with a fine bettween the same partties.

i558, the 29 of Juny and 44 of Queen Elizabeth[37] Jane Coressly, sister and heire of Francis Windham, covenants with Henry Windham to stand seized to the use of her selfe for her life and affter to Thomas Prand, son of Henry Windham, and to his heires intaile, inrolled the seventh of December and forty seventh of Elizabeth.

i602, the i of May and 20 of Jaccobus or James the First[38] Henry Windham and Thomas Windham by deed enrolled in Trinytie tearme the 20 of Jacob the First bargaine and sell to Edmond Bullock and Georg Scott and theire heires in concideration paid by Sir Edmond Bullock a fine exemplyfied between the parties aforesaid.[39]

i625, Juny i and 7 of Carrolus the First[40] Sir Edward Bullock

---

[33] Versions of this history appear in B, fols. 47v–48v, and BL, Add. MS. 45721 A, fols. 1r–v. The third regnal year began on 28 January 1548/9.

[34] Messuages: dwelling, nearby buildings, and adjacent land; tenement: land or real property held and in common law 'lands, other inheritances, capable of being held in freehold, and rents' (Black, 1,316); hereditament: inheritable property.

[35] 10 February 1560/1, in the third of the regnal years beginning on 17 November 1558.

[36] 22 February 1572/3.

[37] 29 June 1602.

[38] 1 May 1624, in the twentieth of the regnal years beginning on 24 March 1602/3.

[39] 'Edmund Bullock, of Norfolk, gen., of Furnival's Inn' entered Lincoln's Inn on 14 November 1601 (*The Records of the Honorable Society of Lincoln's Inn*, 2 vols. [Lincoln's Inn, 1896], i. 133). 'George Scott of Essex, gen. of Clifford's Inn', had preceded Bullock at Lincoln's Inn (i. 128); another, the son of William Scott from Conghurst, Kent, matriculated at Queen's College in 1608, entered Gray's Inn the next year, and died in 1633 (*Register of Gray's Inn*, 122; Venn, iv. 31).

[40] 1 June 1631, in the seventh of the regnal years beginning on 27 March 1625.

and Edmond Bullock and George Scott bargaine and sell to Thomas Benyfield all their intrest to Edward Richerson and Ambross Shepherd and their heirs in trust for Sir Thomas Richerson, Lord Cheife Justice Richerson of the common please.[41]

[W, fol. 111v]

1634, January 16 of Carrolus the First The Lord Cheife Justice Richerson deviseth the saide maner of West Billney to Sir Thomas Richerson, his son, for life and affter to Thomas Richerson intaile, now Lord Thomas Richerson (Baron Gramontt).

1652, Octtober 13, Charls the 2d Sir Thomas Benyfield and his heires (January 7) and Ambross Shepherd leases to Thomas Lord Richerson, Barron Gramontt in Scottland, son and heir of Sir Thomas Richerson and grandson of the lord chiefe justice, for a yeare West Billney and affter.

1652, Octtobr 15, Charls 2d Sir Thomas Benifield and his heires and Ambross Shepherd releases to the said Lord Richerson and his heires West Billney.

1653, Trinyty tearm, Juny 7 The Lord Richerson suffers a recovery to John Tostock, and the seventh of Juny 1653 the lord by deed leases the uses of the saide recovery to him and his heires.[42]

1659, May 27, Carrolus 2d The Lord Richerson, Barron Gramond in Scotland, mortgages the said maner of West Billney together with the demeans and other lands in West Billney to Sir Jacob Garrett for two thousand five hundred pounds for 500 years, and 3000 l. was desired on itt.[43] And by his deeds convey'd itt to him May 27, 1659.

1663, June 3d, Carrolus 2d Sir Jacob Garrett with the Lord Thomas Richerson, Barron Gramond, did sell to my deer father, Ralph Frek, Esqr, of Hanington in Wildshier, on his paymentt of a 1000 l.,

---

[41] Edward Bullock of Faulkbourne Hall, Essex, knighted on 5 July 1609, and the father of Edward Bullock, who resided at Pentney when he entered the Inner Temple in 1628 (William A. Shaw, *The Knights of England*, 2 vols. [1906, reprinted Baltimore, 1971], ii. 148; Blomefield, ix. 40; Venn, i. 252). Thomas Bedingfeld or Beddenfield: associated with Gray's Inn; 'Thomas Beddingfield of Holborn, Midds.' was knighted on 23 June 1638 at Greenwich (*Register of Gray's Inn*, 127, 211; Shaw, *Knights of England*, ii. 206). Ambrose Shepherd, the son of Owen Shepherd of Kirby Bedon, matriculated at Caius in 1614; later, an Ambrose Shepherd became lord of the Norfolk manor of Kirby Bedon (Venn, iv. 58; Blomefield, v. 477). Thomas Richardson, a knight and member of parliament from St Albans who became speaker in 1621, served as lord chief justice from 1621 until his death in 1635 (*Scots Peerage*, ii. 579).

[42] Recovery: restoration or affirmation of right through court judgment (Black, 1,147). John Tostock is unidentified among the Tostockes of Norfolk or at the inns of court.

[43] Sir Jacob Garrard (d. 1666), London alderman from Bishopsgate and Candlewick, was knighted on 3 December 1641 and received a baronetcy on 16 August 1662 (Beaven, *Aldermen of the City of London*, ii. 64; *CB*, iii. 255–6).

thousand pound, more to my Lord Richerson, he did sell all his said maner of West Billney with all itts appurtenances, members, &c., as parcell of the late disolved monastry of Pentney together with Sir Jacob Garretts mortgage of 500 yeares.

1664, Novembr 28 And took itt up of my Lord Richerson as by his lease appeers and paid of to my lord three thousand one hundred fiffty nine pounds **1665, Jully 5**. Which mony was to bee paid back to my deer father by my Lord Richerson with itts intrest of seven hundred thirtty seven pounds, fowrteen shillings, and ten pence (737–14–10) the twentieth day of January.

[W, fol. 111r]

1665[/6], January 20 Which faileing of both princeple and intrest, the Lord Thomas Richerson did sell West Billney with Sir Jacob Garretts mortgage by lease to William Coward, Esqr,[44] viz., all the maner of West Billney with itts apurtennances and members thereto belonging as partt and parcell of the late desolved monastry of Pentney. And with all his rightt the Lord Richerson did convey to my deer father, Ralph Frek, for (5896–14–10) fyve thousand eight hundred ninety six pounds, fourteen shillings, and ten pence; which sume the Lord Richerson owns to have received from my father as by his deeds mentioned and enroled, &c.

1672, Octtober 5 My deer father gave this estatte to my brother Austen for my deer sisters portion for 4000 l. Butt hee nott liking the distance of itt from his own estat in Kentt, my father paid my brother the mony and sould itt to my deer husband, Percy Freke, Esqr, and did then settle itt on me, Eliza Frek, his eldest daughter, and on my heires (as a retreatt from Ireland), my son being then aboutt fowre monthes old. Since which time (1675) to Octtober the 22, 1712, this estate of West Billney has bin in me, his daughter Elizabeth Freke, viz., for thirty eightt years and upward, and in my deer fathers possesion neer fiffty three yeares, iff right reckned by me, EF.

1688, the 1 of Queen Mary and William the 3d[45] My deer husband, Percy Freke, Esqr, boughtt of my Lord Henry Richerson, Barron Gramontt, eldest son to the Lord Thomas Richerson, and of his brother Mr Thomas Richerson their rightt of redemtion of West Billney together with Gander Fenn in Wrongy, or Wormongy, abutting

[44] William Coward (1634–1705), called to the bar from Lincoln's Inn in 1662 and later a sergeant-at-law, was a recorder of Wells, which he represented in a number of parliaments (*HC*, ii. 164–5).

[45] Regnal year beginning on 13 February 1688/9.

on my Decoy,[46] and the five aker peice of Mrs Barns in Winch abutting
on Billney, or rather in Billney, for a hundred guinyes, viz., io7.

i689, King William 3 Which I, Elizabeth Freke, paid him att
Pentney and Mr Frek enrolled in chancery by a new decree. And when
hee dyed in i706, June the 2d (and my sons birth day), hee settled itt
on my son and his grandchildren successivelly. Eliza Freke

[W, fol. iiov]

i688, the i of Queen Mary and William the Third, 3d And
Mr Freke then took a larg deed from the Lord Richerson and his
brother Mr Thomas Richerson with Yelverton Payton, Esqr,[47] and ther
bond for performance of covenantts of three hundred pound aboutt
July i688 or i689. Thus in Queen Mary the first and King William the
3d time I have lived in a quiett possesion withoutt the least disturbance
for aboutt 38 yeares and my deer father before me for neer fiffty years,
viz., from the 27 of May i659, the twentieth of King James the First,
till the seventh yeare of Queene Ann.[48]

i709, Queen Ann 7 year, Jully 22 or thereaboutt The presentt
bishop of Norwich, Doctter Trimnell, did turne outt my minester, Mr
Charls Buck, from offyciatting in my church for nott excepting of his
licence and beinge subjectt to his courts. Which I then held outt against,
I nott haveing in the three foregoeing bishops ever had my right
questioned (viz., in Doctter Sparrows time, Dr Loyds time, and Doctter
Moors time). And to make itt the more barbarous, this was done when
I were att Bristoll goeing for Ireland, [which] forced me home againe
to defend my rightt against this bishop, Doctter Trimnell; Doctter
Jeffryes, the arch deacon; and Docter Thomas Tanner, their chancellour,
who threatned me with excomynication.

i709, Michellmas to Aprill i7io Then I keptt the church seven
month vacantt from Michellmas to Aprill to see whatt there tormentting
of me with ther letters and procttors would come to and to justifye my
right as partt of my estate and itts head – itt being thus used by the
Norwich clargy affter I had outt of my own generossitty for thirty eight
yeares maintained a minester heer outt of my own pockett att twenty

---

[46] Thomas Richardson, the second of Lord Cramond's three sons, died in 1696 (*Scots
Peerage*, ii. 582). The land known as Decoy was on the western side of the estate, west of
the area located on the current Ordnance Survey map as Denton's Farm and north of
Wormgay, which Freke's transcription of Camden's *Britannia* notes is 'commonly called
Wrongey' (BL, Add. MS. 45720, fol. 47r) and Faden's 1797 map of Norfolk depicts as
Wormegay Fen.

[47] Yelverton Peyton, fourth son of Thomas and Elizabeth Peyton of Rougham and
husband of Hannah Roberts, matriculated at Caius in 1669 and entered Gray's Inn in
1672 (Blomefield, x. 32; *Register of Gray's Inn*, 315).

[48] 27 May 1659 was in the tenth regnal year of Charles II.

ounds a yeare besids severall other grattuityes, there being neither
leab or tithes butt whatt my charrity affords to this church of Billney.
But I, Eliz Frek, refused all theire authority and unjust demands, itt
eing a peculier since i547, the 3d of Edward the Sixth, and my
eculler, neither subjectt to institution, inducttion, or licence butt an
npropiation and my donitive, as is Pentny church, putt in by my
ather, Ralfe Frek, Esqr, i675. Butt Pentney church has tithes; this has
othing for itts supportt butt my charity and bounty for above thirty
ight yeare past, who have allowed Mr Adams and Mr Buck twenty
ound a year a peice besids other gratuityes since the yeare i675 to this
resentt Lady Day i7i2, Eliz Freke. Mr Buck, my minester, was prefered
om Gyton and Billney to a better liveing, soe thatt my church is now
acantt againe to see the charyty of the bishop and Norwich clergy
ow to this church, which has cost mee above eightt hundred pound
oth itts minesters since I came to Billney (now 29 years agoe). Eliza
reke

B, fol. 29v]

). Account of Money Freke Lent and Brought to Her Iusband

7i2 A true accountte of whatt I have lentt and brought my deer
usband, Percy Frek, Esqr, since I were marryed to him, being the
ourteenth of November i67i, as I have endorst itt to the best of my
nemory. And I show'd itt my deer husband, Percy Frek, i705, (when
e was angry with me I would nott come up to London) to see iff there
vere any mistake in; who affter reading of itt said I was true and thatt
e could deney noe part of itt butt thatt he had received itt from Eliza.
reke.[49]

i67i, November i4 I were privattly marryed to Mr Frek in Coventt
Garden by Mr Johnson, then my Lord Russells chaplin, in London.

i672, Jully 24 I were againe remarryed by my deer father, Ralph
rek, Esqr, to my deer husband, Percy Freke, Esqr, att St Margaretts
Church att Westminster in London by Doctter Uttram the 24 of Jully
ifter I had bin neer eightt years contracted to him, and my licence 4
ears taken out. Eliza. Freke

First, whatt I lentt him of my own saveings I hadd
ais bond for of payment: l.–s.–d.

i672 I lentt Mr Freke to pay my auntt Frek[50] his fathers
and mothers bond by them contracted aboutt 8 years
efore, which with its intrest came to   320–0–0

---

[49] W, fol. 4ov, has an earlier version ending in i680.
[50] Frances, the wife of William Freke of Hannington.

1673 I lentt him more to pay his own debts for sack and
clarrett, &c.   200–0–

1673 More this yeare I lentt him to pay my brother
Austin, who had kindly arested him for itt (tho drinking
mony), together with itts intrest and charge   150–0–

1674 More I lentt him when he wentt downe into Kentt
to seise Leeds Castle aboutt Xmas with the shriefe and
twenty fowre baylyes   100–0–

1675 More he took up of mine in my aunt Freks
hand to buy goods with the first time I wentt for Ireland   150–0–

Besids a greatt many smaller sumes and aboutt eight
or ten dimand rings of myne in his keeping, all lost
butt my weding ring,   920–0–

                                                                    Eliza. Frek

1674 My deer father gave me then for my portian a
morttgage on Sir Robertt Brooks estatte neer Eping
Forrest, in five miles of London – a mortgage of five
hundred pounds a yeare which my deer husband sould to
Sir Josias Child, a greatt bruer in the citty of London, for   5664–0–
Paid him downe in redy mony with itts intrest and
disposed of greatt part of itt unknown to me or my
deer father, Ralph Frek, my trusttee.

1675 I borrowed of my deer father (Ralph Frek, Esqr,)
on the purchas of Leeds Castle in Kentt on my husbands
and my bond   800–0–
Which in a little time affter my father gave me upp on
Mr Freks promise of settling itt on me, Eliza. Frek.
Which 1677 or thereabout my deer husband sould this
estatt of Leeds Castle to Lord Cullpeper for   2500–0–
(unknown to my deer father or mee), which he
transferred to his beloved Ireland and with itt and its
exchang of 300 l. bought part of his west country estate
in Ireland and 100 l. a year by Rathbary.

1675 Then presently affter the birth of my son, Ralfe
Frek, being June the second, 1675, I bought of my deer
father this estatte of West Billney, which was given to
my brother Austen and by him sould to me, then a
mortgage to my father for above 5768 l. For which I
were faine to borrow of my deer father to compleatt
my purchase   768–14–1
And affter my Lord Richersons death I were att the
charge of sueing outt my decree in chancery; affter
which my Lady Richerson received her thirds or dowre
on itt for 28 years or thereaboutt.

i680 When I came into England to see my deer father, ıe gave mee up this bond of 768 l.–i4–io with three years ntrist due on itt, for which I had mortgaged to him by ꝛond West Billney, now my own againe.

i68i or there aboutts Mr Freke had contracted with the ᴄarle of Barrymoore for the inheritance of Rathbary, of ᴠhich was and is aboutt 300 l. a yeare, of which his lease ᴏf itt for a ioo l. a year for above sixty years. Elce iff not ᴨow bought, to be sould from us. When I weere againe ᴏrced to borrow of my deer father on Mr Freks and my ꝛond aboutt   i200–0–0

ᴠWhich he most kindly and redily lentt me soe I came ᴏr England.

    Errors excepted, sume is, if right reckned by Eliza Frek,   ii852–i4–io
                                                             Eliza Freke

[B, fol. 30r]

i7i2 A further accountt of whatt my deer father, Ralph Frek, Esqr, ᴈave me, Elizabeth Frek, his daughter, since I were marryed, i67i, to Ⅿr Percy Freke; which in the yeare i705 I show'd my deer husband to ᴊee iff hee could contradictt any partt of itt or perticuler. All which he ᴠwas pleas'd to allow to Eliza Freke.[51]

i683 My deer father sentt for me outt of Ireland, when ⱨe was pleased to give me up this bond of Mr Freks and ⅿine to him for the twelve hundred pounds and the intrest ᴏn itt. And with itt he was pleased to give me to buy pins   l.–s.–d. ᴀnd needles   200–0–0

i684 January the first and my unhappy birth day my ᴅeer father sentt me over to Ireland for a New Years guift, ᴀnd bid mee hasten over to him with all speed to meett ⅿy sisters and have his last blesing,   ioo–0–0

ᴠWhich being the hard winter, I could nott gett a shipp; ᴀnd hee dyed the 24 of Aprill i684; and I never saw ⱨim more, tho hee offten sentt to me to come to him ᴀnd have his last blesing. Butt my God prevented me ᴀnd leftt me ever to lament him. Eliz. Freke

    My deer fathers guift   ii232–i4

i687 or thereaboutts Mr Frek borrowed of me of my ᴏwn savings to buy the coppy hold estate in Pentney of ᴆorty six pound a yeare, now lett for by me, Eliz Freke, ᴛhe sume of   700–0–0

---

[51] An earlier version of this account in W (fol. 41r) ends in 1709.

i688 More Mr Freke borrowed of me to buy outt the
right of redemtion of Henry Lord Richerson on West
Billney   107–0–0

i70i More my deer husband took up of mine in my
cosin John Frek hand of my own proper mony and savings,
unknown to me,   500–0–0
For which I was troubled. E Freke

i702 More my deer husband took up of mine of my
Indy stock and of me in mony to cary for Ireland to
compleatt his purchas with the Lord Sidney in Ireland my
own saveings   i004–0–0
Which mony by the unsettled govermentt was great
part of itt lost by the Lord Sidney, then deputy of
Ireland. E Frek

i702 Mr Freke writt to me to bestow on my son, Ralph
Frek, towards the purchas of Dirralone, which with the
200 l. I gave my son, Ralph Freke, for a New Years guift
the day he came of age he would compleat the rest. Soe
I did to teach him his fathers trade of buying Irish land.   407–0–0

i703 My deer husband lett me have noe quiett till he
borrowed of me to buye debenturs to cary for or returne
for Ireland. Which I did and paid itt by my cosin John
Freke, which he carryed over with for his last purchas he
there made in the west of Ireland. And all these severall
sums of my own saveings and improvemtt   2020–0–0

i704 December i703 Mr Frek came for England. I
removed my stock into mony for feare all would be gone
from me for Ireland, and I bought an exchecker order of
the queen for ninety nine years for my second grandson,
Ralph Frek, io3 l.–io s. a yeare cost me   i560–0–0

i706 I did then buy another exchecker order of the queen
for ninty nine years together with a bankers debtt for my
said grandson Ralph Frek, both which cost me, E Frek,   i500–0–0

i7i2, September 2 And still I have by me in mony in
Sir George Nortons hand on his bond and judgment for
my grandson Ralph Frek   i339–0–0
And more on Mr Weston a mortgage[52] of   i200–0–0
All for Ralph Frek, and my grandson.

And more now, September 2d, in my cosin John
Freks hand of mine for my two younger grandchildren   io56–0–0
And more now in my closett above   400–0–0

---

[52] The i7ii mortgage is on Steven Weston's Beaconsfield, Buckinghamshire property;
see above, p. i89 n. 478.

All these severall sums of my own saveing and
ndustry. Eliza Freke

Which iff right reckned and errors excepted comes to	23945‾i4‾io
Of which my deer fatthrs bounty and kindnes to me was	ii232‾i4‾io
And my own industry and savings att Billney, &c., vere	i27i3‾o‾o
Both which sumes, iff right reckned by me, comes to otall	23945‾i4‾io
	Eliz Frek

E. Account of Documents To Be Given Freke's Executors

[B, fol. 31v]

i7i2, September the 7 An accountt of whatt parchments and
papers I have laid in my uper closett in a black trunk sowed up to be
kept by my executors as soon as itt shall please my God to take me,
Elizabeth Frek, to himselfe – who brought this estate of West Billney
to my deer husband, Percy Freke, Esqr, lett for now by me, E Frek,
i7i2, 472 pounds a yeare; and more in Pentney, forty six pound a yeare.
Both which are now lett for this presentt time 5i8‾io‾o or therabouts.[53]
Eliz Frek

i Mr Freks settlemtt of his estatte in Ireland upon me, EF

2 The Lord Burlingtons of Garren James in Ireland for 2i years,
i702

3 My deecree in chancery against the Lord Henry Richerson and
his brothers and Serjantt William Richersons right of redemtion fielled
i688, for which I paid him a hundred guines, paid by me, Eliz. Freke,
viz., a hundred and seven pounds

4 Serjentt William Richersons will[54]

5 The Lord Thomas Richerson lease of 500 years, Barron Gramontt,
to Sir Jacob Gerrald for the paymentt of seventy five pounds the 29
day of November 1659 and two thousand five hundred seventy five
pounds upon the one and twentyeth of May following, i660

6 Five leases of the Lord Richersons of Billney lett to these
severall tennants: the first is Mr Price, the Hall, call'd Billney Hall;
2d is William Bishop or Pawes (now William Knopwood); 3 is
Christopher Pery, now Robertt Ram, is the warren; 4th, the Maner
Farme, William Fisk, now Richard Tafft; 5th is Thomas Turner, the

---

[53] An earlier version dated 7 January 1709/10 appears in W, fols. 39v–40r.
[54] William Richardson, serjeant-at-law, was the younger brother of Thomas Richardson, second Baron Cramond. His will was proved on 24 July 1682 (*Scots Peerage*, ii. 581).

White House, now Cross; 6th is the Wassell Farme, formerly
Plattfoot, now Pallmer.

7 One larg deed datted the 3d of June i663 to Sir Jacob Gerrard by
the Lord Thomas Richerson, Barron Gramountt, who did sell to him
all his maner of West Billney with all itts appurtenances as parcell of
the latte desolved monastry of Penttney

8 And one large lease of the Lord Richersons conveying of itt to Sir
Jacob Gerrerd May the twenty seventh, i659, and from Sir Jacob soule
to my fatther, Ralph Freke, Esqr

9 In i664, the 28 of November, my deer father, Ralph Frek, Esqr
lentt the Lord Richerson, Barron Gramond, a thousand pound on Sir
Jacob Gerrards mortgage.

io, i665, July 5 My father laid downe more on this mortgage 3i5
pounds, which mony was to bee paid to my deer father with itts intres
of 737–i4–io January the twentyeth, i665, who took up Sir Jacob
Gerrards mortgage.

ii, i665 Which faileing of both princeple and intrest, the Lord
Thomas Richerson did sell West Billney by a lease to William Coward
Esqr, for my deer father, viz., all the manner with the appurtenancyes
parcell of the late desolved monastry of Pentney, with all itts rights
members, and appurtenancyes belonging to the said maner of Billney
(and the donitive of Pentney).

i2, i672 One deed in which my deer father sues outt a decree for
his princeple and intrest mony to be paide him in, being 4896–i4–io
which was passed and fielled i672

i3, i672 Two deeds of my fathers conveyance of West Billney to my
brother Austen for my deer sisters portion for fowre thousand pound –
i675, June 30, which my brother not likeing itts distance from his
estatte in Kentt sould itt backe againe to my deer father for 4000 l
Which mony my father had of mee, and I did purchass itt of my
brother Austen.

i4 And my father and I gave him Mr Freks and my bond for what
was more due, being 896–i4–io, and my only son being then aboutt a
month old the 2d June. Hee did then settle itt on me and my children
just before I wentt for Ireland the first time of my goeing over there
Elizabeth Freke – my husband then having all my fathers and Sir Jacob
Gerrards intrest conveyed to him [B, fol. 32r] with itts perquisits and
appurtenancyes as parcell of the late desolved monastry of Pentney and
settled on me and my children June i676.

i4–i5 Two deeds of the sale of West Billney by my deer father to
Sir John Earnly and Goreing Ball, Esq, in trust for me, Eliza Freke
aboutt i676[55]

---

[55] John Ernle or Earnley (c. 1620–1697), a Wiltshire justice of peace and militia

i6 One deed more in trust for me to Sir John Earnly and Goring Ball, Esqr

i7 One large deed of trust of my deer fathers and my husbands, Percy Freke, Esqr, to Sir John Earnley and Mr Goreing Ball in trust or mee

i8 Two deeds of dowre to the Lady Ann Richerson wherin she cleases to my deer father, Ralph Frek, Esqr, all her right and claime o the maner of West Billney with itts appurtenancyes, parcell of the ate desolved monastry of Pentney

i9 One larg deed of the sale of West Billney to William Coward, Esqr, for my deer father with all itts appurtenancyes of the late desolved monastry of Pentney

20 One larg deed of the settlementt of West Billney on my deer husband, Percy Freke, Esqr; and me, Elizabeth Frek, his wife; and our on, Mr Ralph Freke

2i, i688 One large deed tryperly[56] of release of West Billney to my deer husband by the Lord Henery Richerson (son to the Lord Thomas Richerson) and Mr Thomas Richerson and Yelverton Payton, Esqrs, with their bond of 300 l. iff either of them intrude on oure estatte of West Billney

22 One parcell of deeds tyed upp of the estatte Pentney bought of Yelverton Payton, Esqr, bought by my deer husband, Percy Frek, Esqr, butt with my own proper mony, i689, Eliza. Freke

23 One parcell of deeds tyed up of my seven akers peice I bought o enclose the whole estatt of Billney in or aboutt Michellmas i686 of Goodman Curttaine; and I paid for itt, unknown to Mr Frek, with my own mony. Itt being free land, I gave itt my son for a vote in the parliament with. E Freke

24 One deed or lease of my five aker peice and 5 perch in Winch ield called Whittpitt Brack bought by Mr Freke in i688 and lett by the ate Lord Henry Richerson to Mrs Barns, a lease of 83 years for twelve hillings a yeare with powre of reentry. Which land shee enjoyed of nine twenty fowr years and ploughed up my myore withoutt ever paying me any rentt. Att last being like to loose itt by Mrs Barns and her son Thomas Langly affter they had enjoy'd itt 24 years for 4 l., I

---

ommander knighted by Charles II, was a member of parliament, chancellor of the exchequer, and lord of the admiralty. Freke's recipes and remedies include several from Lord and Lady Earnley (*HC*, ii. 271–4). But conceivably Freke could intend his son, Sir John Ernle of Calne, Wiltshire (1647–1686), who was knighted in 1673 and was later a member of parliament (*HC*, ii. 274). Goringe Ball, the second son of the knight and master of the bench Peter Ball, entered the Middle Temple in 1652 and was called to the bar in 1657 (*Middle Temple Records*, iii. 1,033, 1,108).

[56] A tripartite indenture or deed: three copies of an agreement made on a sheet cut in indented lines (Jowitt, i. 960).

then entered on itt by seiseing the corne in the cartt for the rentt whicl
they promised me att Michellmas. Which faileing of I did in my own
right enter on itt the Lady Day affter, 1712. Soe thatt this estate of Wes
Billney has bin in my deer fathers posession and mortgage and me, hi
daughter, from the 30 of June one thousand six hundred sixty fowre to
this 7 of September 1712; I then transcribed itt. Which, iff right reckned
is fortty eight years; of which time the Lady An Richerson enjoyed he
dowre on itt neer eight and twenty years with the head house and the
best of the land and then by some fattall accident was burntt to death
all alone in or aboutt Xmas in her closett att Honingham, my lord he
son and daughter being att Norwich – hapned thatt day 1696.[57] Eli
Freke

September 7, 1712 In the same trunk is putt in more by me

1 In a plod bagg, more, two deeds of trust to me for my hundre
and three pound a yeare for 99, ninety nine, years in the exchecke
for my grandson Ralph Freke. The third parchmentt of itt is in m
cosin John Freks hand as my trustee.

2 And the tallyes are in the same trunk in my closet.

3 Together with the tallys for my bankers debt for 34–10–0 a yea
and for 66 pound a yeare I bought since my deer husbands death
1706, for ninety nine years for my grandchildren succesively, and firs
to my grandson Ralfe Freke

4 More is my renewall of my estate att Pentney, which Mr Frek
[B, fol. 32v] surrendered att his death, June 2d, to the use of his wil
made in Febuary 1705 and renewed by me, Elizabeth Freke, Novembe
14, 1706.

5 More is my deer husbands last will and mine.

6 More is in a little red trunk roled up my sons, Ralph Freks, leas
to pay mee three hundred and fiffty pound a year outt of (850 l.) eigh
hundred and fiffty pounds a yeare my deer husband att his death lef
me in Ireland for my life. All which my son has bin soe unkind to m
as to receive all of itt for aboutt six yeare past and never paid me but
one half years rentt of 170. This is too true. E Frek

7 More is my purchas deeds of Pentney, purchased 1688, of fortty six
pound a yeare.

8 And more is my bankers debtt by actt of parliamentt for thirty
fowre pound a yeare for ninety nine years in the exchecker.

9 More is in this little red trunk Sir George Nortons bond and
judgmentt for thirteen hundred pounds borrowed of me November 20
for one yeare.

10 And more is there my cosin John Freks note and letter wherin he
owns to owe me cleere nine hundred and twenty pounds last Xmas 171

---

[57] Anne Richardson died on 31 January 1697/8.

besids the fiffty pound I gave my neece Betty Austen last Febuary.
Since which my Cosin John Frek has received of mine a hundred
pound more outt of the exchecker due to me last Lady Day i7i2 and
thirty six pound intrest mony for half a years intrest due to me from
Mr Steven Weston on his mortgage. Soe thatt my cosin John Frek has
of mine now in his hand io56 pound. Eliz Frek

ii More is in the biger black trunk Mr Stephen Westons mortgage
deeds for twelve hundred pounds lentt him the first of December i7ii.
Eliz Frek

i3 [*sic*] And more is an appoynttmentt of maintenance for my two
elder grandchildren affter my death till they shall come of age. E Frek

i4 Besids there is severall other letters and papers of my concerns in
the little red trunk.

i5 Besids I forgott amongst Billney deeds is the old regester of Billney
datted i562 to be keptt by which I defend my self in the right of my
church against the bishop and chancellour of Norwich.

i6 Is the field book of Billney and Pentney transcribed by Mr
Brockett.[58] EF

F. Account of Freke's Personal Estate

[B, fol. 35v]

September the 29, i7i2 A true accountt of my personall estate
belonging to me, Eliz Freke, widdow and rellictt of Percy Freke
deceased, late of West Billney in the county of Norfolk, Esqr, in my
powre to dispose of in my will and given me by my deere husband att
his death in his will made Febuary 2i, i705,[59] and confirmed att his
death, June the second, Sunday, i706 – the very day and hower my
son Ralph Frek was borne thirty years before (hee being now, i7i2,
seven and thirty years of age the second of June, last i7i2, Eliza. Frek)

l.–s.–d.

One annuiety of fiffty pounds a yeare perr anum
issueing from the exchecker for the residue of a tearme
of ninety nine years, att first purchased in the name of
Sir Joseph Jekill, knightt, and by him assigned to my
cosin John Frek of the Midle Temple in London in trust

---

[58] A John Brockett resided in the Sedgeford Lane Ward according to the 1705 Lynn
land tax (NRO, KL/C47/46); the Gayton parish register records the marriage of a John
Brockett and Mary Chambers, widow, in November 1709.

[59] Freke signed his will on 3 February 1705/6 (PRO, PROB 11/489/145).

for mee and such of my grandchildren as I shall dereict,[60]
Eli. Frek   50–0–0

One other annuiety of twenty pound perr anum
issueing from the exchecker for the residue of a tearme
of ninety nine yeares purchassed by the said John Freke,
Esqr, on the trust above mentyoned for me and such
of my grandchildren as I shall dereictt, E Frek   20–0–0

One other annuiety of thirtty three pounds, six
shilling, and eight pence issueing outt of the exchecker
for the residue of a tearme of ninety nine years, att first
purchased by Charls Bluntt and by him assigned to the
above saide John Freke on the trust above mentioned
for Elizabeth Freke;[61] all bought in i703   33–6–8

One other annuietty of sixtty six pounds a yeare
issueing from the exchecker for the residue of a tearme
of ninety nine yeares att first purchased in the name of
my said husband, Percy Freke, Esqr, and me, Elizabeth
Frek, his said wife,   66–0–0

One other annuiety or pention of thirty fowre pounds,
ten shillings a yeare payable att the exchecker in leiw
of a goldsmith or bankers debtt, purchased by my
husband and the order for the paymentt made to my
said deceased husband, Percy Freke, Esqr. This hundred
pound a year was purchased in the year i705, E Frek.   34–i0–0

And my cosin John Frek, my truste, has the orders
of them all in his keeping for mee and my disposall,
Elizabeth Frek.

Sume of both is two hundred and three pounds, ten
shillings per anum.   203–i0–0
                                                                        Eliz Freke

[B, fol. 36r]

i7ii, November 2i More aded by me of my own
saveings since my six years widowhood is lentt to Sir
George Norton of Abots Leigh in November on his
bond and warantt till Aprill the 2i, half a year,   i339–00–00

---

[60] A member of Middle Temple called to the bar in 1687, Joseph Jekyll (c. 1662–1738
received a knighthood following his appointments as chief justice of Chester and serjeant-
at-law. He succeeded John Trevor as master of the rolls and long served as a member
of parliament (*The History of Parliament. The House of Commons, 1715–1754*, ed. Romney
Sedgwick, 2 vols. [New York, 1970], ii. 174–6).

[61] John Freke's will mentions a Charles Blunt, his sister-in-law's husband (PRO, PROB
11/559/154).

December 7 And more lentt to Mr Steven Weston
ı his mortgage December 7 — i200–00–00

And then more left of my mony in my cosin John
reks hand — 970–00–00

And more my cosin John Frek has received of mine
alfe a years intrest outt of the exchecker funds of mine
st Lady Day — i0i–i0–00

i7i2, May And more by cosin John Frek received of
ine half a years intrest due last May from Mr Westons
ıortgage mony — 36–00–00

And more my cosin John Frek receives of mine half
years intrestt outt of my exchecker funds September
ᵩ, i7i2, — i0i–i0–00

More is now in my closett in my greatt haire trunke
ᵉer — 400–00–00

In all, iff right reckned by mee, Elizabeth Frek, is
ᵉptember 29, i7i2, of mony, bonds, and bills of my
ᵥn to dispose of at my death — 4i48–00–00

Of this (4i48) fowr thousand one hundred forty eightt
ᵒunds my cosin John Freke owes me last Xmas i7ii
ine hundred and seventy pounds, for which I have his
ᵒte. And September 29, i7i2, is a years intrest from
ᵗe exchecker of 203 pounds and half a years intrest of
Ir Westons last May i7i2 is 36 pounds. In all is i208
ᵒund; outt of which my cosin Frek gave my neece
ᵉtty Austen by my order last Febuary fiffty pounds.
ʰich taken outt of a hundred remaines cleere due to
ᵗe from my kinsman ii58 pounds, September 29. — ii58–00–00

Eliz. Freke

i7i2, September 29 Besids this is more due to me
ᵒm my son, Ralph Frek, of my arears of rentt due to
ᵗe in Ireland from Joseph Jervoise three years charged
ı my son, i706, by him and the account brought me
ʸ my cosin John Frek when he wentt over for me i707,
ᵖril 2i, — i200–00–00

Then there was then due to me from my sone, above,
ᵒok up of mine — i920–00–00

3i20–00–00

And more my son owes me. Mr Freke gave me in
ʳeland att his death, i706, by his will dated Febuary
ᵩ, i705, eight hundred pound and fiffty pound a yeare
ᵗt by my deer husband, i703, when he leftt Ireland.
ᵥhich was by my cosen John Frek when he wentt over
ᵣr me Aprill 2i, i707, to take my accounts and arrears

of rentt hee reduced this my 850 pounds a year to 664
pounds a yeare and the Michellmass affter leased this
my 850 l. a yeare to my son for 350 pounds a yeare in
Michellmas i707 for my life. Which is now this
Michellmas five years rentt due to me cleere and a halfe
besids the half years rentt he paid my cosin John Freke,
i707.   7268–00–e

G. 21 May 1712 Letter to Archdeacon John Jeffery

[B, fol. 51r]

A letter I wrott to the arch deacon of Norwich, Doctter Jeffryes, M.
the 2i, i7i2, Elizabeth Freke:

Reverentt Sir,

Being warned by your procter Clark for my appeerance att yo'
courte amongst all your rable and crue, I did desire Mr Smith, vick
of Winch, by my letter to appeere for me. Butt hee, judging itt mo
proper for me to trouble you with this my complaint under my ov
hand, supprest thatt of his.

Sir, I need nott informe you thatt aboutt two years past the severy
of the bishop of Norwich in my absence did me in displaceing n
chaplin att West Billney church, tho coalatted under his own dereicttic
to Gyton; which is more then the bishop can answer or the chancello'
the trouble given me in itt to force mee to his licence and jurisdictic
of Norwich courtte, my church being nott only a peculer butt n
perticuler peculer subjectt nither to licence, institution, or inducttic
and noe tithes belonging to itt. Butt the church of Pentney, tho und
my church and my donitive, has tithes (or is tributary) both in n
challenge. Which by the barbarous usuage I have lately received fro
Norwich has forced me to take a veiw of my rightt in the head of th
spirittuall courte, where tho in the arch bishops jurisdicttion, yett und
noe command from him as to my tittle, I holding my right of th
church and the donitive of Pentney (viz., Billney-come-Pentney) on
from a crouned head. Nor doe I owe any suite or service or rentt bu
thatt which I dully pay to the queen or king in my Lord Oswellsto
rentt, who bought itt of King Charls the Second.

Now, sir, amongst the severall other mistakes I have as a woma
comitted by my ignorrance is in my payments to you of procuratio

d sinodalls, which I finde are nott your due since the desolution of
e latte dissollved monastry of Pentney, viz., my register says since
6o. However, sir, I question nott your honer and justice in takeing
a advantage of an unhappy widow. And iff you thinke, sir, my stopp
my just due any wronge to you, be pleased to convince me from
ove, and I shall submitt to the queens authoryty, my pattron. Sir, I
ve within these few yeares supprestt severall of these sorts of quitt
ntts, which I by my ignorance, folly, and womanhood have unjustly
id, and challenged their redress for itt. Which rather then oppose itt,
ey submitted to. And grievous itt was and is to mee, tho in my own
rong, to contend with the church and your selfe, perticulerly in itt.
nd now knowing my errors in whatt is past, iff I should committ the
me againe, mightt perhaps be registered against mee. Which tho itt
ay nott breake mee, soe itt cannott be of thatt conveniency to you
r mee to doe actt unjustly to the church and my predicessours in itt.
Sir, I am now soe unhappy againe as to be withoutt a minester to
rve my cure heer; and I must be forced to keep itt soe thatt I may
ve a testemony of the bishops generossity and rightt to itt, which as
am very ill and infirme is most grieveous to mee. And tho I am
fered the advantage the queen now allowes mee of liberty of contience
d could partt with my church to a conciderrable advantage, yett
ing bred and borne of the Protestant church and for which I am for
y husbands being soe above fiffteen thousand pounds a sufferer, itt
ould bee cruell in your courte for to force my contience from the
hurch of England. Therfore, honred sir, be pleased to side with me
little that I may fill my vacancy by sending me a generall release outt
your courts or thatt the bishop and you will maintaine your right
ainst me. Sir, I had nott the confidence of addresing my selfe to you
this butt by the encouragmentt of Mr Smith brought me from you.
nd, sir, itt is nott derogatory from your quallity or funtion, tho a
oman, to help and assist me as I am a widow who plead for the rightt
the church and humbly begg your pardon for this scrole and thatt I
ay continue, sir,

> Your obliged, humble servant Eliz. Frek,
> parson, vicker, and curratt of West Billney
> and donative of Pentny

. Inventories of Household Goods

V, fol. 44r]

ecember the 7, i7io An accountt of whatt bottles I have now in my uper closetts of cordiall waters and sirrups putt in by me, Eliz Frek, for my own use[62]

In the great cubbard by the bed side is
54 quartt bottles of hott cordiall watter of several sorts (first watter).
In the little cuberd just over itt is
i8 pints of stronge aquamirabolus.
In the little open cubord by it is
9 pints of severall sirrups.
In the first cubard of the pewter cases is
34 quarts, of which 6 of aquamy[rabolus].
In the 2d cubard of this case is
24 bottles, all strong waters of there severall sorts.
And on the shelf of the same cubbord is aloft
9 quarts of sirrup of gullyflowrs.
In the long chest by the window is
34 bottles, quarts and pints, of cordiall watter, of which
8 pints of aquamirabolus in the cold still.
In the little cubberd under the window is
i6 of cordiall watter.
In all, if right reckned by mee, is aboutt two hundred bottles o
quarts and pints putt in by me, of which 24 pints and 6 quarts i
the best aquamirabolus. E Frek

More on the shelves is
5 quarts of buck thorn sirrup[63]
2 quarts of sirrup of bulles[64]
3 quarts of sirrup of damsons
3 quarts of sirrup of elderburyes
i quart of sirrup of issop[65]
i quart of sirrup of baume,
i quart of sirrup of purslan[66]
i quart of Eliza sallutas, i708
i quart of sirrup of turnaps, i7io
3 quarts of catrick watter, eyes

[62] Variations of the first and last of the following three inventories appear in W, f
3r, dated 5 December 1710.

[63] Buckthorn berries are purgative.

[64] Bullace: 'The Bullesse ... wilde kindes of Plums' that 'do stay and binde the bel
(Gerard, *The Herball*, 1,498, 1,499).

[65] Isop, isope: hyssop–aromatic herb; mixed with water, honey and rue for inflam
lungs, 'the old cough, and shortnesse of breath' (Gerard, *The Herball*, 580; Pechey, *T
Compleat Herbal*, 107).

[66] Purslane: a succulent herb recommended for, among other ills, 'Coughs, a
Shortness of Breath' (Pechey, *The Compleat Herbal*, 155).

3 quarts of surfitt or popy watter, i7io
i quarte of celeistill for eyes
4 quarts of rosemary water
i quartt of popy water, cold still

In my further little closett is December the seventh, i7io, putt in by
,e, Eliz Freke,

32 quarts of red strek cider
9 quarts of cowslip wyne, i709
3 stone bottles of damson wine, hold two quarts a peice, i709
3 quart bottles of damson wyne, i709
9 quarts of white meade
i three gallon bottle of ellder vinegar, i708

3, fol. 52r]

i7i3/i4 i4 of March, a note of whatt I putt into the high long chest
i my closett above by me, Eliz Freke

5 peices of printed paper to hang a roome with, yard wide
2 gild boys for a bed and there tops to them; six couchins
i yellow cloth counterpoyne, worne; i paire of fine blanketts
i old cloth cloke of Mr Freks; i other counterpoyne, worne
i new grey cloth coat and wascote livery; 5 tassells and some patterns
i new black livery and breeches to itt of shamy; 2 little pillows

arch i4. In the deep narrow deale box is 4 blue curtaines, i paire of
illence to them, 2 new blanketts, and i new blu counterpoyne and
ie coverlid and i other blankett to them.

Recipe for Laudanum

N, fol. 122r]

o make lodynum. The Lady Powells receitt sentt me by my deer sister
usten in my distress; of which she has taken of itt neer two years her
·lfe. September 20. Sent i7i2. For the collicke, &c.

Take two ounces of the best opium and one ounce of fine saffron.
utt the opium very thinn and small, and pull the saffron into small
eices; then infuse them in a quarte of the best sack in a deep earthen
ott covered with a blader pricked full of pin holles. And then sett itt
i a kettle or skillitt of boyleing watter till the quantitye in the pott bee
alfe wasted. Lett itt infuse, still keeping the vessell conveniently filld

up as itt wasts; and when itt is done enough (which will be a gre
while first), iff you please, deer Madam, to straine itt and squeeze i
hard outt and keep itt close stoopt for your use. The dereictions follo
how to use this ladynum.

I have sentt my deer sister the receitt of the ladynum as I make i
puntially, and I have taken itt once a day for almost a yeare and half
And I begin with itt att twenty drops att a time, butt by useing of i
itt must be increased soe thatt now I take five and twenty drops in
day in a spoonfull of wyne or beere or coffy. And in any violentt fitt
the colicke you must double the proportion of drops for itt to mast
the humour (which I hope my deer sister itt will doe) both in yo
head and back. My Lady Powell, who gave me this receitt, says sh
had bin dead many years since butt for itt – shee haveing tryed all tl
conciderable phisitions in London and by them brought to a skellitto
in weakness and to noe effectt. Shee has since taken for severall yea
fiffty drops a day and by soe doeing keeps her selfe in a moderat
degree of ease. And my daughter Judith when shee takes itt has offte
the benifitt of putting her into a sleep for six or eightt howers togeth
tho in the collick. And tho itt has nott that good effectt on me, yett i
composes my rest the better in the nightt. And to give me thatt effec
I take itt aboutt two or three a clock in the affternoone. And I have
neighbour by me tells me she takes itt twice a day thirty drops att
time. All these informations I give my deerst sister thatt you may s
itt is a safe thinge and nott be affraid of itt otherwise then to have
carefully droptt. Whatt ever is taken itt sometimes flyes to the head,
perhaps you may find, [W, fol. 121v] and to the frightning of you; bu
for all thatt I wrightt itt, my deer sister, with pleasure hopeing itt m
doe you good. And then itt is butt a small penance to purchas to o
selves a little ease whilst we live in this world. God send you a sud
and joyfull meeting of your deer familly outt of Ireland is the day
prayer of, &c.,

                                                        Judith Austen

INDEX